Motivating Economic
Achievement

Motivating Economic Achievement

David C. McClelland AND David G. Winter

WITH Sara K. Winter

AND

Elliott R. Danzig

Manohar S. Nadkarni

Aziz Pabaney

Udai Pareek

THE FREE PRESS, *New York*

COLLIER-MACMILLAN LIMITED, *London*

Collier-Macmillan Canada, Ltd., Toronto, Ontario

Library of Congress Catalog Card Number: 69–11373

First Printing

To
R. N. Jai and J. E. Stepanek
formerly of SIET Institute
whose faith in the role of the
behavioral sciences in development
made this book possible

PREFACE

The project described in this book represents an attempt to check a behavioral science theory in the field, in the context of all the urgent practical problems of underdevelopment, institution-building, and provision of assistance where and when it is wanted and can be financially supported. Therefore, readers of different orientations and interests may find different chapters of special interest. The reader concerned with policy for economic development will be particularly interested in Chapters 1, 7, 9, and 12. The behavioral scientist who is concerned with motivation and personality change will find Chapters 2, 4, 7, and 9–11 useful. Readers interested in India will perhaps linger on Chapters 3–6, 8, and 10. Nevertheless, the book follows a connected and sometimes complex line of argument, so that most readers will want to read it straight through.

The project required an integration of scientific procedures with the operations of public institutions, and such a combination created real problems. Since this new type of research is becoming more and more important, we think it worthwhile in this preface to describe and reflect upon our experiences and problems.

To the behavioral scientist, research in the field is at once exciting and chaotic. He is accustomed to rational, orderly procedures carried out by a well-organized scientific team that operates in accordance with a carefully designed plan. In fact, however, such plans rarely work out in the field. One reason is the complexity of the field situation: Neither the subjects nor the environmental conditions can be understood, anticipated, or controlled in the ways that they can be in the laboratory.

Yet there is still a more fundamental problem. Because the research is carried out with the collaboration and support of government and semiprivate institutions, the behavioral scientist often comes to feel that what happens is beyond his understanding and control. Thus we often felt as though we were involved in a game in which chance played a big part. As we tried to progress from "Start" to "Goal," we would land on squares marked with messages such as: "Application being processed, wait six months"; "Initial approval given, hire staff"; "Earlier approval reversed, disband staff and start over"; "Your training program seems unethical, wait three turns"; "Your research is good, collect $5000"; "Your training program discontinued, go back to New Delhi and draw cards until you get another institution"; "Data from Spain mailed out but unreceived, wait six months"; or "Factory building started, move ahead three spaces." As we traveled along this confusing and tortuous path, we experienced many of the emotions of John Bunyan's Pilgrim—the buoyancy of Hope, the Slough of Despond, Anger at being misunderstood or blocked, and Gratitude for Help received along the road.

These emotions have no place in a sober and scientific account, such as we have tried to set forth here. However, such emotions do reflect some of the difficulties and complexities of coordinating scientific research with public institutions and policy-makers: such institutions have needs, standards, anxieties, and a logic of their own which often conflict with the requirements of getting research done. Commitments made in good faith by government agencies are always subject to the caprice of political exigencies, and a government is under no obligation to explain its decisions or justify its ways to man. Perhaps it can never be otherwise, for any institution that is involved with policy and society has to play by the rules of the political process if it hopes to survive.

This perspective suggests some of the reasons for our problems with the United States Agency for International Development mentioned in Chapter 3. The American foreign aid program has been and is now in serious trouble. There is political criticism of the basic idea; the results to date are often unclear; and there is a great need for knowledge of how to get a better return or greater effects for the funds spent. Operating in this context, Mr. Mansfield has been praised in the United States Congress and the press for saving millions of dollars through reducing and cutting off programs. When he over-ruled the strong recommendation of the research section of AID and was responsible for disapproval of our project, he doubtless felt that it was a politically important saving, despite the feeling of scholars that the research was of great long-range importance. Having continued and partially completed the research in spite of this setback, we would hope that the cost/benefit figures reported in Chapter 12 would now lead policy-makers to disagree. What seemed like a saving turned out to be an expense because few AID programs are likely to yield such a high rate of return as ours, although it is hard to be sure because AID continues to support a variety of programs for which no cost/benefit figures exist.

We feel that the "saving" accomplished through discontinuing the achievement motivation training project was analogous to the "saving" of a man who refuses to spend money on a doctor, even though he knows he is sick and likely to die. Yet on reflection the problem appears more fundamental. Administrators are probably not often in a position to judge the merits of proposed scientific research; but every day, of necessity, they must make decisions which weigh the importance of the research as over against the implications for their institution of supporting it. It is certainly conceivable, as some thought at the time, that funding our project, however meritorious, could have so opened the whole AID research enterprise to ridicule as to make the investment institutionally disastrous. We can only hope that the results of the research reported in this book may lead a few more policy-makers to take the behavioral science approach to international assistance and economic development more seriously. So the behavioral scientist must at least entertain the hope that public institutions can respond in the long run to the implications of his work even if they cannot in the short run.

The problems were much the same with the Ford Foundation, even though as a private institution it is freed from many of the constraints of Congressional opinion that affect a government agency. Its funds are limited; its personnel are involved in commitments and relationships with other institutions, governments, and people. Its initial encouragement and then subsequent disapproval for our project were frustrating and perplexing, particularly as there was no satisfactory explanation for the sudden withdrawal of its support. Yet from the point of view of the Foundation, the institution had much more important things to worry about than the fate of a particular piece of research.

Still we want to record our gratitude to the Ford Foundation. It did open up opportunities for the training and research at SIET Institute; it supported Dr. Danzig for two months in India; and it financed a follow-up trip for two American researchers (Drs. McClelland and

Berlew) to Hyderabad, Kakinada, and Vellore to assess the early effects of the training. For this we are grateful, as we are for the encouragement, many kindnesses, and great personal assistance given us by our friends on the Foundation staff in India. Without their help and support the research could never have been carried out.

The obstacles to our reaching the objectives were formidable; there were doubts in our own minds as well as in the minds of the institution officials. All the money in the world would not have made the research task easy. Consider the obstacles: (1) We had no real evidence at the time that motivation could be developed in adults, and many psychologists were convinced that it could not be. Why invest time and money in such a risky enterprise? (2) It was essential that we persuade large numbers of adult businessmen to leave their work and undergo a new type of training that was essentially untested. Could we really get enough important businessmen to come? (3) Some local institution had to provide a base for the project until the follow-up results were in. Why should it? (4) The project was a long-term one, and the results of the training could not be known for several years. How was a research staff to be recruited and kept motivated over such a period of time? (5) Standard business and management courses usually take longer than this training; they involve formal instruction in such topics as work study, quality control, cost reduction, budgetary controls, and marketing research. Could we seriously expect that ten days' exposure to "psychological inputs" (however justified by research) would have a lasting effect on how well a businessman performed? Weren't we proposing to substitute some insubstantial "pep talks" for the "nuts and bolts" of learning how to be a better businessman? (6) Even if we could change men's minds or activate them, wasn't it unethical to try? (7) Above all, wasn't the whole effort trivial in the light of the major factors that demonstrably influence the rate of economic growth, such as availability of capital, skills of the labor force, the laws of supply and demand, fiscal policies, the existence of lending and credit institutions, and so forth? More than one economist was tolerantly amused at the thought that purely psychological inputs might seriously affect the rate of economic growth, if not determined that no money should be wasted on such an obviously risky enterprise.

As we look back on it, the odds against the success of our undertaking did seem formidable. It was our scientific conviction that the theory ought to be tested, as well as the trust and cheerful encouragement of many people, that kept us going.

Thus it is with real pleasure and more than the usual sense of gratitude that we record here the assistance of many people—particularly the former director of SIET Institute, Shri R. N. Jai, and Dr. Joseph Stepanek, Ford Consultant to the Institute. Without their commitment, practical help, advice, and encouragement the study could not have been started or finished.

Of great importance to us was the cheerful enthusiasm for the project displayed by the businessmen of Kakinada and Vellore. We had been led to believe, from all that we had read or had heard from government officials, that small-city businessmen in India were backward, unenterprising, and fatalistic. One high government official in New Delhi worried that we would only encourage the men to undertake impractical schemes, that these schemes would fail, and that the men would blame the government! In our experience, all of these expectations about the entrepreneurs turned out to be wide of the mark. The entrepreneurs had reason to feel discouraged at the outset because of the many realistic obstacles to business expansion, but we found that they did become convinced that they could do better than they had been doing, and that they acted on that conviction. Their enthusiasm and their actions in turn encouraged us and kept our interest in the project alive. Several of the entrepreneurs simply laughed at us when we told them of the fears for their financial security on the part of government officials. They replied in effect: "We are grown men; let us worry about that."

Along with this moral encouragement, we did get financial support in bits and pieces from several sources. We would like to acknowledge with gratitude a small Rupee grant out of P.L. 480 funds released by the United States State Department for our use, on the recommendation of the then American Ambassador to India, Professor John Kenneth Galbraith (Project SC-30023). Although he had considerable doubts about the research hypothesis, he felt that the search for knowledge should be encouraged. We are grateful for the small preliminary grant from the AID research section for training our future collaborators. The Ford Foundation also contributed small sums, as explained above, which we acknowledge with thanks. Finally, the research owes a particular debt to John Gardner, at that time President of the Carnegie Corporation, who literally rescued one of us (D.C.McC.) from major indebtedness, following the AID disapproval, by making him a small grant for continuing basic research on motivation development. In fact, the Carnegie Corporation has been a consistent supporter of the research reported here. It backed the early work in Mexico and elsewhere on the development of the motivation courses; it picked up some of the bills for the Indian training when other funds failed; and after the training in India was completed, it awarded a further grant to Professor McClelland which made possible the collection of all the follow-up data and the writing of this book. So if there is a single institution to which we owe particular thanks for financial support, it is the Carnegie Corporation. Its staff continuously backed what they judged to be research on an important topic—the development of motivation—and repeatedly came to our rescue when other institutions failed us.

Other indirect funding was received in the form of a National Science Foundation Undergraduate Research Fellowship which supported Harry Lasker's trip to India, and a Sheldon Traveling Fellowship from Harvard University for Joel Cohen, which enabled him to visit Kakinada and Vellore as a part of his overseas studies.

The number of individuals who worked hard to make this research possible is large, but we want to start by acknowledging with gratitude the particularly important contributions of Dr. Elliott Danzig, Shri Manohar Nadkarni, and Dr. Udai Pareek who largely designed, organized, and ran the training courses at SIET Institute. Others who ably assisted the project there include: Dr. Aziz Pabaney, who initiated and aroused support for the project in Kakinada in the early stages; Dr. A. K. Pal, whose experience in psychology and Indian business was invaluable to us in running the first courses; Mr. Rolf Lynton, Shri Somnath Chattopadhyay, Shri K. J. Christopher, Shri S. Dasgupta from SIET Institute, and Dr. Prayag Mehta from the National Institute of Education in New Delhi—all of whom served as staff for the courses; and finally the visitors who checked up on progress in Kakinada and Vellore —Dr. David Berlew, Mr. Harry Lasker, Mr. Joel Cohen, and Shri Krishna Kumar, who accompanied several of the others and who worked closely with the Winters on the final evaluation. All of these men are in a sense part-authors of what we have done and written, as are others to be listed below. The authors of this volume are merely those who have attempted to write down what was done in large part by others. Several of the men listed above have also read parts of the manuscript and have made valuable suggestions for additions and changes.

The role of Dr. Sara Winter also deserves special mention. She participated fully in the final evaluation, and spent endless hours typing the interview notes which formed the basis for the coding of the business activity. More than that, her analysis of what "really happened," psychologically speaking, to the men who were trained (see Chapter 10) gave us an understanding of the personality changes involved and a conviction as to their substance that went far beyond what the statistics alone could provide.

We want also to acknowledge with thanks the assistance of others not so directly connected with the SIET Institute project: Dr. George Litwin, who was the first to go to India and develop interest and support for motivation training in the Bombay area; Dr. Winthrop Adkins, who worked hard on the ill-fated AID project until its demise; Sr. José Fons-Boronat, who initiated, and Father Luis Ramallo, who helped him give, several courses in Barcelona at the Escuela Superior de Administration y Direction de Empresas; Dr. John Andrews, who helped with the initial courses given in Mexico; Mr. Minoru Terasaki, who arranged an early course in Japan; Dr. James Ciarlo, who with Dr. Litwin gave the very first achievement motivation development course at the Stanford Research Institute; and Dr. Joel Aronoff, who took on the job of following up what happened to the executives who were trained in a large U.S. corporation.

A particular word of thanks is owed to our many friends in Bombay also: to Mr. T. V. Lalvani, whose early example and lively support encouraged us in the early days; to the Bombay Management Association and its executive secretary, Shri V. B. Tendulkar, for sponsoring our courses there; and to Davar's College of Commerce in Bombay for providing us with space and other assistance in giving the courses.

In the final stages of the research Miss Eva Ungar and Mr. Joseph Pleck helped greatly with the computer analysis of the data, and Mr. Stuart Pizer developed a new scoring system for Efficacy that differentiated between Changers and Inactives after training and proved particularly helpful in interpreting our results.

Throughout the entire period of the research, our secretary, Miss Alice Thoren, was a constant source of loyal service; she put some order in our financial and administrative affairs, she kept in touch with us in the field, she worked in the final manuscript, and she helped us in many small ways for which we are very grateful. We want also to acknowledge a great debt to Miss Lynn Lundstrom, who ably assisted Miss Thoren, and who was largely responsible for the painstaking job of typing the final manuscript.

D. C. McC.
Addis Ababa, Ethiopia
D. G. W.
Middletown, Connecticut

TABLE OF CONTENTS

LIST OF FIGURES AND PLATES

LIST OF TABLES

CHAPTER I

THE TARGET IN DEVELOPMENT: MAN OR SOCIETY?

In the mid-twentieth century few possibilities fascinate man more than that of shaping his own destiny. Scientific knowledge holds out precisely that promise. In the struggle for peace he seems far from achieving such a goal, but in the war on want he may be faring better. More and more studies are accumulating which purport to show what factor or factors are important for economic growth. Among these is D. C. McClelland's *The Achieving Society* (1961), which summarized an interlocking series of empirical studies suggesting that a particular human motive, the need for Achievement, promotes entrepreneurship, which in turn is a key to economic growth. The book ends with the scientist's traditional hope that the knowledge so painstakingly collected will somehow be useful in helping man shape his destiny. At the time it was little more than a pious hope, since it was not at all clear how a development specialist or a leader of a new nation could make use of the knowledge accumulated about the achievement motive. If anything, the general import of the findings was discouraging to anyone attempting to accelerate economic growth: the need to Achieve (*n* Achievement) seemed to be a relatively stable personality characteristic rooted in experiences in middle childhood. Didn't this imply that all a developer could do was to try to change parental habits of child-rearing—known to be very resistant to change—and then hopefully wait for the children to grow up with a stronger need to Achieve? Such a reading of the findings in *The Achieving Society* may be correct, but it was certainly discouraging, not only practically, but scientifically. For the scientist would like to explore further the investigation of the role of *n* Achievement in development.

If *n* Achievement can be increased only through child-rearing techniques, then further scientific investigation is impracticable for a variety of reasons. It is probably too difficult to change parental attitudes consistently enough over time to observe any changes in *n* Achievement. Even if *n* Achievement could be changed, it would be a long wait until the children grew up and showed the expected increases in entrepreneurial activity and economic growth. Furthermore, the study would have to be done on a massive scale, since many of the children would be unlikely to go into business in any case. The final results could scarcely be obtained in the lifetime of the scientist; he could not even expect enough feedback to help give his hypothesis a better test by trying different techniques of developing achievement motivation in children. And if he changed his strategy, he would again have to wait a generation to detect any results.

If a theory cannot really be tested, maybe it needs restatement. Furthermore, the urgent problem of accelerating economic growth in poor nations persists. Is there not some way that achievement motivation can be developed in adults—particularly in those businessmen whose actions are likely to bring most immediate returns in expanded enterprise? Can it be shown that direct increases in *n* Achievement in individuals can have significant economic impact on a community? The studies reported here were designed to answer these questions. Their urgency and interest derive from both the practical and scientific points of view.

Answers to them will also make a contribution to the growing controversy as to whether we can best facilitate development, in Weiner's words, "by a frontal attack upon values [or] by a frontal attack upon institutions and structures that reduce incentives and opportunities and by supporting those institutions and structures which increase them" (1966, p. 12). There are scholars who believe that the key to economic growth is man, and that his values and attitudes must be changed in order to speed up the growth process. Such men argue for the importance of education, the mass media, ideology and charismatic leadership in producing modernization. Man must somehow be persuaded to think and act in modern ways before he will build modern economic and social institutions. A peasant or a small businessman won't save or re-invest money unless he believes in the future and in the possibility of controlling it. A trader cannot become a successful industrialist until he has come to value longer-term investments or until he has been trained in modern management techniques. Certainly the evidence that *n* Achievement is an important ingredient in successful entrepreneurship supports this view. For how can a Syrian businessman or a slum-dweller in America respond rationally to economic incentives and opportunities if his *n* Achievement is low?

But, as Weiner correctly points out, such a view is by no means the dominant one among those responsible for setting policies on how to aid and accelerate the development of communities at home and abroad. They believe that while it may be necessary for a man to change his values and actions, by far the simplest and most effective way to accomplish this end is to arrange conditions in society so that it will be to his advantage to change. Use the carrot and the stick. Reward a man for modern, achievement-related behavior and punish him by removing material satisfactions if he persists in behaving in traditional, inefficient ways. The implication is that most men are or would become rational, achievement-oriented, or utilitarian if only the obstacles to their behaving in these ways could be removed. This argument is so widely believed that it deserves careful examination. Is the evidence for it so strong that any demonstration of the ability to change human values directly would have only marginal interest?

The Role of Economic Opportunities and Incentives

Most economic theories of development start with demand. People want a new good or service. This induces higher investments to meet the demand; higher investments lead to innovations and capital improvements that will better satisfy the demand. Satisfying demand leads to higher income and higher savings, which make higher investments possible, and so on in a beneficent cycle. To be sure, someone, a kind of *deus ex machina*, has to perceive the possibilities of all this happening. He may be a planner, a private entrepreneur, or a government administrator. Consider Schmookler's *Invention and Economic Growth* (1966), in which the economist's argument takes its most classical form. He has demonstrated that in the United States there has been a high correlation between investment and capital goods invention. His explanation of the relationship, which seems perfectly reasonable, is that "inventive activity is guided by the expected value of the solution to a technical problem" (p. 109). In a study of some hundreds of patented inventions he could find not one single instance in which a scientific discovery was "specified as a factor initiating an important invention" (p. 67). On the other hand, inventors frequently explain that the motivation for their new idea was the opportunity to solve a technical problem in a way that would make money. From this standpoint, the problem of how to accelerate economic growth is analytically simple to solve, though it may be practically difficult to implement the solution. The argument runs as follows: There are plenty of potential innovators seeking their economic advantage. All you have to do is make it easier for them to see opportunities—for example, by getting experts to point them out—and supply them with the necessities for setting up a firm that will take advantage of the opportunities, such as capital, licenses, tax advantages, and so forth. But maybe such an approach will work only in a Western or a relatively developed country, such as Schmookler and other Western economists are used to studying. Does it adequately describe what happens in a developing country?

Papanek (1962) has provided us with what appears to be an excellent example of how classical economic opportunities and incentives were apparently sufficient to cause very rapid industrial growth in Pakistan after partition. In some ways conditions were almost ideal to test the role of marked changes in external conditions on the economic responses of potential businessmen. The Hindu traders and industrialists had left, leaving large demands for products and services they had formerly supplied. With the Korean War boom and rising international prices, some Moslem trading communities began to make huge profits in the import-export business, profits which they later invested in industry (1) because trading profits began to fall, (2) because the government prevented transfers of funds abroad, (3) because conspicuous consumption was discouraged by the inadequate supply of luxury goods, (4) because they did not want to invest in agricultural land for fear of land reforms, nor in urban real estate because of shortages of building supplies, and (5) because of the obvious possibility of huge profits from much needed new industries. Here the account of rapid industrialization in Pakistan can be given almost entirely in economic terms. There is no need at all to refer to human motives or values, except the classical desire of everyone to seek material rewards. These same Moslem businessmen had done very little before the change in external conditions, but once the opportunities and incentives were available, they quickly stepped in to do what classic economic theory says that men will do on such occasions. In Papanek's words: "The only obvious major change that took place in 1947 was in the economic environment: the sudden increase in economic opportunity" (p. 55). "It is difficult to interpret what happened in Pakistan in terms of a slow, fundamental change in motivation, or in ideology, or in customs, which then caused alterations in economic behavior. Instead, changed economic incentives were effective in altering economic behavior, given specified favorable non-economic circumstances" (pp. 56–67).

In a sense, this is just a particularly well-documented example of a more general argument that economic theorists have employed for some time. Many have noted that overseas Indians and Chinese appear to be much better businessmen than their compatriots at home. The standard explanation is that opportunity has shifted. An enterprising young Indian may not be able to get ahead at home for a variety of social and economic reasons, but once he migrates to East Africa, for example, he finds the economic opportunities much greater and exploits them successfully. Wharton (1966) has extended the argument and stated it in its most extreme form by insisting that even

> peasant and subsistence farmers *are* indeed "economic men" who respond positively and negatively to economic stimuli as quickly as the most commercialized farmers in the modern world. The evidence is quite clear that subsistence man is fully as responsive to the opportunity for a larger income (higher gain beyond costs and effort spent) as the next man. Such responsiveness takes a variety of forms, ranging from the introduction of new crops to the adoption of new practices—even those that are at odds with existing cultural methods (p. 264).

If it is all that simple, if man's desire for economic gain is so overriding a motive, why is it necessary or desirable to consider other values and motives at all—let alone worry about trying to influence them directly? Isn't it enough just to provide opportunities and incentives and to let men know about them? To be sure, making such arrangements often does involve getting politicians and government leaders to do what they ought to do, which may involve changing attitudes and motives, but even such a residual concern for political development leaves little room for curiosity about the possibilities of developing the achievement motive.

Differences in Responsiveness to Economic Opportunities

However, Papanek (1962) uncovered another remarkable fact in his study of industrialization in Pakistan. He found that over half the industrial investment was contributed by five small Moslem trading communities representing about ½ of 1 per cent of the total population of Pakistan. The Halai Memon, for example, made 27 per cent of the industrial investment though they represented about .3 per cent of the population. This is not a particularly new finding; it has been reported in many other parts of the world. Whenever economic growth begins, some tiny community can nearly always be identified which has played a major entrepreneurial role—such as the Jews or the Quakers in parts of the West, the Parsis and Jains in India, the Antioqueños in Colombia, and so on (see Hagen, 1962; McClelland, 1961). If economic opportunities are such important "motivators," why is it that they affect markedly such a small fraction of the total population? Some human factor would seem to be necessary to explain the responsiveness of the few and the indifference of the many.

Papanek, like others before him, argues that the difference lies in the greater experience of the small trading communities such as the Memon. They alone among the Moslems had any knowledge of how to conduct a business, how to borrow money, how to make investments, buy, sell, and so forth. "Among Indian Muslims few except traders were primarily market oriented" (1962, p. 55). But what does it mean psychologically to be "market oriented"? It means that a person will be practiced in calculating risks and benefits, in figuring out how he may do better by investing here rather than there, by buying this article of goods or bribing that official. If a man's thoughts deal constantly with doing something better, he will by definition score higher in n Achievement. It would not be at all surprising to discover that these small Muslim trading communities scored higher in n Achievement than the remainder of the Pakistani population. Papanek discounts the possibility that their motive level changed in any significant way after partition. There were no marked changes in patriotism, child-rearing practices, or prestige that might have accounted for a sudden increase in motivation. But of course no sudden change in motive level is necessary to explain their behavior. They may have been higher in n Achievement all along than their compatriots, a fact which would be sufficient to explain why they took greater advantage of increased opportunities in 1947. The theory of achievement motivation predicts that it is precisely those with high n Achievement who are sensitive to changes in economic opportunities; whereas those with low n Achievement are not. (See Atkinson, 1957).

Unfortunately test data do not exist on these industrialists, but there is plenty of supporting evidence from other sources. Papanek notes, for example, that "entire townships of Memons left India after partition" (1962, p. 55), and several studies have shown that migrants are apt to have higher *n* Achievement (McClelland, 1961; Kolp, 1965). It is for this reason that the greater success of overseas Indian businessmen cannot be attributed without question to the greater economic opportunities abroad. It is likely that they went abroad in the first place because they had higher *n* Achievement.

Moreover, not only those who migrate can be characterized as more motivated to progress. Even among those who stay behind it is possible to differentiate those who are more progressive in terms of their *n* Achievement scores. Rogers and Neill (1966) report correlations between *n* Achievement scores and agricultural innovativeness in farming communities in both India and Colombia. The correlations were significantly positive in six out of eight Indian farming communities, yielding an average correlation of .25 across villages or a total correlation for all individuals of .32 (N = 702). Among 302 farmers in rural Colombia, in six different villages, the average correlation was .18, indicating that farmers who think about doing better (higher *n* Achievement) do in fact respond more to greater opportunities by adopting new farm practices. Wharton's rather strong statement that subsistence farmers respond as quickly to economic stimuli "as the most commercialized farmers in the modern world" (1966, p. 264) must at least be modified to indicate that while some of them are responsive, many more of them probably are not. And it is precisely those with high *n* Achievement who are responsive to economic stimuli and who find ways of making a better living at farming from adopting new practices.

It is not only among businessmen and farmers that higher *n* Achievement leads to more enterprising behavior. Sheppard and Belitsky (1966) surveyed over 300 blue-collar workers who had been put out of work in Erie, Pennsylvania in 1964. They found that motivational level made a big difference in the way the workers behaved when they were laid off. Those with higher *n* Achievement started looking for work sooner (on the first day they were unemployed or before layoff); they checked directly an above average number of companies, they more often went out of town to seek employment; they looked into getting a different job, and many more of them used at least five of eight different job-seeking techniques. Not surprisingly, more of them found new jobs sooner, unless they had special handicaps. Economic opportunities would have to be rated as poor even among the non-handicapped. Yet some of them, such as those who migrated, made the most of what opportunities there were and found employment. Many more, particularly those with very low *n* Achievement, sat around waiting to be called back or for something to turn up. While opportunities were available—since some people found them—many men did not perceive them or take advantage of them because they were not motivated to engage in the necessary exploratory activities.

A careful study reported by LeVine (1966) illustrates in still another context the importance of motivational differences. He observed, as many others have, that the Ibo in Eastern Nigeria are much more upwardly mobile and economically successful than the Hausa in Northern Nigeria. He predicted and found that n Achievement in fantasy (here in dream reports) would be much higher among Ibo than among Hausa students. Once again he establishes in a totally different context the close association between n Achievement and the entrepreneurial spirit. He attributes the difference in n Achievement levels in the two sub-cultures to differences in their traditional status mobility systems rather than in their child-rearing practices or religious ideologies. However, he also notes that economic rationalists think they can explain this difference quite easily without resort to "naive" psychological and sociological variables. Thus, he quotes Horton:

> the Ibo people in Eastern Nigeria have become renowned in recent years for the value they set on aggressive competition, the struggle for achievement, and the willingness to explore new avenues of power and status. A cultural and personality theorist, whom I talked to about them, took this value as an obvious "ultimate," to be interpreted as the effects of certain causes—possible in the realm of child training. As a social anthropologist, I was suspicious of this. I pointed to the fact that over much of Ibo land there is acute land shortage, that anxious parents quite "reasonably" encourage their children to struggle for a school success that will fit them for some career other than farming, and that when the children grow up, their own "reason" tells them that their only hope of a comfortable existence lies in continuing the struggle in outside trade, or in jobs in government or the big commercial firms (Horton, 1963, p. 11).

LeVine answers that responding as the Ibo did to overpopulation on the land is by no means the only "rational" course open to them. They could have stayed where they were and become "accustomed to increasing poverty," an alternative

> adopted by families in economically depressed areas all over the world. Such families operate on a principle of least effort in which the comfort of remaining in familiar surroundings and doing familiar things, even when faced with starvation, outweighs the future economic benefits that might be gained from drastically changing their way of life. So long as their impoverishment is gradual, they will put up with it, for it affords known and im-

mediate gratifications that would be missing were they to seek new productive activities. Their behavior is by no means totally irrational. (LeVine, 1966, p. 84).

He also points out that the Ibo could have responded as the Hausa did by leaving home but restricting their new activities to traditional trading patterns that did not lead to the marked upward mobility characteristic of the Ibo.

> There were, then, at least three possible courses of action open to the Ibo in response to their acute land shortage: to accept impoverishment at home, to extend traditional trading patterns while remaining as un-Westernized as possible, and to pursue Western-type economic activity with the changes in ways of life that were required for it. Other peoples have adopted the first two alternatives in response to economic adversity; although some Ibo undoubtedly did too, many chose the third course. The difference is not one of rationality, but of energy and effort. In simplest terms, the successful pursuit of a novel occupation involving a high degree of enterprise or education is not for a lazy man, no matter how hard pressed he is financially. (LeVine, 1966, p. 84).

To put it another way, energetic striving to improve one's lot may seem rational enough to a man with high *n* Achievement, but not to a man with low *n* Achievement. Some people are sensitive to changes in economic opportunities and incentives; many more are not. What do we know about those who do take advantage of opportunities?

The Urge to Improve

Many scholars have stressed that economic modernization and growth require a whole new set of values and attitudes, and marked changes in social organization. In a cross-cultural study, Inkeles has identified the following attitudes accompanying modernization: "a disposition to accept new ideas and try new methods; a readiness to express opinions; a time sense that makes men more interested in the present and future than in the past; a better sense of punctuality; a greater concern for planning, organization and efficiency; a tendency to see the world as calculable; a faith in science and technology; and, finally, a belief in distributive justice" (summarized by Weiner, 1966, p. 4). Smelser (1966) points out that these value changes are often associated with political reorganization and changes in the educational system, in religion, in family structure, and in social stratification. No one doubts that man changes his thinking and actions enormously during development, but it is hard to know which of these changes, if any, is crucial and whether any of them precedes or follows development.

The need to Achieve, or to give it a less esoteric title, the urge to improve, ought to be viewed simply as one variable among the many or as an index reflecting various habits or thoughts and actions which are important for economic development. There is no reason to believe that the n Achievement index is unique, that these same key attitudes could not be tapped by some other measure. All one can say is that they have not been so tapped as yet, and as an index, the n Achievement score has certain advantages. Research data have accumulated on it for more than 20 years—in the laboratory, in the field, in history, and in many different countries. Thus when one uses such a measure, he is not talking about some vague psychological quality; rather the quality has been quantitatively measured in a variety of contexts and has been carefully interpreted in terms of a general theory of human motivation (see McClelland et al., 1953; McClelland, 1961; Atkinson, 1958, 1964). One aspect of it as a measure needs special emphasis for social scientists who are used to getting measures of attitudes and values by asking people. The n Ach score is an "operant," not a "respondent" measure. That is, it records how often a person spontaneously thinks about improving things, not how interested he says he is in improvement in response to another's question. The distinction is not a trivial one in psychology, although some people have treated it as if it were. Generally speaking in psychology, correlations between operants and respondents are near zero (see McClelland, 1958, 1966b). That is, a person may say that he is very interested in achievement, but a careful sampling of his thoughts over a period of time will show that he thinks about achieving actually very seldom. Some findings reported by LeVine (1966) illustrate the point beautifully. He also asked his students to write two essays, one on the topic of "What is a successful man?", the other on "How does a boy become a successful man?" He used the regular n Achievement scoring theme for coding the essays and found no differences in the stress on achievement, work, and sacrifice between the Ibo and Hausa students. Yet when the same scoring scheme was applied to dreams handed in by these students, the Ibo dreams scored much higher in n Achievement. The essays seem to be tapping what the boys thought they ought to respond, whereas the dreams reflected more accurately what they spontaneously tended to think about. And other studies have shown that what people spontaneously think about frequently is more apt to spill over into relevant actions than their attitudes and opinions as expressed in questionnaires or interviews. While the operant character of the *n* Achievement response index has real scientific value, it undoubtedly has hindered its general acceptance among social scientists and policy-makers, who persist in thinking that the best, the only, or the most valid way to find out about a person's motives and values is to ask him what they are. It is to distinguish it from what is obtained in interviews or questionnaires that the index is referred to as a motive, rather than a value or attitude. It is given the esoteric label *n* Ach to set it off from measures of achievement orientation obtained by such alternative methods.

What is the evidence that *n* Ach is a key factor in economic growth? It can be briefly summarized (after McClelland, 1961). The *n* Ach content of popular literature has been shown to have increased on several occasions prior to rapid economic growth in a country and to have declined prior to a slackening in the rate of growth. When *n* Ach content is coded among modern nations in children's textbooks, those countries that scored higher in *n* Ach in 1925 and again in 1950 subsequently developed at a faster rate economically than countries that scored lower. These crude measures of general concern for achievement in a nation at a particular time presumably also reflect the number of active achievement-oriented people in the country. And how do achievement-oriented people behave? Laboratory studies of individuals with high *n* Ach show that in general they behave like successful, rationalizing, business entrepreneurs. That is, they set moderately difficult goals for themselves, neither too easy nor too hard, so as to maximize the likelihood of achievement satisfaction. They are more than normally interested in concrete feedback on how well they are doing. In this respect they seem to be particularly like businessmen who, more than professionals, get concrete feedback in concrete performance terms as to their relative success or failure. They like assuming personal responsibility for solving problems, because in that way they can get a sense of achievement satisfaction from completing a task, whereas they cannot if success depends on luck or circumstances beyond their control, or if they are working exclusively on someone else's problem. Finally, those with high *n* Ach generally show more initiative and exploratory behavior, continually researching the environment to find tasks that they can solve to their satisfaction. The similarities in these types of behavior to the actions characteristic of a successful entrepreneur were striking. So it was predicted that entrepreneurial business executives should universally score higher in *n* Achievement than professionals with similar social and educational backgrounds. This turns out to be the case in several advanced and not so advanced countries, including Poland, which is not operating under the free enterprise system (see McClelland, 1961, Ch. 7).

Since these data were published in *The Achieving Society,* more information has come in that fills in the picture a little more completely. It is possible that *n* Achievement is a response to being assigned to a job requiring it rather than a personality characteristic leading people to seek out such jobs or be selected for them. A longitudinal study has shed some important light on the question. College students who were tested in 1947 were followed up in 1961. Those in business were classi-fied as filling occupational roles which could be described as entre-preneurial (sales, managing a business) or not entrepreneurial (credit, traffic, personnel, and office managers). "Eighty-three percent of the entrepreneurs had been high in *n* Ach 14 years earlier versus only 21% of the non-entrepreneurs" (McClelland, 1965a, p. 390). A cross-validation of the finding with some later and less adequate data revealed the same trend. Apparently *n* Achievement, which has been shown by others to be a fairly stable characteristic over a long period of time (Kagan and Moss, 1962), predisposes people to end up in entrepre-neurial occupations.

When people with high *n* Achievement get into such positions, they also tend to behave in more expansive and often more successful ways. Evidence for this proposition comes from two sources. Andrews picked two large firms in Mexico City. Company A had been growing at a very rapid rate in the previous three or four years, whereas Company P had been growing much more slowly. He also discovered in the files of a consultant psychologist Thematic Apperception Tests that could be scored for *n* Ach and that had been administered to the key executives in each company prior to the time period under consideration. He found that the top executives in Company A scored significantly higher in *n* Ach than top executives in Company P (see Andrews, 1967). The important point analytically is that the assessment of *n* Achievement levels was made prior to the marked differences that appeared in the growth rates of the two firms. It is hard to escape the conclusion that the higher *n* Ach of the top executives in Firm A had something to do with the difference in growth rate, though as is often the case in such instances, the top executives in Firm P said that they were prevented from doing better by discriminatory regulations on the part of the city government. Furthermore, Andrews found that executives with higher *n* Ach tended subsequently to get more promotions and pay raises in Firm A than those with low *n* Ach. For example, those above the median in *n* Ach received 3.9 pay raises on the average in a four-year period, as contrasted with only 2.6 such raises for those below the median in *n* Ach (p < .05). In Firm P, by way of contrast, higher *n* Achievement was not associated with more rapid advancement, though a higher concern for power was associated with more promotions. Thus, opportunity also makes a difference. Executives with high *n* Ach will get ahead faster and produce company growth in an achievement-oriented organization, but they cannot do so in an organization such as Company P, which was oriented strongly around loyalty to the president rather than independent entrepreneurial behavior on the part of the key executives.

Kock (1965) has reported a much more extensive study, which also shows the effect of high *n* Achievement on business expansion. He obtained extensive economic data over a period of time from a number of Finnish firms, mostly small, involved in the production of knitwear. In cases where the unit was small, he gave a test of motivation only to the owner-manager; when it was larger and several executives were important in decision-making, he tested them all and obtained a motivational score for the firm by weighting each individual's score according to his importance in the decision-making hierarchy. Some of his main results are summarized in Table 1.1. Clearly *n* Achievement scores of

Table 1.1

Correlations Between Motive Scores of Executives and Measures of Business Expansion (1954–61) in Fifteen Finnish Knitwear Factories (After Kock, 1965)

	n Ach	*n* Affiliation	*n* Power
Increases in Number of Workers	.41*	−.62†	.42*
Gross Value of Output	.39*	−.61†	.49**
Profit (Audited Profit + Depreciation + Interest + Rent)	.27	−.30	.01
Gross Investments	.63**	.20	−.06
Turnover	.46**	−.53**	.41*

* p < .10
** p < .05
† p < .01

the managers of these firms are significantly associated with several measures of business expansion, particularly increases in the number of workers, in gross value of output, in turnover, and in gross investment over an eight-year period. Wainer and Rubin have reported a similar correlation between *n* Ach scores of entrepreneurs and expansion of their research and development firms in the United States (1967).

It is interesting that Kock did not find a significant correlation of manager n Ach with increases in profitability. Such a result would be of considerable importance theoretically, if it could be confirmed by further data. The theory of n Achievement predicts that a person with high n Achievement should be immediately concerned with direct quantitative measures of how well he is doing. In a sense, expansion of labor force, output, and investment are more immediate and obvious indicators of "growth" than profits are. Profits are secondary measures derived usually (but not always, of course) from expansion and growth. While it is unwise to place too much emphasis on the low correlation Kock obtained with profitability, it is certainly not inconsistent with the history of entrepreneurship to argue that entrepreneurs with high n Ach are more concerned with expansion and growth than they are with profits, although some economists assume that the two are equivalent as signs of economic development. In fact, as we shall have reason to point out later, it can be argued that a too narrow concern with profits and returns may interfere with expansion and growth. In a certain sense, n Ach leads to irrational concern with expansion, sometimes at the cost of self-interest. Thus, as McClelland argued elsewhere (1961), it is more correct to speak of the achievement motive as underlying rapid growth, rather than of the profit motive, for two reasons. First, the real motive force in development is probably the concern to improve and expand rather than the concern to make profits; and second, the term *profits* suggests that the motive in question is tied in with a particular economic system, i.e., capitalism, whereas it operates as well in a Communist or Socialist state (McClelland, 1961).

Of particular interest in Table 1.1 is the significant correlation between n Achievement and gross investment, because of the stress laid on investment in the classical economic picture of how economic growth begins. As noted above, Kuznets (1959) and Schmookler (1966) hold that improvement in capital, conceived in technological terms, is obviously the basis for the fantastic increase in the standard of living of the Western world over the past 100 years. Schmookler has shown that improvement in capital or technological innovation is highly correlated with investments (or capital goods output). Capital goods output or investment in turn is determined by present and expected sales, which in turn, if Kock's correlation in Table 1.1 is to be taken seriously, is determined by the n Achievement level of the men running the business.

Kock also measured the need for Affiliation and the need for Power in his Finnish knitwear managers. While Andrews found that higher n Power among managers in one firm was associated with slow growth,

Kock's data suggest that *n* Power, like *n* Ach, may facilitate business expansion, if possessed by the owner-manager himself. Kock's data also suggest that strong *n* Affiliation (concern for maintaining and establishing friendly relations with people) may actually inhibit growth. It is hard to escape the inference that men who wanted to keep their shops small and friendly, as in a face-to-face working group, were less likely to do the things that would lead to rapid expansion in their businesses. Unfortunately, Andrews did not report a measure of *n* Affiliation on the executives in Company P, so that the finding cannot be cross-checked there. Perhaps they too were more concerned about good interpersonal relations than about taking the achievement-oriented actions necessary for rapid growth. French has shown in an experimental context (1956) that students high in *n* Affiliation will choose a friend rather than a technical expert as a working partner—which would hardly be the way to produce a rapid increase in output. But more research needs to be done to discover what motives and values actually inhibit the growth of firms. What is clear is that high *n* Achievement leads to entrepreneurial activity, and when possessed by a manager, to more rapid expansion of his firm.

Relation of Motivation and Opportunity

So far emphasis has been on showing that people with certain dispositions, chiefly a high *n* Ach, are more likely to take advantage of economic opportunities. However, this is not to say that availability of opportunities makes no difference. After all, the Memon traders, presuming they had high *n* Ach all along, had been less economically successful before partition than they were after. The thesis of *The Achieving Society* has been repeatedly criticized (cf. for example, Eisenstadt, 1963) for neglecting social structural variables which may inhibit or elicit entrepreneurial activity. What happens if men have high *n* Ach but no opportunities, or low *n* Ach and great opportunities? Might not manipulation of opportunities actually arouse or defeat *n* Ach in individuals?

In several of the studies just reviewed opportunity played a role, even though it was not specifically discussed. In Andrews' report on two Mexican business firms (1967), he found that high *n* Ach was no advantage in Firm P, which was oriented around power relationships. Men with high *n* Ach were not promoted and either left the firm or showed lower *n* Ach at the end of a three-year period. Absence of opportunity clearly prevented success from greater entrepreneurial activity.

Furthermore, in the cases when high *n* Ach paid off in greater success, there was always some opportunity. There were some jobs available for the unemployed blue-collar workers in Erie, Pennsylvania, with high *n* Ach; there are many opportunities available for the energetic young Ibo in Nigeria. Or in the case of the Finnish knitwear firms or the U.S. research and development firms, all were existing under relatively favorable economic conditions, in which the enterprise of a single man could make a real difference in the success of his firm. Obviously different skills and motivations might be necessary for success where huge firms in an industrial state are competing for near monopolistic shares of a large market. It cannot be stressed too often that all the evidence showing the importance of *n* Ach for business or entrepreneurial success applies largely to situations in which opportunity is held more or less constant across individuals or firms, and where success is at least moderately probable.

But what about other conditions? How does strength of *n* Ach interact with differing opportunity structures? The problem has been worked out in some theoretical detail chiefly by Atkinson and Feather (1966), with laboratory demonstrations of what happens to performance when the two factors covary. Figure 1.1 has been constructed as a simple model of their theory. Atkinson has postulated (1957) that the tendency to approach or continue at a task is the simple multiplicative product of the initial level of *n* Ach (or motive to achieve success, Ms), the probability of success at this task (Ps), and the incentive value of success at the task, which, he has postulated, is a simple function of its difficulty $(1 - Ps)$. That is, Approach $= Ms \times Ps \times (1 - Ps)$. Thus in Figure 1.1 the top curve for a person with high *n* Ach (arbitrarily set at $Ms = 8$) shows his tendency to approach tasks of varying probability of success. Obviously he tends to approach most tasks of moderate difficulty where $Ps = .50$ (Approach $= 8 \times .50 \times .50 = 2.00$). A man with lower initial *n* Ach ($Ms = 1$) also tends to approach moderately difficult tasks more, but the curve is much flatter and, in effect, he may show no differential preference for tasks as a function of their difficulty.

On the other hand, a man with a high fear of failure, the negative aspect of *n* Ach, tends to avoid most tasks of moderate difficulty. If he has other motives for performing a task at all, he will tend to prefer either very easy or very difficult tasks, because, in commonsense terms, he avoids in this way being judged for his capacity to achieve something. He is likely to succeed at an easy task, and if he fails at a very hard task, it is clearly not his fault.

From this simple theoretical model, some very interesting and im-

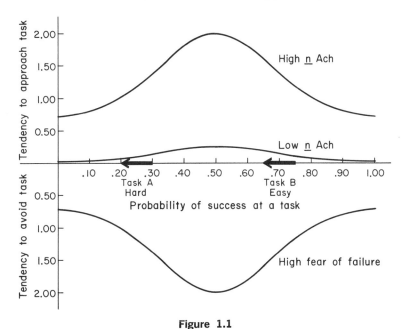

Figure 1.1
The Interaction of Type of Motive and Probability of Success in Determining Approach and Avoidance of a Task

portant consequences flow. To begin with, probability of success obviously makes a big difference in eliciting task performance. Leaving aside the possibility of widespread fear of failure based on past experience, if a government can raise probability of success in business from low to moderate by various aids and guarantees, then it will succeed in getting more people into business activity *regardless of initial level of* n *Ach in* the population. That is, increasing opportunity increases business performance, regardless of motivational levels, under these conditions. This, of course, is the classical assumption made by economic theorists.

But it does not hold under all conditions, according to the model. There are two main exceptions. The first exists when *Ps* in business becomes very high among a population high in *n* Ach. Under these conditions, interest in business should fall off. Such a circumstance may be rare in nature, but it could explain the relatively less vigorous business drive in "mature" economies. The other exception is more relevant to conditions of underdevelopment: Fear of failure may be so widespread in backward economies that improving opportunities may paradoxically make people *less* likely to take advantage of them. To elicit maximum task persistence in such people, opportunities should be either "sure things" or "hopeless." If they perform the tasks at all, it is for non-achievement reasons, and it is best to minimize the achievement aspects of the tasks by making them not personally challenging (moderately difficult).

Another paradox illustrated in Figure 1.1 comes from considering what happens when a person fails at an easy or difficult task. Task A is shown as difficult with a perceived initial probability of success of .30, whereas Task B is easy with an initial Ps of .70. Failure lowers the perceived probability of success at either task, as shown by the arrows pointing to the left in Figure 1.1. But note that for the person high in n Ach, failure at an easy task moves the task into the area of greatest attraction for him, so that he will actually work harder at it. But the reverse is true for what he considers to be a difficult task: failure makes it even less attractive for him. So he will persist more after failure at an easy task than after failure at a hard one.

The man with high fear of failure functions very differently. Failure at an easy task moves him into the area of greatest task avoidance; whereas failure at a hard task makes him less likely to avoid it. So he behaves in a counterintuitive, "irrational" fashion. He is more likely to persist after failure at a hard task than after failing an easy task. Feather (1961) has confirmed all these predictions from the model in a laboratory study.

Consider the implications of these findings for an economic situation such as persistent crop failure or population pressure on resources on peasant farms in Nigeria. The model predicts that the young Ibo with high n Ach will leave the farm (abandon the task) if Ps is really low, sooner than say an equivalent Hausa farmer with lower n Ach. Or if the Hausa farmer is actually high in fear of failure, the more he fails (the lower the Ps), the more he is likely to cling to the farm. Paradoxically if farm conditions improve for such a man, he is more likely to leave (as Ps moves into the neighborhood of .50). The Ibo with high n Ach would be more likely to stay on the farm. In other words, it is a gross oversimplification of the psychological facts to speak as if a man with high n Ach always tries harder at a particular task, no matter how difficult. He will actually quit sooner than a man with lower n Ach if he is failing at something which is very difficult. It even follows that if business conditions in a country are terrible, and the probabilities of success are very low, the higher the man's n Ach, the less likely it is that he will be found in business. Other men with other priorities will be carrying on business transactions and, if they have a high fear of failure, trying to conduct them with the absolute minimum of enterprise —since enterprise involves risk of failure.

It obviously becomes very important for a government that is trying to produce development to know just what the perceived probabilities of success and *n* Ach levels are in various segments of the population. Otherwise, changing opportunities may have the opposite effects from those intended. Improving farm conditions may lead some people to leave the farms for the cities (which may or may not be desirable), whereas letting farm conditions get worse may encourage others to go into business (which may or may not be desirable). We should be beyond the stage in development theory in which policies are set exclusively in terms of either opportunity or motivational changes.

A General Model of Economic Development

Let us take stock of this discussion so far. First, we have reviewed several related theories which, for the sake of convenience, we shall call the rational model of economic development. This model holds that most men—in the West, in developing countries, and in peasant societies— naturally seek to maximize their interests, given the particular situations and constraints in which they find themselves. Hence any attempt to change their economic activity should concentrate on changing the incentives and constraints of their situations. This may involve both closing off some possibilities (e.g., land reform in Pakistan) and creating other opportunities (e.g. improved agricultural techniques). The model is appealing because it is simple and close to our ordinary experience of why men act as they do. It offers clear policy recommendations; in many instances such policies have had important effects on economic development. So it is not surprising that the rational model has considerable repute in academic and policy circles.

However, there is widespread evidence that economic development does not always and everywhere proceed according to the predictions made from the rational model. For one thing, sometimes changing incentives simply doesn't work (see K. Nair, 1961). As experience with development policies and programs has accumulated over the "United Nations Development Decade," some observers now fear that it "may in fact recede into history as a decade of disillusionment"—that "there will be no adequate improvement in living standards in vast areas of the globe for the balance of this century" (George Woods, quoted in Wilhelm, 1966). Surely no man could deny that the problems are enormous and that the efforts, in the form of international assistance, are relatively small. So disappointment with worldwide rates of growth cannot reasonably be counted only against the rational model. One could always hope that things would be different if more money had been available in order to change more incentives.

It is important to turn from a general appraisal of economic development to a careful study of some particular policies. How do different kinds of people act in different situations? Here we begin to question the adequacy of the rational model as it is usually formulated. As pointed out above, only a very small proportion of the potential entrepreneurs in Pakistan took advantage of the changed situation after 1947. In Nigeria, the Ibo responded with unique vigor and success to situational conditions that they shared with several other, less active tribes. Why is it that groups respond differently to similar conditions? If we apply the rational model to these cases after the fact, we can interpret almost any response to a situation as reasonable, under the circumstances. It was rational for the Memon to take advantage of new incentives in Pakistan; yet it was also rational for other communities not to change. How can both statements be true? Surely if we look hard enough we will always find some special conditions faced by the "other communities," which make their inactivity reasonable. Of course the trouble is that it is difficult to specify these special conditions in advance and to be sure that they apply only to the groups who were inactive. That is, the rational model is not very successful at generating clear predictions about any given situation. Rather, it is often used as a schema that leads us to search for special conditions that might explain a man's behavior after the fact. There is almost always some sense in which any man's behavior is rational, in that he is trying to maximize some interest.

We have introduced the psychological concept of achievement motivation, or n Achievement, to account for the differences in response to similar conditions. There is impressive evidence that n Achievement is associated with more vigorous effort and greater success in economic activity: in highly industrialized Western countries such as the United States (McClelland, 1965a; Sheppard and Belitsky, 1966) and Finland (Kock, 1965); in developing countries such as Mexico (Andrews, 1967) and Nigeria (LeVine, 1966); and even among peasants (Rogers and Neill, 1966). The laboratory research on n Achievement shows that different n Achievement (and fear of failure) levels will lead to very different responses to situations and incentives which are externally identical. Certain motive patterns actually lead to withdrawal from "improved" incentives. We are, therefore, suggesting that motivation is an important variable which has to be taken into account in policy as well as theory, if we are to understand the way in which situations and incentives can affect behavior.

Does the *n* Achievement research suggest that the rational model is of no use in understanding and predicting economic behavior? It does not. The model of Atkinson posits motive strength (an individual disposition) as only one factor in the complex interaction of motive, expectation, and incentive that leads to behavior. How can we reconcile the *n* Achievement research with the compelling if ambiguous simplicity of the rational model? Let us review the terms of the rational model: Men act so as to *maximize* their *interest(s) or return(s)* over some *time period,* given the *perceived constraints of the situation.* Each of the emphasized terms of this statement of the rational model contains ambiguities that need to be clarified.

1. *Interest(s) or Return(s).* What is the man trying to maximize? Money? Growth of the firm? His own prestige and power? The Good Life? Leisure? However all of these terms may be defined, it seems clear that pursuing one interest rather than another will lead to quite different actions and enormously different economic effects. The Hausa who were less upwardly mobile than the Ibo may have been trying to maximize leisure. So working shorter hours is rational. An Indian businessman prefers to keep tight control of his company rather than to expand its capital base. So he uses his own funds to buy out the other stockholders, and convert the business to a "Private, Limited" status. Yet given his interest, his action is "rational." A moneylender chooses to loan funds at 24 per cent annual interest to finance elaborate marriage ceremonies, rather than to set up a business. If he wants to maximize his money, he is rational. In short, if the rational model merely says that men try to get what they want, it is of little use in understanding which things they come to want. If it asserts that all men want the same thing(s), it seems clearly wrong. Of course this has been the dilemma of every unitary hedonistic theory of behavior: any category that tries to include all of men's manifest interests—utiles, libido, or pleasure—is either hopelessly vague or else circular.

2. *Maximization.* What strategy or criteria does the man use to maximize the expected value of his outcome? Or does he follow a strategy of minimizing any conceivable loss, no matter what the probability of its occurrence? Is he so optimistic that he does not pay attention to possible negative payoffs? Each of these strategies or decision criteria can be thought of as rational and appropriate, given certain assumptions about the world and about one's own actions (Milnor, 1954). Yet the eco-

nomic consequences of using a particular strategy will be different from those of using another one. For example, a man who operates with a strategy that assumes the world will respond with complete malevolence to any choice that he makes, and who therefore selects the option with the lowest negative payoff, will be very unlikely to risk his money by investing it in a factory, even if the possible return is greater than what he now receives. This is analogous to a high fear of failure as discussed above. Thus it is of little use to know that a man is maximizing some interest—even money—until we know the general strategy that he is using.

3. *Time Perspective.* It is essential to know the man's time perspective, if we are to predict how he will respond to any change in his situation. Is he working for the maximum immediate gain? This is characteristic of the so-called trader mentality, in which the short-run accumulation of highly liquid assets dominates all economic activity. The trader mentality is rational, given a short-run time perspective. However, it is unlikely that this time perspective will be conducive to the long-range planning and extended bearing of risk that is required for economic development.

4. *The Perceived Constraints of the Situation.* What is the man's own view of the situation, in contrast with the judgment of an outside observer? Since a man's actions are guided largely by his own perception and evaluation of the situation, any incentive (advantage) or disincentive (difficulty) must be perceived as such by him in order for it to have its fullest and most appropriate effect. There are consistent individual differences in the ways in which advantages and difficulties are perceived, judged, and acted upon. Considering the patterns of individual difference reported by Atkinson and Feather (1966), we argue here that a man's maximization of interests over time is always with respect to the situation as he perceives or processes it. We cannot anticipate a man's actions until we understand his perceptions.

Our contention is therefore not that the rational model is wrong, but rather that it is only a very general framework for all human action. In order to understand and predict action, we must know the interests, strategy, time perspective, and perceived environment of the man. Our further contention is that when these additional terms are known and fully specified, it is largely irrelevant to ask whether the rational model as such is true. The importance of the model consists in the further specification of its terms: interests, strategy, time perspective, and perceptions.

Now such specific terms as interest in business growth, long-term time perspective, and a cautious but optimistic view of the world are probably widespread in Western industrial cultures. Consequently, development policies which enhanced certain kinds of opportunities and incentives (Keynesian economics, the Marshall Plan) worked well. Theorists concluded that the Western framework of the rational model was itself true—i.e., that it applied everywhere and always to the economic behavior of men. However, precisely because these particular specific terms of the model are so widely diffused and even unconscious in Western industrial culture, they were not fully articulated in the model. Hence they were not included in the specification of policies and recommendations in the developing countries. No doubt some entrepreneurs and managers in other cultures had the same perspectives and interests as their counterparts in the West. Here the assumed framework of the rational model seemed to work by itself, as among a few communities in Pakistan and the Ibo in Nigeria. But in many cases the interests, strategies, and perspectives were different. Thus we have many cases, some of which are mentioned earlier in this chapter, which constitute a kind of territory over which the rational and the motivational theories of development have fought some rather fruitless battles.

We here suggest that for the rational model to be useful, several of its terms have to be specified. Certain patterns of terms seem to lead to economic development, and certain patterns do not. From our review of research on *n* Achievement, we concluded that it was a motive that led to vigorous economic activity. At this point we shall attempt to show how various aspects of the *n* Achievement behavior syndrome are precisely those that are necessary to make the rational model work in a way that promotes economic development. That is, we shall review the characteristics of *n* Achievement in terms of interests, strategy of maximizing, time perspective, and perception of the environment.

First, what interests or desires for return are characteristic of men with high *n* Achievement? The evidence seems clear that these men are interested in excellence for its own sake, rather than for rewards of money, prestige, or power. Men high in *n* Achievement will not work harder at a task when money is offered as a reward (Atkinson and Reitman, 1956). They evaluate roles on the basis of the opportunities for excellence rather than those for prestige. (Burnstein, Moulton, and Liberty, 1963). Their achievement concern is not affected by having to work for the group rather than for only themselves (French, 1958b). They pick experts rather than friends as work partners (French, 1956). Over time they tend to become successful entrepreneurs, rather than equally wealthy men in other roles (McClelland, 1961, 1965a). This connection between entrepreneurial activity and *n* Achievement holds even in Poland, a social system where presumably the direct individual financial return from profits is considerably attenuated (McClelland, 1961, pp. 262–65). So it seems clear that *n* Achievement leads to an interest in entrepreneurial excellence in its most general sense, and not to interests which may be superficially associated with it or confused with it in Western industrial culture, such as wealth, prestige, or individual prominence and influence.

What strategies of maximizing will a man with high *n* Achievement follow? From Heckhausen's summary (1967, pp. 91–103) of many studies of goal setting under conditions of risk, the following propositions seem to be valid: (1) Men high in *n* Achievement are more concerned with achieving success than with avoiding failure. That is, they are not likely to select defensive strategies which minimize failure at the cost of giving up decisive individual action. (2) Compared with men low in *n* Achievement, they pay more careful attention to the realistic probabilities of success which are attached to various alternative actions in a given situation. This suggests that they are more likely to make informal calculations of the expected values of outcomes, and to select over time those alternatives which have the highest expected values. (3) They sharply distinguish situations in which they have some control from situations where results depend largely on chance. That is, they do not assume that the world is unreasonably benevolent or malevolent, but they are aware of what they can do in it. Taking these propositions together, it seems clear that *n* Achievement leads to a strategy of maximization that is most likely to achieve success in the environment of economic decision-making. This particular strategy is no doubt assumed to be a part of the framework of the rational model, although it is by no means a universal strategy.

The evidence is clear that men with high *n* Achievement have a greater future time perspective. They are more concerned with the future, especially the medium- to long-term future. They are more willing to postpone immediate rewards in favor of large future rewards (see studies summarized in Heckhausen, 1967, pp. 42–45). The relevance of this future time perspective to the rational model seems clear. First, men with high *n* Achievement will be maximizing their interests over a longer time span, so that they are less likely to slip into the trader mentality. Second, their greater concern with the future probably enables them to form more accurate estimates of the probabilities of success and failure and this enhances their maximizing strategy.

Are there any general effects of *n* Achievement on the perceptions of the environment? Here we draw together some findings assembled by Heckhausen (1967, pp. 113–14, 122–24, 134–36). First, a man with high *n* Achievement is, surprisingly, better able to recall his failures and the tasks that were not completed and therefore counted as failures. Moreover, given the opportunity, he is more likely to return to these tasks in order to succeed if there is a reasonable probability of success. Even under situational pressures, men with high *n* Achievement are more likely to apply quick perception, practical reasoning, and insight to arrive at new and creative solutions to problems. In perceiving the environment, they are likely to be more independent: They make judgments based on their own experience and standards, rather than become overwhelmed by the perceptual environment or the opinions and pressures of other people. Any integration of these findings must remain tentative; however, taken together, they do suggest that *n* Achievement leads a man to pay more careful and accurate attention to his situation. He is perhaps less likely to rationalize or ignore his failures, and is more likely to maintain independence of judgment. Obviously such a cognitive style has important effects on the extent to which a man can use cues from the environment to maximize his interests over time. So we tentatively propose that *n* Achievement aids the perception of the situation in ways that make economic activity rational.

We have suggested that the *n* Achievement syndrome is associated with a particular configuration of terms in the rational model. Further, we suggest that this particular configuration of terms has usually been a hidden and unacknowledged assumption in the argument that economic activity can be stimulated by improving the incentives and opportunities in the situation. Of course vigorous economic activity has been and can be successfully encouraged by a policy of changing incentives alone; but only if the "target population" (entrepreneurs, managers in public enterprises, and the like) have the appropriate interests, strategies, time perspective, and perceptions—in short, if they have the appropriate structure of response to the situation. Changing the situation works only to the extent that the target population has a structure of response appropriate to the perception, evaluation, and action on these changed incentives. The many and varied experiences with development programs over the past two decades suggest that sometimes it does and sometimes it does not.

The Problems of Changing Men

If we accept the general theory of development outlined above, it becomes important to consider changing the structures of response of people, so that they will respond to changed situations in certain ways.

In psychological language, it becomes important to increase n Achievement. But just how important is it really? That question involves three separate issues.

1. Is it possible at all to change adult behavior—whether this is called changing personality, action, or structure of response? We introduce this question later in this chapter and in Chapter 2. Clearly many people think that changing people is so difficult, time-consuming, and costly compared to changing situations, that we may as well act as if it were impossible, and therefore tactically unimportant. The thesis of this book is that this is not necessarily the case.

2. Is it morally right to change people—particularly if it means changing old, familiar, and comfortable ways of life? Why should we try to export Western culture, with its vestiges of inhumanity and exploitation? Of course it appears, particularly to Americans, that there are no moral problems in changing the incentives and opportunities that are presented to a man, because he remains in some sense free to accept them or reject them. Whether this is the way people actually feel about changes in their situation is open to question, but it is largely beyond the scope of this book. The man who holds a carrot in front of a starving man may be in as complex a moral situation as the man who instead seeks to change the man's hunger drive. Here we suggest that the offering of personality change or increased n Achievement to a person can be made compatible with his preserving his freedom, dignity, and self-respect. Probably the moral aspect of either situational or personality change really depends on the specific program: Who does what, in what manner, and with what sanctions. We urge the reader to study the descriptions of the n Achievement training programs given in the next few chapters and to form his own conclusions. As to the question of disrupting old established ways and exporting the worst features of Western culture, we feel that the issues here are not what they often seem. Many people assume that the whole complex of Western culture is necessary to produce a vigorous, modern economic life; or, in other words, that n Achievement is associated with Western culture. Thus they make lists of various traditional beliefs and practices that in their view have to be changed. In fact, however, little attention and study is usually given to those people who do change and become effective entrepreneurs in developing countries. To preview our own research and conclusions, reported in Chapter 9, we feel that it is by no means proved that economic modernization means the wholesale abandonment of traditional beliefs and practices and the embracing of the worst nineteenth-century Western capitalism. To be specific, n Achievement is a

term that refers to particular qualities of a person's actions, perceptions, and experience. Numerous studies have demonstrated virtually no relationship between *n* Achievement and expressed beliefs and values (see Heckhausen, 1967, pp. 7–9). The characteristic entrepreneurial effects of *n* Achievement have been demonstrated in a wide variety of different cultures and over different time periods (McClelland, 1961). They are not Western, or modern, or associated with white culture.

3. Finally, however, there is a practical question. Granted that changing the structure of response to a situation will enhance the effects of changing the situation, how important is it relative to changing the situation? Aren't there always some men with the appropriate pattern of response already? To judge from the surveys of development program results mentioned above, the answer must be sometimes "Yes," sometimes "No." As an analogy, consider the production of steel from iron and coal. Bringing in iron will help to increase the production of steel, up to the limits of the availability of coal. Coal may exist, but in small quantities, in poor quality, or in relatively inaccessible areas. Existing coal reserves may be under semiautonomous political control or may be used fully for other purposes. In other words, in such a situation there will be immense costs to obtaining and transporting coal reserves to the desired point of steel manufacture. Therefore it is important to try to find nearer or more accessible coal reserves, for the manufacture of steel becomes impossible or very difficult as difficulties and costs of obtaining coal increase.

Let us apply this analogy to the supply of entrepreneurial motivation. A country may have some potential entrepreneurs, ready and waiting, but not enough of them. How many are enough? McClelland (1961, p. 423) gathers data to show that *n* Ach levels are inversely related to the amount of capital required per unit of output. So there is always a need for increased entrepreneurial motivation to reduce other costs. The potential entrepreneurs may have other statuses or functions in the society. They may come from a small geographical or ethnic group, such that it would be politically unfeasible to give them a virtual monopoly of the economy, as in the case of the Ibo in Nigeria or the Indians in East Africa. Finally, if the level of entrepreneurship is low, then development program officers may be driven to such extraordinary costs in providing incentives that the whole program may be jeopardized. For example, if it is "necessary" to provide an incentive of 100 per cent return on investment over a few years, can this be carried out in a political environment where many other people are experiencing acute want? As another related cost, consider the problem of waste. If the structure of response is largely inappropriate, then any manipulation of incentives will incur enormous waste—perhaps well over 90 per cent. How long can an economy of scarcity incur such waste before major resources of finance, foreign exchange, and natural resources are exhausted?

As an example of the costs of incentive programs, let us consider a new intensive program of incentives and opportunities for small industry that is now being carried out by several state governments in India (see Chapter 12). Large amounts of capital and machinery on loan-purchase, together with foreign exchange and raw materials quotas, are suddenly being made available to small businessmen. This is done through widely publicized programs, lasting several days, in the state capital. Decisions on applications are made within days (rather than months or even years), in the hope that bureaucracy and red tape can be cut down. Nevertheless, Indian officials estimate that perhaps 90 per cent of the resources put into these intensive programs may yield no productive return. Yet they feel that the situation is so desperate and stagnant that such a high price of waste is worth the 10 per cent productive return. Whether this is a wise policy cannot be answered here. However, if some investment were made simultaneously in achievement motivation training—that is, in changing the structure of response to these new incentives—the waste could be considerably reduced, perhaps to 75 per cent, 50 per cent, or even less. The productive yield from the programs of improving incentives would be dramatically enhanced. Just how dramatic the enhancement would be depends, of course, on the cost of the achievement motivation program in relation to its effects. In Chapter 7 we consider the measurable effects of the program. It is usually very difficult to calculate the precise yield of any educational or human resources program (see McClelland, 1966a). However, in Chapter 12 we have tried to make some preliminary calculations of cost in relation to these effects for the achievement motivation programs to be described in this book. Our results suggest that attempts to change the structure of response to incentives by increasing achievement motivation, as well as attempts to change incentives themselves, are likely to have significant economic effects.

Increasing the Urge to Improve

How are human values to be changed? Can we rely on social and economic or technical changes in the environment to produce the human characteristics necessary to support them? Many social theorists believe that human beings in the aggregate will adjust to their environment, that certain changes in the environment are more-or-less inevitable, and therefore, that the whole process of development of necessary values and attitudes is more-or-less automatic and can be expected to occur by natural processes. Often economists invoke the "demonstration effect" as the main source of changed wants and values. Poor people everywhere are gradually exposed to modern products such as fountain pens, better seed, or eyeglasses. They observe that the products have real utility for them. They want to purchase such articles, but in order to get enough money to do so, they have to work harder. Their achievement motivation is directly aroused by the promise of material gains. Douvan (1956) found that achievement motivation was significantly aroused in students from working-class backgrounds following failure only when they had been promised a reward in dollars if they succeeded. For the middle-class students, failure alone was sufficient to arouse achievement motivation. Sociologists such as Inkeles stress such major motivation-shaping forces as urbanization, the mass media, creation of the nation state, and the factory. "The city is itself a powerful new experience. It encourages, and indeed to some degree obliges, the individual to adopt many new ways of life" (Inkeles, 1966, p. 147). The individual is exposed to new consumer goods and new ideas. He may learn about being on time to catch a bus, or how to rely almost entirely on money as a means of surviving. He will almost certainly be exposed more to the mass media. As Pool says, "Where radio goes, there modernizing attitudes come in" (1966, p. 100). As the nation state becomes stronger and better organized, the individual is exposed to political rallies, posters, radio messages, the army, the police, the tax-collector—all sorts of influences that will eventually shape him into a man with more modern attitudes. Or if he works in a factory, as Inkeles points out, he should be under powerful influences to change. "There is always an intense concentration of physical and mechanical power brought to bear on the transformation of raw materials; orderly and routine procedures to govern the flow of work are essential; time is a powerful influence in guiding the work processes; power and authority generally rest on technical competence; and, as a rule, rewards are in rough proportion to performance." (1966, p. 149).

The strange part of this argument is that development ought to be fairly automatic, easy, and rapid. Yet it clearly is not. The literature is full of examples of how men have failed notably to be influenced by such factors, have failed to act in their own self-interest. Villagers can be exposed endlessly to radio messages on how to improve their farming practices, with almost no effect unless they are organized into discussion and action groups. In Inkeles's own study, it may be those who are most ready to be influenced by the factory who will expose themselves to it by working there. Thus one can argue that while the factory accelerates change, it may not be considered the primary influence initiating change. Oscar Lewis's reports on the urban poor in Mexico City (1961) show little evidence that they are developing high *n* Achievement from exposure to various "demonstration effects." Over and over again technical assistance has failed to evoke automatically the attitudes it should if it is to be considered a really effective source of attitude change. Consider an extreme case. An airplane is "obviously" a machine that requires careful handling by a pilot, if he is to survive. Anyone given the responsibility for an airplane ought to learn to be careful, precise, and expert in all that he does, because he knows that failure in any respect may lead to sudden death. Yet even the threat of such a severe punishment has not automatically produced the human qualities necessary to keep airplanes flying. For example, in the case of one small airline in Southern Mexico, twelve out of thirteen planes were cracked up by their pilots in the course of a year, and it was not because they didn't know how to fly them. It was because they overloaded, competed with each other to see who could get into or out of an airstrip first, and so forth.

In the town of Kakinada, Andhra Pradesh, India, where the project to be reported here is located, some fishermen eke out a miserable existence with very primitive, easily torn fishing nets in the Bay of Bengal. The government decided to provide nylon fishing nets, which were not easily torn and which could hold more fish. It is true that the fishermen caught more fish, but then one of two things happened. Some of the men stopped fishing when they caught their usual number of fish (a phenomenon well documented in other places by economists) and others caught more fish but used the extra income to buy more liquor and to have more fun. In neither case did technical aid automatically produce the values and attitudes necessary to produce economic development. Even if one argues that such cases are the exception rather than the rule, because in the aggregate general environmental forces and technical change gradually produce an urge to improve, at the very least one would have to admit that the process is slow and uncertain and that it would be worth looking for ways to speed it up.

Most theorists feel that education must be the answer to the problem. And in its more general sense it must be. Man must learn new habits, values, motives, attitudes. And it would certainly be more efficient if he could learn them directly through education rather than indirectly through gradual social and economic forces. But what kind of education? A case can be made for just any kind of education—that is, just the number of years of schooling of any type. Schooling and level of economic development are highly correlated around the world. For example, Harbison and Myers (1964) report that among 75 nations, GNP per capita is correlated .67 with primary school enrollment, .82 with secondary school enrollment, and .74 with third level enrollment. Becker (1964) has made a careful analysis to show that men with more education make more money over their lifetime, even when ability and background variables are equated for those who go on to school as compared with those who do not. The cross-national comparisons do not indicate which came first, that is, whether wealth made more education possible or education led to more wealth. But Becker's individual studies suggest that more education preceded and made possible the increase in individual income. McClelland (1966a) has shown elsewhere on an international basis that countries which invested heavily in secondary education on the average developed more rapidly economically a number of years later, when the educated population would have reached its peak capacity in the working force. It looks as if more of every kind of education would pay off in the human recourses that accelerate economic growth.

But can the type of education that is most useful be specified even further? It certainly cannot be concluded that more of any kind of education will increase *n* Achievement. For example, social class data show that while those with the least education have the lowest *n* Achievement, those with a moderate level of education in the middle classes have the highest *n* Achievement. Those with the most education have somewhat less *n* Achievement on the average than those from the middle classes (Rosen, 1959). The best guess is that education is most likely to produce the kind of people motivated to improve when it takes place in an achievement-oriented atmosphere. The data assembled in Table 1.2 make the point directly. Countries higher in *n* Achievement level in 1950 as measured in children's textbooks showed a higher average gain in rate of economic advance. So did countries enrolling a higher average per hundred thousand inhabitants in higher education relative to their economic level. That is, in this table enrollments in higher education for a given country are compared with those of another country at the same level, to see which was investing relatively more in education. Thus, Turkey is compared with Syria rather than with the United States, which is in a totally different class in terms of its ability to finance higher education and make use of university graduates. But it is the

Table 1.2

Rate of Economic Growth (1952-58) as a Function of n Achievement (1950) and Higher Education Enrollments Relative to Economic Level (1950)

(From McClelland, 1966a)

	ENROLLMENT IN HIGHER EDUCATION PER 100,000 INHABITANTS RELATIVE TO ECONOMIC LEVEL (1950)		
	Relatively High (1950)	*Relatively Low* (1950)	
High n Achievement (1950)** (2.10 or More)	a* USSR +1.62†	a W. Germany + .53	
	a US + .47	b France − .24	
	a Australia + .42	c Portugal + .76	
	a Canada + .06	c Spain + .01	
	b Israel +1.18	d Tunisia −1.87	
	c Ireland − .41	d Syria − .25	
	c Argentina − .56		Mean gain high n Ach = + .49
	d Bulgaria +1.37		
	d India +1.12		
	d Turkey +1.38		
	d Pakistan +2.75		
	Mean gain = + .86	Mean gain = − .18	
Low n Achievement (1950) (Below 2.10)	a New Zealand − .29	a England + .17	
	a Finland − .08	a Belgium −1.65	
	b Netherlands − .15	a Norway − .77	
	b Japan − .04	a Switzerland −1.92	
	b Italy − .57	a Sweden − .64	
	c Poland +1.26	b Denmark − .89	
	c Uruguay − .75	b Austria + .38	
		b Chile −1.81	Mean gain low n Ach = − .46
		c Hungary − .62	
		c Mexico + .12	
		d Iraq + .29	
		d Algeria − .83	
	Mean gain = − .09	Mean gain = − .68	

Mean gain for relatively high levels of university education = + .49

Mean gain for relatively low levels of university education = − .51

* The countries were first grouped by economic level in terms of Kwh electricity per capita produced in 1950. Group *a* includes all countries with a Kwh/cap electricity production above 1,000 in 1950; Group *b*, all countries with an electricity production between 400 and 900 Kwh/cap in 1950; Group *c*, all countries with an electricity production between 100 and 300 Kwh/cap in 1950; Group *d*, all countries with an electricity production below 100 Kwh/cap in 1950. The countries within a group were then listed according to the enrollment per 100,000 inhabitants in higher education in 1950. Those countries in which the enrollment was above the median for their economic level were classified as "relatively high" in higher education enrollment; countries whose enrollment was below the median were "relatively low."

** These are *n* Achievement scores obtained from children's textbooks about 1950. For an explanation, see McClelland, 1961. High *n* Achievement scores are 2.10 or more achievement images per story in the sample of stories coded.

† Positive and negative deviations in standard score units from the regression of the gain in electricity produced between 1952 and 1958 and initial level of electricity production in 1952. Positive scores indicate better than average expected gains in production; negative scores, the reverse (see McClelland, 1961, p. 100).

combination of high n Achievement and greater emphasis on higher education that really produces a high average rate of economic gain. Neither input alone works nearly as well, as Table 1.2 shows.

But how can an education be made achievement oriented? Most of the information on this question has come from studies dealing with a very special form of education—namely, child-rearing or early socialization practices. As noted previously, this research tradition was guided by the theoretical supposition that since motives are formed early in life, one must study how parents treat their children to find out how n Achievement is produced. The studies showed that parents of boys who were high in n Achievement set moderately high standards for them and were warm and encouraging in their attitudes toward their son's efforts to achieve. The fathers furthermore were generally nondominating, leaving the sons free to try things out on their own. But this result only raises another question. How did the parents get that way? What made them achievement-oriented in the first place? Answers have so far been fairly numerous but inconclusive.

For example, Whiting *et al.* (1966) fall back on what amounts to an environmental explanation based on classical economic reasoning. They note that cross-culturally the extended family is associated with obedience training and the nuclear family with self-reliance and independence training, which in turn have been shown to be related to n Achievement. So whenever a household shifts from an extended family pattern to a nuclear family pattern, there ought to be an increase in n Achievement. They note that just such changes occurred in the family in Elizabethan England at the time n Achievement has been shown to have risen, and again in colonial America when families were breaking up to move west. The descendants of these families, the Texans studied by Whiting *et al.*, strongly stress self-reliance and achievement training. Both in England and America, the factor which they feel was most responsible for breaking up the extended family was migration, either to the city or to a new country. Why did people migrate? In their terms, to seek economic advantage. So we are right back where we started: n Achievement is conceived as a kind of fallout from a change in family structure which is caused primarily by economic opportunities. But as noted above, lots of people do not migrate. Many never move and to explain the behavior of the few that do, it appears reasonable to infer that they had higher achievement motivation. So it is just as logical to argue that parents with higher achievement motivation were willing to migrate and break up extended families into nuclear families as it is to contend that the breakup of the family produced their n Achievement.

Other explanations have stressed the importance of ideological factors, derived in various ways. Hagen (1962) argues that it is loss of traditional status respect that gradually, over time, has driven certain minority groups to bring up their children in ways that will give them a strong urge to regain their former status. He cites such groups such as the Jews, or the Samurai in Japan. Unfortunately he has not subjected the hypothesis to an empirical test by collecting a representative sample of such cases to see if there are as many instances in which loss of status respect did not result in such a reaction or in which minority groups rose to the top economically without having been subjected to loss of status respect. *The Achieving Society* presents data showing that religious ideology may be important. Waves of Protestant revival in England were associated with rises in *n* Achievement, suggesting that Weber's argument for the key role of the Protestant ethic in the rise of capitalism may turn out to be only a particular case of a wider generalization to the effect that religious reform tends to increase *n* Achievement. Further evidence for this hypothesis comes from a study showing that villagers converted to radical Protestant Christianity in Southern Mexico were doing better economically and had children with higher *n* Achievement and more schooling than villagers nearby who had not been exposed to religious reform, though they had been the beneficiaries of land reform. Clearly the villagers who had been converted thought of themselves as superior to others around them. This feeling of superiority, however derived, may well be the key factor in leading parents to bring up their children in achievement-oriented ways. However, in both cases it is hard to conclude that child-rearing is really an important causal factor. As Flinn (1966) has pointed out, the Methodist revival occurred in the mid-eighteenth century, just about the same time that the *n* Achievement curve began to rise markedly. There was not enough time lag for the new reform ideology to cause parents to change the way they reared their children so that they would grow up with high *n* Achievement and become active in the industrial revolution decades later. Furthermore, early Methodists were authoritarian in their upbringing and produced few entrepreneurs, in any case, in the early years of the industrial revolution. It could scarcely be argued that Quakers and other dissenters who were more prominent in the ranks of the new industrialists had undergone a marked religious revival in the mid-eighteenth century. There is also not enough time lag in the Mexican village study for child-rearing to be of key importance. The economic effects of the Protestant conversion were noticeable eight years after the first missionary had entered the village, scarcely time enough to have produced a new, economically active generation.

The findings from analysis of children's textbooks published around 1950 also are not easily interpreted in terms of the importance of early childhood training. Variations in *n* Achievement levels in those textbooks were correlated with rates of economic gain very soon thereafter, from 1952 to 1958. Certainly there was no time for a long cycle effect such as a greater achievement mystique leading parents to do the kinds of things that would produce children with high *n* Achievement, who would grow up to be energetic entrepreneurs. A far simpler interpretation of the data is that a greater achievement mystique helps arouse latent *n* Achievement in at least some small segments of the population, which then begin to act in more entrepreneurial ways. If this interpretation is correct, the longer lead times found in earlier historical studies would have to be explained in terms of the fact that it took longer for aroused entrepreneurs to have any significant impact in the economic sphere. But if we now conclude that parental child-rearing is not so important as it once seemed to be, the question still remains: Where does an increase in achievement concern in individuals come from? Variations in national *n* Achievement levels do vaguely fit the "ideological reform" hypothesis. That is, countries such as Russia and China that were swept by zealous Communist ideological revolutions have shown marked increases in *n* Achievement level as measured in children's textbooks (see McClelland, 1961 and 1963). Communist revolutionaries certainly talked and acted like ideological reformers with strong achievement concerns. They also thought of themselves as superior in some sense to traditional bourgeois societies, just as the early Protestants felt in reforming the church. Furthermore, many new nations that have had to fight their way to freedom from colonial rule have elevated *n* Achievement levels in their textbooks (see McClelland, 1961).

But one can still ask: Where do the reformers come from? What sets such a dynamic "revival movement" in motion? LeVine (1966) has sought an answer in social structure. In trying to explain why the Ibo in Nigeria are much more upwardly mobile and achievement-oriented than the Hausa, he points out that the Ibo have traditionally had a social system in which a young man can gain prestige by becoming a member of certain honorary societies. Getting into one of these societies depends on achieving occupational success and wealth. Thus, every parent, or every young man for that matter, sees that he ought to strive for achievement if he is ever to be successful in Ibo society. On the other hand, in Hausa society, the way to gain success is to attach oneself to a more powerful leader in a kind of client relationship, since rewards are bestowed from the top. A young Hausa sees that he is likely to gain recognition by being part of the entourage of a powerful person whose success he must therefore work for. According to LeVine these different traditional status mobility systems promote different ideological systems, which in turn create different personality types. Certainly such social systems should reinforce and help maintain certain patterns of motivation, but one wonders how a system ever gets set up that way in the first place, or more particularly, how it would be possible to change it, once it has been set up. In fact, as noted above, a social-systems analysis is not very helpful in suggesting ways in which a particular pattern can be changed. For instance, suppose someone decided that the Hausa should become more achievement oriented. How could such a change be brought about? One might try to introduce the honorary society system employed by the Ibo, but could it succeed, unless the ideology of the Hausa had somehow been prepared to accept it?

So while the *n* Achievement mystique may have various sources, and while it may be maintained in various ways by the social structure, it is hard to imagine a more effective way to introduce it than by some kind of direct educational technique. Other, more indirect methods may work in the long run. But a brief survey of the evidence suggests that they will work best if there is already some receptivity, some elements of an achievement orientation present among the people to be influenced. Thus, a direct attempt to increase levels of achievement motivation in people and in a community seems to be eminently worth trying. No doubt an economic rationalist would admit that an increased *n* Achievement might add something to the effectiveness of the economic opportunities and incentives he is manipulating. The personality specialist might grant that the evidence does not clearly show that one has to wait a generation until specially trained children grow up. The historian might conclude that ideological reform movements, as in the Protestant Reformation, Communist revolutions, or the nationalism of new nations all have been important sources of increases in social *n* Achievement levels. These reform movements furthermore have usually affected minority groups, which have thought of themselves as superior to the masses around them and which have often had higher achievement motivation and great entrepreneurial success. All might then grant that it is conceivable the same type of dedication could be created among a band of entrepreneurs whose achievement motivation had been directly influenced. Such a project would obviously have great theoretical and practical importance. The ultimate test that *n* Achievement is a key ingredient in economic growth must be an experiment aimed at altering it to see what the effects would be. One must always wonder whether all the studies—historical, experimental, theoretical—have been interpreted in the only possible way. The network of linked findings reported in *The Achieving Society* and since may seem persuasive, but it is nowhere near as persuasive as an actual demonstration that would show the effect of an increase in *n* Achievement on economic growth directly and empirically. On the practical side, if the experiment proves to be successful, planners and policy-makers everywhere who are interested in accelerating economic growth would have a new tool. And planners need new tools; there is no question about that. The normal tools may be working—more investment in everything from schools to roads to banks to steel mills—but they are working slowly and it is difficult to establish priorities among them. It would indeed be exciting if we could discover that a specific short-term educational input in a tiny segment of the population would have far-reaching economic effects. It is for all these reasons that the attempts reported in this volume to increase achievement motivation in entrepreneurs were undertaken.

CHAPTER 2

CAN ADULTS ACQUIRE
A STRONG NEED
TO ACHIEVE?[1]

The research plan requires that achievement motivation be developed in adult businessmen, but is this possible? When the project was initiated in 1960, the dominant view among psychologists was that it was highly unlikely that motives could be acquired in adulthood. The reasons for such an opinion were several and convincing. To begin with, the great majority of psychologists had more-or-less accepted the psychoanalytic view that basic personality characteristics such as motives are laid down in early childhood in a lasting form which could be modified, if at all, only partially by intensive and prolonged psychotherapy. From this point of view, a very strong need for Achievement would be regarded as a neurotic solution to some childhood conflict, such as the desire to surpass the father and replace him in the mother's affection. For instance, Freud reports that it is remarkable how regularly analytic findings testify to the close connection between "ambi-

1. Much of the material in this chapter is a revised and extended version of an earlier paper by D. C. McClelland, "Toward a theory of motive acquisition," *American Psychologist,* 1965, 20, 321–33(b).

[39]

tion, fire and urethral erotism" (1930, p. 54). He argues that the roots of ambition lie in the childhood impulse to surpass other men by putting out fire with a stream of urine. Murray (1955) and Ogilvie (1967) have pursued the idea further in demonstrating a connection between bed-wetting and dreams of soaring high above all others in the so-called Icarus complex.

If some such early childhood problem is at the root of a strong achievement drive, how would it be possible to develop ambition in men long after this period in their lives? Would it not require re-creation of some of the emotional experiences of early childhood, and the reworking of conflict resolutions that had a long history of turning into other channels?

American learning theory is scarcely more encouraging about the possibility of acquiring motives late in life. The culture and personality school (cf. Kardiner, 1945; McClelland, 1951; Whiting, 1961) argued that basic personality structure was indeed formed in early childhood, because associations formed at that time were likely to be stronger and more enduring for several reasons: they were more apt to be unconscious, that is, less represented by verbal symbol systems and therefore less accessible to change later on; they were more likely to be extraordinarily emotional because they are less modulated by adult time, place, and person schemas that limit the impact of a particular event in late maturity; and, above all, they occurred first and therefore would be likely to shape later learning. Thus most writing from this perspective about the acquisition of motives has stressed the importance of various child-rearing techniques and their roles in developing various motives (Sears, Maccoby, and Levin, 1957). And it is a fact that what parents do is associated with variations in *n* Achievement in their sons (see McClelland, 1961, Ch. 9). So the logical inference is that the time to influence motives is early in life, not adulthood when the basic personality structure is already so stabilized that it shapes and distorts whatever might come later in the form of an educational effort. Thus, for example, Kardiner (1945) argues that even a major ideological system such as Christianity does not directly affect basic personality structure, but is shaped by it. He feels that teaching the "Protestant work ethic" to the Alorese would be impossible and absurd because of the deep unconscious personality structure formed in early childhood that would inevitably shape such an education in its own image.

There is still a further theoretical reason why early childhood is the critical period for acquisition of motives. N Achievement is commonly referred to by learning theorists as a secondary or social motive, which has developed out of close association with reduction in primary drives like hunger, thirst, or other physical discomforts. These drives are certainly more urgent in childhood; and if one thinks that some children acquire an achievement need because they have happened to discover that achievement responses bring rewards, say in reducing hunger, then it would be difficult to imagine a training situation in adulthood that could replicate the conditions under which such learning first occurred. Should we make businessmen hungry and give them food only when they make an achieving response? Even proponents of the theory might feel that duplicating these conditions in adulthood would not develop the strong pervasive, undifferentiated drive acquired when the organism was less mature.

Not only did prevailing psychological theories argue against the possibility of developing n Achievement in adulthood, but the facts as to the effectiveness of psychotherapy also made success seem unlikely. Beginning in 1952, Eysenck marshalled some rather impressive data showing how difficult it is to prove that psychotherapy of the more traditional sort has any effect whatsoever. According to his figures, about two thirds of people with personality disorders get well without treatment, whereas with treatment the cure rate "varies between 44% and 70%" (Eysenck, 1960). Although Eysenck's facts and arguments have come under severe attack, they were sufficiently convincing to cast serious doubt on whether short-term efforts to change personality could work when much longer, more intensive efforts apparently had not succeeded. And certainly if the research strategy outlined in the first chapter is to be followed, the training inputs or efforts at personality change would have to be fairly short-term in order to get the information desired within a reasonable length of time. Bergin (1966) has reviewed many of the same therapeutic evaluation studies and come up with an even more disturbing conclusion—namely, that therapy makes a significant number of people worse, while it makes others better. If the two kinds of patients are pooled, the effects cancel each other out, so that it often appears the group as a whole has improved no more than a control group without treatment. In a way, such a conclusion is even more alarming because it raises ethical questions. Is it right to subject a person to a personality change program which might make him worse off than before? It is certainly not always clear that it is as proper to teach a person a new motive as it is to teach him skill like playing the piano. At the time this research was undertaken, Bergin had not yet collected the evidence for his conclusion, but certainly we were aware that this research would run into ethical difficulties as well as theoretical and empirical ones.

Nevertheless, even in 1960, some minority views were not drowned out by the consensus that teaching motivation to adults would be impracticable. On the one hand, a few educators, operating without benefit of technical psychological knowledge, seemed to have been quite effective in changing peoples's lives. Certainly Communist party functionaries, Mormon missionaries, even Dale Carnegie or Billy Graham seemed to be having enough impact on people's lives to make one wonder if the majority view among psychologists about the resistance of adults to change could really be correct. To be sure, the "conversions" obtained by such "nonprofessional" methods have not been adequately studied; they might be superficial, and they might represent no more than what the person would have done without the influence attempt. Yet they certainly made one wonder if changing people was hard for people who thought it was hard and easy for those who thought it could be done.

Furthermore, there was a vociferous minority among psychologists who challenged the consensus that early childhood was so important. They were the radical behaviorists, followers of B. F. Skinner, who did not accept complex ideas about a psychic structure in which deep, underlying, unconscious motives lie buried at the bottom. They retain a faith in the infinite plasticity of human behavior in which one response is just like any other, and any such response can be "shaped up" or strengthened by reward—presumably even an achievement response as produced by a subject in a fantasy test (cf. Bandura & Walters, 1963, pp. 238 ff.). In fact, the "naive" optimism of one such researcher (Burris, 1958) had a lot to do with getting the present research underway. He undertook a counseling program in which an attempt to elicit and reinforce achievement-related fantasies proved to be successful in motivating college students to get better grades. Even Eysenck, who is generally so skeptical about the effectiveness of therapy, is prepared to grant that the so-called "operant conditioners" have been unusually successful in relieving people of symptoms (Eysenck, 1960).

So while most psychologists were pessimistic about personality change, a few were very optimistic, and it was to the optimists we turned for some theoretical guidance as to what we were about to attempt. For if we were to change motives in adulthood, we had to have at least some rudimentary notion as to what was to be changed and why it could be changed at some point other than early childhood. In other words, what is a motive? What would we be trying to change? In connection with the early work on *n* Achievement, McClelland, Atkinson, Clark, and Lowell (1953) attempted an answer to these questions, and while the answer has not been widely accepted (cf. Berelson and Steiner, 1964), it needs to be briefly summarized here to provide a theoretical under-pinning for our attempts at motive change. It starts with the proposition that all motives are learned, that not even biological discomforts (as from hunger) or pleasure (as in sexual stimulation) are "urges" or "drives" until they are linked with cues that can signify their presence or absence. In time, clusters of expectancies or associations grow up around affective experiences, many of which are not connected by any means with biological needs (McClelland *et al.*, 1953, Ch. 2). These clusters of expectancies are commonly labeled motives. More formally, motives are *affectively toned associative networks* arranged in a hierarchy of strength or importance within a given individual. Obviously the definition fits closely the operation used to measure a motive: "an affec-tively toned associative cluster" is exactly what is coded in a subject's fantasies to obtain an *n* Achievement score. Thus, if he writes stories containing many references to doing something well, doing things bet-ter than someone else, or overcoming obstacles to achieve his goal, he is recorded as having a high *n* Achievement score, which is simply another way of saying that he tends to think or free associate a lot along achievement lines.

The strength of a motive (its position in the individual's hierarchy of motives) is measured essentially by counting the number of as-sociations belonging to this cluster as compared to other associations that an individual produces on a given occasion.

If one thinks of a motive as an associative network, it is easier to imagine how to change it: the problem becomes one of moving its posi-tion up in the hierarchy by increasing its salience compared to other clusters. It should be possible to accomplish this end by such techniques as the following (a) Setting up the network—discovering what associa-tions, for example, exist in the achievement area, and then extending, strengthening, or otherwise improving the network that they form; (b) Conceptualizing the network—forming a clear and conscious verbal construct that labels the network; (c) Tying the network to as many cues as possible in everyday life, especially those preceding and following actions, to insure that the network will be regularly rearoused once formed; and (d) working out the relation of the network to superordinate associative clusters, like the self-concept, so that these dominant schemata do not block the train of achievement thoughts—for example, through a chain of interfering associations (e.g., "I am not really the achieving type").

Such a formulation at least takes some of the mystery out of the concept of "deep, underlying, unconscious motives" and helps to define concrete goals for the techniques of change. But what about the techniques themselves? How could we bring about the changes outlined? Here the decision was made at the outset to be *eclectic* and *systematic* in our attempts to develop *n* Achievement. We decided to be eclectic partly because we had no allegiance to any particular school of psychology, but mostly because of our own fears based on all the arguments given above that we would not be able to change motives in adulthood. That is, we decided to leave no stone unturned in searching through the experimental or clinical literature to find variables that someone had demonstrated to be effective in producing behavior change. Thus, from the extensive literature on learning, we noted that such variables as the frequency of reward, the meaningfulness of material learned, and recitation were important in producing rapid alterations in behavior. From the studies of the effectiveness of psychotherapy, we found that warmth and empathy on the part of the therapist seemed to promote more rapid improvement (Bergin, 1966, p. 239). And from the attitude-change research literature, we learned that using reason or prestige to support an argument and affiliating with a new reference group are variables that are crucial for developing new attitudes (cf. Hovland, Janis, and Kelley, 1953; Cohen, 1964). Our purpose, above all, was to produce an effect large enough to be measured. Thus we tried to profit by all that is known about how to facilitate learning or produce personality or attitude change. For if we could not obtain a substantial effect with all factors working to produce it, there would be no point to studying the effects of each factor taken singly. Such a strategy also had the practical advantage of putting us in a position of doing our best to deliver the goods to our course participants, since they were giving us their time and attention to take part in a largely untried educational experience.

Our overall research strategy thus has been systematically subtractive rather than additive. That is, we have tried first to produce a major effect using as many factors as possible. Then, once a substantial effect had been obtained, factors could be subtracted one by one until the effect decreased notably or disappeared. In this way it should ultimately be possible to isolate what variables or what combinations of training variables produce the maximum increase in *n* Achievement in most people.

Obviously, such a strategy shapes the way the training has to be designed and carried out. To begin with, the variables or training inputs, have to be clearly enough defined to be subtractible. Most psychotherapeutic procedures, such as nondirective therapy or psychoanalysis, are all of a piece. It is scarcely possible, at least intentionally, to be a nondirective therapist in one way (e.g., warm) and not another (e.g., empathic). Yet our design calls for therapeutic-like courses in which such inputs can in fact be present or absent without disrupting the whole nature of the relationship to the participants. Secondly, the effects of the courses on the participants must be systematically evaluated over a period of years after training, in order to detect which variable or combination of variables is having the most effect. Measuring the outcome of therapy or personality change efforts is fraught with difficulties, but the design requires that some objective measures be found to evaluate whether *n* Achievement has been appreciably increased following training.

Such an input/output research strategy puts further limitations on how the change efforts can be carried out. If any systematic information is to be gathered on relative effectiveness, the influence attempts could not very well be on a one-to-one basis over long periods of time, as in the model of traditional psychotherapy. They had to be more in the nature of brief courses for groups of individuals. Furthermore, they had to be voluntary, if we were to avoid getting into ethical difficulties. Fortunately, these design requirements matched fairly well with a practice common in the business world, in which managers go off for several weeks to attend a seminar. Thus it has proved practicable to present and give our achievement motivation development courses as variants of standard management-training seminars.

What exactly has gone into these new courses? While each of them requires a large package of training materials—games, paper and pencil exercises, outside reading, tests—it is convenient to summarize the basic inputs under four main headings: the achievement syndrome (A), self-study (S), goal-setting (G), and interpersonal supports (I). As we take up each of these classes of inputs in turn, it is well to remember that their order of impact on the participants is not necessarily the same as the order in which they are described. They are themes which, if included at all, are interwoven throughout the seven to ten days of the course. Even when shorter or longer courses are given—they have varied from two to twenty-one consecutive days—a given theme may be presented in greater or lesser length and detail.

The Achievement Syndrome (A)

Fantasy. The simplest and most obvious training input is to teach the course participants how to recognize and produce achievement-related fantasies. They first take a form of the Thematic Apperception

Test in which they write imaginative stories about a series of pictures. They then learn how to code what they have written according to the standard system for identifying *n* Achievement. That is, they learn when a statement in the story refers to "doing better" (i.e., competing with a standard of excellence), to long-term involvement with a work problem, or to a unique accomplishment. Furthermore, they learn the specific subcategories of the scoring system as illustrated in Figure 2.1. They can

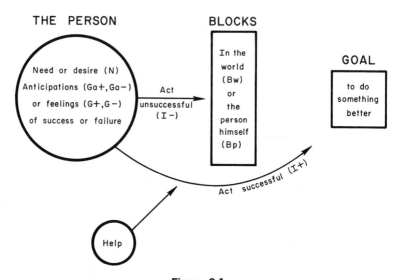

Figure 2.1
The Organization of Subcategories in the n Achievement Scoring System (After McClelland et al., **1953**)

in time distinguish between a *desire* to accomplish something, an *act* designed to achieve the goal, and a *block* either *personal* or in the *world* which stands in the way of success. They then rewrite the stories at various times, trying to maximize the number of scoring categories they can introduce. For instance, under the conventions of the scoring system, it is possible to get a score of +11 for each story, so that if they write six stories, they could in fact obtain a maximum score of 66. Few can do this without considerable practice, but most are able after a few lessons to get much higher scores than they did at first.

The idea behind this training is very simple. It is to form the associative network, which in a certain sense could be considered the motive itself. Most people who take the course think they know what achievement is and how to think along achievement lines, but they soon learn how general, vague, and imprecise their notions are. Here, for example, is a story written by a man who had heard a lot about *n* Achievement and who thought he knew what it involved.

> This man is an architect. It is late at night. He has taken on a job and the deadline is tomorrow but could be extended. On the table, a snapshot of his wife and kids; they are waiting for him. He would like to drop everything and take the train. He could do it, but he decides to meet the challenge. He will call home, take the rap, and complete the job.

Having written the story, he checked with the scoring system to see how much achievement imagery he had introduced. Somewhat to his surprise, he discovered, as most course participants do, that he had produced almost no phrases or sentences that could legitimately be scored for *n* Achievement. For instance, reference to a "deadline" does not qualify as concern with a standard of excellence or doing better, nor does "completing the job." Not even "meeting the challenge" is necessarily achievement related, since it may only mean that he wants to finish on time. There is no explicit statement that he wants to do a better job or to improve the way he is doing his job. Furthermore, much of the story deals with his guilt over making his family wait. The words and phrases in the story must be *explicitly* concerned with achievement in order to be scored for *n* Achievement. Much time has to be spent with course participants in detailed discussions of this sort which gradually shape and refine the meaning of the *n* Achievement scoring categories as separate and distinct from other motive systems, such as the need for Power or the need for Affiliation.

The purpose of this course input is to give the participant a carefully worked out associative network with appropriate words or labels to describe all its various aspects. In fact, if the course lasts an appreciable length of time, participants commonly tend to use the new language of the coding system, including its abbreviations, such as Ga+, I+, and Bw (see Figure 2.1), to describe not only the stories, but also what is happening in their own lives or in the activities of others. The achievement language becomes a kind of framework which can be used to describe almost anything that happens—from what they read in the newspapers during the course to an example someone gives of how he conducts his business.

It is important to stress that not just the label (*n* Achievement) is taught. The person must be able to produce easily and often the new associative network itself. It is here that our approach comes close to traditional therapy, which might be understood as the prolonged and laborious formation of new associative networks to replace old anxiety-laden ones. That is, a patient over time comes to form a new associative network covering his early relations, for example, to his father and mother, which still later he may learn to refer to as his Oędipus complex. Cues that formerly would have produced anxiety-laden associations now evoke the new associations instead; the old ones are blocked out by associative interference. But all therapists, whether Freudian or Rogerian, insist that the person must learn to produce these associations in their new form spontaneously and often, and that teaching the label is not enough. Thus, the training involves far more than simple directive slogans such as "Get out there and be an achiever!" Trying to impose a new construct on an old set of associations is unlikely to be effective unless the whole network of associations itself is revised in detail. The hypothesis behind this instructional input can be stated as follows:

Proposition A-1. *The more thoroughly an individual develops and clearly conceptualizes the associative network defining a motive, the more likely he is to develop the motive.* What reasons are there for believing such a hypothesis might turn out to be correct? It receives backing from quite a number of different sources. As already noted, it seems to describe what in fact is going on in much of psychotherapy—namely, the formation and coding of a new associative network with different transitional probabilities among its various elements. From the radical behaviorist's point of view, the proposition is almost true by definition. That is, if the term *motive* in this tradition has any meaning at all, it refers simply to the associative responses coded for *n* Achievement, and if these are strengthened by reinforcement, the motive itself is by definition strengthened. But support for the proposition also derives from other sources, particularly the so-called "set" experiments. For decades laboratory psychologists have known that one of the easiest and most effective ways to change behavior is to change the subject's set. If he is responding to stimulus words with the names of animals, tell him to respond with the names of vegetables and he can change his behavior immediately and efficiently without a single mistake. At a more complex level, Orne (1962) has pointed out how powerful a set such as "This is an experiment" can be. He notes that if you were to go up to a stranger and say something like "Lie down!" he would in all probability either laugh or escape as soon as possible. But if you say, "This is an experiment! Lie down!" more often than not, if there are other supporting cues in the environment, the person will do as he is told. Orne has demonstrated how subjects will perform nonsensical and fatiguing tasks for very long periods of time under the set "This is an experiment." At an even more complex level, sociologists have noted how quickly a person will change his behavior as he adopts a new role set, as when he becomes a teacher, a parent, or a public official. In all these instances an associative network may be said to exist, usually with a label conveniently attached, which we call a set and which, when it is aroused or becomes salient, proceeds to regulate behavior very effectively. Obviously the person who is told "This is an experiment" must have a cluster of ideas as to what an experiment involves and what the proper behavior for a subject in an experiment is, before he will perform according to instructions. The label by itself is not enough: it symbolizes the associative network which does control behavior.

But why should a change in set or its corresponding associative network be so influential in controlling behavior? The explanation lies in part in the symbolic character of thought. Learned acts may have limited influence because they often cannot occur without reality supports (as in typewriting or swimming), but learned thoughts (symbolic acts) can occur any time, any place, in any connection. They may be applied to whatever the person is doing. They can be more readily generalized than actions.

They also are less easily inhibited than actions. Isak Dinesen tells the story of the oracle who told the king he would get his wish so long as he never thought of the left eye of a camel. Needless to say, the king did not get his wish, but he could easily have obeyed the oracle's prohibition if it had been to avoid *looking* at the left eye of a camel. Thought sequences are simply harder to control voluntarily than act sequences. One may learn to swim, dance, type, make a public speech, read a book, and yet with relative ease avoid doing any of these things. On the other hand, it does not appear to be so easy to stop thinking in achievement terms once one has learned specifically what is involved, unless some new thought sequence is learned which blocks out achievement thinking through associative interference.

But what does it matter what a person thinks about? Isn't it possible that he might think about achievement all day long and still never do anything? What reason do we have for believing that changing the frequency with which a person thinks about certain things will have an effect on what he does? To begin with, motor learning experiments have shown that symbolic practice facilitates actual performance (cf. Hovland, 1951, p. 644). If a person stands still imagining himself performing a certain motor task, he will actually perform that task better when he tries than if he had not engaged in imaginary practice. Thus, in a sense achievement thinking is symbolic preparation for achievement acting. And in fact Skolnick has reported some data (1966), reanalyzed by McClelland (1966b), to show that in general there are low positive correlations between frequencies of thinking about certain activities and frequencies with which they are carried out. But given our overall research goal of producing a large training effect, it would obviously be unwise to leave the matter of performing achievement actions up to the individual to work out for himself. Therefore achievement actions became the subject of the next training input to be described.

Action. Years of research have shown that people with high *n* Achievement tend to act in certain characteristic ways. By analogy one might conceive of their "thought-stream" as showing a high concentration of "virus *n* Ach," and then ask how people with such a high "infection level" tend to act in real life. According to studies summarized in *The Achieving Society* (1961), they display four characteristic modes of acting, each of which becomes the focus of training in the course.

1. They tend to set moderate goals for themselves and to work harder when the chances of succeeding are only moderately great. The reason seems to be that they are trying to maximize their achievement satisfaction, since obviously if the task is very easy they can feel no sense of accomplishment from succeeding at it, whereas if the task is very difficult they are unlikely to succeed at it. The point can be made easily with a ringtoss game, which is actually used as a training input. Each man is taken out of the room, shown a peg some distance away, given three rings, and asked to see how many he can throw over the peg. He is further instructed that he may stand at any distance he likes from the peg. The examiner's task is simply to record where he stands and how many ringers he makes. After each man has performed the task, the instructor reports the results for each individual to the group, explains why research has shown that men with high *n* Ach tend to stand at moderate distances from the peg, and uses the results obtained in a general discussion. What is immediately apparent is that individuals have reacted to this simple task in very different ways. Some have stood very close to the peg and others impossibly far away. A few have probably calculated very carefully where they were most likely to succeed, and have adjusted that throwing point to their success and failure on previous tries. These are the men who have shown the behavior typical of men with high *n* Achievement, and they provide a concrete example of the type of action that the participants ought to learn to make if they want to behave like a man with high *n* Ach. What is most important at this point is the

group discussion which occurs as men are called upon to explain why they set goals the way they did and why some reacted as they did to failure to make ringers from where they were standing. Other variants on the game are often introduced, such as playing it in front of other people, or for various money payoffs at different distances, in order to illustrate other training points to be taken up later.

2. Men with high *n* Ach prefer work situations in which they can take personal responsibility for the performance necessary to achieve the goal. In fact, they typically avoid gambling situations in which they have no control over the outcome. In such situations they prefer taking no risks at all, which underlines the fact that their preference for moderate goal setting applies only to achievement situations in which they are responsible for producing the outcome. In fact, some studies have shown that they have high confidence in their own ability to perform an unknown task, and thus, from a subjective point of view, they may not feel that they are taking much of a risk in setting a moderately difficult goal for themselves. They may recognize objectively that the goal may not be reached by everybody, but subjectively they feel that they are better able to reach it than most people. This also tends to make them dislike committee situations in which others set goals for them or in which others must do the work to achieve the goals that they have set. In either situation they are less personally responsible for the outcome than they would ideally like to be.

The meaning of personal control, as of the next two characteristics, is taught largely in connection with a business game to be described below. It is also taught by discussing feelings throughout a game of chance as contrasted with a game of skill like ringtoss, or by getting reactions to a work situation in which goals are set by others or a committee.

3. Men with high *n* Ach like to get feedback as to how well they are doing, and are responsive to that concrete feedback. One of the simplest illustrations of this tendency is provided by the correlation reported by Kagan and Moss (1962) between *n* Ach in middle childhood and skill at "constructional activities." In other words, boys with high *n* Ach like to build or make things. On the other hand, they are neither especially good nor bad at intellectual activities or academic work. What is the difference between building a radio set or a bridge and handing in a theme to be graded by the teacher? In both cases the child gets feedback, but in the former instance it is much more directly tied to the performance input. That is, the boy knows that if he wires the radio correctly, it will work, or if he does something wrong, it won't work. In

contrast, the tie-in of performance on an English theme with the grade may appear a lot less direct and specific to him. He may find it much harder to identify the response that produces the reward and, in fact, the teacher is probably a lot more variable in providing concrete feedback for specific types of behavior than a model radio set is. This is probably one of the chief reasons that men with high *n* Ach tend to gravitate toward business rather than the professions (McClelland, 1965a). In business, feedback tends to be very concrete in terms of profit margins, costs, per cent of the market, and so on, and the tie-in with performance often seems to be direct and immediate. In the professions, feedback may be either very general or nonexistent. How well does a teacher know the extent to which she has accomplished what she set out to accomplish in a given class? How can she tell whether she is actually improving in her ability to provide instruction over the years? Doctors, lawyers, ministers all receive some kind of feedback on how well they are doing, but usually it just tells them whether they are behaving appropriately, not whether they are actually getting results (see McClelland, 1968).

As a consequence of this general desire for feedback, men with high *n* Ach react to money in a way which at first seems paradoxical. On the one hand, they do not work harder for financial rewards—partly because they are apparently working as hard as they can already (see Atkinson and Reitman, 1956). On the other hand, in the ringtoss game just described, they say they would award even more money for a ringer from a very difficult distance than a man with low *n* Ach would award for a ringer from the same distance. The interpretation of this apparent paradox seems to be that the man with high *n* Ach thinks of money as a concrete symbol of how successful a man has been, rather than as a motivator. Money incentives are often used in the ringtoss game to illustrate how they get some people to try harder and to be more successful (usually those with low *n* Ach) and also to show the difference in action between pay-offs as rewards and as motivators.

4. Men with high *n* Ach typically show more initiative in researching their environment. They travel around more (McClelland, 1961), and they generally try out more new things. Again the purpose seems clear: They are searching for new opportunities to try out their achievement skills, or to find ways of realizing the goals they have already set for themselves. Andrews has demonstrated nicely (1966) that in a college setting they tend to score much higher on an "entrepreneurial acts" index that he developed. College students with high *n* Ach tried out more courses and club activities to see if they would like them; they

checked with the teacher more often to understand better how well they had done on a paper; they started more businesses of their own on the side; and so forth.

Most of these action patterns characteristic of a man with high *n* Ach have been taught in connection with a business game invented by Litwin and Ciarlo (1959). In it, each participant is presented with the task of constructing by himself various models made out of Tinker Toys. He first assembles one on his own according to a pattern given him; then he times himself to discover how long it takes him; finally he decides how many he will attempt to make in a five-minute period. He is also presented with norms as to how long most other people take to construct the model in question. Finally, he is given information as to the cost of parts for the model, the selling prices, and the penalties for changing production targets at a later point. Various payoffs are arranged in the game, which can make profits larger or smaller depending on the number of units produced in relation to the number contracted for. Basically, what the participant has to do is to set his goal in terms of his knowledge of all the factors that should influence him in choosing a production goal. Next, he actually performs the task and carefully calculates his profits or losses. Then he repeats the process on a second and on a third model. Since all the men are working at the task together at the same time in a room, they have many opportunities to observe how other people are responding to stress, achieving their goals, or modifying their targets, depending on how well they have done. As in the ringtoss game, it can be pointed out in the discussion that follows the task that practically all of the action characteristics of the man with high or low *n* Ach have actually been illustrated by the behavior of someone in the group.

Thus the principle of *moderate goal setting* is readily illustrated by the targets various men set for production. Several usually set too high targets and several too low targets, the former losing a lot of money and the latter not making very much. *Personal responsibility* is not always well illustrated by this game, since the players do not have an opportunity as it is usually played to delegate responsibility to others; but it may come up indirectly, as when some player makes the mistake of copying his neighbor's model incorrectly rather than checking with the original. Or the game can be restructured to have "managers" setting goals for "workers," to see what effect that has on the reactions of all concerned. The use of feedback is readily illustrated, just as it was in the ring-toss game, by the extent to which men modify their targets upwards or downwards depending on how well they have performed on the previous task. And, finally, it is easy to observe that one or two among ten or twelve men have taken unusual initiative in researching the environment—by finding a way to beat the system, such as arranging their parts in advance of actual production so that it is easier for them to produce more units. What the game provides is an opportunity for many people to display their own action characteristics and to observe those of others in a lifelike performance situation. In short, it provides them with the opportunity to acquire the actions associated with high *n* Achievement.

Proposition A-2. *The more an individual can link the newly developed associative network to related actions, the more the change in both thought and action is likely to occur and endure.* The evidence for the importance of action for producing behavior change consists of such diverse findings as (a) the facilitating role of recitation for human learning, (b) the repeated finding that overt commitment and participation in action changes attitudes effectively (cf. Berelson and Steiner, 1964, p. 576), and (c) early studies by Carr (cf. McGeoch and Irion, 1952) showing that simply to expose an organism to what is to be learned (e.g., trundling a rat through a maze) is nowhere near as effective as letting him explore it for himself in action.

Theoretically, the action is represented in the associative network by what associations precede, accompany, and follow it. So including the act in what is learned enlarges the associative network or the achievement construct to include action. Thus the number of cues likely to trip off the *n* Achievement network is increased. In commonsense terms, whenever he works, he now evaluates what he is doing in achievement terms, and whenever he thinks about achievement he tends to think of its action consequences.

Early achievement motivation development courses consisted almost entirely of these two training inputs. Litwin and Ciarlo gave the first course at the Stanford Research Institute as part of its international training program for managers in the autumn of 1960. Similar versions of the course were given by Litwin in the spring of 1962 for a group of staff members of the Japan Management Association in Tokyo, and for a group of businessmen from Ahmedabad, India, though by this time some other inputs had been added. These courses demonstrated that such a program of training was of interest to businessmen and felt by them to be relevant to their performance as executives. Largely in response to their need to apply this fairly theoretical material to everyday life, another training input was soon added. This consisted of case materials drawn from everyday business life to illustrate the various aspects of the achievement syndrome.

Cases. The Harvard Graduate School of Business Administration has traditionally used the case method as a major educational technique. Cases are not presented to illustrate effective or ineffective handling of administrative problems, but to provide opportunities for classroom discussion. The technique was simply adopted here as a means of illustrating how *n* Ach thought and action could be displayed in everyday business life. Actual examples of the development of the careers or firms of business leaders are written up in disguised form and assigned for discussion to the participants. After these cases have been discussed and analyzed, individuals are asked to bring in problems from their own business activities for analysis in terms of the achievement syndrome.

For example, in a ten-page summary of the career of an investment entrepreneur, the class must learn to pick out and correctly label statements such as the following:

> In deciding whether a company merits all the aches and pains of putting together private capital, I look to see if it is a company with a product that is being successfully marketed. This means that the company has shown the ability to sell its products to final customers, and that the products have been accepted by these people and found adequate for their purposes, and that the customer either wants to buy some more or will recommend its purchase to a friend. Many companies, particularly in the scientific field, come up with wonderful gadgets that they have "working in the factory" but which they have never actually sold to a customer who has used it and found it acceptable. Although occasionally he can be successful in this type of investment, more often than not, the product, several million dollars later, never does work out.[2]

This seems to be a clear statement of how an investor-entrepreneur goes about establishing a moderate risk. He knows that any company involves a risk, just as throwing a ring at the peg from any distance involves a risk of missing, but he tries to find many concrete ways of reducing the risk. In particular, he is not here impressed by whether a gadget works or not, but points out that its actual marketability must first have been demonstrated.

2. This and subsequent quotations are drawn from the "Jefferson E. Towne case" prepared by Joseph F. S. Pampel and Fred Richards, Jr. under the direction of Herbert Stewart of the Harvard University Graduate School of Business Administration. Copyright © 1961 by the President and Fellows of Harvard College. Comments here about the case carry no implication of how this and other cases would be used at the Harvard Business School.

Or again, in another part of the case, he describes how as an underwriter he screened

> perhaps a hundred or more companies coming in search for funds each month, most of which were too small or speculative for a firm of this stature to handle. Separating the firm's business from the small speculative opportunities is easy, but occasionally I find a small company with good potential, suitable as a speculative investment. I spend perhaps 50% to sometimes 90% of my time weeding out and analyzing these small firms. When I find a good small firm, I arrange private financing for it.

We note here his *initiative* and exploratory behavior in carefully weeding out the best investment opportunities. In one such case, he became convinced of the future prospects of the firm, but could not sell his superiors on underwriting it. He therefore recommended it to another firm where he had friends. They took on the job, but managed to place only 40 per cent of the issue. At this point our entrepreneur had responded to a *block* in the world by trying an alternate instrumental activity (sending the business to another firm), only to find that he was blocked again. Now his sense of *personal responsibility* as a man with high *n* Achievement came to the fore: He quit his job at the old firm, joined the new firm, and sold the remainder of the issue to private investors within a few weeks, also purchasing some of it for himself. Here he showed what he had believed all along—that the issue could be sold, though he had to do it himself in order to prove it. It was a difficult task, too difficult for others but not for him, as he had correctly estimated.

Dozens of examples like these, developed and discussed in the course, can give the participants a concrete idea of how the achievement syndrome functions in everyday business life.

Proposition A-3. *The more an individual can link a newly conceptualized association-action complex (or motive) to events in his everyday life, the more likely the motive complex is to influence his thoughts and actions in situations outside the training experience.* It seems almost unnecessary to give either theoretical or empirical evidence to back up such a hypothesis. Since the goal of the training is to transfer it to everyday life, it seems self-evident that such a transfer will be easier if it is made explicit during the training. Certainly this is the way most interview therapy operates when the patient reworks during the session old memories, events from the past twenty-four hours, dreams, and hopes for the future. Such reworking should at the very least expand

and clarify the associative network and increase the number of cues in everyday life that will re-arouse thoughts about the achievement syndrome.

Self-Study (S)

The training inputs so far described can be taught in ways that do not involve the participants very much at all. That is, the orientation of the teacher can simply be that the goal of the course is to give people an idea of what *n* Ach is and how it influences people's behavior. Many individuals sign up for the course with little more in mind than satisfying their curiosity about some new idea the psychologists have come up with. But if the training is to set personality change in motion, the individual must begin at some point to confront how the achievement syndrome relates to his own life, his own career, his. main goals and values. There are three distinguishable types of training inputs that are designed to make this possible.

Career Relevance. Men with high *n* Achievement not only act in certain ways, they also tend to gravitate towards certain occupations and to play key parts in getting economic growth started. They are salesmen-entrepreneurs. The evidence for these assertions is carefully reviewed for the participants, based on findings reported in *The Achieving Society* and elsewhere. It is explained in theoretical terms why men with high *n* Ach gravitate toward entrepreneurial roles: because in such roles they are most likely to find opportunities for taking moderate risks and personal responsibility, or for getting concrete feedback on how well they are doing. Participants want to know why *n* Achievement should fit people for business roles particularly, and why not for high achievement in any role? Why shouldn't eminent generals, research scientists, or statesmen all have high *n* Ach?

The problem here is partly semantic. It is natural to assume that any high achievement is caused by a high need for Achievement. But this simply represents a defect in the English language, for *n* Ach as it is defined and measured in the technical sense does not and should not motivate all types of success in the real world. Eminent scientists, for example, do not in fact score high in *n* Achievement (McClelland, *et al.*, 1953), perhaps because they have been willing to wait for long periods of time without getting concrete feedback on how well they were doing. Politicians are known to have a need for Power (Browning and Jacob, 1964), and it is very likely that generals have too. At any rate, empirical data clearly show that it is only the salesmen-entrepreneurs who on the average score high on this measure of *n* Achievement. Of course individual professionals may score high, as when, for example, a professor of English literature decides actually to stage Shakespearean plays, sets up his own company to do so, and takes it on tour (see McClelland, 1965a). In such cases the man is occupying a professional status—that of a teacher—but he is behaving in an entrepreneurial way. He is playing an entrepreneurial role when the status (his job) does not actually require it. That is, it is entirely possible for a professor of English literature to do an excellent job without putting on plays—or becoming entrepreneurial in the sense of taking moderate risks, worrying about concrete feedback (from audiences), and so on.

All of this, and much more, is explained in careful detail to the course participants through outside reading, lectures with illustrations from the research literature, the television film called *The Need to Achieve*, which summarizes the findings of *The Achieving Society*, and group discussions. The goal is to make as clear as possible what kind of a role a person with high *n* Achievement likes to play and plays well and what his function is in a business or in society, so that the participant can at some point ask himself whether he wants to be that kind of person. It is necessary to make the description of the person with high *n* Ach very specific and explicit so that the participant will not make the mistake of assuming that *n* Achievement will help him be better at accomplishing whatever he wants to do in life. Furthermore, the negative aspects of the entrepreneurial role are also stressed: it may result in restlessness, overwork, neglect of family, and less time for friendly interaction. People with high *n* Ach, for example, prefer to spend their time working with experts rather than friends (cf. French, 1956). They may not be ideal team members, or good accountants: After all, who wants an accountant who takes risks of any kind? They probably do not make good employee relations managers, because they are not interested in the seemingly unending intricacies of interpersonal power struggles which seldom lead to permanent accumulative achievements. They may not even make the best top managers in big corporations, for the same reason.

But the implication of this discussion is clear: Most of the men taking the courses are, in fact, businessmen who are in a position to become more entrepreneurial if they decide it is relevant to their job. The scientific implication of the research findings is inescapable. If they want to do a better entrepreneurial job, then the scientific evidence shows that the means to that end is to learn to think, talk, and act like a person with high *n* Achievement.

Proposition S-1. *The more an individual perceives that developing a motive is required by the demands of his career and life situation, the more educational attempts designed to develop that motive are likely to succeed.* The word *required* is used here in the sense of being required by logic and reasoning based on all the evidence, including scientific evidence. The stance of the psychologist when he confronts a businessman with this evidence is the same as that of the public-health doctor who confronts a group of villagers who are constantly troubled by stomach disorders and dysentery. The doctor may conclude that the water supply is contaminated and that there is clear evidence linking their discomforts to the contaminated water supply. He can then say that if they want to decrease their discomfort, they must clean up the water supply, put chemicals in it, stop washing clothes in it, or what not. Once the problem is scientifically diagnosed, then the doctor can prescribe what is required to solve it. Whether the villagers want to feel better or not is a separate question. It is up to them to decide, but if they do, there are "required" methods of going about it. It is explained to the course participants that the situation is analogous here. If they want to behave in a more entrepreneurially successful way, and in fact many of them are in jobs where that behavior would seem to be demanded of them, then this is the way the evidence shows they must learn to think, talk, and act.

This training input is interesting in that it represents an appeal to reason in a century in which psychologists and social theorists have been impressed mostly by the power of unreason. Yet it is well to remember that research has shown that rational arguments do sway opinions, particularly among the doubtful or the uncommitted (cf. Hovland, *et al.*, 1953). Reality, in the form of legal, military, or housing rules does modify white prejudice against Negroes (cf. Berelson and Steiner, 1964, p. 512). The associative network that organizes reality—that places the person correctly in time, place, space, family, job—is one of the most dominant in the hierarchy of schemas a person carries around. It is the last network to give way in psychosis. Thus any proposed change in an associative network should be tied in with this dominant schema in such a way as to make the change consistent with reality demands or reasonable extensions of them. In commonsense terms, a man seems more likely to develop higher *n* Ach if he clearly understands why and how his job requires it.

Motives. It is still possible for a course participant to understand all that has happened so far and still not have made any kind of a personal decision as to whether he wants to do anything about his own *n* Ach. He knows a lot about *n* Ach; he knows his own *n* Ach test score (usually low at the outset); he knows more or less what his job requires of him. But how is he to decide whether he wants to get personally involved in changing? For obvious ethical reasons, the instructors make it very clear that the choice is up to each participant and he will be respected no matter what it is. A man is free to drop out of the course at any time or, as has occasionally happened, he may decide after finishing it that he really does not want to be like a person with high *n* Ach. In fact, in one early course, a man decided that he did not want to continue in his high-level managerial position. He subsequently resigned and became a chicken farmer, to the relief of his associates in the business in which he had been an ineffective manager—his family firm. The training goal is to get each man to study himself honestly and to make a decision as to what he wants to do.

Obviously, participants come into possession of considerable information about themselves—e.g., their fantasy test characteristics (Figure 2.1) and the types of behavior they have exhibited in the ringtoss or business games—but group sessions are also arranged which specifically promote self-examination. They begin normally with an exercise in which each participant tries to answer in writing the question "Who am I?" in as many ways as he can. After each person has had an opportunity to think about what kind of person he is, the leader opens up a general discussion to which anyone may contribute as much or as little as he desires from what he has already written down. Usually a rather open discussion develops about individuals' hopes, fears, desires, and limitations, much in the manner of T-group, sensitivity training, or self-analytic group sessions described elsewhere by Mills (1964); Bradford, Gibb, and Benne (1964); and others. Experience has shown that the level and nature of these group discussions can be determined somewhat by the leaders. Thus, some self-analytic groups can deal with quite superficial matters, whereas others, usually through interpretation provided by the leader, can deal with quite extraordinary or normally "secret" matters (cf. Slater, 1966). Since it is not the purpose of the *n* Ach training to get into psychotherapy, that is, into dealing with individual neurotic difficulties, anxieties, or family problems, the leaders attempt to set the tone for the discussion at a motivational level. They start the discussions themselves by talking about their own careers and what they have always wanted to get out of life, how successful they have been doing so, and what they feel dissatisfied about in their performances so far. The talk is not exactly superficial because it is not common for people to speak openly about their motives in public, but, on the other hand, it does not deal with "depth" material such as neurotic complaints or anxieties.

In the course of these discussions and at other times, it is necessary to define and describe other main types of human motivation—such as the need for Power, the need for Affiliation, and so on. In more extended courses, the participants may even be taught the coding schemes for those other motives so that they can distinguish them clearly from *n* Achievement. For example, it is common for people to confuse *n* Power with *n* Ach since both may lead to assertive behavior. But the motivation of a person with high *n* Power is quite different: he wants to have impact on others, to control and persuade them. Whereas a businessman with high *n* Ach would do whatever is necessary to get his factory built, another man in the same position with high *n* Power might get so involved in controlling others and being the boss that he might not even care if the factory never got built. On the other hand, the person with strong *n* Affiliation wants to stay on friendly relations with other people at all costs. He, too, might never get the factory built because it could involve spending a lot of time away from his friends or perhaps even hurting their feelings. When a participant has analyzed where he stands on some of these other motives, he ought to be in a better position to judge the context to which he is willing to develop his own *n* Ach, perhaps at the expense of some of his other goals in life. Just where does an increased *n* Ach fit into his self-picture? Other devices are used to facilitate making a decision—for instance, silent meditation or writing the epitaph on one's own tombstone—but the goal is always the same: understanding what one ultimately wants out of life.

Proposition S-2. *The more an individual can perceive and experience the newly conceptualized motive as consistent with the ideal self-image, the more the motive is likely to influence his future thoughts and actions.* Evidence on the importance of the ego or the self-image for controlling behavior has been summarized by Allport (1943). In recent years, Rogers and his group (Rogers, 1961; Rogers and Dymond, 1954) have measured improvement in psychotherapy largely in terms of improvement of the self-concept in relation to the ideal self. Indirect evidence of the importance of the self-schema comes from attempts of hypnotists to get people to do things which are inconsistent with their self-concepts or values. Investigators now agree that hypnotist's suggestions are likely to be successful only if the subject perceives the action suggested as consistent with his self-image or values (cf. Berelson and Steiner, 1964, p. 124).

The same logic supports Proposition S-2. It seems unlikely that a newly formed associative network such as *n* Achievement could persist and influence behavior much unless it has somehow "come to terms" with the pervasive, superordinate network of associations defining the self. The *n* Achievement associative complex must come to be experienced as related to or consistent with the ideal self-image; otherwise associations from the self-system will constantly block thoughts of achievement. The person might be thinking, for example: "I am not that kind of person; achievement means judging people in terms of how well they perform and I don't like to hurt people's feelings."

Values.   But it is necessary to carry the self-study further. A man is not only his work or career, and his motives or what he wants to get out of life. He is also, in a very real sense, what he values. The subculture, the family, the religious group to which he belongs all shape what he believes is important, and a higher *n* Achievement may conflict with some of the values which he has come to hold most dear. Again the problem is one of seeing how consistent or inconsistent a higher *n* Achievement is with the superordinate associative networks representing values.

The original impulse for this training input came from the study by Rosen and D'Andrade (1959), which shows that authoritarian fathers tended to have sons with low *n* Ach. The fathers of boys with high *n* Ach, on the other hand, tended to set high standards, to be encouraging and rewarding, but not directive in telling the boys exactly what to do. Other data reported in *The Achieving Society* have shown that authoritarian family structures, as in Turkey, tend also to be associated with low *n* Ach, unless the boy manages to escape his father's dominance. Some of the early *n* Ach training courses were given in Mexico, where patriarchal social systems are the ideal type. That is, in the traditional social order, the father is very much head of his family, expects to look after them, and to be obeyed and shown loyalty in return (cf. Kluckhohn and Strodtbeck, 1961, Ch. 6). The same pattern exists in many traditional businesses in Mexico, so that the organizational structure does not encourage *n* Ach (cf. Andrews, 1967).

To open discussion of how respected values may oppose the development of *n* Ach, the participants in the Mexican course were asked to re-enact the test situation originally used by Rosen and D'Andrade in their study of the families of boys with high and low *n* Ach. Three participants are asked to role-play a mother, a father, and their son respectively. The boy is asked to pile as many blocks on top of each other as he can left-handed and blindfolded. The "father" and "mother" are asked privately how high they think their "son" can pile the blocks this way, and then he goes ahead to see how well he can perform the task in front of them. What is interesting to the observers and to the participants themselves is how much direction and of what kind the parents give their "son," and how the "father" and "mother" relate to each other and to the boy. Very often in the Mexican situation the "father" follows the traditional patriarchal pattern in which he gives very precise and detailed instructions to the boy as to how to pile the blocks. The subsequent discussion by the group then easily gets into the question of why research has shown it is difficult for a boy under such conditions to develop high *n* Ach, which requires a great deal of initiative, personal responsibility, and checking on his own to get feedback on how well he is doing. It is pointed out that a patriarchal system is not necessarily authoritarian and bad, as many Americans think it is. Rather it served, and still serves, many important organizational functions. Anyone wanting to increase *n* Ach in himself or others needs to consider the extent to which such a need will run counter to values which emphasize helping others and loyalty rather than initiative and independence.

Another technique used for studying values involves the study of the children's stories collected for *The Achieving Society* to assess national *n* Achievement levels. These stories are simple—they come from third- and fourth-grade public-school readers—and provide therefore an amazingly straightforward introduction to what the culture thinks is important. Consider these Indian stories, for example, translated from a third-grade school reader:

> There was a big tree in the village. It was full of leaves and fruit. Therefore many birds came and built their nests on the tree. They lived happily in their nests eating the fruit. Some time went by. The birds ate away all the fruit. Some fruit ripened and fell down below. All the leaves on the tree turned yellow and began falling down. Then within a few days all the leaves fell down. The tree was bare with just its branches.
>
> At that time all the birds in the tree left the tree and went to another tree that was full of leaves and fruit. On seeing this, the tree spoke as follows: "Till now the birds were living happily with me. Now I have neither leaves nor fruit. Therefore these birds forget the help I gave them and leave me. Only if we possess something people will go after us. Nobody will go to a person who has nothing."

Another story tells about a kindly king who considered it his duty to be good to all living beings. One day a dove that was being pursued by a hawk fell in his lap and asked for protection. The hawk demanded of the king that he give up the dove because it was his food. "I am dying of hunger. How can you take away my food? If I die of hunger, you will be guilty of the sin of killing an animal." The king then said he would get him any other kind of meat, but the hawk asked for some of his own flesh in return.

> The king agreed. He immediately got a balance and placed the dove on one of the pans and on the second one he cut the flesh from his thigh and placed it there. However, as much flesh as he put, he could not balance the weight of the dove. Then he said, "Eat me."
>
> Immediately the Gods were pleased and sent him to heaven. To test the king's good deeds, the Gods had come down in the guise of the hawk and the dove. As the king proved his noble character they were pleased with him and made him a man of virtue. So whenever a man trusts you, don't disappoint him. You must protect the man who craves protection.

These and other Indian stories make very clear that an important Indian value is having something to give and giving it to those who ask for it. One must have things to give—wealth, wisdom, power—and the highest virtue is attributed to the man who sacrifices even himself for others. To be sure, children's stories from a number of countries mention the virtues of self-sacrifice, but the theme is emphasized unusually often in the Indian stories. For a group of Indian businessmen the question then becomes: To what extent are we personally committed to living up to this ideal of accumulating wealth in order to gain virtue by being in a position to help others? And where does *n* Achievement fit in with this value? At a concrete level, there would probably be very few Indian businessmen who would use accumulated family capital to build a factory if the money were needed to pay for expensive family obligations like weddings. Such matters come up for discussion in the group. The trainers obviously can take no position as to what is the right thing to do, because the goal of the exercise is simply to have a person confront common values in his culture and decide for himself how, for him, they would combine or conflict with a higher *n* Achievement.

Proposition S-3. *The more an individual can perceive and experience the newly conceptualized motive as consistent with prevailing cultural values and norms, the more the motive is likely to influence his future thoughts and actions.* The cultural anthropologists have argued for years how important it is to understand one's own cultural values in order to overcome prejudices and adopt more flexible attitudes, but there is little empirical evidence that understanding changes a person's behavior. Some findings from the field of attitude change may be considered indirect support for the hypothesis. Many studies have shown a close link between attitudes and the reference group associated with them. For example, a man's attitudes toward a question will vary significantly depending on whether he is asked, say, as a Methodist, as a public official, or as a private citizen. Similarly his views of a particular enterprise will vary depending on whether he is told that it is a Jewish, a Negro, or a Yankee enterprise. Other studies have shown that detaching an attitude from its reference group by any means will tend to make it more amenable to change. Thus, if a voter moves from the city to the suburbs, he is more likely to vote Republican. If he gets more detailed information about ethnic groups, he is less apt to show prejudice (Berelson and Steiner, 1964, p. 517). If he role-plays a new attitude, he is more likely to shift in that direction (Berelson and Steiner, 1964, pp. 566 ff.). In the course of discussing a country's cultural values as revealed through its children's readers, the individual may detach himself from his cultural milieu sufficiently to gain some perspective on it and some freedom to choose whether or not he fully accepts the values he has unconsciously absorbed.

Yet there is always the possibility that treatment of cultural values may only confuse the participants and, as a matter of fact, this particular input has been less often dealt with in our training courses so far than any other. Its most common application has been to the problems of authoritarianism, because the research evidence is so clear that a powerful controlling relationship discourages self-reliance and *n* Ach.

Goal-Setting (*G*)

Another set of inputs involves what might be called the dynamics of the training situation. Why do people take the training course? What do they expect to get out of it? What reasons do they have to believe that it will produce a change for the better in them? How will they know if the course has actually had an effect? In the first place, the courses have to appeal enough to prospective participants for them to enroll. They often arrive with rather vague hopes and expectations as to what they will gain. Some want to satisfy their curiosity, to find out about something new; others go along because their friends are going; probably all have a vague expectation that the course will lead to self-improvement of some kind. The task of the training then shifts toward helping them to define more precisely what goals they will set for themselves and how they will go about measuring progress toward those goals. It is convenient to divide this goal formulation process into three distinguishable training inputs.

Prestige Suggestion. We obviously had to convince businessmen to take the courses, if we were to study their effects. We were not in the position of an animal psychologist who can order a dozen rats, or an academic psychologist who has captive sophomores in his classes, or even a psychotherapist who has disturbed people knocking at his door every day. In the language of business, there was a selling job to do. As our sales pitch broadened and improved, it obviously became itself a major training input that might be in part responsible for any changes that might result. The term *prestige suggestion* covers loosely all the reasons explicitly or implicitly given to the participants as to why the course would change or develop their motivation. To illustrate the reasons actually used, let us focus on a particular set of courses offered in Bombay in February, 1963.

Prospective participants received a nicely printed brochure, the cover of which contained the following announcement:

MOTIVATION
DEVELOPMENT
for
MANAGEMENT

Programme by

THE CENTER FOR RESEARCH IN PERSONALITY
HARVARD UNIVERSITY, U. S. A.
Under the Auspices of
BOMBAY MANAGEMENT ASSOCIATION

The course title, Motivation Development for Management, was printed on a blue background, since blue is a color preferred by people with *n* Ach (see McClelland, 1963, Ch. 8). Such a point would, of course, be lost on a potential recruit, but it could be referred to later in the course as an indication of the careful and detailed research that had gone into understanding the achievement motive.

On the first page, the intent of the training program was outlined as follows:

> The purpose of these courses is to increase the entrepreneurial spirit and managerial effectiveness of the participants, by considering the motivation and thinking necessary for effective management, rather than the technical skills. We assume that most managers already have the necessary business and technical skills; this program attempts to provide some of the other, less tangible but no less important resources. We want to create a new awareness of the importance of motivation and thinking; we want to stimulate new ways of thinking that will result in a more effective approach to management problems.

Note that the sponsors of the course are stating clearly that they want to "increase," "create," and "stimulate" the entrepreneurial spirit and managerial effectiveness. Thus, hopefully, the prospective participant signs up with the expectation that his motivation will increase and that this, in turn, will make him a better businessman.

The brochure goes on: "There is no attempt to manipulate the participant: we state openly that we want to demonstrate *how* a person can change his thinking and *why* he might want to do so. Any change is a result of a commitment by the individual."

There are three reasons for this simple statement: First, it is a matter of ethical propriety to state emphatically that the course does not manipulate or brainwash anybody. Second, Hovland *et al.* (1953) report that the less manipulative the intent of a communicator, the greater the tendency to accept his conclusions. Third, the suggestion is clearly made that outsiders cannot change a person; he must take responsibility for changing himself. The implication is that he can change himself by adequate commitment.

The brochure then states that "the courses are a new development in management training" and this point is stressed at several other places throughout the seven-page booklet. It is further made clear that the courses are based on some new research findings and that the "goal is to establish pilot programs and courses in several countries; to assist people who are interested and willing to pioneer in developing and expanding this new approach to management training." The appeal here is to be in on the ground floor, to be first, to find out something new, to satisfy one's curiosity.

The major section of the brochure stresses the importance of the ten years of research that have spelled out empirically the relationships of achievement motivation to entrepreneurship and economic growth.

> Two major findings of this research are: (1) achievement motivation is a key factor in national economic growth, since a rise in achievement motivation generally precedes an accelerated growth period, and a fall in achievement motivation generally precedes a decelerated period; and (2) individuals who are high in achievement motivation are more often found in the business or industrial spheres and are usually much more successful than individuals low in achievement motivation.

Here the appeal is to the high prestige of scientific research.

Who are the sponsors of the courses? Here again, there are several opportunities for prestige factors to influence expectations as to the worth and efficacy of the training. The program in Bombay was identified as originating at Harvard University, a prestigious academic institution, in association with the Bombay Management Association, a local organization that enjoys a considerable reputation for sponsoring useful management training courses and for gathering together some of the leading businessmen in Bombay for cooperative efforts. The value of the training may also be enhanced by enlarging on the qualifications of the instructors, although this was not done, particularly in the brochure for these courses. The faculty was listed simply as Mr. David Winter from Harvard University and Dr. Elliott Danzig, a consultant from Mexico City, plus members of the Educational Committee of the Bombay Management Association. More could have been made of the qualifications of the men, and in other courses greater efforts in this direction have been made. Finally, the location of the courses can be a source of prestige suggestion. That is, the courses can be held in some prestigious retreat, as they have been on other occasions. However, the Bombay courses could not be residential and were held at Davar's College of Commerce in the central business district of Bombay.

The brochure also reported that the course had already been given elsewhere and that "most of the participants report great satisfaction with this course and have recommended expansion of such programs in their companies. Some participants report deep changes and improvements in their life and work." Here the expectation is created that the course has produced satisfaction and is therefore likely to have the same effect on the new participant.

Finally, broader appeal is made to more altruistic motives. It is mentioned that not only is the course designed to develop the participants as individuals, but also to "consider how India's resources of human motivation may be discovered and used." In other words, self-development may also be altruistic: by developing himself and by developing motivation in others, each participant may make a contribution to the economic development of his country. But the wider significance of participation does not end there. The international aspects of this research and development are specifically mentioned: the original course at Stanford Research Institute for the International Program in Small Industry Management; the training programs already undertaken in Mexico City; earlier work in Ahmedabad, India; the course given by the Japan Management Association in cooperation with Mitsui in Japan; and similar seminars in large corporations in the United States. In other words, it could reasonably be suggested that the significance of participating in the program extended from themselves to their nations, to, in a small way, economic development in a number of countries around the world.

Finally, they were asked to pay Rs. 30 to take the course. This was not a large sum of money (then the equivalent of about $6.00) for attending 11 training sessions scheduled over a period of three weeks, but it was introduced as an additional motivational factor. That is, it was considered that having to pay something to attend the course would make the course seem more worthwhile than if it had been given free, and also would increase the commitment of the individuals to take what they were doing a bit more seriously.

These inputs concerned with forces intended to get the participants to set high goals may be summarized under the following proposition:

G-1. *The more reasons an individual has to believe that he can, will, or should develop a motive, the more educational attempts designed to develop that motive are likely to succeed.* The empirical support for this hypothesis from other studies is impressive. Empirical research on attitudes has shown again and again that the prestige of a source is extremely important in influencing what people will believe or do (cf. Hovland, *et al.*, 1953). Years ago Roethlisberger and Dickson described a phenomenon in industrial management which has come to be known as the Hawthorne effect, after the plant in which it was first observed. Management was conducting research on what environmental conditions improved the performance of workers. They found that if they increased the lighting, the workers' performance improved. Just to be sure, they later decreased the lighting and found that worker performance improved still more. The explanation of these and similar findings in other studies seems to be that if research changes are expected, by the subjects, to have a certain effect, they will tend to have that effect.

Rosenthal and Jacobson (1968) have collected a large number of illustrations of these effects from a variety of different fields, varying from hypnosis to psychotherapy, physical therapy, or self-fulfilling prophesies. As they point out, there is solid empirical evidence to back up the wise physician's admonition to "treat as many patients as possible with the new drugs while they still have the power to heal." If patients think they are getting a new and powerful drug, it does relieve symptoms, even though carefully controlled experiments in the laboratory show that it has little physiological effect. In psychotherapy, Frank (1961) refers to this result as the "Hello—Good-by" effect, since patients who merely speak briefly to a prestigious psychiatrist improve significantly over waiting-list controls, and almost as much as those who get prolonged psychotherapy. Rosenthal's numerous studies in this area are particularly impressive. After extensive psychological testing, he has sent classroom teachers the names of three to five children in their class who, according to a "Harvard Test of Inflected Acquisition," are likely to bloom intellectually in the coming year. He found that communicating this simple expectation about children who were actually chosen at random did in fact lead to great improvement in their intelligence and achievement test scores on the average, as contrasted with control children in the same classes. Somehow the teachers communicated to the children named the expectation, based on the "Harvard Test," that they would improve greatly during the year—and this expectation was sufficient to produce dramatic improvements. There are few phenomena in psychology which are as well documented as the effect of prestige on change. The difficulty psychologists have had in taking it seriously is that it has commonly been treated as error or bias or mere suggestion. These words imply that the phenomenon is some kind of a scientific nuisance which interferes with objectivity, rather than a powerful source of personality change to be understood in its own right.

One clue to what is happening when such effects are observed is provided in studies reported by Kausler (1959) and Mierke (1955). They have shown that setting goals for a person, particularly in the name of prestigious authorities such as science or research, can sharply improve performance. These findings are reminiscent of those reported by Rosen and D'Andrade, which show that parents who set high standards for their sons are more likely to have sons who develop high *n* Achievement. The primary function of such goal-setting is probably to arouse what exists of an associative network in the achievement area for the person affected. That is, studies have shown that if an instructor talks about achievement or affiliation or power, individuals in his class tend to think about achievement or affiliation or power more frequently (cf. Atkinson, 1958). And the stronger and more frequent the talk, the more the relevant associative networks are developed and aroused (McClelland *et al.*, 1953). Such an arousal has several possible effects, which would facilitate creation of a new motivational network: (a) It elicits what response exists in the person, thus making it easier to strengthen that covert response in subsequent learning; (b) It creates a discrepancy between a goal (*Soll-lage* in Heckhausen's theory of motivation, 1963) and a present state (*Ist-lage*) which represents a cognitive dissonance that the person tries to reduce (cf. Festinger, 1957). In commonsense terms, he has an image clearly presented to him of something he is not but should be; (c) It tends to block out by simple interference other associations which would inhibit change, such as, "I'm too old to learn," "I never learn much from going to school, anyway," "What do these academics know about everyday life?" or "I hope they don't get personal about all this."

Work Plan. As a course proceeds, individual participants are encouraged and helped to refine their vague expectations that their motivation will be increased into something far more specific. What exactly is the relevance of achievement motivation to their present life situation and how, if they believe it is relevant, would it lead to specifically different activities or outcomes in the next six months to two years? Toward the end of the course, they are asked to fill out what amounts to an achievement plan for the next two years. It is patterned after the coding system for *n* Achievement as outlined in Figure 2.1. In abbreviated form, the following are the questions participants must answer for themselves:

What do you want to accomplish in the next two years? (Be specific.)
What specific steps (instrumental acts) do you plan to take to achieve that goal?
What blocks in yourself will you have to overcome to achieve that goal?
What blocks in the world will you have to overcome to achieve that goal?
How do you feel about the possibility of achieving that goal?
How do you feel about the possibility of failing to achieve it?
Where will you go specifically for help in accomplishing your goals?
How strongly do you want to achieve this goal?

How important is this goal to you as compared to other things you want out of life?

The plans are filled out individually and then are subjected to discussion in groups of four or five, with occasional help from the group leader. The reason for the group review is that nearly always the plans start out by being far too general. For instance, a man may state that his goal is to increase his sales by 50 per cent over the next two years. How will he accomplish that? He says he will try harder, that he will feel very happy if he succeeds and very unhappy if he doesn't. At this point the group usually expresses dissatisfaction with the lack of specificity in his plans. Exactly what does he mean by "trying harder"? What will he do concretely? What kinds of new clients will he visit? What new sales appeals has he thought of? Is a 50 per cent sales increase a realistic goal in the moderate risk-taking sense? Has he improved his performance by anything like that much in the last two years? After a lot of detailed discussion of this sort, the man then goes back and revises his plan, hopefully in the much more specific directions indicated by the discussion.

The purposes of this document is in part to formulate for each participant the practical implications of the course before leaving it, but even more to provide a basis for the evaluation of his progress in the months after the course. The participants are told that they are to regard themselves as "in training" for the next two years, that the ten to fourteen days of the course itself are obviously too short to do more than present a new way of acting. They are now to set about changing themselves along the lines they have chosen and they are to report back approximately every six months on how well they are progressing toward their goals. The instructors will help them in this self-evaluation by contacting them approximately every six months and asking for a report on progress. An important part of this future orientation is that each individual is more or less forced to define in advance the objective evidence he will try to provide later that he has progressed toward his goal.

Proposition G-2. *The more an individual commits himself to achieving concrete goals in life related to the newly formed motive, the more the motive is likely to influence his future thoughts and actions.*

Proposition G-3. *The more an individual keeps a record of his progress toward achieving goals to which he is committed, the more the newly formed motive is likely to influence his future thoughts and actions.* These hypotheses are both related to what was called "pacing" in early studies in the psychology of work. That is, committing oneself to a specific goal and then comparing one's performance to that goal has been found to facilitate learning (cf. Kausler, 1959), though most studies of levels of aspiration have dealt with goal setting as a result rather than as a "cause" of better performance. Learning theory gives ample support for the importance of specifying symbolically in advance the response to be made and getting concrete feedback as to whether, in fact, it has been made or not. A person can gradually, by trial and error, learn to push a stylus through a slot maze blindfolded, but he can run through the task almost without error if he memorizes the turns—right, left, right, right, and so on—before he starts. Furthermore, if he is clearly told when he is right and wrong, he learns much more quickly than if he has only general information as to what is right and wrong (McGeoch and Irion, 1952). If he has no feedback on whether he has made the right response, he will not learn at all. In these terms it is scarcely surprising that many patients do not improve after psychotherapy, since they have not specifically defined what changes in behavior they want to show and therefore have no way of knowing whether they are in fact showing changes. A basic principle of the more successful behavior therapies is their careful specification of the responses to be strengthened and weakened. There is ample evidence that such specification does facilitate change (cf. Eysenck, 1960).

In terms of the associative network theory proposed, these training inputs serve to keep the newly acquired associative pattern salient over the next two years. The participant knows in advance that someone will come back and check up on him. This expectation should guide his behavior. He knows he is still part of an experimental training group which is supposed to be reflecting in everyday life the results of a motivational increase (Proposition G-1). Revisiting the participants after six months, either personally or by letter, should serve to rearouse the associative network and remind the person of the goals that he has set for himself.

Actually, it has not been possible to follow up all the courses as carefully as intended. In the Bombay case, for example, a visit was made by Professor McClelland in early October, 1963, approximately seven months after the completion of the course. The participants were asked to report their progress; they met and exchanged notes; and it was clear that one or two had some astonishing progress to report. This, in turn, may well have spurred others to do better. But another follow-up was not made until two years after the courses, when one of the instructors, Dr. Winter, returned for a final evaluation of progress in January, 1965. Here, as in the case of other training inputs, practical exigencies dictated variations in practice that could become part of the overall research strategy of trying to isolate by subtraction which of the training inputs was crucial to producing the most effects.

Interpersonal Supports (I)

As described so far, the course could be conducted by correspondence or taught through a programmed text. Yet nearly all efforts to change people, certainly at the personality level, have stressed the importance of interpersonal relationships. In theory, emotional as well as cognitive learning ought to take place. A motive has been defined as an *affectively toned* associative network. Since the courses were set up from the beginning as group experiences, led by teachers or trainers, several interpersonal training inputs can be identified.

Warmth. The first input concerns the attitude assumed by the course instructors toward the participants. It can best be described as warm acceptance of each individual as a person, combined with a scrupulous avoidance of telling him what he ought to do or making suggestions as to choices he ought to make. Dr. Elliott Danzig and Shri Manohar Nadkarni, who were most responsible for formulating the nature of this relationship explicitly, have described it in a series of advice to trainers, summarized in Chapter 5.

The role is similar to the one recommended by Rogers for non-directive therapy (1961). Other distinguished therapists from St. Ignatius to Freud have similarly avoided telling clients what to do, apparently in the belief that it is only what the adult emotionally commits himself to by himself that will really affect his future conduct. For example, in his famous spiritual exercises, which have played a key role in producing and sustaining personality change in the Jesuit Order, St. Ignatius writes:

> The director of the Exercizes ought not to urge the exercitant more to poverty or any promise than to the contrary, nor to one state of life or living more than another . . . [while it is proper to urge people outside the Exercizes] the director of the Exercizes . . . without leaning to one side or the other, should permit the Creator to deal directly with the creature, and the creature directly with his Creator and Lord.

In general, the group leaders or instructors are there to help the person clarify what he wants, to provide him with information that will make his self-study more complete, and to give him the warmth and respect he needs, particularly when he is going through an honest period of self-searching.

Proposition I-1. *Changes in motives are more likely to occur in an interpersonal atmosphere in which the individual feels warmly but honestly supported and respected by others as a person capable of guiding and directing his own future behavior.* Bergin (1966) has summarized quite a bit of empirical research which supports the hypothesis that such therapist characteristics as warmth and empathy facilitate therapeutic progress. "Analyses of recorded therapist behavior and ratings by clients of their therapist during the process of treatment have yielded a consistently positive relationship between empathic understanding and outcome" (Bergin, 1966, p. 239). It is noteworthy also that parents of boys with high n Achievement are warmer and more encouraging, and fathers are less directive, than parents of boys with low n Achievement (Rosen and D'Andrade, 1959). In other words, it made sense in trying to develop n Achievement to model trainer behavior after the behavior of parents whose sons had high n Achievement. Nondirectiveness and positive regard do not imply, of course, permissiveness and promiscuous reinforcement of any type of behavior. Actually, the demands set for careful self-examination in the training courses were quite high, just as they are in Rogerian nondirective therapy, and just as they are in families of boys with high n Ach. High standards are maintained, but the person is encouraged and helped to decide for himself how or whether he will try to achieve them.

In theoretical terms, why should warmth as an interpersonal variable promote personality change? One simple argument is that the possibility of change involves disruption of existing patterns of thought and action, which causes anxiety, which in turn prevents change. Warmth, then, could be conceived as a means of reducing the crippling anxiety introduced by the prospect of change. Or, alternatively, warmth could be conceived as the means of developing a close interpersonal relationship which inevitably comes to be used as a means of reinforcing the new types of thought and activities presented to the participants for consideration. That is, while the explicit ideology of the course is that the person can choose what he wants to do, the implicit message is undoubtedly that it makes sense for most of the people to begin to behave like people with high n Ach. And undoubtedly, since the trainers have this goal in mind, they will tend to reward or "be warm" whenever a participant shows achievement-related behavior. And certainly there is ample evidence that rewards of this type will shape behavior, even if they are provided unconsciously (cf. Bandura and Walters, 1963, pp. 283 ff.).

Or warmth and respect may facilitate change for quite a different reason. They help give emotional support for the idea, expressed repeatedly in various ways, that each individual is a powerful person, capable in his own right of redirecting his own life (course input G-1). In other words, to respect someone is by definition to treat him as an *origin,* to communicate emotionally that he is important, worth while, and full of promise.

Retreat Setting. Sometimes the experience of "going through something together" is dramatized by holding the courses in a retreat setting, usually in a resort hotel or conference center. This makes it possible to define the training as an experience apart, or an opportunity for self-study, which can be carried out with few distractions from the outside world or from other people not involved in the experience. Such isolation promotes an atmosphere of total concentration on the objectives of the course, including even informal interaction at meals and late into the night. Again to quote St. Ignatius, "The progress made in the Exercises will be greater, the more the exercitant withdraws from all friends and acquaintances, and from all worldly cares." Such a withdrawal was not possible in the course sponsored by the Bombay Management Association, although it had characterized a small course given for some executives from Ahmedabad by Dr. George Litwin at Mount Abu ten months earlier. Most American companies favor this approach to management training, so that courses given in the United States have usually been held in a retreat setting.

Proposition I-2. *Changes in motives are more likely to occur the more the setting dramatizes the importance of self-study and lifts it out of the routine of everyday life, thereby creating an in-group feeling among the participants.* Actually, there is only indirect empirical support for such an hypothesis. It is known that establishing a new reference group promotes and supports attitude change, and it seems reasonable to infer that a retreat setting will promote formation of a new reference group. That is, the individuals live, sleep, eat, and talk informally with each other in a very intensive way. Furthermore, going off and living in a hostel-like setting may have some of the qualities of an initiation experience. Thus, having lived through an unsettling experience together, the participants are likely to regard it favorably, according to the theory of cognitive dissonance (see Festinger, 1957). Enduring a somewhat uncomfortable, strange experience may be perceived as an additional reason to develop *n* Achievement, to justify having undergone the experience.

On theoretical grounds, removing the person from everyday routine should (a) decrease interfering associations, to say nothing of interfering appointments and social obligations, and (b) heighten the salience of the experience by contrast with everyday life and make it harder to dismiss with the usual defense that it is "just one more course." The network of achievement-related associations can be more strongly and distinctly aroused in contrast to everyday life, making new learning easier. In fact, recent theorizing about learning suggests that half the problem is getting the person's attention focused on what is to be associated or learned (cf. Kagan, 1967).

It follows that the dramatic quality of the experience cannot be sustained very long in a ten- to sixteen-hour day without a new sense of routine developing. Experience has shown that a period somewhere between six and fourteen days is optimal for maximizing the effect of this particular training input. St. Ignatius sets an outside limit of 30 days, but for a less intensive schedule consisting of only a few hours a day spread over a longer period.

A New Reference Group. Many aspects of the courses tend to heighten the participants' sense that they are joining a new reference group. The *n* Ach coding system helps. It becomes a kind of secret language that only those who have gone through the course know. Shorthand terms such as Ga +, Bp, Bw, I — (see Figure 2.1) are learned and the participants continue to use them in talking with each other, even when they slip back into their native tongue. The retreat setting also helps create a new reference group, as do the intimate self-revelations that often occur in group discussions of motivation. The participants feel closer because they know each other better; they have been through a strange experience together. They have learned to support and respect each other even though at the outset they may have been strangers.

In some cases, it has been possible for participants to form an alumni association, which continues to meet after the course has ended to keep alive individual and community goals set in the course. In the early courses, participants were drawn from different companies, so that it was not possible or practicable to form a follow-up association, although individuals were occasionally brought together to meet the trainers later. In the major project to be reported in subsequent chapters, however, such associations were formed, which continued to function for a number of months after the termination of the course. The model here is that of the political party cell, which, experience has demonstrated, is one of the most effective ways to sustain attitudes and behavior. Furthermore, therapeutic groups such as Alcoholics Anonymous or Synanon have also found such continuing small group organizations to be one of the essential parts of maintaining personality change.

Proposition I-3. *Changes in motives are more likely to occur and persist if the new motive is a sign of membership in a new and continuing reference group.* Fewer principles have stronger empirical or historical support. Many empirical studies have shown that people's opinions, attitudes, and beliefs are a function of their reference group and that different attitudes are likely to arise and be sustained primarily when the person moves into or affiliates with a new reference group (cf. Berelson and Steiner, 1964, p. 580 ff.). In theoretical terms, a reference group should be effective because its members constantly provide cues to each other to rearouse the associative network they have learned; because members will also reward each other for achievement-related thoughts and acts; and because members label themselves as belonging to a group with a distinctive name and achievement-oriented set of goals. These characteristics will prevent assimilation of the new associative network to bigger, older, and stronger networks, such as those associated with traditional values.

In summary, then, the achievement motivation development courses include the achievement syndrome (A), self-study (S), goal-setting (G), and interpersonal supports (I). Some twelve different training inputs, three under each of these headings, may be identified. What is unusual is that each is designed in such a way that it can be omitted without destroying the viability of the treatment. This has never been true of other studies of the psychotherapeutic process (cf. Rogers and Dymond, 1954). That is, it is entirely feasible to conduct a training course without any aspect of the achievement syndrome being formally presented, without engaging in goal-setting, without self-study, or without any of the interpersonal supports normally provided in a group experience. Each of the training inputs, however, has some justification in past experience in attempts to change people, in empirical findings, and in the basic associational network theory that underlies our conception of motivation. The basic research strategy has been to run courses which included a fairly large number of these inputs, to insure obtaining a significant effect, and then to subtract the inputs or refine them, with the intent of discovering which of them is most effective in producing personality change.

Effectiveness of Achievement Motivation Training

Do the courses work? How can their yield in terms of changing motivation be measured? It was decided at the outset that satisfaction of the participants with the courses, while important, would not provide a sensitive guide to their actual change. The participants were always asked at the end of the course how much they liked various parts of it and the total experience, but their comments were more useful in helping improve the presentation of course materials than in providing an index to personal change. The whole experience with psychotherapy evaluation supports this view. Obviously it must be satisfying its customers or there wouldn't be an ever-increasing demand for psychotherapeutic services. On the other hand, hard empirical personality change data have often failed to back up the subjective impressions of personal change (cf. Eysenck, 1960; Bergin, 1966).

So it was necessary to look for long-term changes in thoughts and actions of the sort being taught in the course as characteristic of the man with high *n* Achievement. After the course, participants should think more often in terms of improving their business activities, take more successful moderate risks, use feedback, explore the environment, and so on. There should be many concrete signs of these changes in behavior—such as unusual pay raises, promotions to jobs of higher entrepreneurial responsibility, increased profits, decreased costs, larger sales volume, and the like. Such measures of yield, while nicely concrete, presented two major methodological difficulties. Even though a man started behaving more like an entrepreneur right after the course, it would usually take some time for these changes to affect any of the business indicators involved. Second, how could the various measures be made comparable for different people? How could an unusual pay raise for one man be put on the same scale with a new business started by another who was in a different life situation?

The first problem was met by extending the period of follow-up evaluation to two years. It was felt that if any concrete business improvements had not by that time resulted, it was unlikely that any significant motivational changes had occurred. Unfortunately, such a decision only created another problem. It meant that all of the courses, in the first two years of the project at least, had to be designed without any real feedback on the yields of earlier courses. It was obviously impractical to give one course and wait two years to discover its effects before giving another. So the early courses had to be designed "in the dark," with almost no knowledge as to whether the training was working at all. Fortunately for our morale, there were a few striking examples of change: one businessman, within a couple of months after taking an early Bombay course, decided to quit his excellent job and go into the construction business. He was well-to-do, well thought of in his company, and admired in the community, but he was restless because he found his job more and more boring. At the time of the course, his original *n* Achievement score was not very high and he was thinking of retiring and living in England, where his son was studying. In an interview eight months later, he said the course had served not so much to motivate him, but to crystallize a lot of ideas he had vaguely or half-consciously picked up about work and achievement all through his life. He decided he wanted to be an achievement-oriented person, that he would be unhappy in retirement, and that he should take a risk, quit his job, and start in business on his own. He acted on his decision, and in six months had drawn plans and raised more than one million dollars to build one of the tallest apartment buildings in Bombay. Such an immediate impact of a course is extremely rare, because it is seldom that a man is in the precise position necessary to move ahead as this man was. Nevertheless, it served to encourage us and other Indian authorities to go ahead with the major training project to be described in subsequent chapters.

The problem of comparability of measures on different people could not be solved at a very sophisticated level. The original plan was to give detailed follow-up questionnaires to course participants every six months for two years, which assessed their change on a number of psychological and business-activity variables. Unfortunately, we could not get enough of the men to fill out the questionnaires often enough for the measures to be meaningful. Furthermore, there was sometimes a spurious objectivity about the figures they reported. A man might state that he had been given a double jump in promotion to head some new branch of the company, whereas a talk with his superior in the company, or even with some of his friends, would show that actually he had been "kicked upstairs" into a position of lesser responsibility. Finally, there was no conceivable way to decide precisely questions such as how much more significant a raise of 1,000 rupees a month in a small company was than the same raise in a large company. The procedure actually adopted was crude, but more practicable and probably fairer than trying to develop comparable scales based on answers given to a questionnaire. Each man was rated on the activity score sheet reproduced in Table 2.1

Table 2.1
Business Activity Code

I. Activities Scored as −1

1. Increased activity with family or religious organizations, at the expense of business.

2. Decrease: less pay, fewer responsibilities, demotion, firing.

II. Activities Scored as 0

1. Person appears blocked, helpless in the face of an overpowering situation, e.g., family runs firm. Government restrictions prevent expansion, or personnel policies of firm block advance.

2. Firm improves, but not due to his specific acts, e.g., gross income higher because of rising prices.

3. Improvements in family or personal life.

4. Routine job advancement of the firm or of the man in his own job. Normal pay increases or bonuses.

III. Activities Scored as +1

1. Specific plans to improve his qualification or his business with some relevant preparatory action taken (e.g., taking a course in accounting which qualifies him for a better job, planning to set up a new plant, getting information in a way that involves some expense).

2. Increased activity with voluntary business organization, such as Rotary Club, or a professional organization.

3. Specific change in his interest, concern or involvement in his business, such as going to work more often, or earlier.

IV. Activities Scored as +2

1. Specific action taken which has improved procedures, e.g., he has simplified reports of agents so that they can post them daily, or he has put new product in production. Hiring a salesman, where it results in a rise in business.

2. Unusual increase in firm's business due to man's activities.

3. Promotion or salary increases above 25 per cent for a two-year period which are unusual (although the latter must always be evaluated in terms of the prior level and the reasons for the increase).

4. Goes into business for himself.

---

after he had been assessed, usually from several different points of view. The categories of this system are rough groupings of different kinds of business activity which can be thought of as approximately equivalent. Ideally, he filled out a questionnaire giving concrete information about changes in job activities and pay raises; he was also interviewed at length about what he had been doing since a given date; and finally, one or more of his friends or work associates was interviewed to check on the reliability of his report. Sometimes one or more of these sources of information was either unavailable or unnecessary. For instance, if a man took the interviewer down to show him the new apartment building he was constructing, it was not always necessary to check on the activity with someone else. Or, on the other hand, if a man could not be found for an interview, but his company superior could be interviewed about his progress, this was often sufficient. For each man a paragraph was written summarizing the relevant information for the time period in question, and this information was subsequently coded according to the activity score outline provided in Table 2.1. A man's rating could range from 0 to + 2. Some examples from how the procedure was applied to the Bombay course participants will help illustrate the concrete nature of the information on which the ratings were based. In reading these summaries, it is important to remember that the *n* Ach training courses were given around February, 1963. The Before ratings refer to the period 1961–63 and the After ratings to March 1963–January 1965.

A

Source: Interview.

His company finally made him sales manager of the All-India branch, giving him the scope he felt he needed for his ideas in September, 1963. Since then sales are up 35 per cent rather than the usual 15–20 per cent. He credits his ideas as follows: (1) He brought in field representatives for orientation courses; they now are better appreciated and can understand and plan their work better. (2) He told them to make frequent regular calls on dealers, since this is even more important than prices, delivery, and service. (3) He simplified reports of agents, so that they post them daily on tours rather than writing them up when they get back. The result is that clients get word from the head office instead of feeling forgotten. (4) He asks for quarterly reports on new accounts, so that the field representative gets a chance to realize what he's done. He now knows how much he's accomplished. His management was at first reluctant, but he tried out a few ideas, the results of which panned out so that he was given a free hand.

Before: 0   After: +2

B

Source: Mr. C. and Mr. G., both managers in his company.

B. joined the firm in 1954, after the London School of Economics, through connections with the family owning the firm. Pleasant person, but not pulling his weight initially. Steady, improvement over the last four to six years helped by marriage to a clear-headed girl in the office, and death of his father who was mentally unstable. Manager reports that up through the end of 1962 he must have been frustrated because he was not fully utilized. In 1963 he was put in charge of sales in Bombay. He improved dealer relationships through emphasis on courtesy, sending out supplies on time, and initiated policy of regular circulars and contacts about new products. Later promoted from No. 2 man in Bombay to No. 1 in large North Indian city.

Before: 0 (normal progress)   After: +2

C

Source: Questionnaire and interview.

He was promoted to overall charge of sales and administration from Maharashtra and Gujarat States in July 1963, but is a little vague about specific changes. "Control including follow-up, is now based on facts, including the gathering of relevant facts, consultation before taking action, and new approaches to problems which did not exist previously." Could not get more specific instances from him of changes in his own activities. Normal pay increases. He says two suggestions he has made are under consideration by his general manager. Believes that n Ach leads only to frustration in organizations like his.

Before: 0   After: 0

D

Source: Questionnaire.

In 1960 he started up the consultancy department of a firm and had a large but "normal" salary increase in 1962. Says "for this change I had to fit myself, school myself, and am still working on myself." He reorganized the consultancy side and gave up the auditing side in 1960. He sounds very busy and happy and enthusiastic about the achievement aspects of his work. But there is no concrete evidence of a change after the course.

Before: +2   After: 0

E

Source: Questionnaire and Interview.

He had been doing very well in his company before the course, as indicated by his very high monthly salary compared to other participants. He feels that the course has not been of great value to him. He doesn't seem to have done anything extraordinary in his work. He says he got the idea during the courses that he ought to leave his company, but he decided not to and it was the best decision he could have made. He doesn't say why or mention any specific changes. However, he was invited to give some lectures on industrial development, of which he gave me a copy. In addition, because he stood up for certain things as a matter of principle in the professional association, he was persuaded to be a candidate for a high office. He was defeated, but feels he was probably ahead of the normal pace in this anyway and will do all right later. In any case, his name is now known in professional circles and his ideas and statements are quoted.

Before: +2   After: +1 (increased
                           activity with voluntary
                           business organization)

It is important to note from these examples that it is activities that are scored, not outcomes and not reasons for activities. Thus a rapid promotion is not enough to give a person + 2 for increased activity, since it is an outcome which may come about for other reasons, such as resignation of a superior or intervention of the family in the firm. Furthermore, the coding is independent of what the man says the course did for him. The last man, E, says he doesn't think it helped him much, but the code is based on his actual behavior—the fact that he ran for a high office. Obviously, the course may have had nothing to do with this, but the research question is whether people who have had the course are more or less active afterwards on the average than people who have not had the course. It is conceivable that people's opinions as to the effects of the course may be wrong in either of two ways. Either they may think it has more effect than it has, or they may think that it has less effect than it has. *The activity level is coded here, not the person's or the judge's opinions as to the reason for the activity.*

The difference between a + 1 and a + 2 score is largely determined by whether a specifiable increase in activity has had a financial impact that can be assessed in terms of increased income, sales, profits, decreased costs, and so on. All plans, improving one's abilities by taking courses or joining in professional activities, receive a + 1 score until they result in concrete financial improvements. Agreement on these ratings between two judges working independently from the same material runs around 92 per cent.

Table 2.2 describes in summary form the training inputs characteristic of various early courses and their later yields in activity levels, so far as they could be determined. The earliest comparison of the effects of two types of training courses was carried out in Mexico City with the assistance of Dr. Elliott Danzig in late summer 1961 and February, 1962. Through his consulting firm, Dr. Danzig arranged to give two courses to a number of Mexican businessmen. The *n* Ach training materials were brought to Mexico by Dr. John Andrews, then a graduate student, who helped members of Dr. Danzig's firm give the course. The training inputs for the experimental course, all of which were in Spanish, consisted mostly of learning the *n* Ach coding system, practicing the business game, discussing authoritarianism in the Mexican family and business life, and thinking through the role of *n* Ach in the participants' working life. Sessions were held in a classroom setting after hours during the regular business week. The control course was arranged some six months later. It was held at a local club in town and consisted of a variety of techniques for self-study, such as the "Who am I?" exercise designed to help a person decide what he wanted to be and do. Both courses contained some elements of prestige suggestion of the sort described for the Bombay course above, since they were described as based on some new scientific research ideas coming from Harvard. An engraved certificate of course completion, signed by a Harvard professor, was awarded at the end.

The average age of participants in both courses was slightly over 35, with a range between 28 and 53. About 30 per cent of the participants in each course worked in banks, 60 per cent in various executive capacities in manufacturing, and 10 per cent in other occupations. Though it was not noticed at the time, the participants in the control course unfortunately represented a higher occupational level, since about two thirds of them earned over 76,000 pesos a year as contrasted with only about one third of the participants in the *n* Ach course.

The yield measures obtained some three years later give no indication that the *n* Ach course or the self-study course had any significant effect on the mean activity level of the participants. Both groups had been fairly active in the two years before the courses; they were on the average slightly more active in the two years afterwards, but the increase is not significant. There is no difference between the two courses and it is quite possible that the increase might be due to the generally accelerating rate of economic development in Mexico City. It is difficult at this distance to explain why no effect was obtained. There are several possible explanations: this was the first full-length course to be given. The instructors had to learn not only how to present the material, but also how to present it in Spanish. The classroom setting created a rather academic approach to the subject which may not have engaged the attention of the participants sufficiently to lead them to accept the notion that they could change. There were also more bank employees in these courses than in any of the subsequent ones. It is clear that the *n* Ach

Table 2.2
Course Inputs and Before-After Activity Levels for Early Samples of Businessmen Trained

Course Designation	Date	ACH. SYNDROME			SELF-STUDY			GOAL-SETTING			INTERPERSONAL SUPPORTS			N	MEAN ACTIVITY LEVELS*		
		Fantasy A-1	Action A-2	Cases A-3	Career S-1	Motives S-2	Values S-3	Prestige G-1	Ach. Plan G-2	Check-up G-3	Warmth I-1	Retreat I-2	Group Ref. I-3		2 Years Before	2 Years After	p diff
Mexican businessmen																	
n Ach	8/61	1.5	2	0	1	0	1	2	0	0	0	0	0	13	.69	.85	n.s.
Self-study	2/62	0	0	0	1	2	0	2	0	0	1	0	0	13	.77	1.00	n.s.
Bombay businessmen																	
n Ach	2/63	1.5	2	2	2	2	1	2	0	1	2	0	0	29	.48	1.21	<.01
Waiting List†		0	0	0	0	0	0	0	0	0	0	0	0	21	.42	.62	n.s.
Large U.S. firm																	
n Ach	10/62	2	2	1	2	2	0	2	2	0	2	2	0	11	.55	.82 ⎫	<.05
Company course		0	0	X††	0	X††	0	2	1	0	2	2	0	11	.64	.27 ⎭	

* Rated so that −1 = poorer performance, demotion; 0 = normal progress; 1 = increased plans and activities; 2 = specific improvements, usually having notable financial impact.

** Rated so that 0 = not present; 1 = partly present; 2 = fully present.

† 11 out of 21 applied to enter the course but were put on the waiting list; the remaining ten yielded almost identical Before-After mean scores.

†† Company-sponsored course on how to maintain the "corporate image," which stresses competence, soundness, clear-headedness, and progress.

concepts are not particularly relevant to many banking roles, which do not generally have entrepreneurial components. Finally, the follow-up measures themselves are based on less adequate information than in the other studies summarized in the table.

Bombay Courses.   Three courses were given in collaboration with the Bombay Management Association in a six-week period starting in late January, 1963. They met for 11 sessions of two to two and one half hours each, approximately every other day in the evening after work, for over three weeks, with two sessions and a luncheon meeting on Saturdays. Thus the total training time was approximately 25–30 hours including personal counseling conferences. Although the results of the Mexican courses were not known at that time, it was decided to strengthen considerably the self-study part of the courses in order to get individuals to work harder at applying what was being learned to their own lives. This process was also helped by introducing case materials showing how business activities could be coded for the various aspects of the *n* Ach scoring system. In other words, the key instructor, who was again Dr. Danzig, decided to combine the two approaches he had used in the Mexican courses. He taught *n* Achievement in the context of a self-development course, with much personal counseling and feedback on performance. He was assisted by Dr. David Winter, then a graduate student from Harvard spending a year in India carrying out motivational research. The help and encouragement of the staff of the Bombay Management Association and several key executives who took the first course designed for future trainers was particularly useful. Not all the people who applied to take one of the courses could be admitted, and 11 of these were followed up in January, 1965, along with the graduates of the courses, by Dr. Winter, who returned to Bombay to interview the men and their associates. As noted above, the coding was based in part on personal history questionnaires filled out before training and two years later, and in part on information gathered about both time periods from the man himself and his associates. These 11 men who were not admitted to training might be considered to be matched with those who took the course, in terms at least of their desire to participate and improve. Their average activity level in the two years before the course was similar to that of those who did take the course (mean = .36), and two years later they had shown almost no change (mean = .54). To make sure that the result was not due to the small sample size, the activity levels for an additional group of ten subjects were added, when it became apparent that even though they had not volunteered to take the courses, their mean pre-course activity level was almost identical to that of those who had volunteered.[3] Furthermore, the fact that the additional subjects had not volunteered did not mean they had not wanted to, for most of them did not know about the courses at the time they were given. Before and After activity level information was collected for them at the time of the final roundup, two years later (January–February, 1965).

The mean age was 36.1 years for the trained subjects and 37.8 for the controls, with a range between 27 and 47. Approximately 47 per cent of those who took the *n* Ach courses held sales or marketing positions, since we had stressed in particular the appropriateness of *n* Ach training for such entrepreneurial roles. The remaining participants were divided almost equally between manufacturing and other occupations. The proportions in various occupations were about the same for the control subjects, with 43 per cent in sales and marketing and the remainder divided about equally between production and other occupational roles. Median income for all subjects in 1963 was about Rs. 2,000 per month, with a range from Rs. 400 to upwards of Rs. 7,000 per month. The distribution was skewed upwards, so that the average monthly income was around Rs. 2,500 in 1963. Follow-up information was obtained in January, 1965 on 29 of the 34 men who took one of the three courses offered. These 29 men were significantly more active in the two years after the course than they had been in the two years before, as the mean scores in Table 2.2 show. The control subjects, who had no course, showed no significant change, suggesting that the improvement among the course participants could not be wholly due to the effects of inflation in the economy nor to general business improvement in the Bombay area in 1963–65. The differences also show up in the proportions of men who showed a marked increase in activity (score of $+2$). In the two years before the course, about an equal proportion of the trained and untrained men received a $+2$ score—24 per cent and 19 per cent respectively. In the two years after the course, 16 out of 29 of the trained men received a $+2$ score (55 per cent) vs. 6 out of 21 of the untrained men (29 per cent), a difference which could hardly have arisen by chance ($x^2 = 4.08$, p $< .05$).

Thirteen of the course participants reported salary levels for 1961, 1963, and 1965. The average increase in salary was considerably greater for the 1963–65 period (approximately Rs. 13,000 per annum) than for

3. The authors are indebted to Dr. R. M. Shah of Bombay for obtaining these additional data.

the 1961–63 period (approximately Rs. 10,000 per annum). But the difference could easily be due to a generally accelerating rate of economic growth in the Bombay area. The consumer price index for Bombay rose from about 100 to 110 in the earlier period and from 110 to 130 in the later period.[4] Consequently, a careful attempt was made to match these 13 individuals with 13 nonparticipants with equal salaries at the time of the course (1963). Each man's starting or 1963 salary was plotted against his finishing or 1965 salary. A regression line was then drawn, showing the expected average rate of salary improvement for all of these men in that particular two-year period in Bombay. Sixty-two per cent of the men who had had the course had higher salaries than the average regression predicts, contrasted with only 36 per cent of the men who had not had the course. The difference is not significant ($x^2 = 1.64$, p $< .20$), and one cannot be sure that the 13 from the course who reported their salaries are representative, but the trend is certainly encouraging and in the predicted direction. It adds weight to the significant trend based on a more general rating of all the cases, showing that those who took the n Ach training course subsequently showed a higher activity level score.

It may also be noted that Dr. George Litwin gave a brief course in Tokyo to nine management consultants. The pattern of its training inputs was more similar to the Mexican n Achievement course than any other, since it was given soon afterwards in the spring of 1962. A checkup five years later showed that five of the nine trained (56 per cent) received a $+ 2$ rating within two to three years after the course. Four of them had left the firms for which they had been working for some time in order to take better jobs. Moving from one firm to another is much less common in Japan than the United States, because in Japan greater stress is placed on loyalty to and continuity in the firm. The average post-course activity level score is 1.1 for the nine men involved, which is very close to the average post-course activity level score for the group trained in Bombay. There was no control group in Japan, but the movement out of the company into better jobs seems definitely unusual and the improvement rate is about the same as for the trained group in Bombay.

A Large U.S. Firm. Another comparison involved a special course given for a large U.S. company in a retreat setting in October, 1962. As Table 2.2 shows, there were more training inputs included for this course than for the others so far discussed. Stressed, in addition to the

4. Data from the *Reserve Bank of India Bulletin*, March, 1967.

achievement syndrome and the self-study inputs, were goal-setting and the interpersonal supports that developed in the retreat atmosphere. The instructors for the course were Dr. McClelland from Harvard and Drs. Litwin and Ciarlo, assisted by the staff of the training division of this large company. The company involved is highly successful and maintains a mystique of achievement and progress, so that the participants understood the concepts of the *n* Ach training course better than either the Mexican or Indian businessmen.

The fact that all the participants came from the same company made it easier to measure subsequent progress precisely and to obtain a carefully matched control group of subjects who had taken the usual company executive development course. The company course lasted longer and, if anything, had somewhat greater prestige, since the participants knew that they were selected for it as a probable route to future advancement. The *n* Ach course, on the other hand, could not be introduced as fulfilling this function. Rather it was described as an experimental program developed on the basis of some Harvard research that ought to be of assistance to them in their careers. The company course gave a good deal of academic and technical business information which was designed to prepare the men for their future roles as representatives of this large corporation and of the American business community. While it is doubtful that the training directors intended it, the implicit message that the course may have conveyed was that if a man was to be promoted to high responsibility and visibility in this company, he ought to be above all competent, sound, clear headed and forward looking. While it is certainly understandable why the company would want to promote such an ideal image, it may have given the men the impression that they ought not to behave in any way that would rock the boat.

At any rate, the activity level measures show that 11 of those who took the *n* Ach course advanced more rapidly than they had previously, whereas the 11 men who took the company course advanced less rapidly than they had previously. The difference between the two groups of men was significant two years after the course. Originally 16 men took the course, but three of them had had to reduce their activities because of serious medical disabilities, and two left the company. Of those who had left the company, one was doing extremely well in another company and the other's whereabouts was not known. Aronoff and Litwin (1968), who conducted the follow-up study, carefully matched each of the 11 remaining cases with a "twin" in the company. "The match was reached solely on the basis of function (manufacturing, sales, engineering), division within the company (the type of product made), job level (e.g., assistant branch manager for sales), and the man's age (obviously there are different opportunities open to a thirty-five-year-old assistant branch manager as compared to one sixty years old)" (Aronoff and Litwin, 1968). The age ranged from 31 to 59; all had major management responsibility. The authors give more details, but the central conclusion remains the same: the n Ach training course seems to have promoted the careers in this company of the participants more than the company course did for those who took that course.

While the results summarized in Table 2.2 are not so clear-cut as one would like them to be, they do suggest six rather encouraging conclusions. (1) It is practicable to run n Ach training courses for businessmen with varying training inputs and to compare their yields, at least roughly, in terms of an activity level score. (2) There is encouraging evidence that n Ach courses may increase the subsequent activity levels of the businessmen who take them. The skepticism characteristic of most psychologists concerned with personality change does not seem wholly warranted in the light of the significant changes in activity levels of the Bombay businessmen and the executives in the large U.S. corporation who were given n Ach training.

It may be countered that the results are not due to the training at all, but just to selection factors or mere suggestion. Yet (3), it seems unlikely that all the results obtained could be due to selection or "volunteer error," in the sense that those who signed up for the course were already those who were more likely to change. In Bombay some effort was made to control this source of bias by using as controls other subjects who had volunteered for the course.

In the U.S. company it is difficult to see how the differences could be explained in terms of a greater motivation to change of those who signed up for the n Ach course. The procedure followed was the same for the two types of courses. A man was chosen and was given the opportunity to attend the training sessions at the country estate maintained for this purpose. All had the opportunity to accept or refuse. Nearly everyone accepted, with the exception of a very few who had important personal reasons for not going at that time.

Nor (4) does it seem likely that mere suggestion produced the changes in activity level, if by "mere suggestion" is meant any course designed for self-improvement. Certainly the company-sponsored course in the U.S. had a markedly different effect from the n Ach course in the same company. Also, neither course produced a significant and measurable effect on activity levels in Mexico. So not just any course will "suggest" improvement. It is not possible yet to specify what aspect of training produces a change in activity levels, but it is safe to conclude even at this stage that not just any course will make a difference.

(5) On the other hand, even the preliminary data in Table 2.2 suggest that there are a number of training inputs which do not seem to be essential. The interpersonal support inputs were certainly at a fairly minimal level in the Bombay courses, yet the courses seem to have had a significant impact. Furthermore, repeated checking up on progress does not seem to be absolutely necessary. In the Bombay courses, only one follow-up session was held for some of the participants, when Dr. McClelland happened to be in that city about eight months after the course was given. Even then, the checkup reminded the subjects of their participation in an experiment more than it checked on progress. In the large U.S. company, no further formal contact took place with any of the course participants at any time after the course ended.

Nor can one argue that the results can be obtained only through the personal influence of a particular instructor. Dr. Danzig was a key leader in the unsuccessful Mexican *n* Ach course and also in two of the three successful Bombay courses. A totally different group of trainers were involved in the successful *n* Ach course given for the large U.S. corporation.

(6) Finally, experience bears out the theory that the course probably is more useful to men who occupy an entrepreneurial (sales) role or can move into one. It may be less useful to people occupying non-entrepreneurial roles. The evidence for this is quite sketchy, but there were a great number of bank employees in the Mexican courses who were unaffected and a large number of sales and marketing executives in the Bombay courses who were affected.

The findings are more suggestive than conclusive. In each case it is not possible to rule out absolutely any other possible interpretation of the increased activity level scores obtained after *n* Ach training. Yet, to have any results at all is encouraging in a field where follow-up findings are usually not sought or, if they are sought, as in the case of recent studies of psychotherapy, generally show no great effects as compared with findings on groups who have not received special treatment. At any rate, the approach seemed sufficiently promising to be worth a serious try at a community-wide level.

CHAPTER 3

PLANNING A COMMUNITY BUSINESS DEVELOPMENT PROJECT

The early attempts to develop motivation reported in Chapter 2 concentrated on trying to find out whether individuals changed following specialized training. The focus of attention was on whether course participants subsequently became economically more active. Yet even demonstrating their increased activity does not enable us to conclude anything definitive about the relationship between achievement motivation and economic development. For the main question to be answered is whether increasing achievement motivation in individuals will contribute to the economic growth of a *collectivity*—a firm, a community, or a nation. And it is quite reasonable to argue that the advancement of some individuals is always made at the expense of others, resulting in no net gain in collective welfare. Foster (1965) has pointed out that among peasants the "image of the limited good" is often dominant. They believe there is a limited supply of resources to go around, so that the entrepreneur who works harder will simply get more than his share, forcing others to make do with less. Is this what happens when achievement motivation is increased in a small segment of a community?

It is certainly conceivable that the businessmen discussed in the last chapter who were promoted more rapidly after *n* Achievement training may have been promoted at the expense of others who did not get the training. Or the salesmen who subsequently sold more of their products may have taken a share of the market away from somebody else. Or if a new firm was founded or expanded, it may have been at the expense of other firms. Sinha (1967) has carried the argument one step further. He notes that if resources are really limited, increasing competitiveness may actually lower collective output over what it would be without such increased competition.

> The theory that *n* Ach leads to economic growth seems to be based, although never explicitly stated, on a philosophy favoring decentralized decision making, where individuals are in a better position to think what is best for them; and since it is they who constitute a society, their individual attempts at achievement maximization will lead the society to growth and prosperity. But what seems overlooked is the possibility that attempts to better one's achievement (which may be just control over resources) may put others at a serious disadvantage especially in a resource-limited condition. . . . Even if the output levels are better for a few with plenty of resources, the loss to the remaining ones may offset the gains by a few, thus showing less than the maximum output possible in a society.

He quotes with favor C. Wright Mills' statement that "a competitive spirit which is conceived to be the source of all virtue, abounds only where there is consciousness of unlimited opportunity. Whenever there is consciousness of scarcity, of a limited, contracting world, then competition becomes a sin against one's fellows." Sinha has furthermore carried out an experiment in the laboratory which clearly shows that if competitiveness is increased when resources are limited, the output of the group is less than what it would be if cooperation is stressed. "When resources are limited, not only is the total group output reduced (both time- and error-wise), but experiences with the task result in lesser liking for the group and the task, and more negative evaluation of the partners. Even one's own self-esteem suffers." While his research also shows that a competitive attitude is conducive to increased output when resources are plentiful, he wonders whether trying to increase achievement motivation in a poor country like India might not be very dangerous, since the country's resources are limited.

On several grounds the argument represents an oversimplification of known facts about *n* Achievement. For instance, competition cannot be equated with *n* Ach in any simple way. One of the scoring criteria for *n* Achievement involves competition with others, but the primary emphasis is on "competition with a standard of excellence"; on *doing better than one has done before,* either in terms of some objective standard or the standard of someone else's behavior. Furthermore, one of the results of increased *n* Achievement should be an increased search for new resources, rather than a fight to get a greater share of the old ones. All that we know about *n* Ach reveals that a person high in it does not restrict himself to presently available means of achieving his goals, but seeks for new and alternative means. Competition perceived exclusively in terms of fighting for limited resources is a power image. For when the primary motive is for power or influence, then the person is playing a zero-sum game: what A gains in influence over B, B loses in influence over A. But in the achievement game, when A gains, this helps B gain because more resources are created.

While several such theoretical objections to Sinha's line of reasoning may be made, nevertheless its possible implications need to be taken seriously, as far as empirical research is concerned. Even though data collected in *The Achieving Society* show a low positive correlation between national levels of *n* Ach and rates of economic growth, the relationship is far from being understood in any detail. It may exist only where resources are relatively unlimited. And in any case, very little is known about how individual changes in activity levels are translated into collective outputs. Clearly, a study is needed in which the effects of changes in *n* Ach levels of individuals can be traced over time throughout the social and economic life of the community. Accordingly, a search was made to locate a site where a development project could be initiated for a collectivity. The goal was to find a community where a significant proportion of the key leaders could be exposed to *n* Ach training so that a study could be made of the effects of the training, not only on their own careers, but on the economic output of their total community.

If such a field study was to lead to any definite results, obviously the collectivity involved had to satisfy certain criteria. It could not be too underdeveloped, or else not enough infrastructure would exist for economic development to show up in any reasonable period of time. That is, it seemed unwise to choose an extremely backward area, populated only by illiterate peasants without business experience, or an area without any of the conditions necessary for business such as credit, transportation, or literacy. Some minimal level of social overhead capital and business organization seemed necessary if motivational inputs were to have any observable effects in the short run. On the other hand, the collectivity ought not to be too large, too developed, or too complex. If it were, then it might be very difficult to prove that a single input such as motivation training was responsible for any changes in collective growth. The motivational inputs might be swamped by the large number of changes naturally occurring in a highly developed, specialized, urban complex. Other criteria for selecting a location for the project included: a very slow economic growth rate over a long period of time; some receptivity locally to motivational training; an educational institution with access to the community where the motivational training could be carried out; and enough political stability so that it seemed probable that the long-term evaluation could be carried out without disruption.

At the time the search for a site was instituted, the U.S. Agency for International Development (AID) was interested in finding new methods of improving the effectiveness of its world-wide program to help poor countries develop economically. It was particularly interested in new methods because some of the traditional economic approaches which had worked so well under the Marshall Plan did not seem to be having the same effect in really poor countries. Economic theorists and planners like Rostow (1960) were arguing that it was not so much that the methods were ineffective but that they could not be used on a large enough scale to get a backward economy moving at an accelerating rate. Such a line of reasoning would seem to call for massive economic aid in many countries. But it seemed unlikely that Congress would try to cure what seemed to be a faltering AID program by making even larger sums of money available so that economic aid could reach the critical mass necessary to stimulate a "take off" into rapid growth. So the research office of AID was searching for methods of using more efficiently what seemed to be a diminishing supply of money. And it seemed at least plausible that one possible reason why traditional methods had proven less effective in some countries than in Europe was a difference in motivational orientations. At any rate, it was widely believed among commonsense observers that in some countries, the business leadership did not seem to be strongly motivated to make use of the aid offered in the most entrepreneurial ways possible. Thus a pilot project, to test whether n Ach training might be a relatively effective and inexpensive way of accelerating economic growth on a community-wide basis, seemed to be a worthwhile venture.

The research section of AID in November and December of 1962 encouraged our project application. The purpose of the project would be to test the effectiveness of n Ach training in a number of different locations and countries receiving assistance from AID. The agency agreed to finance an initial training conference in the United States for representatives from various underdeveloped countries who themselves might help with the research and *n* Ach training back in their own countries. The conference was held in the summer of 1963 at the Harvard Business School. It was attended by sixteen participants from ten countries: India, Egypt, Colombia, Tunisia, Algeria, Spain, Chili, Italy, Mexico, and Thailand. After discussions and an extensive study of possible locations for training in these various countries, it was decided that further feasibility studies would be carried out primarily in India, southern Italy (which was still classified as underdeveloped), and Tunisia. India was chosen not only because we had had considerable previous experience there already, but also because it presented opportunities for studying the effects of *n* Ach training on two types of collectivities at different levels of complexity. At the simpler level, it was proposed to study the effects of training on the productivity of firms. In several places in India there are associations of a number of fairly large textile mills. Preliminary contacts suggested that it would be possible to interest the key executives in some of these mills to attend motivation development seminars. Since careful comparable records of output of all the mills are kept, it seemed possible to discover fairly promptly whether the motivational training had had any effects on the output of the affected mills.

At a more complex level, it was proposed to train a significant proportion of the key leaders in a small city dominating a district in India to see if this had any significant effect on district indicators of economic growth. Such an effort was made feasible by the possibility of collaboration with the Small Industries Extension Training Institute, a Government of India Society located in Hyderabad in the state of Andhra Pradesh.

Southern Italy was chosen for study because the Cassa di Mezzogiorno, a governmental development agency, had already set in motion a plan by which business leaders from centers of four underdeveloped regions were to be specially trained in Naples. It seemed feasible to add motivation training to the program for leaders from one or two of the regions, to observe whether such training would make any difference in the rate of development of these regions as compared to the others, the leaders from which had not received *n* Ach training.

Finally, and more ambitiously, initial contacts had suggested that Tunisia was a small country whose political leaders might be particularly interested in introducing achievement motivation training for a number of leadership cadres in various sectors of the government. Thus, if all went well, it might be possible to observe the effects of motivation training on the rate of development of the country as a whole as compared with a number of similar countries, the leadership cadres of which had not been exposed to n Ach training. In sum, the research design of the project called for further investigation of the feasibility of observing the effects of achievement motivation training introduced at the firm level, the district level, the regional level, and even at the national level. In the Fall of 1963, Dr. McClelland set off to visit these various sites and explore the possibility of setting up the planned programs with the financial support of the research section of AID.

When he reached India, however, he learned that AID would not be able to support the project, which had been in the planning stages for nine months. For fear of the ridicule that such a large scale "psychological" enterprise might be subjected to in Congress, the AID leadership in Washington had decided that it could not provide funds for the project after all. David Bell, AID administrator, felt it might seriously jeopardize "developing a strong research program as part of the U.S. foreign aid effort" (personal communication). He was acting on the advice of the Inspector General for Foreign Assistance, J. K. Mansfield, who wrote to him on August 20, 1963: "We find it very difficult to see how the large cost of this proposed project can be justified in terms of its contribution to the Agency's work, and we strongly recommend that AID not enter into this contract."

Essentially this decision led to the abandonment of three parts of the proposed program, but left one opportunity alive—the possibility of collaborating with the Small Industries Extension Training Institute in Hyderabad, with support from the Ford Foundation. SIET Institute had been brought into being with Ford Foundation assistance as a Government of India Society designed to train extension workers who would serve to help small industries develop all over India. Two of the chief Ford Foundation consultants to the Institute, Drs. R. P. Lynton and J. E. Stepanek, had written a monograph entitled *Industrialization beyond the metropolis: A new look at India.* Their analysis of India's economic situation and manpower needs pointed to the great importance of developing a more entrepreneurial spirit at the district level in the smaller cities. Thus there was some eagerness at SIET Institute to see whether achievement motivation training would help meet India's need by creating entrepreneurial spirit in such places. Thus, to pick up that part of the original AID proposal, and in collaboration with SIET Institute, an application to the Ford Foundation was prepared, with the strong support of its India representative, Douglas Ensminger.

Planning at SIET Institute

Since the project was ultimately carried out in collaboration with SIET Institute, the Institute needs to be understood. Its dominant orientation was reflected in the Lynton and Stepanek monograph, whose premises were simple: India was in dire need of a much more rapid rate of economic growth. For political and humanitarian reasons, it had to accomplish this goal by providing also for an accelerating rate of employment to keep up with the rapid population growth. Traditional economic planning was not sufficient to do the job. According to Lynton and Stepanek's figures, even if the targets of the third five-year plan were met (1961–66) and 14 million additional jobs provided, the total unemployed would still be around 12 million. Obviously some new approach was needed. What could it be?

One approach favored by many Indians was to provide as many jobs as possible at the lowest levels of technology—to go right where the unemployed were, so to speak. This meant, essentially, development of cottage industries using traditional technologies, a course of action which had been recommended by Gandhi. But to the leaders of SIET Institute this approach seemed wasteful. It provided employment, but dissipated resources without creating the capital surpluses needed to accelerate growth. The opposite approach was also favored by many Indian planners—namely, working primarily at the most modern advanced level of Western, labor-saving technology. The reasoning was that India needed to use what few resources it had as efficiently as possible to create the surpluses which in the long run could only lead to the accelerating rate of growth necessary to provide full employment. The difficulties with this approach were also obvious: India did not have the capital (and particularly the foreign exchange) to invest in advanced levels of technology in a sufficiently massive way to get the whole economy moving more rapidly. Furthermore, starting up huge, technologically advanced factories in the urban communication centers would tend to draw workers at an accelerating rate from the countryside in search of employment, when such migration was already threatening to overwhelm the major cities of India. The cost of providing services for such huge population agglomerations would more than offset the gains in efficiency from setting up a relatively small number of factories using advanced technologies.

A better approach seemed to lie somewhere between these extremes. It would employ modern, but capital-saving technologies in small factories located in the smaller cities. Developing secondary cities would slow the mass migrations to major cities like Bombay, Calcutta, Madras, and Delhi. Concentrating on small factories employing from 20 to 100 workers (rather than cottage industry) would guarantee at least some minimal level of management skill and experience and often some private capital. The strategy was one of transferring attention from cottage to modern, small-scale industry, while at the same time continuing to encourage the growth of large enterprises in smaller cities. Thus, relatively inexpensive assistance given to men operating such firms would most likely pay off fairly rapidly by creating capital surpluses that would lead to expansion and increased employment. Furthermore, these men not only had management skills and some money, they could also often employ middle-level technologies that did not require extensive training or lots of capital or foreign exchange. Lynton and Stepanek (1963) provide the following examples:

> In a small town the manufacturer of truck drive shafts got tired of waiting for a Rs. 3500 forging hammer from Germany under a hire purchase scheme, invested Rs. 200 in locally available capital equipment and started producing the shafts by hand. The shafts are higher in price but of acceptable quality. Above all they get made and are a straight gain to the economy over waiting. . . . A second proprietor is using hand looms to manufacture wire screens and sells it over the whole state. No doubt he could be forced out of business by a competitor using power looms. But what would be the advantage of that compared to using the power-looms or equivalent capital for more essential products of greater complexity? (p. 29).

It was this type of analysis of the situation that led to the setting up of SIET Institute. Its purpose was to train development officers to assist small industries in smaller cities and towns in every conceivable way: by helping them find middle-level technology as a substitute for more advanced methods of production requiring foreign exchange; by helping arrange for credit; by making economic surveys that would show what products could be made advantageously under local conditions, and so on. Everyone realized the need for a more entrepreneurial spirit among all the people involved in development both in the public and private sectors in the district. Again Lynton and Stepanek sum up the prevailing situation succinctly:

> When it comes to questions of development, people in the districts, officials included, talk mostly about the seemingly endless problems of getting anything significant moving. Entrepreneurs speak of interminable delays and unfathomed uncertainties

connected with getting loans processed, buildings constructed, electricity connected up even well after the machines are installed, and with obtaining regular supplies of raw materials. Officials speak of being desk-tied by piles of paper work, much of it connected with raw material control and dictated by policies too distant to query. In the villages, craftsmen join officials in talking about little else than the inadequacies of finance, by which they mean finance granted or loaned by the government; not a word about markets or about improved technology.

The most natural thing in the world for the official is to be part of this relentless stream toward insignificance. It rushes without response past the first, hesitant inquiry of a potential entrepreneur, the wealthy farmer who might come forward and invest in industry if he knew how, the skilled workman who has the itch to start out on his own but needs a little capital and lots of reassurance. Far from encouraging this urge the prevailing stream is more likely to kill it. (p. 11).

In view of this analysis, it is scarcely to be wondered that the hope of increasing achievement motivation either in public officials or private entrepreneurs was very appealing to the leadership at SIET Institute. At any rate, they entered enthusiastically into planning activities designed to pick districts where the training might affect the whole community. While the application to the Ford Foundation was being processed in New York, two Indian staff members were recruited for the project and paid out of a small rupee grant to Dr. McClelland, which had been released previously by the U.S. State Department. One staff member, Dr. Aziz Pabaney, had attended the AID-sponsored training conference the previous summer at the Harvard Business School. He served as the project initiator, coordinator, and planner. He was joined soon by Shri Manohar Nadkarni, whose task it was to collect information on a number of small cities throughout India in preparation for deciding exactly where and under what conditions the training was to be carried out. The initial plans called for selecting three pairs of small cities matched on a number of variables such as size (set at about 100,000 inhabitants); per cent literacy and growth in literacy over the past decade; number of persons of various ages in school; total number of firms employing twenty or more people and the growth in number of such firms over the past decade; level and growth rate in electricity consumed, transportation, and communication facilities; pattern of agricultural, industrial, and commercial employment; and so on. The search was limited to cities of about 100,000 because it was felt that in the Indian context they were neither too large nor too small. That is, they were large enough to provide the infrastructure necessary for rapid economic growth, but small enough to be relatively unaffected by major economic inputs which might be introduced by government or major private enterprises. It was necessary of course to eliminate certain cities because they were affected by certain special factors, such as major central government spending or the presence of a single, dominant environmental condition (such as one would find in a mining town or a small city in the desert).

After preliminary investigation of 1961 census data, seven comparable small cities were selected in three different states as sites for the project. Information on five of them is summarized in Table 3.1.

Table 3.1
Comparative Statistics on Five Small Indian Cities Initially Chosen for Study

State	ANDHRA PRADESH		ARCOT	MADRAS	
District	EAST GODAVARI			MADURAI	THANJAVUR
Town	Kakinada	Rajahmundry	Vellore	Dindigal	Kumbhakonam
Population (in 000s)					
1941	75	75	72	56	67
1961	123	130	114	93	97
Per cent Literacy (1961)	44.5	45.6	48	48	59
Per cent of 1961 Workers in					
Manufacturing	14.2	19.8	25.5	23.1	20.0
Trade	19.3	22.4	20.5	23.1	20.0
Agriculture	3.4	1.5	2.5	3.3	6.6
Mining	5.0	.8	—	3.3	—
Transport	12.4	15.2	7.7	6.6	6.6
Other	45.7	40.3	43.8	40.6	46.8
Factories					
1957 No. Units	93	99* (1958)	32	87	57
No. Employees	2437	2865*	644	3643	1696
1963 No. Units	94	90*	51	112	85
No. Employees	2413	2343*	745	3560	2753
Industrial Electricity Consumption (in 000s kwh/annum)					
1956–57	953	614 (58–59)	295	736	401
1962–63	1180	1077	516	713	403

* Excluding four tobacco units employing 3–4,000 workers.

Kakinada and Rajahmundry seemed particularly well matched in East Godavari District in Andhra Pradesh. They are located in the same ecological area only some forty-five miles apart and they are inhabited by very much the same kind of people. In Madras State three cities were chosen because it did not seem possible to get any one pair that were closely matched in size as well as the other variables. Finally, two cities were chosen in Maharashtra State, Akola and Amravati, but as no further work was done there, information on them is omitted from Table 3.1. It was decided to start with the pair of cities in Andhra Pradesh where the match was best, then move on to Madras State, and finally to Maharashtra State. In each case a city was chosen by chance as a place where *n* Achievement training was to be introduced— Kakinada for the first comparison, Vellore for the second, and Akola for the third. The selections were actually made by Dr. McClelland thousands of miles away in Rome, without any personal knowledge of conditions in any of the cities. The other cities were to serve as control cities, whose progress was to be followed to provide baseline change data against which developments in the treated cities could be compared.

Actual visits to the cities by Shri Nadkarni in November–December, 1963 revealed a number of problems. Statistical summaries of the sort provided in Table 3.1 did not always correspond to data obtainable in the field. New factories had appeared, old ones had disappeared. Definitions differed so that similar figures were not comparable when obtained from different sources. For instance, the census purports to record all industrial workers, while the factory inspectors only record those units registered under the Factories Act. Yet even a little local observation revealed that a number of owners avoided registering new production units because they found it hard to observe all the provisions of the Factories Act, particularly when they were getting started. A number of important local industries in some of the cities depend heavily on agricultural products, which in turn depend on the weather. Thus, there can be major annual fluctuations in city economic indicators—even in the electricity consumed by such industries—which strictly speaking have nothing to do with the entrepreneurial drive of business leaders in the town.

Furthermore, close inspection made one doubtful about the comparability even of two cities like Kakinada and Rajahmundry, which seemed so superficially similar in terms of the statistical data. It seemed impossible to rule out special economic inputs which might favor one town over the other or in some way make the two not comparable. For instance, in Table 3.1 it is clear that the tobacco industry in Rajahmundry contributes heavily to employment and income in a special way not matched in Kakinada. Furthermore, it seemed unlikely that outside economic forces would hold off influencing either city for the two or three years' duration of the project. As a matter of fact, no sooner had we chosen Kakinada at the site to introduce *n* Ach training, than the central government announced that it was going to build a huge bridge across the Godavari River into Rajahmundry—a project which could not fail to increase employment and income in the city in a major way. Finally, the more we investigated conditions in the cities, the more convinced we became that it was unlikely that even a major increase in entrepreneurial activity would show up in city-wide economic indicators until a long time had passed. Ultimately, of course, major increases in business activity would have to show up in general economic indicators, but it seemed likely that this would happen six to ten years after the training inputs were introduced. The reasons were all those given by Lynton and Stepanek above: delays in getting licenses, the red tape required to get permits, raw material shortages, slowness of communication among all the regulatory agencies involved, and so forth.

For all of these reasons, we concluded that the main measures of the effectiveness of the *n* Ach input could not very well be differential changes in the community economic indicators in terms of which the cities had been matched. Even if, for example, Kakinada showed a much more rapid gain in electricity consumption after the training input than Rajahmundry, which seemed unlikely in any case, it would be very difficult to attribute it to our intervention. The weather might seriously harm the tobacco crop one year in Rajahmundry or there might be a strike of government power workers, or a license might have suddenly come through for a new generator to supply the electricity for which connections had been made long ago. Instead, it seemed more sensible to focus on the effects of the training inputs on the activity level of individual businessmen and changes in the rates of growth of their firms. Thus we decided to select three comparable groups of businessmen whose activity could be studied over a five-year period—starting roughly two years before we began the project and ending with its completion three years later in the Spring of 1967. Group A would consist of the men who had received *n* Achievement training in a target city—say, Kakinada. Group B would consist of comparable businessmen from the target city who had not received *n* Ach training. The idea was to see whether *n* Ach training increased the business activity level of the men who receive it as compared with other men from the same city who do not receive it. Group C would consist of comparable businessmen from a comparable city—say, Rajahmundry—who had not received *n* Ach training. It seemed reasonable to suppose—in fact, it was part of the whole rationale for introducing n Ach training on a community-wide level—that creating increased entrepreneurial spirit in a significant portion of the business leadership of a community would help create a more "go ahead" atmosphere for all businessmen in the city. Thus one would predict that even Group B—the untrained group from Kakinada —would show a higher level of activity than Group C—the untrained group from Rajahmundry.

In studying the businesses of these men, it would obviously be necessary to go far beyond the simple rating scale adopted in Chapter 2, if further light was to be shed on the relationship of n Ach training to general economic activity. Thus it would be necessary to pay attention to whether previously unproductive capital had been mobilized, new equipment created, or new businesses started that made use of material resources or technologies not already in use. Otherwise we could not answer the question of whether by increasing the competitive spirit we had only succeeded in getting one group of businessmen active enough to take resources away from others who might employ such resources more effectively. Overall evaluation of such data might still be difficult, but it seemed an essential first step to collect detailed information on just what various groups of businessmen did with and without specialized motivation training. The quality of what some of them did might turn out to have more long-term economic significance than the quantity of workers they employed, if their expanded business and employment was only at the expense of somebody else in the same field.

The project proper started with visits by Dr. Pabaney to Kakinada in January, 1964. The first two training courses for especially prominent businessmen were scheduled to be held at SIET Institute in late February and early April. An outside consultant arrived at SIET Institute in mid-February to help organize the training. He was Dr. Elliot Danzig, who had already organized such courses in Mexico and Bombay, and then had helped run the AID-sponsored conference at the Harvard Business School in the summer of 1963. Dr. McClelland, who had proceeded on to the Mediterranean after helping organize the program in Hyderabad, was to return for the first course to participate in the first important step toward carrying out the project, which had been in the planning stages for over a year. Then the blow fell. The Ford Foundation at the last moment turned down the application for grant support of the project, possibly because it had just given SIET Institute a very large grant that in its view could be used to finance our research. Nevertheless, since public commitments had been made in Kakinada, and

Dr. Danzig was already on the scene, the Institute decided to go ahead with the n Ach training as best it could without special funding. It is a tribute to Shri R. N. Jai, Principal Director of the Institute, and the SIET Governing Council, that this decision was made, since the results of n Ach training were at that time still quite unknown and since the Institute did not have funds in its budget for this type of project. Nevertheless, the lack of Ford Foundation support forced some major revisions in the way in which the research was carried out. The first two training sessions for leaders from Kakinada were carried out more-or-less as planned, except that because of lack of funding it was impossible for Dr. McClelland to join in the training and for any case material to be written specifically about the local scene. Thereafter very little outside staffing was possible for the training. Dr. Pabaney had to leave. Shri Nadkarni was appointed a regular member of the SIET Institute staff and various other regular staff members had participated enough in the first two training sessions to become skilled as trainers themselves. Two more training courses for Kakinada, for a total of four, were run in the summer and fall of 1964 and the program in Vellore was initiated in January, 1965 by a special visit from Dr. McClelland, who had been appointed special consultant to The Ford Foundation to study the progress of the n Ach training program at SIET Institute. However, after two courses for Vellore had been run, there was a change in staff and overall policy direction at SIET Institute. Dr. Stepanek had left as the chief Ford consultant. Shri Jai was replaced as Principal Director by Shri Malgavkar, who recommended that the entrepreneurial motivation project be discontinued on the grounds that the research had not been properly designed or carried out and was therefore unlikely to yield results of any use to the Institute. A grant from the Carnegie Foundation to Dr. McClelland made it possible to do the follow-up studies on the businessmen trained in Kakinada and Vellore and to take comparable business histories of leaders in Rajahmundry over a two- to three-year period. Thus, of the original ambitious plans, all that was carried out in reasonably complete form was the first phase of the India program, involving comparisons of the activities of trained and untrained businessmen in Kakinada and Rajahmundry. The second phase was started somewhat tentatively in Vellore and then stopped. No comparative data were obtained from Dindigal or Kumbhakonam. The Vellore experience will serve more as an index of how effective a less intensive training input is, as compared with the more intensive one managed in Kakinada. The plans for the comparison in Maharashtra State had to be abandoned altogether for lack of money, just as the plans for studies in southern Italy and Tunisia had had to be dropped earlier.

The gap between what we had hoped to do and what we were actually able to do is obviously very great. It forced us to the conclusion that the kind of research we were attempting to carry out is actually much more difficult than we had at first supposed, because it involves collaborating with institutions in order to attempt to introduce changes in the motives and attitudes of people. Certainly it is far more difficult to carry out such research than it is to observe people as they are—whether that involves taking case histories of Bombay businessmen or sound motion pictures of the traveling Bushmen. Even such observational studies probably introduce changes in their lives, but unintentionally. Our goal, on the other hand, was to try consciously to introduce new ways of thinking and new types of motivation into people's lives. Initially change agencies are eager to try out motivation training and other programs of psychological education, but in our experience, they all suffer from afterthoughts as to whether such attempts can or should be tried. Psychological education appears to threaten in some way those committed to more traditional and well-established programs for accelerating development.

In any case, whatever the real reasons were our ambitious expectations had to be scaled down considerably. What remains is little more than a pilot study—a demonstration of the lines along which a large-scale project might be carried out with more solid support in the future. It cannot hope to give final answers to the urgent theoretical questions initially raised as to the community economic impact of increases in entrepreneurial motivation in a small sector of the business leadership of the community. It will report, however, in some detail just what happens to the business activities of men after they have been exposed to achievement motivation training. Perhaps the findings of even a pilot study will be sufficiently interesting and reassuring to make it possible to carry out the major project originally planned.

It remains to describe in more detail the cities where the study was actually carried out.[1]

1. The description is based on the following sources:
Hemingway, F. *Madras District Gazetteers: Godavari*. Madras: Government Press, 1907.
Imperial Gazetteer of India, Vols. 5, 24. Oxford: Clarendon Press, 1908.
Glamann, K. *Dutch-Asiatic Trade, 1620–1740*. Copenhagen: Danish Science Press, 1958.
Raychaudhuri, T. *Jan Company in Coromandel, 1605–1690*. The Hague: Nijhoff, 1962 (*Verhandelingen van het Koninklijk Instituut voor Taal-Land-en Volkenkunde*, 38).
Lasker, H. M. Factors affecting responses to achievement motivation training in India. Unpublished B.A. thesis, Harvard University, 1966.

KAKINADA AND RAJAHMUNDRY: HISTORY

Kakinada and Rajahmundry, each with a population of about 125,000, are the two principal cities of the East Godavari District in the Telugu-speaking state of Andhra Pradesh. Kakinada is a port on the Bay of Bengal, while Rajahmundry is an inland city on the Godavari River, forty miles away. Both are about 300 miles northeast of Madras city.

The Godavari district area was on the periphery of several ancient Indian empires, including that of Ashoka (260 B.C.), the Pallavas, and the Cholas. Rajahmundry was made a dynastic capital of the Reddi clan in 1385. Over a hundred years later, the area was involved in the rivalry between the Moslem kingdom of Golconda and the South Indian Hindu empire of Vijayanagar. Golconda finally captured Rajahmundry in 1571–72, but it in turn was absorbed into the Moghul Empire a hundred years later. As the Moghul Empire ties began to loosen, the ruler of the region became independent as the Nizam of Hyderabad, in 1724. During all of this time, Rajahmundry remained an important district administrative center.

Meanwhile, European influence slowly began to penetrate the coastal area after the early seventeenth century. The Dutch established a "factory" (a fortified trading post and warehouse) at Jaggananthapuram around 1650 (the present Jagannaickpur, a part of Kakinada city). This factory was one small part of a string of bases used by the Dutch to purchase the cloth that financed their spice trade in Java and elsewhere. The English made several settlements in the area during the late seventeenth and early eighteenth centuries. The French started a factory at nearby Yanam around 1750. However, the influence of these European outposts on the district as a whole was probably rather slight. The kingdom of Golconda was in a continual state of unrest, and local chiefs usually created difficulties for the European traders. Hence, the amount of trade was a good deal smaller in the Godavari District than in other, similar trading outposts elsewhere in India. The trade-based economic activity had slowly withered away by 1825, when the Dutch finally left Jaggananthapuram, and at that time the British rulers took steps to encourage other kinds of economic activity.

Godavari district was directly involved in the English-French commercial rivalry of the eighteenth century, the military outcome of which left the English in complete control of the coast after 1765. Over the next hundred years, the English consolidated their hold on the district through revenue collections and direct political administration. In the middle of the nineteenth century, the economic structure of the district began to assume its present outline. Agricultural commodities, such as rice, pulses, fibers, and hemp had always been important products. Construction of an *annicut* (earth dam) across the Godavari in 1850 increased the amount of land under irrigation and gave protection from floods, thereby helping to increase output. Cotton became an especially significant export during the period of the American Civil War.

This trade enhanced the position of Kakinada, as it was the only major port of the district, and indeed the principal port for several hundred miles along the coast. Shipping and allied commercial ventures grew in importance, although Kakinada was handicapped by having only a spur connection to the main-line Madras to Calcutta railway. The danger of silting in the harbor was recognized, and plans were made to improve harbor facilities, although these plans still have not been fully carried out. Kakinada's mercantile importance encouraged Indian businessmen to enter commerce in a vigorous way, and they set up their own local chamber of commerce. Furthermore, the city's relatively great contact with Western ideas and influences was reflected in the early enthusiasm for social reform and education. Kakinada was one of the first towns in India to have a local chapter of the *Brahmo Samaj,* an important nineteenth-century Hindu reform movement. Today, Kakinada has a large number of educational institutions: colleges, medical colleges, and technical institutes.

Rajahmundry also developed into a commercial center in the nineteenth century. Although it was not an ocean port, its location on the main-line railway between Madras and Calcutta, as well as on the Godavari River itself, made it a center of internal communications and commerce. By 1900, it was an established center for the manufacture of brass vessels. Gradually the making of graphite crucibles developed as an allied industry. A large paper factory was established in the 1920s, and this has been greatly expanded recently.

KAKINADA TODAY

While the two towns are quite similar in size, history, and general economic conditions, at first sight they appear quite different to the visitor. Kakinada presents a spacious, open pattern of wide, straight streets, while Rajahmundry is made up of crowded, narrow, twisting lanes. The road into Kakinada parallels a narrow canal in which barges coming from the Godavari River and canal network are pulled by workers clad in loincloths. On either side of the road are vast, brilliant, green fields of rice, fringed here and there by graceful, curving palm trees. At the edge of the city are the rambling stucco administrative offices of the district government: the Collector (chief district official), the Planning Commission, and the government Travelers' Bungalow. Next are some old, pillared mansions which are now the homes of wealthy merchants. Finally, there is the bazaar, which is clustered along a straight, wide Main Road that leads down to the port and then across a bridge to the older section of the town, where there are factories, residences, and a community of poor fishermen. Bullock carts, bicycle-rickshaws, cows, people, cycles, motor scooters, and occasional cars and trucks fill the Main Road during most of the daylight hours. Down near the port, large wooden barges with massive sails move slowly out into the roads of the harbor, where ocean-going vessels are anchored, about three or four miles offshore. Back from the Main Road are residential areas, many cinema houses, temples, thatched huts where the poorer families live, and several small engineering works, foundries, and other factories. Away from the port, towards the other end of the town, are the municipal offices and more small factories (see Plates 1 and 2).

The economy of Kakinada may be divided into four principal activities. First, there is the port and its related businesses, such as shipping, insurance, and stevedoring. Since the large ships must anchor several miles offshore, many boats and hundreds of workers are required to transport the cargoes in small batches from the railhead and the town itself out to the ocean-going vessels. While this system provides a good deal of employment in the town, its inefficiencies and delays have tended to retard the development and use of Kakinada as a major port. Port improvement has long been a political issue of greatest concern to the community, and there have been repeated attempts to have Kakinada included in the national plans for the development of ports. The second major activity is the palmyra fiber industry, which is closely related to the port. The fiber is collected from several villages in the area and brought to Kakinada for processing, combing, cleaning, drying, cutting, and baling. From Kakinada the fiber is exported to Japan and several European countries. Four or five large firms and many smaller firms handle this trade. Perhaps several thousand workers in the town and in the surrounding community are directly or indirectly employed in this business. However, the future of palmyra is uncertain. The overseas markets are not expanding, and there are persistent rumors that Japanese customers will convert to using synthetic fibers in the next few years.

Kakinada used to be a center for the shipment, both export and domestic, of various kinds of food grains, edible oils, and the like. This trade has been severely curtailed by shortages and recent government controls on the grain trade. Nevertheless, processing and distribution continues to be an important part of the economy of Kakinada. Considerable retail trade with the surrounding area continues in all commodities. Kakinada is also a distribution center for manufactured goods and agricultural supplies.

Finally, there is the growing industrial sector. The earliest industries started up around the processing of agricultural products. Gradually, foundries were established to produce castings for irrigation projects and equipment for sugar and rice mills. Today there is a major factory for the manufacture of automobiles and truck spare parts.

A typical industrial establishment is small, employing from ten to thirty men, and earning a gross annual income of from Rs. 10,000 to Rs. 300,000.[2] A foundry may consist of a one- or two-acre plot, part of which is covered by an open shed (see Plates 3 and 4). Casting is done, by semiskilled workers, in clay molds dug in the ground. Lathing, drilling, and other finishing work is done on machinery which is sometimes imported, but more often is a locally made replica of foreign equipment. Most foundries own five to ten pieces of such equipment. Cupolas for the melting of pig iron are usually of local design and have been built in the foundry itself. When sufficient supplies of coke and pig iron have been gathered, clay molds for whatever part is to be constructed are dug, the cupolas are fired, and the molten iron is cast. Casting usually is done a few times each month. After the castings have cooled, they are machined and finally assembled. A typical foundry can produce one or two large pieces of equipment, such as a sugar-crushing apparatus, per month.

The commercial establishments fall into two principal categories. Businesses dealing in grain and other agricultural commodities are among the oldest Indian-owned enterprises in the area. They are usually owned by men who possess considerable lands outside of the town, either in their own name or through their joint family. Many of these men belong to the *Vaisha*, or trading community.[3] Their land holdings may trace back to the times of the early British revenue settlements, or may be based on a succession of intermarriages with other landholding families. These men refine or process agricultural goods before selling them, in order to secure the higher and more stable prices that the finished product will bring. They may obtain the original crops directly from tenant farmers, if they own considerable land; but if they do not own

2. There are approximately 7.5 rupees to the United States dollar at the 1967 rate of exchange, and 4.85 at the 1964 rate.

3. The word community here refers to the *varna* (grouping of subcastes) of which an Indian considers himself a member.

land, they may instead lend money to small farmers against the purchase of the harvested crop.

Nonagricultural commercial establishments are rather different. For one thing, they usually consist of one office or store located along the Main Road. For another, they usually employ only three or four salesmen, since they are primarily involved with distribution only. These businesses tend to be relatively new. Most have been established since 1940, as the demand increased for the wide variety of products that they offer: cooking utensils, textiles, drugs, pastry products, cameras, radios, bicycles, and automobile parts (see Plates 5 and 6). In most cases, these nonagricultural establishments were started by their present owners or their fathers. Often the owners were immigrants to Kakinada, and they established this line of business both because of the promise of returns and because of the difficulty of entering any other line. Entering industry requires considerable initial capital, while entering agriculture-based commerce usually requires land, which is in short supply near the town. Selling practices in these shops vary widely. Some men feel that their principal task is to open the shop each day and then to be in constant attendance, in case a potential customer should enter. Others employ vigorous sales techniques, decorate their shops attractively, try to use rudimentary market research, and go in for advertising and other promotional devices.

The businessmen of Kakinada are very active in organizations and clubs, both the business-oriented and service clubs such as Rotary, Lions, and the Chamber of Commerce, and more purely social organizations. These clubs, in turn, have been responsible for characteristic improvements in local amenities and civic life. Nevertheless, a good deal of charitable activity is carried out by various religious groups and communities, principally for the welfare of their members, as well as by the beneficence of wealthy private individuals.

RAJAHMUNDRY TODAY

The most spectacular approach to Rajahmundry is over the railway bridge coming from Madras. As the train rolls over the mile-and-a-half span, built in 1900, the visitor looks down on the mud-colored waters of the massive Godavari River, one of the seven sacred rivers of India. About a half-mile downstream, construction is progressing on a highway bridge that will greatly improve transportation with the regions to the west and south. On the Rajahmundry side of the river, *dhobis* (washermen) are busily at work. Immediately after crossing the river, the visitor alights at one of the town's two railway stations, and then walks out to the head of the Main Road. As in Kakinada, this road contains most of the important shops; it, too, is filled during the daylight and evening hours with every sort of person, vehicle, and animal (see Plate 7). However, the road is much narrower, and has been made into a one-way street. A bicycle-rickshaw journey can be formidable. Textiles, jewelry, and a variety of other consumer goods are sold along the bazaar. Factories are located about a quarter-mile back of this road, away from the river. Far beyond these factories and adjacent residential areas are the green fields, not as accessible and visible from the city as they are in Kakinada. Several miles to the south, along the river, is the suburb of Dowleshwaram, famous for the manufacture of weighing scales. Finally, to the north is another residential area, which strings out along the road to Kakinada.

Rajahmundry industry produces brassware, and more recently, aluminum utensils. Most of these small factories have been modernized since 1950, so that they now have oil burners and use some electric power. The manufacture of iron products, such as scales, nails, and the like, dates back to the establishment of a government-sponsored training center in the nineteenth century. Several firms produce graphite crucibles, which are used in the foundries for holding, transporting, and pouring molten metal. More recent products include bicycles and metal furniture. The large paper factory, recently expanded and reorganized as a government-private cooperative venture, is the most important single economic unit in the town, but it is quite apart from the local industrial structure and entrepreneurs. It is managed by outside experts, and was financed by outside capital. It does not obtain raw materials from the other industries of Rajahmundry, nor does it sell its products to them. Thus the small industry sector of Rajahmundry is quite similar in size, organization, and appearance to that of Kakinada, although there is some variation in the assortment of things produced. Rajahmundry commerce is quite similar to Kakinada, although there is no palmyra industry in Rajahmundry.

VELLORE: HISTORY AND TODAY

Vellore, also with a population of over 100,000, is located about eighty miles west of Madras city in a region infused with the Tamil language and culture. It was part of various South Indian empires and kingdoms, until the first Moslem conquest around the middle of the sixteenth century. The Marathas (a west Indian Hindu empire) captured the city in 1676, but Moslem forces under the control of Delhi regained the city in 1710. For the next eighty years, Vellore was in the center of a region that was fought over by various groups, with the British finally moving into the city in 1760 and defending the fort in a two-year seige by Haidar Ali, starting in 1780. The British took full control of the region in 1801, although their Indian troops mutinied at Vellore in 1806. Most of the officers and several English soldiers were killed.

Vellore was a major center of foreign missionary activity from the middle of the nineteenth century. The American Arcot Mission had a center in Vellore and founded the Christian Medical College, with its affiliated hospital. Today the hospital is famous throughout India, and patients come from all over the country—even from the overseas Indian communities. Apart from the medical college, another mission college, and a new government polytechnic institute for boys, however, Vellore does not seem to have the proliferation of educational facilities and institutions characteristic of Kakinada and, to some extent, Rajahmundry. The general mood of the community is perhaps more conservative; certainly Vellore was never a comparable center for advanced ideas in the nineteenth century.

In part this may be due to Vellore's geographic and economic situation. Trade flourishes, but industry has never taken hold to the extent that it has in Kakinada and Rajahmundry. Some brass utensils are produced. *Bidis* (a cheap type of cigarette) are widely manufactured in small units throughout the region, and are collected and sold by a few large firms in Vellore. There is a leather-tanning factory that is part of a larger firm based in Madras. There are a few printing presses and a few foundries. Mostly, however, the economy of Vellore is based on trade, especially the food grains trade. This has been somewhat handicapped since the railway was constructed, since Vellore is four miles away from the main line, connected to it by a smaller, narrow-gauge line. Furthermore, the proximity to Madras has probably worked against the development of local industry: resources and skilled, innovative people may be drawn off to that large metropolis.

The visitor enters Vellore from the north, on the road from the main-line railway station. Large, rather barren hills are visible in the distance. A bridge crosses the Palar River, which is completely dry much of the year. Then there are sheds of some small industries and automobile parts distributors. Soon the road turns, passes a large bus station, and open out into the Main Bazaar. The bazaar is so wide that some small huts with miscellaneous articles for sale are set up along the middle. The larger, well-established shops are on either side of the street. Because of the hospital, there are many pharmacies and lodges for relatives of patients. Off to one side is the hospital itself, with new buildings under construction. Down the Main Bazaar and to the other side is a vast, open park, where hundreds of people gather in the evening for entertainment, for political rallies, or just to walk and talk. At the edge of the park is a very old, very large, and very famous fort, now used partly as a police training school. Inside the fort is a temple, although it has no images within. The people of Vellore are fond of quoting a humorous saying, which expresses the peculiar nature of the town:

> Vellore is a city of paradoxes: It has a fort without guns, a temple without a god, a mountain without trees, a river without water, a college without knowledge, and women without beauty.

PROBLEMS FACED BY THE ENTREPRENEUR
IN KAKINADA, RAJAHMUNDRY, AND VELLORE

It is appropriate to conclude this social and economic description with some account of the common problems faced by small entrepreneurs in the three towns. Each town is slightly different from the others, of course, but the major problems seem to be the same. In fact, these problems are probably faced by businessmen all over India, and in most other developing countries as well.

First is capital. A common impression is that developing economies suffer from an absolute lack of required capital. Many economists with knowledge of India challenge this assertion (Lewis, 1964; Lynton and Stepanek, 1963). In our three towns, the real capital problem seems to be as follows: What wealth there is, is largely unavailable to the entrepreneurs. Much capital is invested in nonproductive, prestige possessions, such as gold and jewelry. Money-lending, at very high rates of interest (often greater than 24 per cent a year) draws in a lot of wealth. To be sure, money-lending may be necessary, in the absence of adequate government-sponsored agricultural credit, to finance farming and the distribution of farm products. It remains debatable how efficiently the needs of farming are served by the system, and also how much money is actually lent for that purpose. Often the pattern is simply that the people who are wealthy are neither interested in nor competent at business (see Chapter 8). Yet joint-stock companies are very difficult to start in towns of this size, because people are often very reluctant to trust someone they do not know well. Hence a man with knowledge and motivation may not be able to get finance from a wealthy man, because each travels in different social circles in the town. Even banks are unlikely to lend on any security except present wealth. This means that available bank loans go to the very businesses that may need them the least.

A second problem is the scarcity of almost every kind of necessary material. Sometimes there are simply genuine and insoluble problems, such as the lack of available foreign exchange, which forces businessmen to make do with old equipment or local replicas. Often, however, the problem involves materials which are not in constant short supply, such as pig iron or coke for foundries. What is particularly annoying is that delivery of promised supplies, once the appropriate permits are secured, may still involve great delays and unexpected caprice. Thus the tremendous proportion of an entrepreneur's time that is spent obtaining licenses, permits, quotas, and fiscal clearance often goes to waste, because rational plans still cannot be made.

Sometimes government action taken to help entrepreneurs inadvertently creates another obstacle. For example, the government decided to open an "industrial estate" in East Godavari District, so that small industries could have a good location, cheap power, low rent on buildings, and so forth. However, the estate was built at Samalkot, about ten miles away from Kakinada and at a very inconvenient place, in part because the government already owned land there. In retrospect, the decision has helped no one, and most of the sites at the estate have remained unoccupied since the day they were built. Paradoxically, until this estate flourishes, which does not seem likely, there is almost no chance that another one will be built nearer to Kakinada.

Finally, many entrepreneurs need advice, but they do not know where and how to seek it. Consequently many of their plans are unrealistic: they do not realize the resources required, they overestimate the potential market, and they are not aware of possible government restrictions. The Government of India has tried to increase extension work in the field of small industries, but most of these services still do not reach the average businessman or potential industrialist.

These are some of the major problems that all of the businessmen in the three towns have to face in the ordinary course of things; the problems become even more intense if they try to expand or improve their businesses.

CHAPTER 4

RECRUITING BUSINESSMEN FOR THE PROJECT

Once the small cities had been selected for study, our next objective was to interest local business leaders in participating in the project. Obtaining information from a number of them about their businesses did not seem too difficult, particularly in view of the excellent cooperation men like Berna (1960) had obtained on previous occasions. But would it be possible to persuade really influential men to leave their work for ten days to go to Hyderabad for an "experimental" course designed to increase their "entrepreneurial motivation"? The recruiting task seemed formidable at the time. Why should they take the course? Many of them were extremely busy; yet it was the busiest ones we were most interested in obtaining, because they were often the most influential. Some would undoubtedly be the sole proprietors of a shop. Could they afford to close the shop or to leave it in the hands of an assistant for so long a period? What would they think of a course designed to change them rather than just to give them the technical skills that would make them better businessmen? Experience had shown that recruits could easily be obtained in Bombay, but would the situation be different in small cities in South India, far removed from metropolitan influences? In particular, would there be enough businessmen who spoke sufficient English to make the training feasible? It was decided that the courses had to be given in English partly because SIET Institute gave all its courses in English and partly because none of the Indian staff members who participated in the project at the outset spoke Telugu, the language of Andhra Pradesh.

The difficulties seemed great enough to warrant a careful and systematic approach to enlisting the support of the leadership of the town. Dr. Aziz Pabaney went to Kakinada in January, 1964, having first obtained a personal introduction to the Collector of East Godavari District, who was the chief administrative officer for the central government in the area. The collector in India occupies a unique position of very high prestige. His title derives from the fact that under British rule he was the collector of taxes. Under the present Indian government he is the chief administrative officer of the district, in charge of implementing all central government schemes at the district level and controlling the issuing of permits, licenses, and the like. Men who rise to this position in the Indian administrative service are highly educated and talented, since they are selected by a stiff competitive examination process set in motion by the British years ago. It would certainly not have been practicable to undertake a major development in Kakinada without the prior knowledge and approval of the Collector. Fortunately, Dr. Ram K. Vepa, Collector for the East Godavari District, turned out to be very interested in the project and quite willing to introduce Dr. Pabaney to some of the leading men in the town. After several informal conversations with these men, he was invited to give a short speech to the Rotary Club to outline the proposed project.

In all of his conversations he found it was quite important to stress the solid credentials of those sponsoring the project. For as he wrote at the time, "In India any new project, particularly one sponsored by outsiders, is not easily accepted and is apt to be looked upon with suspicion." The fact that Dr. Pabaney had been introduced by the Collector and other influential men in the town helped. So did the fact that the training would be carried out by a Government of India Society, the Small Industries Extension Training Institute in Hyderabad. Yet it was also necessary to make it clear that while the project was known to and approved by the government, information would not be collected and passed on for use by government officials. Businessmen in Kakinada, as everywhere else in the world, did not want to get involved in a project which would mean giving information about their businesses which might be used against them in subsequent tax or licensing investigations by government officers. Thus, it was also necessary to stress that the project was an independent research enterprise, the records from which would be kept confidential and presented only in a form in which no person could be identified. The fact that the sponsoring educational institution was Harvard University also undoubtedly helped in enlisting the interest and support of men in the town.

Dr. Pabaney found a real interest and considerable enthusiasm for the project. He concentrated on recruiting influential men for the first course, scheduled to begin February 26. He wrote to Dr. McClelland at the time:

> It is important that those who attend the first course should be persons who will not only start on new lines of enterprise, but who can influence the growth of the whole program in Kakinada, help in the recruitment of other participants, and be able to sustain and develop the achievement mystique among other entrepreneurs and potential entrepreneurs in the city. Their selection for the first course is therefore important. Under Indian conditions, it is also necessary to get the support of leading persons, entrepreneurs or others for a successful beginning and a more successful continuation of the program.

While occasionally he met skeptics, men who felt that entrepreneurs are born, not made, even they seemed willing to entertain the notion that psychology might have discovered a new way to develop the entrepreneurial spirit, and several promised to try to rearrange their schedules so that they could attend the first course. More felt that the project was godsent, that they should be doing more than they were to develop Kakinada economically. In fact, many of them said this was an ideal opportunity to take up the challenge to break through the stagnation that all felt they were in. As Dr. Pabaney wrote, "It is a pleasure to talk to the entrepreneurs for they seem to recognize the fact that if anything moves, they would have to do the moving."

On January 30 the Chamber of Commerce organized a meeting attended by about fifty persons, at which three men spoke: Dr. Pabaney for the project; Mr. Harry Wolfe, an American consultant from SIET Institute; and Professor Ayyar, the director of the prestigious Institute for Economic Research in Hyderabad. The theme was Kakinada and its economic growth. The following day a panel of four persons including these three and the Collector discussed the same topic before another large group at the Rotary Club meeting. A summary of Mr. Wolfe's remarks follows:

> The immediate impression that everyone surely forms on coming to Kakinada is of the resources of the area combined with its

loveliness and the friendliness of the people. In many respects this is like a typical southern town in the U.S.A. There are ample resources, high talents, and a favorable environment, but apparently a shortage of an intensive drive for progress. However, as I met with individual businessmen, bankers, professional men, and industrialists, I got somewhat the impression of steam boilers standing at maximum pressure ready to blow off steam, but without the engine to convert this steam to constructive power.

The question then becomes one of how to devise the mechanism to channel this potential power for the use of the town, rather than to simply let the boiler exhaust its steam into the open air.

At the present time it appears to me that some of the most capable men in Kakinada are exhausting their efforts in complaining about the government, or in pursuing advantages or privileges from the government. Kakinada must come to recognize that nothing constructive—or even profitable in the long term—will come from this application of the town's better talents. India does not have a totalitarian socialistic government, but one which says that the people are determined to achieve economic and social progress by national methods if free enterprise cannot achieve this goal alone. It is true of course that the government does not always act with certainty, a good sense of administration, and complete competence.

However, the government would not need to exercise either a check-rein or whip if private enterprise would concentrate its talents on national purposes and on ways in which national objectives can be accomplished—along with maximum freedom for private enterprise and for generating profits. For men of talent, there must be an acceptance of responsibility for decision and for action. From the outstanding examples of such men in Kakinada, it obvious that the men of Kakinada have been exposed to good examples of enterprise. Kakinada needs only to broaden its base of men who are prepared to decide, and to act.

As a final part of the recruitment effort, another general meeting was arranged by the Chamber of Commerce on February 4, which was addressed by a leading businessman who had taken the course in Bombay. He was the man described in Chapter 2, who shortly after taking the course had become a successful entrepreneur in the construction business. He testified to the value and interest of the course to a gathering of about fifty persons, demonstrating by his own example not only that the course could prove useful but that it was adapted to Indian business and that there was nothing peculiar about it that might make people hesitate to sign up for training.

The initial approach to Kakinada had two goals—to help create more of an achievement mystique, a sense of forward motion, in the town and to recruit participants for the courses. The first goal seems to have been attained. Nearly all of the key men in the town, both businessmen and others, learned that a project was to be started there, designed to improve business, employment, and economic welfare. As news of it spread, more and more people began to show an interest. In fact the head of the Chamber of Commerce reported that many people whom even he had not seen or talked with for a long time were coming forward and showing an interest. As he left Kakinada, Dr. Pabaney reported to Dr. McClelland:

> the whole program of personal contacts and public meetings has helped to develop confidence among the people. At yesterday's meeting several of the citizens came forward publicly to "own" the project as having been adopted by the city. The public expressions by local leading citizens have also become definitely more positive and achievement-oriented, unlike earlier expressions of constant complaints against the government. "Let that be a thing of the past, now it is for us to act" seems to be the general feeling as summarized by the head of the Chamber of Commerce. Even at a theosophical meeting, the speech last Sunday was achievement-oriented and Mr. Harry Wolfe seems to have made a big hit here. The speech by the Bombay businessman has, I think, clinched the issue. All in all this has been a very heart-warming experience both for us and for the entrepreneurs of Kakinada.

As noted in the second chapter, one of the major training inputs thought to produce change is creation of a strong expectation that one can and should change. Obviously the public meetings and private conversations in Kakinada during the precourse period have to be considered part of the training itself. In fact, they produced a major effect on one small businessman who for some time had been considering opening a factory. He wrote Dr. Pabaney on February 8 that after being exposed to all this talk of achievement, he decided that he would go ahead immediately. After talking personally with Dr. Pabaney on February 8, he decided to find a site for his factory and succeeded in obtaining it that same evening and occupying it the next day. In order to pay for it, he left town immediately "to finalize an account which has been kept pending, unsettled for fifteen years."

He obtained the money needed and immediately set about organizing a factory. He could not attend the first course for this reason, but did attend the second. In his own words: "All these transactions had been so easily finalized because I worked with determination to get the things done at a certain time. I am cultivating this habit of determination in going ahead only because of my having listened to your valuable advice and public lectures." The observer might feel that this man exaggerates the importance of a few public meetings in producing the change in his behavior, but the tone of his letter is certainly characteristic of many things that were being said in Kakinada at the time. The climate had become somewhat more hopeful and forward looking.

The second goal of the preparatory work was also achieved. Fourteen men attended the first course at SIET Institute in Hyderabad, 350 miles away, which started February 27. Among them were a member of the state legislative assembly from Kakinada and several leading bankers and businessmen.

The instructors for the course were Dr. Elliott Danzig from the United States, Dr. Pabaney, and Dr. A. K. Pal, a psychologist from Hindustan Lever, Ltd., in Bombay. He had attended the special training course at the Harvard Business School the previous summer and was of great assistance to the project on this and other occasions. The instructors felt that the course went well, in the sense that they had presented what they had planned and found that it was understood and liked by the participants.

Dr. Danzig wrote Dr. McClelland soon after the course was finished:

> Their openness was striking, after an initial period in which they were very hesitant to speak out about their plans. They got plenty of practice in realistic goal setting, most of which revolved around actually getting going industrially. Their cooperative behavior went up about 400%. One man decided to sell off part of his plant (he had been non-operative for lack of capital, having bought too much machinery) and to use the proceeds to get into operation on a more realistic scale. For some time he had just been sitting on his hands, lamenting the "unfair competition" and other blocks. He then offered his power permit to another man who has claimed that he was held back by lack of electric power. About three different combines were arranged which will provide capital, since we had a bank manager and a money lender in the group. They formed a Kakinada Entrepreneurs Association, with place and date of the first meeting determined. And we will get there right afterwards to see what they have done. They are planing to create a combined fund to get government help, technical know-how, etc.
>
> To give you some idea of reactions: a 60-year-old ex-Gandhiite, who invented a Telugu typewriter in 1935, on his own initiative, without any suggestion from us, worked up a history of his successes and failures in trying to get the product on the

market, breaking it down chronologically in terms of the scoring categories.

Lack of self-confidence proved to be a dominant theme in the group. There was much fear of responsibility and of failure. Counseling helped this superficially, the group support helped, and our backup in terms of requiring concrete planning and giving them positive support may help. Many of them were not very realistic in their initial plans. They would start out with ideas like, "I want to open an oil refining plant," or "I want to make three lakhs of rupees (1 lakh = 100,000) next year." When asked what they were going to do about problems like permits, competition, and so forth, they initially had not thought through the concrete steps they had to take and tended to fall back on such generalities as "I hope I succeed." It was the practice in realistic goal-setting and concrete specific planning which hopefully will reduce their general worries and help them actually get going.

An important factor in the favorable reception of this course was the strong support given it by the Principal Director of SIET Institute, Shri R. N. Jai. As noted in the previous chapter, the expected grant from the Ford Foundation was cancelled. Shri Jai responded by adopting the project as SIET Institute's own, though with greatly diminished resources. He welcomed the participants on behalf of the Institute, attended the training sessions, and participated throughout, drawing heavily on his own earlier experience in business. The high expectations already created in Kakinada were fully supported and confirmed by what happened at SIET Institute during the first course. With such a good start it was considered feasible to adhere somewhat more strictly to certain standards for admission to the course.

The following points were stressed in recruiting for later courses: (1) The person had to want to go and to become a more active entrepreneur; he should not attend just out of a sense of duty as a leading citizen; (2) He had to be reasonably proficient in English, since simultaneous translation by fellow participants, while possible, was difficult and disruptive; (3) He should be in the 30–45 age range with allowances up to five years at either end; (4) He should be either an independent businessman or a person with a good chance of becoming one in the near future. It was also stated unequivocally that the course was serious and intensive and involved much hard work, and that those who came had to be prepared to live in, do homework, and attend all meetings on time. As a further guarantee of the seriousness of the intent of the participant, SIET Institute began charging participants Rs. 150 for board and room for the ten days they were there. Since all participants, including those for the first course had also to pay their round-trip travel fare to Hyderabad (about Rs. 100) this meant that from the second course onward participants were putting up Rs. 250 each to attend the course (about $50 at the 1964 rate of exchange).

Further visits to Kakinada were made in March by Shri Jai, Dr. Danzig, Dr. Pabaney, and Shri Nadkarni, the chief staff members at SIET Institute concerned with promoting the project. They recruited an excellent second batch of men who were trained for ten days, beginning April 4. During this course Dr. Danzig, who had been the chief instructor, was able to turn more responsibility over to the Indian staff who would continue after he left. At the end of the second course, which was also very well received, Drs. Danzig and Pabaney left because there were no outside funds to support them. Shri Nadkarni was added to the regular SIET Institute staff to share responsibility for continuing the project in collaboration with Dr. Udai Pareek, a psychologist who was already a member of the SIET Institute staff and later became chief of its extension division. Shri Nadkarni returned to Kakinada in early July after the recess at the Institute to recruit for the third and fourth courses, to be given beginning July 16 and October 17. He reported that he did not have to do much to sell the courses, and readily succeeded in getting participants signed up. Apparently interest in the project was still strong in Kakinada, although obviously a good deal of the glamour of the early days had faded with the departure of the outside consultants and the return to the routine of daily life. Some evidence for this falling off is the fact that while 20 signed up for the fourth course in early July, in fact only 10 attended it in October.

Characteristics of the Businessmen in the Project

Who attended the courses from Kakinada? What kinds of businesses did they represent? What resources did they have available to expand their businesses or start new ones? These and other questions are answered in a general way in the summary figures presented in Table 4.1. For comparative purposes, the table also presents the summary figures on two control groups of businessmen who were not trained, one from Kakinada and the other from Rajahmundry. The goal was to study intensively the business activities of these three groups of men in an effort to determine whether the *n* Achievement training had an effect over and above what one would expect from similar groups of men operating in the same city, or a nearby city totally untouched by the public excitement over an entrepreneurial motivation project. The method of recruiting the untrained businessmen for study will be described below.

The course participants averaged about 36 years of age. The oldest was 60 and there were several in their early twenties. The general level of education averaged a year or two beyond secondary school, which in India includes from ten to eleven years of education. About two thirds were judged to be "in charge," that is, in a position where they were free to make decisions more-or-less on their own as to the future conduct of the business. In this part of India most of the businesses are joint family firms in which several members of the family may have capital invested and in which a son frequently works in collaboration with his father or several of his brothers or brothers-in-law. It is sometimes difficult to be certain how much freedom of decision a man has, but extensive interviewing usually made it clear as to whether a man was the leading member of the family so far as making business decisions was concerned. If he was, usually this meant either that his father was dead, or inactive, or actively operating another business, and he was the oldest son; or that if he had older brothers, they lived somewhere else and were in some other occupation. It was the intent of the recruiting effort to get primarily decision-makers, since it was hoped that the results of their decision could be detected fairly soon after the training ended. Obviously if a man was in a subordinate position in a business or was a youngest son with two older brothers ahead of him in the business, it might take some time for him to show any entrepreneurial activity. On the other hand, a secondary goal of the training was to broaden the base of active entrepreneurs in the town so that some younger men were admitted to training who might branch out and become active on their own.

A little over a third of the men were in industry and about half of them in commerce, the remainder being professionals such as teachers or lawyers. A very few were not working at the time of the course, living off inherited income and spending their time at the clubs. The industrialists were of two types: they were either involved in processing agricultural products such as palmyra fiber, rice, and sugar, or they ran small foundries that cast parts for various types of machinery, particularly sugar and rice mills. The men in commerce were more diverse. Several were large-scale wholesalers dealing in grains, edible oils, and timber. A number were proprietors of cycle shops, which were quite numerous in Kakinada at the time, because cycling was the main method of transportation and because Kakinada is an educational center with a large student population. Others operated clothing stores or radio shops. Bankers and men in the transportation business were also classified as being

Table 4.1

Characteristics of Businessmen Studied in Kakinada and Rajahmundry (as of 1964)

Kakinada Course Participants	MEAN YEARS			Number "in charge"*	NUMBER IN		MEDIAN (IN RS. 1000s)	
	Number	Age	Educ.		Industry**	Commerce	Annual Firm Gross Income†	Personal Capital††
Batch 1 2/27–3/7/64	14	45	11.6	9	8	5	100	210
Batch 2 4/4–4/14/64	16	37	12.1	15	4	10	200	150
Batch 3 7/16–7/26/64	12	32	13.5	6	4	8	150	33
Batch 4 10/12–10/26/64	10	28	12.4	6	4	3	150	30
A. For Total Trained Group	52	36.3	12.4	36	20	26	150 (N=47)	100 (N=35)
% of total				69	38	50		
B. Kakinada Controls	22	34.1	12.4	15	7	14	110 (N=16)	75 (N=13)
% of total				68	30	64		
C. Rajahmundry Controls	35	36.6	11.3	23	13	17	120 (N=27)	90 (N=22)
% of total				66	37	49		

* Number of individuals in chief decision-making role in business.

** "Industry" includes all manufacturing or processing of raw materials; "commerce" includes wholesaling, retailing, renting, shipping, land transport, banking, theaters, etc. A few men are in neither category—e.g., as professionals or as not working at the time.

† Rs. = Rupees; Rs. 100,000 = approximately $20,000 (1964 rate of exchange). Estimates are approximate; based chiefly on figures given by the men themselves, occasionally supplemented by general knowledge.

†† Personal capital is estimated only for those "in charge," i.e., in a position to allocate what they have.

in commerce, in the sense that they were not involved in transforming raw material into finished products.

The size of the firms they represented is indicated roughly by the column in Table 4.1 showing the estimated median annual firm turnover in thousands of rupees. Most of the men were willing and presumably able to give estimates of the gross annual income of their firms, from which these medians have been computed. Median figures seem appropriate since the firms actually varied tremendously in size—all the way from the large wholesale dealers who grossed Rs. 50 to 70 lakhs (1 lakh equals 100,000 rupees) down to those who grossed only about two thousand rupees a year. Obviously the median businessman had a substantial amount of experience since his firm was grossing in the $20–40,000 range, though to translate rupees into dollars in this way tends to underestimate the amount of business done in Indian terms. The last column in Table 4.1 attempts to estimate the amount of capital the median man had available to invest in a new enterprise, should he decide to undertake one. These estimates are even more wobbly than those for gross income, because we could not reasonably expect the men to tell us their net personal worth. Furthermore, in many cases the money was tied up in joint family holdings which made it very difficult to estimate what a given person's share might be. However, crude estimates were made based on figures they gave as to capital investments they had made between 1962 and 1967 and general knowledge in the town as to how wealthy a man was. The estimates again seem to be meaningful only for those men who were actually judged to be in charge. Even though a younger son in his twenties might come from a very wealthy family, it did not seem possible to estimate what personal capital he might be able to talk the family into giving him to start a new enterprise.

Certainly a number of the men were quite well-to-do by any standard. Conservatively, four to six men who attended the course had assets totalling at least a million dollars in land, bank deposits, or cash. At the other extreme were several who earned as little as 1,500 rupees a year (about $300), though this should be evaluated in terms of the average annual wage of an unskilled worker in Kakinada at that time, about 400–700 rupees, and in terms of the fact that even these men often had sources from which they could raise capital if necessary (e.g., from ancestral land holdings). In short these men were not poor. Nearly all of them had some means of obtaining capital if necessary, and our best estimate is that the median businessman in the group could raise about one lakh of rupees in capital (about $20,000), if he wanted to.

Fifty-two men representing 49 different Kakinada firms attended the four courses in achievement motivation given at SIET Institute. How representative were they of the total business community in Kakinada? The two largest firms in town—one an automobile parts factory and the other the largest foundry—were not represented, although executives from these firms were included in the control group from Kakinada. Two thirds of the remaining major businesses in town were represented by at least someone in one of the courses. If it is further estimated that there are perhaps 100 key businessmen in a community of 100,000 people, then we might have trained around one third of this group in Kakinada. These figures are approximate, but if anything, they are on the conservative side. They are based on the fact that we actually included 36 key decision-makers in the trained group and 15 in the untrained group, and the assumption that there were probably at least as many again that we did not interview. That is, in several of the larger firms we interviewed only one person, whereas there were perhaps two or three others in the top management group. Even conservatively, then, the project succeeded in gaining the attention of a significant proportion of the business leadership of the town.

The characteristics of the participants changed markedly from the first two to the last two courses. As noted already, every effort was made to get the senior business leaders to attend the first two courses. The success of this effort is indicated by the fact that only one of the thirty attending the first two courses was below 30 years of age. In contrast, in the last two courses the majority (14 out of 22) were in their twenties. In the fourth batch, eight out of ten were under 30 and the oldest man attending was 36. The comparative youthfulness of the third and fourth batches is also reflected in a significantly lower number of participants who were in charge (54 per cent versus 80 per cent, $p < .05$), in the lower financial resources available to them, and in their slightly higher educational level. The shift to a younger age group represented partly the falling off in senior staff available for the project after the second batch and partly the desire to recruit younger men into the business leadership group.

Table 4.1 also summarizes the characteristics of groups of untrained businessmen in Kakinada and Rajahmundry who were intensively interviewed to get data on business activities to compare with similar data obtained from the trained businessmen. In Kakinada these men were contacted and interviewed by Dr. David Winter and Shri Krishna Kumar in March, 1967 at the same time as the final follow-up interview was conducted for the trained businessmen. The primary reason why a man was contacted as a control subject was that he was on the list of names

collected by Dr. Pabaney and others at the outset of the project as someone who wanted to go to SIET Institute for training. That is, the primary criterion for matching the untrained businessmen with the trained
businessmen was motivational—the desire to take the course. It was
considered desirable to match the subjects for motivation because if the
controls had been largely people who did not want to attend the course,
that might have meant they were a less motivated or progressive group
to start with. Then any differences in business activity might be attributable not to the training but to differences in the initial impulse to
modernize and progress. It might be thought that because the controls
had not attended the courses, they were less motivated to go, even
though they had said at one time that they wanted to attend. Careful
reading of their individual case histories does not support such a contention strongly. The great majority could not attend because they were
out of town on other business, because they could not leave their shops
unattended, because of illness or death in the family. While hopefully
the two groups are fairly well matched on motivation to progress, they
also are very well matched on the other variables in Table 4.1. (Compare
the summary figures for Groups A and B.) On the average they were
about the same age and had the same amount of education; the same
proportion was in charge; slightly fewer were in industry and more in
commerce and the size of their firms and financial resources seem
roughly comparable. This was more good luck than good management,
because the primary criterion for selecting a control subject was, as we
said, initial interest in the training.

Since most of the untrained subjects in Kakinada had attended at
least some of the meetings organized by Dr. Pabaney and others at the
outset of the project or had heard about the project from friends, it
seemed desirable also to get a comparable group of businessmen from
the nearby city of Rajahmundry to check on their business activity levels
over the period of time being studied in Kakinada. The Rajahmundry
control subjects were selected in the following manner. In the spring of
1966, Shri Kumar went to the district Assistant Director of Industry,
who gave him a list of all industries in Rajahmundry. These were
grouped into general categories and firms were picked at random from
each category. The result was an approximate cross-section of local
industry. There were a few confusing factors like Rajahmundry's massive paper mill, which was simply ignored because it was so different
in scope from anything in Kakinada. Shri Kumar interviewed about
30 businessmen from this random sample from industry, with eight to
ten refusals.

Unfortunately it was more difficult to obtain a representative sample of men in trade or commerce, since no master list could be obtained. He therefore took general categories of commercial establishments, e.g., clothing stores, cycle shops, radio stores, and so on, and searched for ones comparable to those in Kakinada. Within each category he made up a list and picked some randomly. The secretary of the local small-scale industries association scrutinized the list and suggested additional names.

When entering a shop, he would ask for the managing partner or proprietor. Sometimes the second man passed himself off as in charge, but that in effect provided about the same proportion of men not in charge as in the sample from Kakinada. He noticed as he proceeded that age distribution was running roughly comparable to what it was in Kakinada. From this group there were a few refusals and five or so who avoided. He obtained 57 interviews in all. One year later he and Dr. Winter returned to Rajahmundry to reinterview the men and obtain further information. The total sample of 57 was divided into random thirds and the first two-thirds were reinterviewed *in toto,* which seemed to provide enough cases, as time was running short and the figures being obtained were quite stable. Finally it was necessary to seek out some additional cycle shop owners, since there are fewer of them in Rajahmundry than in Kakinada, and to eliminate five businessmen on the grounds that their interviews had to be conducted in Telugu. As noted previously, it was necessary to insist that those attending the courses at SIET Institute speak English fairly well, although one or two did not know much English and had to be helped by their friends. The random method of selection used in Rajahmundry turned up a number of men who did not speak English. Since speaking English might be a factor indicating a more modern orientation to business, it was decided to eliminate all save a couple of businessmen who could not respond in the interview in English. The five who were eliminated were the five oldest with the least education, since it was apparent that the Rajahmundry sample was generally somewhat older and less educated than the Kakinada sample.

The results of these efforts are summarized as Group C of Table 4.1. Once more the control sample of untrained subjects seems to be comparable to the trained group from Kakinada as to age and the percentages in charge, in industry, and in commerce. Both groups come from businesses of about the same size, as judged by annual gross incomes, and seem to have at their disposal about the same estimated amount of personal capital. At the time of the final interview most of them had been interviewed a year earlier, so that if repeated interviewing affected the figures in any way in Kakinada, the same factor had a chance to operate somewhat in the Rajahmundry sample.

Only in education do the two samples differ significantly. Whereas only 30 per cent of the course participants from Kakinada reported 11 years or less of education, 54 per cent from Rajahmundry had this little education ($p < .05$). The difference is almost certainly due to the fact that Kakinada has more educational institutions and is more education minded. At any rate, the absolute difference is small and does not exist at all at the lower end of the educational distribution (five years of education or less), where it might be supposed to make the most difference. It is hard to see how an extra year or so of education once one gets above the secondary school level would make a person into an appreciably better businessman. So the 35 untrained businessmen who were interviewed in Rajahmundry seem as comparable to the trained and untrained businessmen from Kakinada as one might reasonably expect.

The Vellore Project

In late 1964, the governing board of SIET Institute, on the recommendation of its Principal Director, Shri R. N. Jai, authorized offering two courses for businessmen to be recruited from a new town, Vellore, in view of the favorable experience in Kakinada. By this time the general approach to advertising and describing the project and the courses was well worked out. It is best summarized by quoting from the brochure which was mimeographed at the time and taken by Shri Nadkarni to Vellore in his initial attempts to recruit participants.

Small Industry Extension Training Institute
General Information on "Entrepreneurial Motivation" Training Course

The SIET Institute, a Government of India Society, offers two types of regular training courses three times a year: one in industrial management and another in area development. Both the courses are fully residential; their duration is twelve weeks and they run concurrently.

A special course on entrepreneurial motivation is a part of a research project on entrepreneur motivation and economic growth. After investigation of relevant factors, the towns of Kakinada in East Godavari, Vellore in North Arcot, and Akola in Akola District have been selected as the experimental towns. In these towns we propose to give this course to a sizable number of important persons. During 1964, 52 persons from Kakinada have taken the course in four batches.

*For Vellore two courses are scheduled for ten days
from 1st March and 1st April 1965*

THE NATURE OF THE COURSE:

The main purpose of the course is to increase the entrepreneurial spirit of the participants. This is thought to be achieved by focussing on the motivation and realistic goal-setting which are necessary for effective development and management of an enterprise.

The participant is encouraged to make a frank appraisal of himself. Through a series of lectures, discussions, assignments, case studies, business games, and demonstrations, he is given an understanding of his underlying motives, which are involved in successful entrepreneurial behavior. There are practice sessions in which the participant relates his thoughts and creative imagination to action, for achieving his personal objectives.

While the program is basically one of SELF-DEVELOPMENT, the importance of group cooperation is emphasized. It is intended that the experiences shared during the course will enable the members of the group to encourage and reinforce one another and to continue to utilize what they learned on return to Vellore so that each may benefit and so also the community.

The training course is intensive in content. Each item of the course and every day's work are a definite part of the whole course. Therefore, the participants must be present and participate right from the beginning and through the whole course.

THE BASIC REQUIREMENTS FOR THE SELECTION OF A PARTICIPANT ARE:

A. Good knowledge of English is essential. The entire course is in English and involves reading and expressing oneself in English, both in discussions and in writing.
B. He should preferably be in the age range 30 to 45 years.
C. He must have high motivation to expand and improve his existing business/industry, or to start a new industry.
D. He must be willing to engage in ten days of an intensive, residential course involving taking tests, doing assignments, observing the work/time table and the routines of living and working together.
E. He must commit himself to continue to participate in the research project, which requires completion of certain forms periodically for the next three years.

Participation in the training course (and the research project) will be by *invitation* from the Principal Director of SIET Institute. The participants have to pay Rs. 150 towards boarding, lodging, and other incidental expenses.

Armed with this description of the project, Shri Nadkarni approached the Collector of the district, following the procedure successfully adopted by Dr. Pabaney in Kakinada. Again the Collector understood the project, thought it might be valuable for Vellore, gave it his blessing, and introduced Shri Nadkarni to some of the leading businessmen in the town. One of these, an influential doctor and ex-member of Parliament, was particularly enthusiastic about the project and put in a considerable amount of time interesting others in participating in the courses. Names of prospective course participants were obtained from these men and also from the Chamber of Commerce. Two public meetings were arranged, at which the nature and purpose of the project were described in much the same terms as they had been described in Kakinada.

Finally, a large public meeting was arranged on Republic Day, January 26, 1965, which was addressed by Professor McClelland, who had just come from visiting SIET Institute and the project in Kakinada as a Ford Foundation consultant. The occasion turned out to be a fairly dramatic one. Despite the fact that it was Republic Day and there were many other activities in progress, plus a good deal of public disturbance over the fact that the central government had begun to force the use of Hindi in place of English in official documents, the meeting was attended by 75 to 100 persons. The Collector was able to attend to introduce Professor McClelland. The dramatic element was introduced by some graduates of the Kakinada courses. Before leaving Kakinada for the 500-mile drive to Vellore, Professor McClelland had suggested that it might help sell the courses in Vellore if one of the Kakinada participants could come along and speak about the effectiveness of the training. The Kakinada Entrepreneurs Association was enthusiastic about the idea, but could not decide who should go. They asked the visitors to pick someone, but we felt that we ought not to make that decision for them, that it was desirable to emphasize here as we had throughout the course that they could not expect to continue to get help from the outside, but must rely on themselves to make collaborative decisions and move ahead on their own. They accepted the responsibility for the final choice, but still could not arrive at a decision by the time the visiting party had to leave for Vellore, the day before the public meeting was to be held. We were disappointed that no one was coming from Kakinada, but felt that it was more important to leave the responsibility with the Kakinada participants. The decision turned out to be an unexpectedly wise one.

Table 4.2
Characteristics of Businessmen Studied in Vellore (as of 1965)

Course Participants	MEAN YEARS				NUMBER IN		MEDIAN (IN RS. 1000s)	
	Number	Age	Educ.	Number "in charge"	Industry	Commerce	Firm Gross Income	Personal Capital
Batch 1 3/1–3/10/65	12	30.3	12.8	6	5	7	210 (N=8)	110 (N=4)
Batch 2 4/1–4/10/65	14	30.8	13.9	5	2	8	300 (N=9)	45 (N=4)
D. For Total Trained Group	26	30.6	13.4	11	7	15	250 (N=17)	80 (N=8)
% of total				42	27	58		
E. Control Subjects	16	37.4	12.1	8	4	11	270 (N=11)	100 (N=5)
% of total				50	25	69		

The public meeting in Vellore the next day was scheduled for 4:00 P.M. At 3:00 P.M. a telephone call came in from a nearby town stating that a party of men from Kakinada was driving through and hoped to arrive in Vellore at 4:00 P.M., in time for the meeting. As it happened, the meeting had just opened when five participants from Kakinada arrived dusty, tired, but triumphant. Late in the afternoon of the preceding day, after the visitors had left, several had gathered together to express their concern that they had let the project down. After discussing the matter a bit, they decided to rent one of the half dozen taxicabs available in town and depart immediately for Vellore. The car was not in very good condition. They had to stop several times for repairs and drive all night almost without food and rest in order to arrive just as the meeting opened. Their public testimony to the worth of the project and the type of motivational training received was obviously greatly enhanced by what they had just gone through in order to be present at the meeting.

The build-up for the project was certainly not as extensive or impressive in Vellore as it had been in Kakinada, but it was sufficient to gather a good group of participants for the two courses that were given as planned. The first course went off with the full support of Shri Jai, Principal Director of SIET Institute, Dr. Pareek, Director of Extension Training; and the staff. However, some changes affected the second course. The recruiting visits between the first and second courses were made by two new members of the SIET Institute staff, since by this time Shri Nadkarni began to feel that he was going stale. Furthermore, during the course itself, there was evidence that the project was in some difficulty. Shri Jai was unable to welcome the participants on behalf of the Institute or to participate in the course sessions as he had all along up to that point. The staff knew that policy disagreements at the highest level might lead to discontinuation of the project, and their uncertainty probably communicated itself to the participants. At any rate, soon afterwards the project was discontinued, Shri Jai left as Principal Director, and no further courses were given for participants from Vellore, even though there was still a considerable list of interested men.

What were the characteristics of the men actually trained from Vellore? Table 4.2 summarizes the relevant information in the format used for Kakinada and Rajahmundry. They were, on the average, younger and less often in positions of key responsibility than the participants from Kakinada. Forty-six per cent were in their twenties, as contrasted with only one of the first thirty men trained from Kakinada. Fifty per cent in the first batch from Vellore were in charge, whereas only 36 per cent from the second batch were. This contrasts sharply with the over-all 69 per cent in charge among the Kakinada participants. On the other hand, the Vellore participants were better educated on the average and represented somewhat larger firms. The proportion in commerce was somewhat higher in Vellore than in Kakinada, which would be expected from the general nature of the business base in the two towns. Since Vellore is an important medical center, many of the commercial estab-lishments were pharmaceutical firms or drugstores.

Once again the two largest businesses in town—a tannery and *bidi* cigarette manufacturing—were not represented in the courses, though they were represented in the control subjects interviewed. Obviously the impact on the business community was much less than in Kakinada. There was less pre-course preparatory work, fewer visitors from the out-side, fewer men actually trained. Undoubtedly a much larger percentage of firms and key individuals in those firms never heard about the project except possibly through items in the local papers at the time of Dr. McClelland's visit. Also, whatever momentum might have been achieved through the first two courses was dissipated by SIET Institute's dis-continuing the project before it was completed.

At the time of the final checkup of the trained men in the spring of 1967, the control subjects were also interviewed by Dr. Winter and Shri Krishna Kumar. Again they were chosen primarily because their names appeared on the list of those interested in attending the courses. As it turned out, this group was considerably older and somewhat less edu-cated on the average than those who actually attended the courses, a fact which supports the view that fewer of the older, really influential men in town were trained in Vellore. In other respects, the control group seems comparable to those trained. About equal percentages were in charge in the two groups. They came roughly as often from industry and commerce, and from firms of about equivalent size. They had equivalent amounts of personal capital, so far as this could be determined from the very small number of estimates available. It is unfortunate that the two groups from Vellore are not more comparable in age, but it seemed unwise to try to make them more comparable for a number of reasons. To throw out cases in the trained or untrained groups would be to make already small samples even smaller and the figures based on them even less reliable. In any case, age is not strongly related to several of the indicators of business activity and when it is, it tends to favor those who are older. Thus, if anything, the untrained subjects from Vellore represent a group which is in a better position to show an in-crease in business activity level than the trained group.

So much for the recruitment process. It obviously left much to be desired. In fact it was carried out at the level initially planned only for the first two batches from Kakinada. Thereafter, lack of special financial support led to a considerably diminished effort, although Professor McClelland's visit to Vellore helped create some momentum at the start of efforts in that town. Also, lack of research staff made it impossible to obtain detailed business histories from the untrained subjects at the beginning of the project, as had been originally planned. But social researchers must do the best they can under actual field conditions. They are not working in a laboratory where everything can be laid out carefully in advance and controlled. Given the actual conditions under which the project operated, the five groups of businessmen studied—two from Kakinada, two from Vellore, and one from Rajahmundry—seemed reasonably comparable. The next question is: What was the nature of the training some of them actually got at SIET Institute?

PLATES

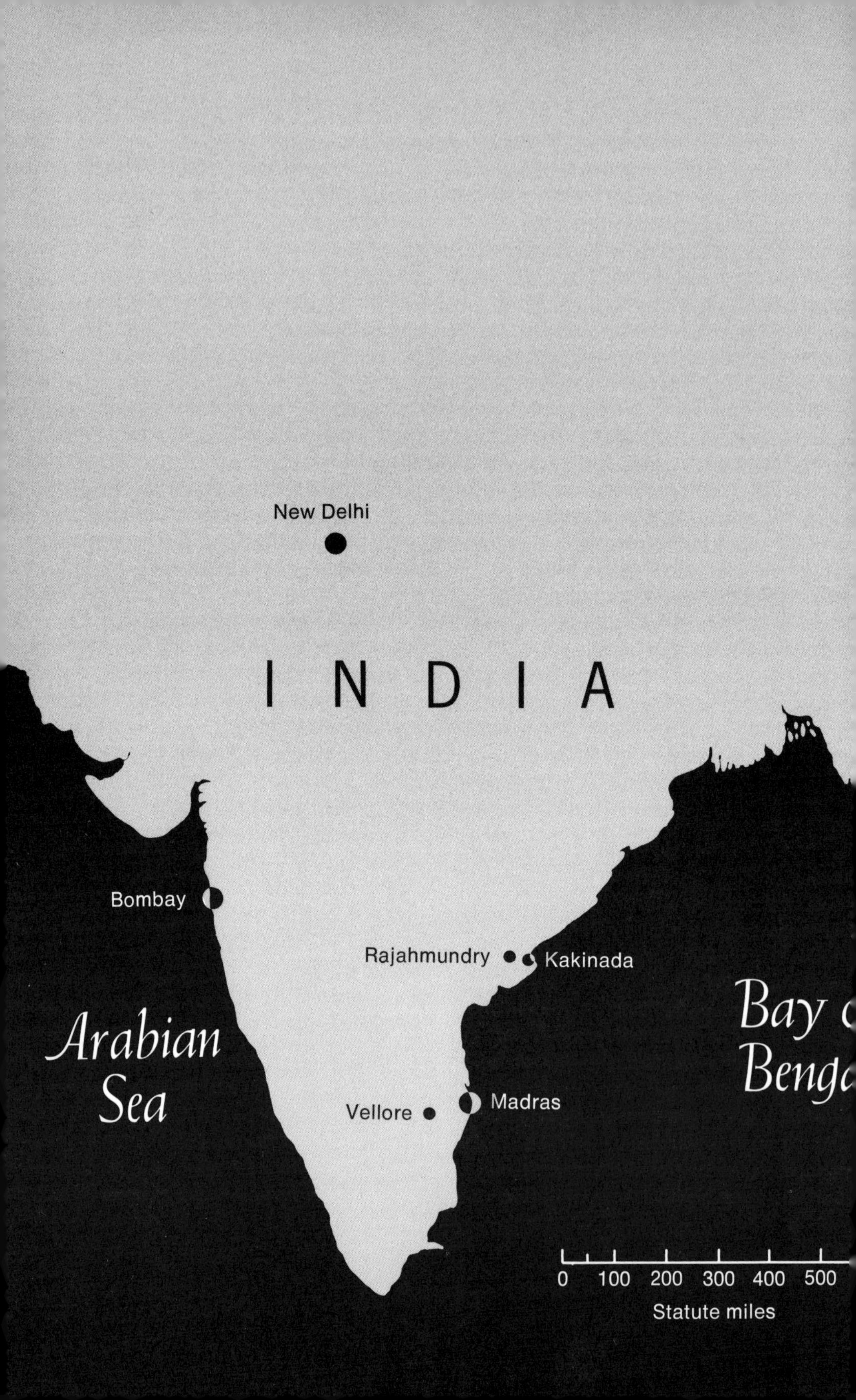

New Delhi
INDIA
Bombay
Rajahmundry
Kakinada
Arabian Sea
Vellore
Madras
0 100 200 300 400 500
Statute miles

Plate 1. The lower end of the
main road in Kakinada.

Plate 2. The canal opening into the
harbor at Kakinada. The boat is typical
of those used to transfer goods
from the port to ships anchored
in the roads of the harbor.

Plate 3. A Kakinada foundry.
The pipes are being produced for
an irrigation project.

Plate 4. Production under way at a
newly established small factory.

Plate 5. A typical cycle shop owned by one of the course participants.

Plate 6. The sari section of
a renovated textile shop.

Plate 7. The main road at Rajahmundry.

Plate 8. Participants and staff at the second Kakinada course, SIET Institute.

First row (l. to r.): S. Chattopadhyay, M. S. Nadkarni, A. D. Pabaney, R. N. Jai, E. R. Danzig, U. Pareek, P. Mehta, P. S. Hundal.

Middle row: P. Krishna Rao, D. Raghavendra Rao, Ch. Sreeramulu, R. Subba Rao, B. Venkataratnam, G. Raju, K. Chinna Rao, N. Mankani, H. Jain.

Back row: V. Sreshti, P. Vishwanadham, C. Srinivas Rao, V. Subbaraju, K. Ramana Rao, P. Sastry, G. Venkataratnam.

CHAPTER **5**

THE NATURE OF THE ACHIEVEMENT MOTIVATION COURSES AT SIET INSTITUTE

The twelve educational inputs designed to increase achievement motivation have already been described in Chapter 2. They represent the scientist's way of abstracting and conceptualizing what he thinks he is doing, so that he can gain some systematic control over the educational process and measure the comparative effectiveness of various combinations of course inputs. However, such abstract inputs have to be fleshed out and made practicable and interesting for a group of adult businessmen. How did the courses function in actuality? What kinds of sessions took place from day to day?

In describing the sessions, full credit should be given to their chief architect, Dr. Elliott Danzig. He had had some experience in designing such courses in Mexico and Bombay, but on a more limited basis. Here, for the first time, he had the opportunity to collaborate fully with an Indian staff in a carefully organized, full-length, residential program solidly backed by an important Government of India training institution. Furthermore, since this was the first community-oriented program that had been undertaken, it was necessary to revise the training to take into account the opportunity for collaborative effort among the participants afterwards. Finally, since Dr. Danzig's stay was limited, he had the task of helping develop Indian staff leadership and an instructional manual for the courses, which would ensure the successful completion of the project. Fortunately, it was part of the philosophy of the program from the outset that training should be turned over to Indian staff members as soon as practicable, on the same ideological basis that *n* Achievement development is turned over to the individual as soon as possible: in the end, both ethically and practically, the individual person (or country) must be responsible for his own development. Dr. Danzig responded with vigor, skill, and imagination to all of these opportunities and essentially shaped the courses as they became a part of the regular offerings of SIET Institute.

After the first course for participants from Kakinada had been given, Dr. Danzig and Shri Nadkarni outlined "A Manual for Instructors" (Danzig and Nadkarni, 1964), and in collaboration with Drs. Pabaney and Pareek, other Indian staff members at SIET Institute, further revised it after the second course. It summarizes very well the objectives and nature of the instruction as they were perceived by the staff managing the program. We can scarcely do better than to quote extensively from this manual.

April, 1964

Goals of the Course

1. The course seeks to increase entrepreneurial spirit and improve interpersonal competence among the participants by emphasizing motivation, planning, and cooperative effort, rather than technical skills.

2. The course is basically one of self-development. Attention is focused on the self, and methods are presented for self-directed motivation change. Attention is given to three approaches to greater self-knowledge and understanding of motives:

I. The roots of values, attitudes, and motives are examined. Here the familial and cultural effects on the individual's images of himself and his world are examined.

II. Each individual is guided in examining his characteristic modes of behavior as perceived by those about him.

III. He is also encouraged to examine his fantasies and his aspirations in relation to this actual behavior.

3. A continuing theme throughout the course is that participants can initiate and control change by setting reasonable goals for change in themselves, in their firms, and in their area, and that this can lead to rapid economic growth for the individual and for the area.

Nature of the Program

To begin with, evidence is presented showing how achievement motivation or the "entrepreneurial spirit" is related to performance and success, and how such a spirit has contributed to national economic growth. Participants spend some time studying these research findings and how and why achievement motivation is related to improved performance.

1. Participants are given an opportunity to analyze their own spontaneous thinking or imagination and to score this material for motivational content according to well-defined scoring procedures. The purpose is to help them recognize achievement thinking in its various aspects so that they can reproduce it in their thoughts and, therefore, in their actions.

2. Participants are encouraged to use the understanding of their own motivation and thinking to evaluate their approach to their work; to set realistic challenging goals for themselves.

3. Participants practice "Achievement Thinking" by learning to perceive job situations, problems, and possibilities in achievement terms. They engage in achievement-related activities in a simulated business situation. Here they become aware of the relationship between achievement thinking and entrepreneurial actions.

4. Cases of successful entrepreneurs and sometimes entrepreneurs in person are presented to the group to enable the participants to see the relationship between successful business functioning and achievement thinking and also to understand the origins of entrepreneurial behavior.

5. Participants are, throughout the course, given an opportunity to experience and internalize the characteristics of a successful entrepreneur. This is done through (3) and (4) and by lectures, discussions, and demonstrations involving creative problem-solving and risk-taking.

6. The individual is encouraged to write an autobiography, to make plans for his future, to take the practical steps and make the commitments necessary to fulfill the personal goals he has set for himself. Personal counseling sessions are arranged for individuals to obtain better self-knowledge, more realistic appraisal of goals, and more creative ways of attaining them.

7. Participants are encouraged to examine their relations with others in the group throughout the course. In small and large groups, they are given opportunities to understand the needs of others and to help them in solving their problems.

8. The participants are given practice in aiding and supporting one another in group activities. This is designed to increase cooperation upon their return to their area and to increase the probability of mutual reinforcement for one another in the future.

Follow-Up

Any training course to be truly effective and vital has to maintain contacts with the participants. This program is particularly concerned with helping participants to bring new ways of thinking into their work. It is intended to maintain contact with the participants for a couple of years at regular intervals after the course to check up on the progress they are making toward accomplishing their objectives. The participants are expected to continue to analyze their own thought processes and behavior and to look for concrete feedback as to how well they are doing. A procedure has been developed whereby participants will regularly submit written progress reports which will be analyzed and commented upon by the faculty in writing. This will reinforce the participants' achievement thinking and planning.

In creating an achievement climate in the town, the participants support and stimulate one another in their individual and group activities. The instructors of the course are also involved in creating an expectancy on the part of other business people in the community that changes have taken place in the participants.

It is expected that the participants on their return will organize themselves into a formal association designed to stimulate economic growth for the purpose of maintaining the achievement spirit.

Evaluation

It is intended to find out the extent to which this type of program affects the economic development of a given area, in comparison with a similar area where such a program has not been presented.

Accordingly, studies will be made of control and experimental areas, prior to training, and the subsequent economic changes in these communities examined. Changes in individuals who have undergone the course will be observed in comparison with a similar group who have not undergone the course.

It is important to realize that the ideas in this manual reflected in a variety of ways not only what the staff understood about the program, but also what they told the participants it was about, repeatedly, throughout the courses and follow-up visits in Kakinada and Vellore. Thus, for instance, it was considered important to let the participants know from the outset that they would be followed up over several years (Input G-3, Chapter 2), that they would be compared with other men who had not had the course or that the growth of their town should exceed the growth of a comparable town (Input G-1).

It should also be noted that in points 7 and 8 under "Nature of the Program," great stress is laid on collaborative effort among leaders in the community. The emphasis was new for the courses at the time, but obviously very important for several reasons. Indian businessmen tend to be very competitive and secretive, anyway, since most of them accept the philosophy of the limited good as outlined by Sinha (1967), and in Chapter 3. That is, they believe that everyone works solely for his own good, that resources are very limited, and that therefore working with someone else means that he will be likely to take your share of the resources away from you. But from the practical point of view, it seemed essential for the businessmen to work together if they were to develop their city—if only to solve such obvious community problems as providing better port facilities, which would benefit all of them. From the ethical point of view, stressing cooperative effort was also desirable since the program was attacked then, as it has been since, as a selfish device to help the rich get richer at the expense of others. It is common among intellectuals in India, as in other countries, to sneer at industrialists and businessmen. The well-known Indian critic Nirad Chaudhuri says, for example:

> Behind the industrial revolution in India, in fact the only positive force, is the Hindu's insatiable greed for money. King Dollar who is inciting King Paisa does not know either himself or his new "Royal Brother." The American industrialist, even when he is aware of no other motivation except acquisition of money, is the old European Conquistador in a new incarnation. He is the Genghis Khan of the age of economics. But the Hindu money-maker can never be anything but his paisa-counting sordid self. He is the worshipper of money in the absolute manner. Believing that money can do everything, he is prepared to do everything for money. (1966, pp. 83–84)

To be sure, Chaudhuri is considered to be too much of an irresponsible cynic to be taken altogether seriously; nevertheless we did not want to be considered promoters of unbridled economic selfishness, in a basically idealistic nation. So we felt it important to emphasize over and over again that: (1) a man's personal development should benefit not only himself, but his firm, his community, and ultimately his nation, and (2) benefits to the community and nation obviously had to come from collaborative effort.

Optimal Psychological Conditions for Change

It is one thing to lay out the nature of an educational program, to describe what is supposed to happen. It is quite another to create a climate in which what is supposed to happen will happen. Danzig and

Nadkarni in their 1964 manual also had quite a lot to say about the process by which personality change is to be brought about. They were concerned with such matters as how the instructors should behave, how the participants could be encouraged to take responsibility for self-development, the sequence with which ideas should be introduced, and so forth. It will be useful to summarize what they had to say under several main headings to give some notion of how they thought they were bringing about the expected personality changes. They were much influenced also by the philosophy of training then prevalent at SIET Institute, which has since been fully explained in a book by Lynton and Pareek (1967).

The Image of the Faculty Member. First they considered the characteristics of the instructor. What sort of a person should he be? How should he behave in a way most likely to facilitate change? They felt that almost as a precondition he should be *worthy of respect.* That is, he should be perceived by the participants "as capable of producing desirable changes in their lives." Such a perception depends obviously on his personal qualities—his honesty, his concern for them as individuals—on his specialized knowledge, or relevant experience, and on the nature and extent of the institutional support he had. In brief, he should have a certain prestige in the eyes of the participants because, in line with Proposition G-1, Chapter 2, he may be one of the main sources of the participants' belief that they can and will change. Furthermore, "In order to maintain this image, the faculty members must continuously demonstrate mutual respect for one another and a high sense of purpose." Such a corollary seems so obvious as to be hardly worth stating, but numerous studies have shown that when staff members are in serious conflict or disrespect each other, participants also become confused and conflicted, even though the staff may outwardly present what appears to be a united front (see Caudill, 1958).

The staff member must not only be perceived as capable of producing change, he must himself believe that he can help others to change. The self-confidence of the instructor helps the participants believe that they are likely to change. But the instructor also must not believe he is God. The simplest antidote for such self-intoxication is a deep and honest concern for every participant in the course as an individual—with unique characteristics, problems, and goals. Included always in this concern is the conviction that developing achievement motivation may not be right for a particular person. In other words, the instructor is not like a salesman who is pressing his product on everyone, regardless of need or condition in life. The instructor must be far more sensitive to individual differences than that, far more respectful of the human being's capacity to choose his own goals and to decide whether or not he wants to develop achievement motivation. The instructor is more like a salesman who is enthusiastic about his product, but clearly recognizes that it is appropriate only for certain people in certain life situations and that in the end, anyway, it must be the person himself who decides whether he wants the product or not. Without such a commitment, the product cannot be "sold."

Finally, "the faculty member has to communicate a healthy model of the behavior expected." He must be honest, realistic, and enthusiastic. Above all, he should support and encourage the participants rather than criticize them. The reason lies not only in the extensive psychological literature showing that reward is a more powerful change agent than punishment, it derives also from the simple observation that adults trying new modes of behavior after years of doing something else are fearful of appearing ridiculous. They are timid, uncertain, anxious, and in much need of encouragement. The faculty members by being cheerful and supportive are displaying behavior that they expect from the participants not only toward their work, but toward each other.

The faculty should also display another characteristic expected from the participants—namely, openness to change and new ideas. As Danzig and Nadkarni put it, "The faculty member presents the program as one of change by exchange, i.e., he, as well as the participants, expects to be changed by the program." The point to be made is that everyone can always learn something new, no matter how old or how experienced he is. The instructors are no exception. Each new participant's problems are unique. There is always something to learn, no matter how often the instructor has been involved in change programs. Being open-minded and humble before the participant is particularly easy for a foreign consultant who knows little about the country in which he is working. So far as this aspect of the course was concerned, Dr. Danzig found it a positive advantage to know very little about Indian philosophy, religion, culture, or economic life in a small city. These were obviously all areas in which the participants knew far more than he did, and he was eager and excited to sit as a student at their feet. It is sometimes argued that a person should not try to become a change agent until he "understands thoroughly and completely" the language, customs, history, and so forth of the group of people he hopes to influence. Our experience with these courses does not support this contention. Rather it is our belief that if the instructors had been extremely knowledgeable about the background and life conditions of the participants, they would have found it much harder to assume the role of "learner" and to shift responsibility to the participants for their own self-development. The consultants' very ignorance at times prevented them from being put in the position of the wise man or magician who has an answer to every question. Instead they could honestly say that they knew only certain general facts and principles and that they were as interested as the participants were in seeing how such generalizations applied under local conditions.

Defining the Goal of Change. Technically, the change process can begin only when the participant perceives clearly a new pattern of thought and action for himself that would have beneficial consequences for his life. The faculty member then should "bring out the bright prospects that lie in change." He helps the participant conceive and develop a more satisfying self-image. He traces carefully the connection between changes in thought and action, a more satisfying self-image, brighter prospects for the firm in which he works, and the potential contribution of an improved business to economic development of the area and the country. As Mierke has shown (1955), "bright prospects" that are wholly selfish are much less effective in motivating people to action than more altruistic goals that embrace one's family, friends, community, or nation. The prospects of change, both in their narrow personal sense and in their broader altruistic sense, must be vividly and accurately set before the participant. One of the serious errors that the folk psychology of the West falls into is to assume that either man is basically selfish and forced to consider the community only under pressure or that he is basically, or ought to be, only "good" and altruistically devoted to the good of society. The historical and cultural reasons for splitting man into selfish and altruistic parts have been described fully by McClelland (1964, Ch. 4). But the fact is that the split is more in man's perception of human nature than in human nature itself. At any rate, it is when goals appeal to both types of motives that human thought and action are fully mobilized and sustained.

Understanding the Real Self. Just as the instructor sets forth the image of an ideal self, of the person the participant might become, he helps everyone understand at the same time accurately and realistically how closely he approximates that ideal at the present time. The discrepancy between the real and the ideal selves sets the process of change in motion. Therefore "the participant is encouraged to see and present himself frankly by reviewing his failures and successes, his values, his fears, and his aspirations." In order to increase his self-knowledge, the roots of his values and attitudes and motives in the family and culture are examined. He is helped to see "the relation between his own values and what society, i.e., his family or the culture, expects. Then he must make some decisions as to the role he really wants to play in society." How much of what he wants does he want really out of his own decision and how much does he want merely because he has fallen into a certain pattern of thinking or because he is afraid of what others will think if he behaves differently? To what extent is he avoiding decisions because it is too uncomfortable to move in one direction or another?

Nor is it sufficient for him to discuss his attitudes, opinions, and beliefs as he is aware of them and might discuss them with an intimate friend. He must also be "guided in examining his characteristic modes of behavior as reflected in the understanding of those about him." Most people have a well-formed idea of what they are like, how they are acting, and what other people think of them. However, if properly guided to discover the opinions and perceptions of others, they may discover to their surprise that others do not see them as they see themselves. Danzig and Nadkarni contend that it is an important part of the role of the instructor to give the participants the power to see themselves through the eyes of others. It is one of the most effective ways of making clear the gap between the real self and the ideal self.

Finally the participant "is encouraged to study his fantasies and his aspirations in relation to his actual behavior, and to his potentialities as realistically appraised." This may reveal important discrepancies between what a person believes about himself and what he spends his time dreaming about. He may think of himself as achievement-oriented, but may discover that in six consecutive creative stories, he has not once introduced the notion of achievement. Or he may observe that he has fantasies of becoming a great benefactor to mankind, when in real life he is a harassed younger son completely under the domination of his older brother and father. What actions can or should he take to fit his aspirations to his life situation? Should he change his aspirations, leave home, or find some alternative course of action? Helping the participant realize the existence of such issues is certainly an important step in initiating the change process.

Ways of Closing the Gap Between the Ideal Self and the Real Self. Danzig and Nadkarni also recognized that it is not enough to present a person with his problems, to create discontent. The instructor must also help him find solutions. He presents "alternative ways of thinking and acting, and factual information in relating to the consequences of these choices." For instance, he describes in detail the entrepreneurial way of acting—taking moderate risks, personal responsibility, and so on. "The participant is furthermore encouraged to try out the new ways of thinking and acting, in a safe atmosphere where the consequences of a mis-step are not serious." He is encouraged to write stories high in *n* Achievement or to play a game in which he can make decisions that fit the entrepreneurial model. "The faculty member insures that the participant receives quick feedback concerning his new behavioral patterns and understands their significance." The feedback may come from the instructors or the other participants. The main point is that he should receive support and encouragement immediately whenever he makes the appropriate response.

"The faculty member and participant then collaboratively work out ways of evaluating progress in the desired direction in the future after the course." That is, the participant will not be able to rely after the course on feedback provided by other participants or the instructors as to whether he is continuing to make the decisions and actions characteristic of the new way of behaving. Some method must be devised in advance so that he can know whether he is making progress. Thus the participant "is encouraged to try out his new behavioral patterns in the real world outside the training experience" and to keep and examine feedback on himself in this real world. In short, the method of closing the gap between the ideal and the real follows the tried and true path of all good problem solving: new methods of acting are presented, tried out, reinforced, and generalized to all sorts of situations in the real world, the whole process being made as explicit as possible with respect to the actions taken and their consequences.

Strengthening the Belief in the Power of the Self to Change. Fundamental to all the other conditions for change is a growing conviction on the part of the person that he can change, that he can take control and direct his life. As most psychotherapists have realized, there is a "double bind" in personality change programs. The client comes seeking help from someone but that someone must get him to realize that he can only help himself. There are a variety of ways in which instructors can help a person realize how powerful he is, or how he really is an "origin" rather than a "pawn" being pushed around by others more powerful than he (de Charms, 1968). For instance, when the instructor insists he has much to learn from the participants, he is helping the participants believe in their own power to help others. The way the course is set up helps reinforce the idea that the participant is a strong person who has already taken an important step in deciding to come to the course. It has cost him some money; he has had to leave his work for a number of days; he is subjecting himself to living with other adult men as though he were in school again; he is told that he is expected to take the course very seriously and to do a lot of hard work; he is required to expose some of his inner thoughts under somewhat embarrassing public conditions. The fact that he does all of these things already shows that he is a man who can overcome difficulties, who is capable of decisive acts of will. Furthermore, at some point during the course the participants are given a clear and open invitation to withdraw from the program if they find it uninteresting or irrelevant to their lives. The opportunity is provided as unobtrusively as possible so that they will not stay on out of embarrassment, but can exercise their own free will, as origins rather than pawns. Even if a man decides to stay, he must face another decision, "whether to continue as in the past or to commit himself openly to strive to change." In fact, at the end of the course he writes a contract with himself for change—not necessarily to be better in entrepreneurial ways, but at least to improve in some ways. It is he who makes the contract and the decision, not the instructor or anyone else. Similarly, it is he who has set his own goals, analyzed his present characteristics, and tried out in action new ways of achieving a more satisfying self-image.

Furthermore, the instructors find many ways in the group to shift responsibility to the participants—by asking them to evaluate various course inputs, by asking individuals to rotate as leaders of small groups, by commenting as supportively as possible about one another's behavior. As Danzig and Nadkarni put it: "The faculty member continues in the role of the change agent in gradually diminishing degrees; however, effort is made from the beginning to develop the group to take over and be accepted as the change agent." That is, the instructor must start out as a person responsible for initiating change, but he gradually shifts responsibility to the group and to the individuals who make it up. In some cases he may even be able to prepare people "in the community of the participants to expect a change in their behavior." It is obviously helpful if not only the participant sees himself as an origin, but if those around him expect him to act like one. But perhaps most important of all, instructors strive to convince the participants that they can and should "seek and utilize other stimuli for change outside the group and the training program." In other words, having become origins, they can continue to research their environment and to find other means for promoting personal growth long after the course. The attitude of the instructor throughout toward a participant is something like this: "You are a strong person, worthy of respect. You can make your own decisions, having obtained help and guidance from others. You can change and redirect your life if you want to badly enough. Don't believe those philosophers who say that you never can be anything but what you are. All we can do is give you some new techniques, discovered by psychological science, which will help you define your goals and find ways of achieving them."

A Day in the Course

What went on has still been described only in fairly general terms—either as educational inputs abstracted for scientific purposes, or as an outline prepared for prospective participants, or as a set of psychological conditions created by the instructors to facilitate personal change. What actually happened is still disturbingly elusive and difficult to describe in sufficient, concrete detail. In an attempt to provide a better picture of what happened, we have picked a particular day in one of the courses and have described the proceedings from start to finish, to show how various sessions illustrated some of the general points already made. In other words, we will reverse the procedure we have been following so far. Instead of making generalizations and finding concrete illustrations for them, we will start with the concrete events in the life of a particular group of people on a particular day and seek to relate what happened to various generalizations about the courses. Since the participants were promised confidentiality, it will be necessary to be a little vague about some points and to make minor changes in the narrative to avoid identification of some of the characters involved. However, the facts are in the main as they actually happened and were recorded by an observer at the time.[1]

The group that assembled for this course had come a considerable distance from home to attend. They had heard something about the course before they left, but they did not know quite what to expect. They arrived at SIET Institute to discover that it consisted of a set of new and impressive buildings located in the country on the edge of the large city of Hyderabad. It was hardly feasible to walk even to a nearby store, and transport to the city itself could be arranged only occasionally

1. We are very grateful to Shri Somnath Chattopadhyay for keeping the detailed daily record on which this portion of Chapter 5 is based.

through Institute buses or by specially ordered taxis. So they found themselves living essentially in isolation in a dormitory, dependent on their own and the Institute's resources. They were curious about what these new psychologically oriented courses would be like, impressed by the excellent facilities of the Institute, and prepared initially to wait to be told how they should behave in this novel situation. In effect it was as if they were back in school again with all of the supports, activities, and distractions of their normal adult lives removed. In short, conditions were nearly ideal for new learning. The staff had their full attention at the outset.

In this particular group there were small clusters of people who knew each other fairly well, but for the most part they were only casual acquaintances. They knew of each other, but were certainly not in the habit of discussing their business affairs with each other. In fact, in the early sessions they tended to be rather formal and correct and naturally hesitant to discuss in public their private business affairs. As we have mentioned, it is usually considered unwise in such communities to talk openly about one's plans, for fear that others will take advantage of such knowledge. One of the first tasks of the staff was to encourage participants to loosen up and talk more freely about themselves. Part of the "unfreezing" occurred quite naturally through informal discussions that took place outside of class in the dormitories or living rooms or at their separate table in the dining room. Here acquaintances could be formed based on purely social rather than business interests—e.g., living conditions at the hostel, the possibility of visiting night clubs in Hyderabad, talk about sports, and so on. Two smaller groups tended to form initially based on common earlier experiences. One consisted of representatives of older, well-to-do families in the town and the other of a number of self-made men. One or two men did not belong to either group but were brought in gradually only as the course progressed.

At the opening session of the course, Shri Jai, the Principal Director of SIET Institute, reminded the participants of the seriousness of India's economic need and the importance of the role they could play in helping develop the national economy. It was a mistake to assume that development occurred automatically as the result of a happy combination of circumstances. Grit, determination, and purposefulness had developed great nations in the past and would develop India in the future. They must, therefore, take the course on which they were about to enter with high seriousness of purpose, attending all the sessions and arriving on time. They were privileged to be part of an important new effort to find a way to speed India's economic growth. Furthermore, growth was obviously not the result of individual efforts alone. They had to learn to cooperate with each other and to share the responsibilities for developing their community.

After this orientation, the participants settled down to filling out a number of questionnaires and test forms with the explanation that all of the results would be used as part of the training later in the course. They wrote six imaginative stories to pictures, wrote answers to the question "Who am I?" in as many different ways as they could, wrote a brief essay on why they had attended the course, and rated their feelings about a number of different concepts—e.g., themselves and their businesses—on a Semantic Differential Test Form. On the second day, some history of the research on achievement motivation was introduced, the nature of the project and courses was explained in full, and the participants spent a good deal of time discussing publicly their answers to the question "Who am I?" On the third day, lectures were given on the nature of motivation and values and on the nature of the achievement motive in particular, with all its attendant thought and action characteristics. On the morning of the fourth day, which will be described in full, all arrived on time for the 9:00 A.M. opening session despite the fact that several had been up late on a trip to Hyderabad the night before. The first thirty minutes were spent giving the staff feedback on what they had thought of each of the sessions that had taken place the day before. Some said that the lectures had been too abstract. They had found it difficult to understand exactly what was meant by motivation. Furthermore, the scoring for *n* Achievement which had been introduced had gone much too fast and they had failed to grasp the meaning of several categories. What, for example, constituted a "unique" accomplishment—one of the scoring categories for determining whether achievement imagery was present in the stories? They had seen a film on "time" the day before, which seemed to them to be quite irrelevant to the course. Why had it been introduced? Some even went so far as to comment on mannerisms or modes of delivery of individual staff members.

These critique sessions, which were held daily first thing in the morning, were introduced for two reasons. First, they undoubtedly did give the staff guidance as to how well they were getting certain ideas across. But second, they provided one of several means of reinforcing the idea contained in Proposition I-1 (see Chapter 2) that each individual in the group should be warmly respected as an origin rather than a pawn. That is, in India, as in other countries, it is quite common to turn a class session into an authoritarian situation in which the instructor gives out information and the pupils write it down and recite it back to him. The pupil becomes a pawn to be manipulated by the instructor. Even though these pupils were adults, in many cases very responsible businessmen, they were all too ready to fall into the passive role of accepting what they were told. So it was thought desirable to encourage them to take a quite active role in criticizing and commenting on the course, even though this might make a staff member's job more difficult in terms of changing his plans or accepting criticism.

CREATIVE THINKING SESSION

Shri Jai then gave a brief lecture on creative thinking. It is important here to say a word about his background, because it was known to the participants and undoubtedly influenced their response to him. He was a businessman with extensive experience in a large company in Bombay. He had taken a leave of absence at some personal sacrifice from his company to become director of SIET Institute because he believed in its great potential for contributing to India's economic growth. Thus both his background and his motives gave him prestige in the view of the participants. They saw him as a businessman with experiences like their own, rather than as a bureaucrat speaking wholly from a theoretical point of view. He obviously spoke from real conviction and knowledge backed up by the rather unusual action he had taken in coming to the Institute. He noted that curiosity and creativity are words which both begin with c and end with y—a fact that gives a clue to their basic meaning—c = "see," y = "why." As everyone can observe, children are naturally curious. They actively explore everything in their immediate environment. Studies of great men have shown that they have never ceased being curious, because curiosity means essentially continuing to learn, continuing to try and find out why things are as they are. Most of us lose our questioning urge as we get older either because we become satisfied or because our failures tend to make us cautious. To the truly curious, creative person, a failure can be a stepping stone to success. We can see why it occurred and can correct our behavior in the future. Unfortunately, far too many of us accept our failures as being due to fate, and do not try to learn from them. The question is: How can we maintain a questioning, curious, learning attitude throughout life? Shri Jai ended with a quotation from Einstein, "Imagination is more important than knowledge."

Then Shri Nadkarni took the floor to run a group demonstration showing how imagination and creativity could be aroused and strengthened. Again his background is relevant to his message. He did not have

any formal degrees in psychology but had worked with Professor Gardner Murphy on research for his book on India years before. After that
he worked for a number of years for the Khadi Commission, which
attempts to encourage the growth of cottage industry throughout rural
India along lines suggested by Gandhi. Thus he knew village India
intimately and had had much experience living and working under very
difficult conditions and getting people to participate and cooperate with
one another in community programs. However, he had come to agree with
the position taken by SIET Institute and by Lynton and Stepanek in
their monograph "Industrialization Beyond the Metropolis"—that the
most effective way to speed India's rate of economic growth was to work
neither at the very top nor at the very bottom of the economy but somewhere in the middle, with businesses both large and small, in medium
sized cities. He was somewhat skeptical about the possibilities of changing people in any very fundamental way in a short period of time, in
view of his long and rather discouraging experiences with cottage
industries in villages. But he was willing to be convinced, and certainly
willing to participate in the research designed to evaluate the effectiveness of this new approach. His first experiences as a participant in the
training itself converted him to considerable enthusiasm for the approach.

The demonstration itself was based on an article by Dr. Danzig on
creative problem solving which had appeared in *The Chemist* (1953).
Shri Nadkarni began it by explaining why they had been shown the
film on "time." It had been designed to loosen up their thinking by
showing how a simple idea like time can be perceived in many different
ways. The film showed how perception changes if time is speeded up
or slowed down, as when the projector presented motion as faster or
slower than normal. Time is infinitely divisible or expandable. An in-
individual's life can be measured in years, months, days, or moments.
Time can be perceived as going in circles, in spirals, or marching off in
a single direction to an unknown future. What is the significance of a
man's life in time? The permutations and combinations of ideas about
time are endless. They illustrate the infinite capacity and flexibility of
the human mind.

He then explained that all were going to play a game to see for themselves how imaginative even they could be. The game involved what is
sometimes called brainstorming or wild thinking (*cf.* Osborn, 1953).
Someone in the group was to present a problem he had. Then the others
would contribute imaginative solutions to it. However, there was one
rule all were to follow: they were not to be critical either of their own

ideas or those offered by others, or to be influenced in the slightest by considerations of practicality. Imaginativeness and creativity are too often stifled by doubts, fears, and critical thinking. Here the goal was to stimulate imaginative ideas, no matter how wild they were.

Someone said that he had the problem of how to stop the damage to the seats in his movie theater caused by college students who often did not hesitate to write on them or carve the arms. Someone suggested he might have his seats made of tough plastic that would not be so easily defaced. Then others began to get more into the spirit of the thing suggesting that he close the theater, burn the chairs, or stand at the entrance shooting the boys before they entered. The staff entered in with equally wild suggestions and soon everyone was enjoying the game. As the ideas got wilder and wilder, there was much joking, and an atmosphere of playfulness in which imagination could soar to new heights. In fact they enjoyed the game so much that they continued playing it on their own throughout the day whenever they were free. Some even used it as a kind of projective test in which they realized they were revealing things about themselves. For instance, the man who suggested the students be shot mentioned, in response to some kidding, that he wouldn't mind doing it himself.

What was the purpose of these sessions on creativity and imaginativeness? Actually a great many of the theoretical course inputs were involved. The sessions increased openness and self-knowledge (Input S-2), improved in-group feeling (Input I-3), gave the participants practice in part of the achievement action syndrome, i.e., taking personal responsibility for varied instrumental acts (Input A-2), and demonstrated that everyone could be imaginative to an extent that was probably a surprise to himself. Once again they were being taught that each one of them had the power within himself to be extraordinarily imaginative, to think creatively on his own, even though he might not have done so for a long time either out of habit or caution. They were helped in this way to believe that the human mind is a tremendously powerful instrument which they could use to change themselves (Input G-1). In the course of the brainstorming sessions, they even thought of some practical solutions which were of help to the men who had raised the problems in the first place. Thus they had experience in helping one another and in seeing how wild ideas can sometimes lead on to practicable ones—another aspect of the achievement action syndrome. Above all, they could feel the exhilaration and joy that comes from throwing caution and criticism to the winds, at least for the moment. As they themselves were quick to point out, this was an uncommon state of mind for them to be in, since it is all too common in India for people to spend their time criticizing each other, the government, or even themselves. Thus, the exercise gave insight into a cultural value which can inhibit optimistic, forward-looking achievement planning (Course Input S-3).

FAMILY VALUES ROLE PLAY

After a long morning of study, the group broke up at 12:30 for lunch and some rest and relaxation during the hottest part of the day. The next session began at 2:30 with Dr. Udai Pareek in charge. Dr. Pareek has a Ph.D. in social psychology and a national reputation in India as one of the leaders of the middle generation of Indian psychologists who have thoroughly absorbed the values and skills characteristic of modern psychological science. He is well grounded in modern psychological theory and experimental and statistical methods and has had considerable experience as a teacher and researcher in psychology. What is more, he had become interested in an experience-based approach to education through his participation in sensitivity training or T-groups. The characteristics of these groups have been fully described elsewhere (Bradford, Gibb, and Benne, 1964) as they have been developed by the National Training Laboratories, which hold workshops in Bethel, Maine. Dr. Pareek, who was then head of the extension division of SIET Institute, saw the possibilities of combining T-group methods with some of the more structured techniques employed in n Achievement training. In short, he was a thoroughly trained scientific psychologist with a strong interest in experience-based methods of psychological instruction such as those employed in these courses.

He spoke first of the relationship between motives and values. If motives belong to the individual, values are the cultural norms of a society. The individual learns what the values of the society are and how they shape his beliefs, attitudes, and motives. Much learning about values takes place in the family. A demonstration might help the participants understand what some of the key values are in the Indian family.

He then described the following situation: A father has just learned that his son has failed an important examination. He talks to the mother about it and then she talks to the son. Who will play the part of the mother, father, and son? He found no difficulty getting volunteers. They entered into the role-playing with enthusiasm. Then he staged a more elaborate drama based on the Rosen and D'Andrade experiment (1959) already described in Chapter 2. A boy is asked to see how many blocks he can stack up in a tower with his left hand while he is blindfolded. The psychologist is testing the manual dexterity of the boy, while the mother and father watch. A popular dry goods store owner volunteered to be the "mother," a tall well-to-do-farmer, the "father," and a small, rather unassuming cycle shop owner, the "son."

The psychologist reported that the average number of blocks piled up by boys in this situation is eight. How many does the "mother" think her "son" can pile up? She says seven. The "son" also gives the same number as his estimate of what he can do, but the "father" says he thinks the boy can only pile up six blocks. The "son" goes ahead and attempts to pile the blocks as the "parents" comment on how he is doing.

After it is over, the psychologist asks each member of the "family" why he chose the goal that he did. The "mother" said she was concerned about the possible failure of her "son." She felt he must not fail. She never wanted a son of hers to fail at whatever he undertook. Therefore she felt that he should take no chances. The "son" reported that he had chosen a below-average goal because he thought it was better to be below average and succeed than to shoot too high and fail. The "father" simply reported that he thought his "son" was below average, that he would be too anxious to reach the goal if he set a high one, and would certainly fail. Then the observers were asked to report what they saw, what they thought of the comments made by these "family" members, and whether they thought the behavior shown was typical for similar situations in their hometown. That is, do parents generally encourage their sons? Or do they doubt their ability to do well? Do they let sons take the initiative or do they continue to attempt to control them in order to keep them from making mistakes? Most of the participants felt that the reactions spontaneously given in the role-playing situation were typical. Parents would be concerned about failure and would try to keep their children from getting into situations where they might fail. They would be quite critical of their sons, as the father was in this case. While all agreed more or less on the facts, two points of view began to emerge slowly. Some felt it was clearly the duty of parents to give children this kind of guidance—in fact, that was precisely what parents were for. Others felt strongly that children should be left freer to make mistakes on their own. They complained that all too often in the Indian family sons never had a chance to take initiative so long as a father or an older brother was alive to exercise this controlling, guiding role.

Without attempting to take sides on the issue of what was the right role for parents to play, Dr. Pareek then pointed out how the demonstration and the discussion afterward showed how important values could interact with the development of a particular motive like *n* Achievement. He referred to the research findings of Rosen and D'Andrade and others, showing that in general, families and societies which value highly an authoritative role for the father tend to produce sons with lower *n* Achievement. It is clearly not for the psychologist to say whether a society, a family, or an individual ought to value such a role for the father, but it is his duty to point out that research findings show a clear connection between holding such a value and low *n* Achievement. If a person wants to develop high *n* Achievement, he will have to consider whether he wants to modify his attitudes towards such an authoritative role relationship, either in his family or business.

The same choice faces him over whether he wants to continue to follow the common Indian practice of using criticism almost exclusively in order to correct or guide behavior. Expectation of failure was common in everything they had seen and heard in the role-playing: the "mother" did not think her "son" would do well; neither did the "son" nor the "father." The "father" had criticized the "mother" for failing to correct the "son" earlier so that he would not have failed his examination. Many observers of Indian life from the lowest village level up to the most sophisticated urban centers have noted the widespread use of criticism, the rare resort to praise or enthusiasm for the performance of another. Minturn and Hitchcock (1963) recorded five hundred consecutive remarks of a mother to her child in a village in rural India. Four hundred and ninety-nine of the remarks were critical of what the child was doing; only one could be coded as rewarding the child. Perhaps the ratio of blame to praise is not so extreme in urban Indian newspaper editorials, but at times it seems almost as high. It is almost as if it is bad luck to say something good about a person in public, just as the villagers feel it is bad luck to praise a child (see Minturn and Hitchcock, 1963). A sophisticated Indian intellectual such as Chaudhuri (1966) uses criticism almost exclusively in his obviously deeply felt concern to do something about India's present predicament. He excoriates every conceivable target—the English, the Americans, the Hindus, the villagers, the city people, the businessmen—even such widely respected politicians as Nehru. He hardly has a good word to say for anyone, except possibly the aboriginal inhabitants of India. It is one thing to talk about such norms in Indian life in the abstract and give illustrations of them in the course of a lecture. It is quite another to have participated in a role-playing situation in which you have displayed those very characteristics in a form clearly observable to you and to your friends. Thus Dr. Pareek was in a better position to relate what they had observed to the general points he was trying to make about how a human motive like *n* Achievement must always function in a cultural context which may support or inhibit it.

The purpose of this section was obviously to confront the participants with some of the Indian cultural norms which might conflict with the development of *n* Achievement (Course Input S-3), and to give further illustrations of aspects of the achievement action syndrome (Course Input A-2). That is, the "boy" in the role-playing situation was actually engaged in goal-setting—which in this case was not moderately optimistic as expected of a person with high *n* Ach, but rather on the low side. He also could not very well show personal responsibility if his actions and goals were set for him by his "parents." Nor could he concentrate on feedback from his performance if he was constantly involved in trying to act primarily to please his parents. These and other such matters came up in the course of the discussion, which lasted until tea-time.

MEMORIAL STATEMENT

Just before the tea break, Shri Nadkarni distributed to each participant a white cut-out pasted on a dark background, which purported to represent a man's tombstone, complete with a bust in profile on top. Each man was to meditate on what words he would like to have engraved on his tombstone, write them on the cut-out and turn it in the following morning. The purpose of this exercise was to get each man to thinking about the relevance of what he had learned during the day to himself. What kind of a life did he really want to lead? What career would be recorded on his gravestone? Is achievement motivation relevant to that career (Course Input S-1)? How close is his present condition to that ideal? (Course Input S-2). How much of that final goal for himself has come from unexamined acceptance of Indian norms for family and social life (Course Input S-3)? The day had begun with a discussion of time and eternity. Here was another chance to collapse time and to look back at his life as he would have liked to have lived it, as if he were already dead. There was much joking about the assignment, of course, but most of them took the task quite seriously and the next day handed in memorial statements, some of which were quite moving.

ACHIEVEMENT MOTIVATION SCORING PRACTICE

After tea Dr. Prayag Mehta led a session which gave the participants more practice in scoring imaginative stories for *n* Ach content. He was a young research psychologist attached to the Department of Psychological Foundations of the Ministry of Education in New Delhi. He came to the courses at SIET Institute because he was interested in learning the techniques for possible use with underachieving high school students. He began by reminding the group that they had felt their initial introduction to the scoring system the day before had been insufficient for them to understand what was really meant. So he reviewed each of the scoring subcategories (see Figure 2.2) and then read a number of stories aloud, sentence by sentence, stopping to ask after each one whether anything in it should be scored. The class was then divided into groups of three or four each and given their own stories to score, which they had written on the first day of the course. Most of them were quite interested in finding out how much of this new "mental virus," which they had been hearing so much about, they had possessed on arrival. In fact they were so interested that they spent most of their time trying to get the staff member assigned to the small group to help score their stories for them, so that they could find out who had the highest score. With some judicious reminders that they had to learn how to score if they were to know how to think easily along achievement lines, most of the participants managed to learn the scoring system fairly well and also to satisfy their curiosity as to how much achievement imagery they had spontaneously injected into their stories. Some of those who scored low had to be reassured that they were in a better position to show improvement. They were told that near the end of the course they would be given a chance to take the test again and to show how much they had learned.

The purpose of this session was quite simple and straightforward; it was to help the participants understand in concrete, specific detail just exactly what responses constituted "achievement thoughts" as defined by the psychologists (Course Input A-1). Most of them only had very general and vague ideas as to what n Ach, in the narrow, technical sense, meant. They began by wanting to score almost any wish to be big, important, successful, of service to others, as indicating a need for Achievement. Gradually they learned that for n Ach to be scored there had to be actual statements about improving, doing better, or wanting to do well, and that one could not infer from a desire to be important that there was any concern for improvement involved.

After dinner they had an opportunity for further practice in using the n Ach scoring categories. The staff had recorded a talk by a successful entrepreneur from Hyderabad. Shri Nadkarni introduced the session by stating that such a man, according to the theory they had been hearing about, ought to have high n Ach. The question was did he in fact talk spontaneously in ways that could be coded under any of the categories of the n Ach scoring system? Did he report actions that would be characteristic of the n Ach action syndrome—moderate risk taking, attention to feedback, assuming personal responsibility, showing initiative? Shri Nadkarni played the tape and stopped it when any one of the participants felt that he had heard something that related to the achievement syndrome. Or if the whole group missed such a statement, he stopped the tape and asked them whether what they had just heard could be coded under any of the categories they had just been learning in the afternoon. The participants found the exercise very engrossing because they were listening to a man who was very much like themselves, who had succeeded, and who, without knowing anything about the achievement syndrome, was spontaneously displaying many of its characteristics. Thus, the session contributed not only to learning the achievement thought characteristics (Course Input A-1), and the achievement action characteristics (Course Input A-2), it also showed concretely how these abstract categories functioned as parts of successful business behavior in real life (Course Input A-3). When the man talked about the initiative he had had to take in order to get cement released for his use, or the obstacles he had had to overcome to get his factory built, categories came to life. Participants also were helped to think about similar ways in which the abstract categories might be reflected in concrete plans they could make for expanding their own businesses. In other words, they were encouraged to believe that what they were learning about n Ach might be relevant to their own lives (Course Input S-2). Later in the week they visited the speaker's factory in Hyderabad and some of them undoubtedly felt the satisfaction of thinking that they had inside information as to why he had managed to be so successful. The psychologists had given them specialized knowledge that explained his success. Since they knew the secret, so to speak, they could be like him. In this way they were encouraged in their belief that they could change and become more successful than they had been (Course Input G-1).

FILLING OUT LIFE HISTORIES

After the tape-listening session broke up about 9:00 P.M., there was still quite a lot of informal work to be done. Several participants had not completed the personal history questionnaires which they had been asked to fill out on the first day of the course. That is, they had been told that they would find it useful to write out an autobiographical statement, particularly as it related to their business life, since later in the course it would be helpful to them to re-examine what they had been doing in the light of what they were learning. All also had to write their memorial statements for the following morning. And finally, everyone had to report to his small group leader what his reactions had been to each of the sessions of the day. That is, the staff had decided that in order to get efficient feedback reports the first thing in the morning on each day, it would help if each participant gave his report to the leader of a small group of four or five at the end of each day. Then it was the leader's task to synthesize and summarize these comments and to report on them during the first half-hour of the next day's session. Three such summary reports could give the staff a good sample of group opinion as to how the course was going. What was also important about this procedure was that the reporters for each of these groups were rotated from day to day so that everyone had to speak for the group once or twice during the ten days. This prevented those who were more fluent in English from dominating the session and encouraged those who had initially been very shy to speak out. In the beginning, several who had been trying to sit in the background as much as possible found the task of speaking out very difficult, but instead of being criticized by the members of their group, they were often encouraged and supported in what they said. Again this procedural device contributed to several of the theoretical course inputs. It treated every person as an origin (Course Input I-1). It helped form in-groups which actually provided practical support for their members (Course Inputs I-2 and I-3).

While the staff generally had mixed freely with the participants in informal discussions throughout the day, it withdrew late at night for a private evaluation session to discuss how the sessions for that day had gone and to make some rough plans for the next day, which had to be flexible enough to be changed in the light of the critique the participants were preparing. Both before and after this staff meeting individual staff members counselled individual participants who felt they had problems that they did not want to talk about before the other group members.

Obviously the day had been a very strenuous one both for the staff and the participants. And so the course continued for six more days. Any particular session or procedure might strengthen one or several of the theoretical course inputs. A particular course input would often be returned to again and again from different angles in a more-or-less spiral fashion. Thus, for instance, the n Ach scoring system was first described in a general way; then, as in the fourth day described here, used by the participants to score their own stories; used again to code the remarks of an actual entrepreneur; and then returned to much later in the course when the participants tried to write stories as high as possible in *n* Ach. The staff tried to alternate theoretical discussions with games involving action or role-playing, to keep general interest from lagging. Attention also had to be given to what the participants themselves wanted. This led to variations from day to day from course to course depending on the mood and atmosphere in the group. Each group was given a day off from regular sessions—the seventh day. This group decided it wanted to spend its day visiting the plant of the man whose speech they had coded for *n* Ach. Often they liked a particular exercise so much that they wanted another session of the same sort. This group asked for and got further a session on brainstorming which yielded some interesting solutions to practical and impractical problems. Toward the end of the course, more and more attention was naturally given to the concrete individual plans that each person was making for what he would do when he got back. The staff was particularly concerned that these plans be realistic and based on careful research. Initial drafts of the plans were criticized in small groups. Suggestions were given as to books or institutions where information might be gained about a particular problem. It would certainly be a mistake to think that mere enthusiasm— mere wanting something—would enable a person to carry out a plan successfully. This was not achievement thinking, as participants had learned about it over the past week and a half. The importance of co-operation was stressed by a demonstration involving one-person groups, three-person groups, and six-person groups. Dr. Pareek explained some of the theoretical background on how small groups function: the limitations of group decisions, the way groups could be organized to insure efficiency and get maximum individual involvement, the way group discussion of feelings may often facilitate working together, whereas secrecy and gossip may lead to the breakup of groups.

CLOSING SESSION

Finally the last session arrived. Its atmosphere was charged with considerable emotion and excitement. Everyone felt, staff and participants alike, that he had made many new friends, that he had had a warm and exciting experience, and that the program had great promise for the future. Staff and participants posed for a group photograph (see Plate 8). Two men had been chosen to speak on behalf of the participants. One said with conviction that they had undergone a transformation. So far as self-confidence was concerned, they had been turned from "mice into men." The training had been practically free, but they all would have been glad to pay for the important effects that it had had on their lives and thinking. He felt that others should get the training and that it was going to have a major impact on his hometown. He was delighted his town had been chosen for the experiment and had high hopes that it would be in the headlines in the future as a pacesetter for that part of India.

The second man stressed the feeling of cooperation that had developed in the group. He felt sure that they could do something together for their community. Furthermore, it would be something practical and realistic, not too ambitious to be realized or too trivial to make any difference. He mentioned some of the steps that had already been planned for starting new industries. He and his friends now realized that there were many places they could go to get information and help from the government or SIET Institute whenever they ran into difficulties. He thanked the staff on behalf of the participants for what they had done, for all their hard work and skill in carrying through the project with such success and enthusiasm.

The staff also responded with their expectations about the future. The real task lay ahead. They expressed themselves as grateful for the enthusiastic response to the course, but reminded everyone that they were still "in training" and that for the next two years they would be visited every six months to see how well they were able to live up to the goals they had set for themselves. The real measure of success would be whether they were able to accelerate the rate of economic growth of their home community. If they could build their town into a better place, they would be helping to build India. India had a great and important past but today it needed self-confidence, and self-confidence ultimately is rooted in the hearts and minds of people like those attending the course. Progress would certainly result from the increased self-confidence and the specialized knowledge the participants had gained, but such progress need not be at the expense of others. The progress of one contributes to the progress of others so that the whole community can rise. Shri Jai closed the session in which many were obviously deeply moved, by reminding them that it was motivation, participation, and cooperation which produced growth.

It is difficult to find the words to re-create long afterwards the intensity of the feelings of nearly all concerned; the sense of high purpose, commitment, and involvement with which this course ended. Not all the courses reached such a high point, but most approached it to some degree. Participation had been an unsettling experience for some, an enlightening experience for more, an emotional experience for nearly all. Conservatively estimated, the participants had spent about one hundred hours each thinking, talking, and experiencing achievement motivation as it related to their individual lives and community growth. One hundred hours is about the classroom exposure time of an average college course spread over an entire year. Here the exposure was condensed into a ten-day period, which was a "total immersion" in which there was almost no time or energy to think about anything else. Furthermore, much of the learning was emotional, or experience-based. Formal barriers between people, the ordinary conventions of everyday living, tended to drop away as people got deeper and deeper into thinking about what they wanted out of life and why and how other people differed from or were similar to themselves, as they listened to them discuss their goals in group sessions. Some of the participants thought more deeply about these matters than they had ever thought before in their lives. It was small wonder that many of them felt the training had had a major impact on them. Comments such as these were sprinkled on their final evaluation sheets: "I feel I am a better man," "I feel bolder now," "I am extremely happy," "I can't express the things I learned—so useful!"

Certainly if consumer satisfaction were the main criterion for judging the courses' success, they would have to have been considered first rate. The participants were impressed by them. The courses could be sold by a consulting firm on the basis of being worthwhile experiences in themselves. However, it remains to be seen what happened afterwards. Were the courses just emotional binges, or did they have long-term effects?

CHAPTER 6

CHANGES IN BUSINESS
ACTIVITIES AFTER TRAINING

Plans for the community development project called for a very careful study over time of how the businessmen behaved following the training. Repeated interviews with the course participants were necessary to find out what they were doing and why. The goal of continuously following business activity was two-fold. On the one hand, it was an additional training input which had not been extensively used in any of the earlier studies. That is, it reminded the participants that they were being watched, that they were still "in training," just as the course had explained they would be, and that they had the responsibility as taught in the course to compare their actual progress with the goals they had set for themselves. On the other hand, we felt continuous progress reports ought to provide some knowledge of how economic growth begins, at least on a small, community-wide scale, if the training proved effective. That is, it might show what kinds of plans the participants made and how they tried to execute them; what difficulties they ran into; whether they expanded their old businesses or tried to set up new businesses; whether they cooperated or competed with each other, shared plans or went off on their own. This kind of detailed knowledge on what actually happens during the early stages of an "economic growth

[177]

spurt" scarcely exists in the literature. Scholars have nearly always had to rely on recollections of what happened long after the events took place. In this case we were determined to follow the events as they occurred so that even if nothing significant happened, the historical record of what happened would be complete.

Early staff reports on what was happening in Kakinada after the courses revealed considerable disappointment. Perhaps some letdown was inevitable after the high expectations built up during the emotional excitement of the last days of the course, when nearly all the participants were promising to go back to work with renewed vigor and a stronger spirit of enterprise. For instance, when Shri Nadkarni visited Kakinada in July, 1964, a month or so after the second course, he wrote, "I was sorry to find that our past associates have not yet proved to be a good advertisement for the courses. Nearly all of them it seems have forgotten their resolutions and are sliding back into their old ways. The Entrepreneurial Association seems to have become only a place where people gather to drink tea once a month." The same theme appeared, though less strongly, in a report written by Dr. David Berlew based on a visit he made to Kakinada in January, 1965. His trip to study the immediate effects of the training was financed by The Ford Foundation, because his background qualified him in a number of important ways for appointment as a consultant to SIET Institute. He not only knew a good deal about achievement motivation, but also was a member of the staff of the Massachusetts Institute of Technology, primarily concerned with training businessmen in the Sloan Fellow Program.

He found that many of the course participants were unhappy that they had been unable to achieve their objectives.

> One subject that came up on several occasions was the obligation participants felt to The Ford Foundation, to SIET Institute, even to David C. McClelland, to expand or start a new industry. One man even introduced the notion of "dharma" to describe his agitation and discomfort when he was unable to achieve his goals on schedule. Several spoke of their anxiety and worry since the training: anxiety which could only be eliminated by achievement. It was important to them to have a chance to explain to me the intensity of their feelings and the reason they had not yet achieved something significant.

There was even some feeling that perhaps the course had been oversold as something that would change a person's life overnight. The staff at SIET Institute was beginning to feel slightly uncomfortable about this "because (a) the course often doesn't lead to miraculous changes, and (b) people's hopes are so high that disillusionment is almost inevitable. The issue here seems quite clear cut. On the one hand, faith in the training program may be necessary for a really significant change and failure to change may be due in large part to a lack of faith. On the other hand, trainers don't like to promise more than they feel they can deliver." Dr. Berlew found: "The Kakinada Entrepreneurial Association has not been a thriving organization. The group has an office, stationery, and regularly scheduled meetings, but programs have not always been carefully planned and attendance is not always good." He thought "it should not be difficult to increase the effectiveness of the Entrepreneurial Association by giving it some clear cut objective and suggestions for and even help with programming. The Association, if it has any vitality, may provide an ideal vehicle for reminding participants of their training . . . or for sponsoring programs for other Kakinada entrepreneurs." Partly because of the lack of vigorous response from some of the older men who participated in the early courses the staff at SIET Institute decided that perhaps it should try in the later courses to include more younger men, who might find it easier to change their habits.

Nevertheless Berlew's report was not all negative. He noted that "many trainees meet frequently in small groups, often members of the same [course] batch, to discuss business problems, opportunities for new industries, etc. Some of these sub-groups even have invited speakers and carry out study projects. . . . My overall impression is that the training has made a significant impact on the lives of many of the men I talked to and that these changes will be reflected in economic growth." But he also noted that economic changes would not be noticeable for a number of years, and in the meantime he thought it might be difficult to maintain staff motivation and excitement, particularly in the face of cases where the training obviously didn't seem to be "taking." Dr. Berlew was joined in late January, 1965 by Dr. McClelland, whose visit was also financed by The Ford Foundation, since SIET Institute had clearly demonstrated its interest in continuing the project by allocating its own resources to it. Dr. McClelland's visit served several purposes. It gave a boost in morale to both the staff and the course participants. All had heard about him throughout the project, but none had actually met him, so that there was a good deal of interest and curiosity aroused as to what he was like and what he would have to say. It was thought that his presence would strengthen training input G-1 (Chapter 2), that is, it would strengthen individuals' faith that they could and should change.

Furthermore, Dr. McClelland was to prepare a report evaluating progress to date. Such an evaluation was important to the participants themselves. It contributed to training input G-3 (checking up on how well they had done in comparison to the goals they had set for themselves); it was important to the project as a whole to find out whether anything at all seemed to be happening; and finally, it was important to The Ford Foundation and SIET Institute since they had to decide whether to continue to support the project as a limited research enterprise, to expand it as a more-or-less regular Institute program, or to terminate it.

The visit to Kakinada was arranged by the course participants with considerable ceremony and warm expression of appreciation for the role that the project was playing in helping them promote the best interests of their community. The party from SIET Institute, Dr. and Mrs. McClelland, Dr. Berlew, and Shri Nadkarni, were met by representatives of the Kakinada Entrepreneurs Association who had been waiting for some hours outside of town to present them with garlands and welcome them officially. The guests were treated like visiting dignitaries throughout their stay. They were taken on a personally conducted tour of the shops and factories belonging to participants in the courses. Dr. McClelland spoke at the Rotary Club to a large gathering of the leadership in the town. Later, a special public meeting was arranged by the Kakinada Entrepreneurs Association, at which both he and representatives of the town spoke about their hope for the future development of the city. A number of informal parties, both large and small, heightened the sense of belonging to a common enterprise. On one memorable occasion, nearly the entire group of course alumni went on a trip with the visitors around the Kakinada harbor in rented launches, ending with a picnic on an island in the middle of the bay. A formal picture was taken by a photographer who had attended the courses. In every way they could, the course alumni made their guests feel welcome and turned the visit into a public occasion, which could serve to remind themselves and others in the town that Kakinada was committed as a community to developing itself rapidly in the economic sphere. Undoubtedly the visit served to recommit individuals, both publicly and privately, to the goals they had set for themselves. It also served to bring the group together, to reinforce bonds of friendship that had been formed at SIET Institute, and to make everyone realize that they had group as well as individual goals to achieve.

When the visitors left to inaugurate the courses in Vellore, as described in Chapter 4, they felt that many of the entrepreneurs of

Kakinada were deeply committed to improving business conditions locally.

Back in Hyderabad at SIET Institute, Shri Nadkarni, Dr. Berlew, and Dr. McClelland took stock of the business activity levels of each of the 52 course participants before and after the training, according to the scheme outlined in Table 2.1. The information available included business history questionnaires filled out at the beginning of the course, and a great deal of personal knowledge gathered about the participants during and after the course by Shri Nadkarni and by Drs. Berlew and McClelland. Since the time elapsed after the training was short, emphasis was naturally placed on planning activities (Category +1) rather than activities involving major financial changes (Category +2). In a report to Shri Jai, Principal Director of SIET Institute, dated February, 1965, Dr. McClelland summarized the results of this first attempt to evaluate the effects of the courses as follows:

> As of January 1965, a careful review of subsequent activities of the course participants showed that two thirds (36 out of 52) have been active either in promoting their own businesses or planning to establish new ones. The remaining one third (16 out of 52) have so far shown no discernible effects of the attempt to increase their entrepreneurial motivation.
>
> Is such a high rate of entrepreneurial activity above what one would expect under normal conditions? Would it be as high for any comparably selected group of entrepreneurs who had not taken the course? Ultimately we hope to get similar data for the same time period for another town and from other entrepreneurs in Kakinada who did not attend the course, but for the moment we must attempt to estimate whether the activity level recorded subsequent to the course was higher or lower than it had been in the previous year for the same person. Note that it is possible for a person to be scored high for entrepreneurial activity subsequent to the course and yet not show actual "improvement" if he had been expanding his activities prior to the course. There were several such cases. There were also several men who had just initiated some new activities in the year before the course so that they could not very well be scored again for "increased" activity in the period after the course. In other words, the course happened to fall at "favorable" or "unfavorable" periods so far as the development of particular individuals was concerned. But in a reasonably large sample, one would expect that these chance events would balance each other out and we may properly ask whether significantly more men were active immediately following the course than had been active in the two years preceding it.
>
> For such an analysis it seems best to restrict attention for the

moment to the thirty men involved in the first two courses, since only for them had enough time elapsed (8–10 months) for new economic activities to have been actually started. We decided to record (1) whether the person had undertaken concrete plans to expand his economic activities, e.g., by taking trips to investigate new products, writing for information, meeting with others to draw up plans for joint ventures, etc. Or (2) whether he had undertaken some new or some special economic activity which had resulted in expansion of his personal or business income. In the two years prior to the course 13 out of the 30 men (43%) had shown activities which could be classified under either (1) or (2). In the eight to ten months after the course 21 out of the 30 men (70%) had shown increased entrepreneurial activity, an increase of 27% which could hardly have arisen by chance. ($\chi^2 = 4.2$, p $< .05$).

These figures refer almost entirely to Category $+ 1$ activities undertaken either before or after the course. In the final evaluations reported in the next chapter, the emphasis shifted almost exclusively to Category $+ 2$ activities, i.e., business changes with major financial impact. Furthermore the information obtained later in the spring of 1967 was much more accurately dated and sifted for errors of various kinds. Thus the later, more accurate figures show that only five out of the thirty men should have been classified as active before the course as contrasted with the 13 mentioned in this memorandum. The discrepancy is explained by the tighter definition of "planning" adopted in the final evaluation. If the looser definition used in January, 1965, were applied to the information available in the final evaluation, ten out of thirty of the men in the first two courses would be judged as involved in some planning activity before the course. The remaining three, judged to have been active at the time but not later, were all men who were reputed to be active and successful, but whose unusual activities turned out on more careful examination to date from a period prior to the two years before the course. Thus the activity levels of the businessmen before the course were slightly exaggerated in January, 1965, but the error was in the conservative direction. What happened after the course, on the other hand, was much more carefully scrutinized and better known, although in the final analysis much of the planning activity reported at every evaluation visit was simply disregarded. It was hard to evaluate how serious it was and how much it represented the individual's need to tell the visitor that he was living up to his obligation to become active.

Nevertheless, this early report on increased planning had an important morale-building function, so far as the project itself was concerned. The information was fed back to the participants themselves and to the staff at SIET Institute as concrete evidence that there already was an increased level of activity in the town, even though some of the early reports had been discouraging. Furthermore, several individuals reported that their behavior had been markedly influenced by the course. For instance, a bank manager reported that before the course he had been primarily interested in the security provided for a loan. He said that during the course he realized that he ought also to evaluate the quality of the man applying and the likelihood that the project for which he wanted the loan would succeed. He had begun acting on these new principles since the course, and reported with pride that the business of his commercial loan department had increased so markedly that he had received a special letter of commendation from his superior. Another man had helped start a ceramics factory in Hyderabad. One man had opened a new factory, as noted in Chapter 4. The proprietor of a cycle shop was making plans to manufacture bicycle stands locally, rather than import them from a distance. Three course participants, a banker, a manager, and a craftsmen, had joined in planning a small unit to manufacture handmade paper. The palmyra fiber processers and exporters were talking about finding ways of making finished palmyra fiber products locally, since they realized that it didn't make business sense to export the raw materials to Japan where they were made into brushes that were then sold back to India. While Dr. McClelland noted in his report to Shri Jai that these changes or prospective changes might have an impact on the community in the long run, larger effects ought to come from several more elaborate plans, which were then under active consideration.

> One group is working on plans for a new foundry to make castings for which there is a local demand. Another is designing an industrial estate for the town. Still another group of about five men have been very active in looking for new industries that might be started in Kakinada. They have corresponded extensively with firms and government agencies, and have taken trips to investigate concrete possibilities for making new products. Most of these plans are being worked on by sub-groups within the Kakinada Entrepreneurs Association which was set up explicitly by the alumni of these courses to promote the activities they were committed to undertake.
>
> One of the main effects of the courses seemed to have been to bring together small informal groups of men who are encouraging and helping each other to plan new activities. One prosperous money-lender is being urged by his friends to invest in the industrial estate, despite the greater risk involved for him. Several of the most active entrepreneurs in the town are "outsiders" (a

Sindhi cloth merchant, two overseas businessmen returned from Burma, a migrant from Kerala, etc.) who have become "insiders" by attending the course in company with members of the established families in the town. In any case, in the course of my visit to Kakinada I was greatly impressed by the commitment and eagerness of most of the course alumni to do something both individually and collectively.

On the basis of these generally encouraging trends, Dr. McClelland's report recommended that SIET Institute not only try to complete the original training plan by offering a similar set of courses for Vellore and Akola, but also arrange for a continuous research evaluation of progress made in all of the three cities and provide enough staff time to make sure that training materials were continuously revised, field visits to the communities involved were regularly undertaken, and policy implications of the project were written up for presentation to governmental authorities. Since the project had been largely under the direction of psychologists, it was considered important to add to the staff an economist-sociologist, who would be more knowledgeable about tracing the economic and social effects of planned community change. Finally, to insure a continued high-level direction of the program, the report recommended that Shri Nadkarni be brought to the United States for a year for further training and that one of the regular Ford Foundation consultants to SIET Institute be someone with interest and experience in this area. Of all of these recommendations only Shri Nadkarni's visit to the United States was actually carried out. The training was discontinued after the first two courses at Vellore. Shri Jai resigned as Principal Director, and his successor Shri P.D. Malgavkar, recommended that the project be discontinued as an activity of SIET Institute (as of the Fall of 1965).

Mr. Harry Lasker's Visit

Consequently, considerable improvisation was necessary to carry through the schedule of a follow-up visit every six months, from 1965 to 1967. Relationships with the businessmen in Kakinada and Vellore remained good and they continued to regard themselves as part of an ongoing project, whatever SIET Institute's attitude might be. Thus they gave a very warm welcome to another visitor from Harvard, Mr. Harry Lasker, when he arrived in July and August, 1965, to undertake the second set of follow-up interviews for Kakinada and the first set for Vellore. Mr. Lasker had been studying contemporary Indian society at

Harvard and had decided to do a senior thesis on whether traditional religious beliefs and practices interfered with business development among those who had attended the courses. It has been frequently argued that traditionalism in its various guises is one of the main obstacles to rapid economic growth. Here was an opportunity to see whether in fact it was the most traditional participants in the course who changed least afterwards. So he constructed a long questionnaire-interview on traditionalism, which he administered to the course alumni in Vellore and Kakinada while getting their reports on their activities in the past six months.

With the assistance of Shri Krishna Kumar, a researcher associated with Dr. Pareek at SIET Institute, Mr. Lasker was able to interview 25 of the 26 course alumni in Vellore in only two and one-half days. Despite his comparative youth, he was well received. He found that the Entrepreneurs Association was not functioning particularly well, as it had not in Kakinada earlier. He observed that the men in Vellore had not yet developed the group spirit which seemed to characterize Kakinada. There was still a split between the first and second batches trained from Vellore and less willingness to consult with other members of the Entrepreneurs Association. However, it was his overall impression that the traditional distrust among Indian businessmen had been diminished by experiences together at SIET Institute.

> One of the most significant unsought by-products of the training was the fact that men who had shops along the same bazaar met, communicated and became friends for the first time. There is no doubt that there is a hard core of the Entrepreneurs Association who are now very close friends, and who, in the future, could easily pool their resources to start new industries. As far as I could tell this is a dramatic change from the way life has been conducted in Vellore in the recent past. There is reason to believe that this group spirit is a characteristic by-product of the courses. . . . There is great enthusiasm for a third and fourth course. Men were genuinely disappointed when I revealed to them that the courses would not be coming soon, and I believe it would be easy to recruit at least another two groups from Vellore.
>
> . . . A group of four men in widely diversified fields—an auto mechanic, a photographer, and two others—financed [a] trip to Madras where they talked with officials of the Small Industries Service Institute to come to some understanding of what types of industries could be set up in Vellore. They have three possibilities they are considering at present—iron casting, sugar refining, and shoe making. Their rather well planned approach to trying to understand what types of industries can be started in Vellore con-

trasts with the tendency of men everywhere to decide to begin a business without proper study and guidance. I was perhaps most intrigued by a young man of about twenty-five who had completely reorganized and made much more efficient his father-in-law's business of manufacturing ceramic sinks after he had returned from the course. The sinks were produced by making molds which were fired in the kiln and later glazed. Before the course apparently 50% of the sinks produced in this small factory in Vellore cracked in some point of the process and had to be scrapped. I saw a large heap of them piled up behind the factory. The young man did some research to see if there was some other way to make sinks which would result in less cracking and discovered that sinks could be produced by pressing instead of molding. The new technique proved not only more effective in that fewer sinks cracked in the firing process but also more economical in that it took less time to produce a sink ready to be fired. The son-in-law has also figured out a way to make use of the sinks which are cracked in the process of firing and is selling some of them at lower prices so that they are not completely going to waste.

. . . There is in my opinion little doubt that the courses have had an effect on the participants from Vellore. It is too early to assess the full extent of this effect or its duration, but there are unmistakable signs that things have changed.

However, he felt that in the long run changes in Vellore would be considerably less marked than in Kakinada, partly because fewer men had been trained, and partly because the opportunities for industrial expansion were considerably less favorable than in Kakinada.

In Kakinada small factories and industries are rather common. Foundries were owned by several men who had participated in the courses and there are at least two very large scale industries in the town. In Vellore, however, the situation is quite different. The vast majority of business people are employed in commerce and industrial know-how seems lacking. Only a few members of the two batches from Vellore were involved in any type of small industry. Thus, innovative behavior in Vellore may well be limited primarily to commerce where the effects on employment and investment will be less conspicuous.

Subsequently in Kakinada, Mr. Lasker, with the help of Shri Kumar, managed to interview forty of the fifty-one course alumni in one week. (One had died the previous autumn.) Here, too, he was welcomed cordially and made a speech bringing greetings from Dr. McClelland and outlining possibilities for future growth and expansion. He found that many of the plans discussed with Dr. McClelland six months earlier had developed further; some had been abandoned; and new ones were being considered. For instance, the following possibilities were mentioned to him by various businessmen in Kakinada.

> A paper mill, a solvent factory, a brick factory, a new foundry, a starch factory, a pharmaceutical plant, a cement factory, a unit to assemble umbrellas and another to print theatre tickets for Delhi and Jaipur. These various plans are in different stages of development. All the entrepreneurs concerned have at least secured detailed information about the machinery needed and the economics of the unit concerned and have usually consulted with the Small Industries Service Institute. Some men have actually purchased land. Although there is a tendency to talk in very optimistic terms among the men I interviewed, I believe that perhaps half of the projects just listed actually will get started in the next year.

As it turned out, this estimate was far too optimistic.

Typical of Mr. Lasker's report are his remarks on the reactions of a middle-aged, wealthy theater owner.

> He said that he felt very deeply the philosophical effects of the course. He felt that he had been "bitten" and "awakened" by the philosophy of the course and that he tries to put more hours into his work now and to make better use of his profits so that "they will benefit him and his nation." More specifically he has begun three different projects at the same time which are entirely new activities for him. The first is an attempt to manufacture cement products in Kakinada. He has visited the SISI in Hyderabad and talked with men about the promise of starting such a manufacturing unit. He is now applying for permits to begin the industry, and has interested two other businessmen in investing in the project. Secondly, he gathered information at the same SISI in Hyderabad about a more simple industry that he himself could control entirely and he is thinking about attempting to assemble umbrellas. He decided upon this project because he wanted something that he could supervise himself which would not require a major investment. His third project is to start printing cinema tickets locally not only for his own theatres but for others in Delhi and Jaipur. He believes there is a good market for tickets and since he is already in the theatre business, he is in a position to know about the problems of marketing theatre tickets. I was surprised at the depth with which he seemed to be moved by the ideas he had been exposed to in the training courses. He has undoubtedly taken them to heart and is almost religiously trying to fulfill them.

Mr. Lasker also coded the activities of all the men he contacted and again estimated that about 70 per cent of them were involved in extensive planning for expanded business activities.

Mr. Lasker happened to visit Kakinada shortly after a major community calamity, which evoked a rather unexpected response from the Kakinada Entrepreneurs Association. "In July of 1965 a fire destroyed about 300 homes and left something like 3,000 people homeless and without possessions." The president of the association and one other member were very active among the small group that took initiative to raise nearly Rs. 8,000 within a few days, to provide clothing for those who had lost everything in the fire. Much of it was raised by going from door to door, so that something like a thousand donors contributed to the total. New clothes were provided quickly for all the victims of the fire. Mr. Lasker felt that this action was part of a growing community consciousness among the members of the Kakinada Entrepreneurs Association, resulting from the ideology of their training. That is, while the achievement motivation development courses had sometimes been criticized for helping "selfish" businessmen to get richer, the ideology of the course had stressed not making money for selfish ends, but investing to develop the community and the nation. Apparently some key members of the courses had caught the idea and felt that the fire, even though it did not represent a personal loss to them, did represent a setback for the community which they should do everything they could to overcome.

Mr. Joel Cohen's Visit

The next evaluation visit was also the result of a happy coincidence, as Mr. Lasker's had been, since by this time the project had no staff either in India or in the United States. On his graduation, Mr. Joel Cohen was awarded a traveling fellowship by Harvard University and decided to take a trip around the world to investigate a variety of research stations primarily dealing with primate social behavior. However, he also wanted an introduction to field research in India and agreed to serve as our emissary to interview the Kakinada participants for the third time and the Vellore participants for the second time. His main task was simply to ask them what progress they had made in their business plans since the last visit, but he also asked a number of questions about the nature and composition of their families, in view of our growing interest in whether family structure could inhibit independent action. He inquired about the persistence of friendships formed during the course, since they seemed to be a possible source of help and encouragement for a new venture.

He went first to Kakinada where he was warmly received and managed to interview 43 of the 51 course alumni beginning in the last week of December, 1965. He wrote as follows:

> Once the entrepreneur is located, the interview takes from one to two hours. The interviews at the place of business take longer because of constant interruptions from customers and visiting friends. The interviews in my room here and at the homes of the entrepreneurs are much more straightforward. Working from 8:30 in the morning to 10:30 or 11:00 at night I have been able so far to manage four or five interviews a day. The secretary of the Kakinada Entrepreneurs Association has been extremely helpful; he shepherded me around on his motor scooter all day yesterday, and has been sending people to my room.
>
> I must admit that I've enjoyed the interviewing immensely. Even though it's sometimes frustrating to try to get to the entrepreneurs, even though it's sometimes a little boring to sit while a long answer is being written out, still I've always wanted just to drop in to a strange town and find out what people are thinking and talking about, what they have been doing and what they want to be doing, how they see themselves and what they think of others. Interviewing these entrepreneurs, and talking with them before and after the interviews, gives me a chance to do just some of these things. It's exhausting, but great fun.
>
> My estimate of the net result or effect of the courses within the last six months in Kakinada in this: for a few individuals, mostly young, the course is a conversion experience; for the first time they thought about goals and action toward the goals; the course had a pervasive and more beneficial effect on their business activity within the last six months and probably will continue its effect in the future. For a much larger group of young to middle-aged men, the course has generated a great deal of talk among themselves about planning; it has also led to several actual site visits to factories which are being considered for purchase; and in a favorable environment may lead to some really considerable business action in the next six months. For another large group of men, the course either had no effect or generated only lip service and an occasional guilt feeling when somebody from Harvard comes around.

Mr. Cohen's summary views are quoted not because they were accurate in particulars, but because they represented the impression an objective visitor would get from visiting the town at this time. He had no strong preconceptions as to the value of the project nor experience with social-science research. In fact, his major interests were in applied mathematics and music. Nevertheless, he captured very well the pleasure that all visitors felt in visiting these towns and the general sense that something was going on of considerable importance.

Three major historical events were agitating the local community at the time of his visit. First, border disputes with China and Pakistan had aroused a great deal of patriotic sentiment throughout India. In Kakinada, the secretary of the Entrepreneurs Association had organized a rifle club which a number of the entrepreneurs attended regularly to get practice in shooting. There was a feeling of excitement in the air; people felt locally that they wanted to do something to show their solidarity with their country in its confrontation with China and Pakistan. To a certain extent this excitement distracted some of the men from their concern for business expansion.

The second major event was a boycott declared on October 25, 1965, by the Japan Control Association of palmyra fiber importers and dealers against fifteen of the nineteen Kakinada shippers of palmyra fiber to Japan. Cohen writes:

> These fifteen shippers were boycotted for shipments which were damaged due to rotting and which were excessively short in weight, both offenses resulting from adding water to the fibre before sending it off. At least two of the trained entrepreneurs are on the list of fifteen. . . . I learned of the boycott from an entrepreneur who is one of their competitors who was elated because his firm was not on the list of those boycotted.
>
> His elation in my opinion is premature. Near the end of its letter, the Association says, "we believe that a strict quality control on your side is absolutely necessary to maintain the market share of palmyra fibres in Japan because, as you probably know, several consumers are already looking for suitable synthetic substitutes of an even running quality."

The local businessmen did know of these dangers. One of them showed Mr. Cohen two brooms in which the bristles were made of plastic.

> The bristles are not as stiff as the best palmyra fibre ones, but this seemed to me a meager difference on which to rest one's livelihood. I pointed out that it would probably require at the most another five years of chemical research to produce a plastic with the required stiffness; such a plastic would then be a very serious and probably successful competitor with Indian palmyra fibre. The problem is serious not only for those of our entrepreneurs in the fibre business, but for the whole city: I was told that perhaps

10,000 people are dependent for their livelihood on the industry in one way or another.

The actual news of the third event came my last full day in Kakinada, January 22nd, at the meeting of the Entrepreneurs Association which had been called for me to present impressions of what I had found in my interviews. The attendance was 19. To the surprise of everyone, one of those attending was the local member of the state legislative assembly (MLA). When I began to talk about the possibilities of port expansion to offset the possible palmyra losses, he rose and asked for permission to talk which I was glad to give him. He said he had just talked that morning with the District Port Officer, who had just returned from an all-India official meeting in Calcutta to decide about the development of ports on the East coast of India; it was decided at the meeting, he reported, that since it would cost Rs. 50 crores (1 crore = 10,000,000) to expand the other port to handle the ore flow beyond its present capacity, but would cost only Rs. 32 crores to develop Kakinada to handle the excess, an investment of Rs. 32 crores would be made in developing Kakinada into an all weather mechanical-loading port. Another man had earlier told me that some large amount had already been sanctioned for the purpose of a deep dredger to dredge a channel so that ships could come right into the harbor, and according to the MLA there will be direct loading from the railroad cars to the ocean vessels. The passage of two million tons of ore through the port won't sop up all available labor under this new system as it would under the present inefficient system of hand carrying from the railroad cars to small boats and hand loading from the boats to the big ships. Nevertheless the expansion and increased activity may probably bring increased prosperity to the city as a whole by the "trickle down theory" which may ameliorate the lives of those 10,000 people whose jobs now hang by a plastic thread. One immediate good effect his announcement did have: I had been talking about the wealth of good ideas the entrepreneurs had described to me for new ventures, new industries, new businesses, and how it was now necessary to go ahead and act on those ideas. The MLA then made the point that since the prosperity of Kakinada was now assured, the entrepreneurs could feel confident and could proceed with security. His presence there with that news then was a very lucky coincidence for the entrepreneurs, I think. The meeting ended with a general air of enthusiasm and preparedness for action.

This episode is a good illustration of the fluctuations of high hopes and deep disappointments that accompany economic progress in India. More than a year after this announcement, when Dr. Winter visited

Kakinada in the spring of 1967, most of the entrepreneurs felt that the port changes would be a long time in coming, if they came at all. There was no evidence that work on the port had begun and no certainty that the appropriation for it was either finally approved or planned. Nevertheless, one cannot be sure that the announcement made at the time did not influence individuals to make decisions that they might otherwise have postponed because of general uncertainty about the economic future of the city.

Mr. Cohen interviewed 22 of the 27 men in Vellore but came away with a negative impression as to what was happening there.

> As far as I can see, the training courses have had no observable effects here. Most of the entrepreneurs seem to look on the course, in the words of one of them, "as a jolly tour," a chance to see Hyderabad, get away from home, and little more. One man may be an exception, but then he left Vellore. Another intelligent man said there is no place for entrepreneurial behavior in government civil service. There is none of the fighting spirit there was among the Kakinada entrepreneurs; the Vellore Entrepreneurs Association, theoretically in existence, has not had a single business meeting since its foundation; its only meetings have been social dinners for guests or departing members. Of the three committees assigned to chart the course of the association, none have come forward to report.

It began to look as if we might get some clues as to how to increase entrepreneurial behavior by contrasting what was done in Kakinada with what was done in Vellore.

The Return Visit of Shri Nadkarni

After a year at Harvard University, Shri Nadkarni returned briefly to India during the summer of 1966, six months after Mr. Cohen's visit. He arranged to spend a considerable amount of time both in Kakinada and Vellore with Shri Kumar, who had accompanied Mr. Lasker on an earlier visit. He had not seen any of the men for over a year and was curious to find out what the long-term developments in the two cities had been. He did not bring any special new tests or questionnaires with him, but he held large meetings in both towns to explain recent developments in achievement motivation training in the United States, and he interviewed about 80 per cent of the men personally, some of them a number of times. He found that activity was continuing at a fairly high level;

that is, about two thirds of the men in Kakinada had been vigorously doing something, just as previous visitors had reported. He also discovered that more people were active in Vellore than Mr. Cohen had found on his earlier visit. But he concentrated primarily on trying to figure out just how the men had changed since he had first come to know them. He had one distinctive advantage over the other visitors. From years of experience, he knew in general what businessmen in cities like this were like and furthermore, he knew what these men in particular had been like when they came for training. Thus it seemed wise for him to try to define as carefully as possible ways in which they had changed, leaving the final statistical evaluation until later.

His first observation was that many of the men seemed to have a changed *perception of risk*. Before the course they had often had an idea for a new venture, but they felt that they could not undertake it, that somebody else would have to do it or help them do it. On this visit he found that "without any change in the objective situation, people had started seeing the same things as involving much less risk, and as something they could handle." He likened the situation to one in which a man hesitates to jump into deep water when he has just learned to swim. For days he may not be able to get himself to jump in. Then finally one day he acts, and finds himself in the water. Something has happened to change his perception of the risk involved. Shri Nadkarni felt the men were more willing to make investment decisions than they had been previously. The change seemed to be a result of the training they received in moderate risk-taking during the course. They had learned to minimize the real risks by studying the situation thoroughly before deciding, and then to act on their own initiative rather than waiting for someone else to take responsibility.

Some of the increased willingness to make decisions probably also came from a number of small working groups that had coalesced out of the training experience. Shri Nadkarni found that "small groups of three or four people would meet often in their houses or offices to discuss business. Previously similar small groups had met often, but for entertainment, not to discuss business or technical matters connected with business." He felt that this activity was as intense in Vellore as in Kakinada. "In Kakinada they are still hoping to make the Entrepreneurial Association itself a force in the town. In Vellore they are not looking upon the Entrepreneurial Association as an organization which can have an impact on the town. Rather it is the small group activity in Vellore, as in Kakinada, which has been mainly responsible for increased entrepreneurial activity." Within these small groups, the individuals trust each other more, go on trips together to explore new possibilities, and pool their skills at times to make new ventures possible.

When the men discussed their lives and what had happened over the past few years, he found that they could still talk about certain things they had done in achievement terms, but the type of achievement imagery involved was neither "competition with others," "unique accomplishment," nor "long-term involvement." These three aspects of the scoring definition for achievement imagery did not seem to have as much relevance for their actual lives as another aspect which might best be described as "proving oneself to oneself." The basic scoring definition for achievement imagery is "competition with a standard of excellence," and the standard of excellence in terms of which a person evaluates his performance varies considerably from person to person and situation to situation. A person may set up a standard of doing better than others, or sticking to something for a long period of time, or doing something different or unique. Here the standard was clearly overcoming difficulties or doubts, proving that one could do something despite all obstacles. The general tendency of Indians to be critical has already been mentioned. And these men had their share of doubts as to whether they could accomplish anything. After all, they had had considerable experience with critical family members, with friends who said they couldn't do it, with government which often delayed endlessly in acting on a request, and with partners who had misappropriated funds. The standard of excellence that seemed most relevant in this situation was proving that one could achieve in spite of all such concrete difficulties and the generally prevailing tone of pessimism.

Furthermore, they were more able to speak about specific difficulties that had to be overcome than they had been. Mehta (1967) has reported that imaginative stories written by Indian students almost never mention difficulties in the way of achieving a goal—whether the difficulties lie in the external world or in some inability of the person to function properly. It is almost as if many Indians are counterphobic about difficulties because there are so many of them. They are afraid that if they even mention difficulties, or think about them, they may fail. Rather, one overcomes difficulties by will power and concentration, by not thinking about them. But as McClelland has shown elsewhere (1961), those countries which are realistic about difficulties in their children's stories are the very ones which are most likely to develop more rapidly economically. Thus the achievement motivation training course had stressed the importance of facing difficulties realistically and trying to find ways to overcome them. Roughly two years later, Shri Nadkarni found that in fact the men were talking much more openly and concretely about difficulties that had to be overcome.

The nature of their achievement imagery had also changed in one other respect. Before the course, they had nearly all seen business success as being almost wholly materialistic and selfish. Thus they were somewhat ambivalent about pursuing it too seriously. In their hearts, many of them agreed with Chaudhuri that the pursuit of money is shameful at the highest moral level. It is best to do one's duty, if one's *dharma* is business, but not to pursue it too vigorously, since that would be a sign of selfishness and disregard for higher values in life, such as serving others. After the course more of the men saw increased business activity not primarily as a selfish way of making more money, but as a way to develop the whole community and ultimately, India. Thus Shri Nadkarni found that when they talked about doing something in business, they nearly always coupled it with the notion that they were doing something for the community. Some critics may regard this new stance as hypocritical, as a cover for their increased greed. But the critic would have to admit that a repeated expressed concern for the welfare of the community as a personal achievement goal is better than no such expressed concern. And in fact, in many cases it seemed to be leading men away from activities which would gain them more money more quickly (e.g., as in traditional money-lending) and toward more risky, long-term investments in industry, because industry would provide more employment in the town.

As a side effect of the participants' increased thinking about achievement and planning ahead, Shri Nadkarni wondered whether many of them weren't more imaginative in all respects than they had been before the course. He recognized that some of their increased imaginative fluency might have come from his growing intimacy with them, but nevertheless he felt that practice in thinking about achievement seemed to have generalized to other areas as well. The men seemed looser, more imaginative on all sorts of topics than they had been before the course.

Finally, he noted that some of the men who had been most enthusiastic during the course had done very little afterwards. Some of them just seemed to be interested in any new thing that comes along. They were fascinated by n Ach training at the time, but since then they had become equally enthusiastic about some other new idea.

"There are some people who are very eager for all kinds of development programs, that is, people who, if a new cult comes along, would be the first to go and embrace it." They may have a function in encouraging others at the outset, but in the long run they shift their interests elsewhere.

On the whole, the follow-up visits were successful either as training inputs or as a means of getting information as to what transpired after the training. The visits served to remind the participants of the project and of the need to show concrete results of the training. They brought people together for public meetings to get new information and to recommit themselves to their personal goals. The participants learned that others were continuously interested in them and expected change. Most of the men were personally interviewed on at least three of the four visits. For instance, in Kakinada 27, or over half of the people, were seen by all four visitors and 41, or 80 per cent, were seen by at least three of the visitors. Only two were not seen at all after the courses ended. The figures are roughly the same for Vellore. In each case the one or two who were not seen had moved away from town.

As the amount of factual information increased from successive visits, it became more and more evident that it did not provide a solid basis for evidence of changes in business activity levels. Reports gathered from the same man on the same business activity at different times yielded different results. For instance, Cohen's report on the plan to develop the port at Kakinada seemed very clear, detailed, and definite at the time he wrote it. Yet six months or a year later, no one seemed to know anything about it. In many cases this was not anyone's fault. It was just that plans that seemed definite at one time might suddenly have to change because of unforeseen events. A banker told one interviewer that he had invested Rs. 2 lakhs in a metal rerolling mill, but six months later he made no mention of it. It turned out when he was questioned about it in the final evaluation that he had not actually made the investment but was just on the verge of doing so in the next day or so. Then he found that licenses could not be obtained to open the mill and he was forced to abandon the project.

Consequently, it was necessary to go into all these matters in much greater detail in the final evaluation conducted in the spring of 1967 by Dr. Winter. To prepare for these interviews, he took with him a running record of what each man had reported when interviewed at different stages in the previous two to three years. These records also provide factual documentation as to what it was like to try to expand business activity in this section of India in the mid-1960s. A few cases will illustrate the process by which some individuals got into the statistical summaries of success to be reported in the next chapter or failed to do so. Details have been altered or omitted to prevent identification of individuals.

Sample Records of Business Developments
After the Course

Case 283 was a serious, hard-working, rather quiet partner in a machine sales and service firm. The record on his activities follows:

1/65

He reported that his plan for manufacturing glazes for pottery and other ceramics, conceived during the course, had fallen through. He had talked with prospective purchasers and calculated that it wasn't a very profitable business. Furthermore there was a government factory already making the necessary chemical compounds in Rajahmundry. So he had begun to think about the possibility of making graphite crucibles.

7/65

The plan to make crucibles had fallen through. He had had difficulty in obtaining licenses for graphite from the government, and he did not think there was a sufficient market anyway for the product. However, the turnover in his business had gone up markedly.

1/66

He was planning to improve his machine repair shop. Starting in 2/66 a new branch for the business is to be constructed in a nearby town at a cost of Rs. 50,000. The lease had been signed in 12/65. He also reported that he had been a partner in a rice mill in two nearby towns.

8/66

The branch was actually under construction and about to open.

This record is interesting but leaves much to be desired. It seems to show that the man tried setting up a couple of new businesses, but abandoned them in favor of expanding his original business. But how much of the expansion is actually due to his interest and participation? Exactly what kind of a "partner" is he in the business? Can he be credited with increased activity if the expansion in the firm's growth is really due to the activity of someone else? How large an increase in the firm's growth actually occurred? Was he active in managing the rice mills, and if so, when did he become active?

With questions like these suggested by the record, Dr. Winter was able to clear up 283's business history reasonably well. He had worked for three and one-half years for a company in Madras, but since he wanted to work on his own, he invested thousands of rupees in the machine repair shop in 1961. The additional capital had made it possible to improve the location of the business and add a repairs and spare parts division, of which he was in charge, and to get a distributorship for another product manufactured under license in India. (June, 1963, before the training.) Thus, he was clearly active before the course (score = + 2) and "in charge" of at least some important part of the firm's activities. He gave Dr. Winter the figures (shown in Table 6.1) on the firm for the past five years.

Table 6.1
Firm's Figures, Case 283

	1962	1964	1966
Capital (in Rs. 1000s)	80	90	150
Gross Income (in Rs. 1000s)	100	150–200	350
Employees	22	22	22
Hours a Day at Work	11	11	11

He noted that the increase in gross income between 1964 and 1966 (after the course) was due to getting the new distributorship, and since this had taken place before the course, it did not seem reasonable to give him credit for improvement. His firm had wanted to construct a new building where they were, but their principals in Bangalore had insisted they open a branch at the nearby town instead. They had originally planned to open the branch in 1967 or 1968, but they started earlier and the branch opened in November, 1966, the capital investment being considerably less than the Rs. 50,000 originally estimated. It is not clear that this advancing in the date of opening the new firm, or the decision to open it, is clearly attributable to anything 283 has done as a result of his achievement motivation training. However, after he had to abandon his plans for manufacturing glazes, or graphite crucibles, he expanded his present business to take on still another machine product which can be sold and serviced essentially with the same staff. The company had sold six of the new machines at the time of the interview and new capital had been raised from new partners, so that this activity seems to warrant giving him credit for starting something after the course (score = + 2). Clearly, here is an active man who is constantly searching for new types of business to start. His family owns land from which he derives some income, though the rice milling business is managed by his older brother. He thought at one time of manufacturing shredded coconut for chocolates in a nearby town where this brother had a rice mill, but the mill closed. He had been very active before the course and continued so afterwards, so that all the training can claim credit for is encouraging him to continue along lines he was already pursuing.

Case 285 is a printer whose firm prints cards, booklets, and stationery. His record follows (amounts and locations omitted to preserve confidentiality):

1/65
    He reported that his plan is to install a rotary press large enough to print three-color children's magazines in the state's language. He is also actively planning to expand his book-selling business.

7/65
    Routine business improvement.

1/66
    He is thinking of moving to a site purchased in 10/64 after the course. In 9/65 he purchased a new flat-bed platen press, foot-treadle operated for Rs.————. In 10/65 he had applied to the State Electricity Board for a three-phase, ten horsepower connection. The press is still at G———— where it was purchased. It will be installed at the new site if the building is constructed there. The press will print in three colors as planned.

8/66
    Business for his press is increasing and now requires two shifts. He still wants to remodel his building and move the press purchased in G———— to the new site. He is planning to start a type foundry.

Dr. Winter confirmed these developments and added additional information. He had actually been running the press since 1942, when he took it over from an older brother who had gone into military service. But little had happened of particular importance since that time. The firm had continued small. It had supplied him with a reasonably good living when supplemented by income from family land. Since the course, he has been definitely more active, though not nearly so much as he would like to be. The press he purchased remains at G————, where it is operating under its own name employing four workers. He wants to move it to the new site he purchased, but it is in the suburbs and must first be incorporated into the town electricity and water connections. The commissioner's approval is necessary and that apparently must wait until after the municipal elections. He wants to purchase a rotary press, which requires an import license and foreign exchange. A friend from the course offered to help him with this, and he plans to go ahead as soon as he can raise Rs. 100,000 in a government loan, but he does not feel he should apply for the loan until he has managed to incorporate the new press into his present business. The type foundry also requires imported materials, so that he has not been able to proceed on it, either. He believes the government will lift the printing machinery import ban in April, 1967.

The figures he gave for his current business are as follows:

Table 6.2
Firm's Figures, Case 285

	1962	1964	1966
Capital (in Rs. 1000s)*	15	15	15
Turnover (in Rs. 1000s)	20	20–25	30–35
Profit (Index Number)	100	125	180
Employees	3	4	6
Hours a Day at Work	8–9	8–9	8–9

* Invests Rs. 3–4,000 annually to replace type.

In many ways, the history of 285's activities is typical of what the course was supposed to accomplish, what it did accomplish, and the difficulties that an increasingly active man runs into. He set some new goals for himself after the course, which he had pursued more-or-less vigorously. His larger plans have not yet really come to fruition, for a variety of reasons, although he has taken at least one definite step toward realizing them. On the other hand, his own business seems to be benefitting somewhat from his increased activity. Larger developments seem to depend on whether he can get his new site incorporated into the municipality, a risk which may be too large for him to have undertaken. On the other hand, he is already beginning to explore the possibility of locating a branch in a nearby town where the municipality has shown an interest in helping him.

Case 292 is a cloth merchant who moved to this part of India several years ago. By the time of the course he owned a fairly large dry goods store.

1/65

He reported that he had started taking his business more seriously himself, since previously he had left it pretty much to his assistants. His business has improved. He is preparing to invest in some new business and is discussing possibilities regularly with other course participants.

7/65

Since his business is already well established and operating more efficiently, he has been giving more time to social service.

He was active in collecting money and finding clothing for victims of the fire.

1/66

His own business continues to improve markedly. He is a key man in the group of five course participants who are actively thinking about buying a leather processing factory in Yanam. The same group also wants to build a steel rerolling mill. They have figured out that since the iron ore comes through the port of Kakinada anyway, the raw materials are present and there is a good market for steel. They have settled how many shares each will purchase in the joint venture. They had located a technical man at Tata Steel who was to come and get the project going, but at the last moment he decided to stay where he was. So the whole project is still pending.

8/66

He has opened a branch at a nearby city, turning the management over to his son. He is thinking of expanding his present shop into a department store in the near future.

As Dr. Winter determined in his final interview, this man had always been a good businessman, since he had built his shop up from very small beginnings in 1949 to its present position. In 1955 he had doubled the size of his premises and in 1960 had moved to the current location, which was larger still. However, from 1960 to the time of the course, the turnover, the number of workers, and the profit had remained more-or-less stable. He had turned his attention primarily to other matters. After the course, in the period 1964–66 his gross income increased 40 per cent, the number of workers from eight to twelve, and his gross profit 70 per cent. He attributes the sharp upturn in business to many factors, all of them in some way depending on what he learned in the course. (1) In December, 1966, he invested in a new sari section for the shop which upped gross income 30 per cent. (2) He replaced six staff members and hired better ones. (3) He radically changed his dealings with his staff: "I don't keep any secrets from them now." He tells his staff what the cloth costs him, lets them set prices, and consults them on what to stock, so that dead stock is no longer a problem. "Even the small boy who is drawing Rs. 50 knows how much my profit margin is." (4) He reduced store hours so that staff would be motivated to work harder during a shorter work day. Gross income is up even with the shorter hours. (5) He spends more time outside the shop in clubs, activities, personal contacts, "promoting relations," because he says this definitely helps business. Also, he has become less suspicious of other merchants: the general policy in town is to be wary when a competitor enters the store. He is hospitable, explains things, and shows his stock. This helps the other man, doesn't hurt him, and builds good will. He feels he is very different from other shopkeepers in the town in this respect.

While this man's personal business has greatly improved, he has by no means achieved his goal. As the record shows, he was one of the leaders in the small group that was determined to set up a moderate-sized new industry for the town. Yet, so far, extensive negotiations and hard work in studying markets, production possibilities, and finance have still been unable to get such an industry going. The negotiations for the leather factory and the steel rerolling mill both fell through, though there is still some hope that the latter project may be revived if a man with the necessary technical skills can be found.

These case records illustrate most of the key characteristics of the information collected about business activities after the courses. Many of the men started working much harder after the course. They explored new plans for starting businesses, most of which came to nothing, either because the ideas did not prove to be profitable, because they could not get the necessary permissions, or because they were not as involved in carrying out the plan as they were in assuring the interviewers they were trying to do something. Generally speaking, the men were better able to expand their own businesses than they were to start new ones or to collaborate in introducing major new enterprises. Many of the reports given to the interviewers involved very complex business and family relationships, the dates and exact natures of which needed careful examination. It was particularly difficult to determine in many cases whether the man himself was responsible for what he reported. For instance, Case 294 said that after returning from the course he suggested to his boss (the proprietor) that he should start a sugar factory, making the machinery at the plant at the engineering works where 294 was a salaried supervisor. The proprietor did as he suggested and invested over Rs. one lakh in building a sugar mill in a rural location not far from the town. Production began in late 1964, with 40 to 50 workers and four staff members. He was involved to the extent that it was his idea and he supervised making the machinery as part of his regular job. Could he get credit for this increase in business activity? We decided that he could not because it was not his final decision, his money, or his company. The course may have contributed to this development, but since we could not be sure of how much a participant had contributed to the decision, it seemed more conservative not to give him or the course credit for it.

The final evaluation, the results of which will be presented in the next chapter, was designed to conduct a thorough investigation into all such matters, to get as precise information as possible under the circumstances. Clearly most of the men were trying harder, but what, in the end, did they accomplish?

CHAPTER 7

EFFECTS OF THE COURSE: STATISTICAL SUMMARIES

What effects did the achievement motivation development courses have on their participants? A variety of quantitative data concerning these effects will be presented in this chapter, while Chapter 8 will describe in more detail the ways in which some participants made changes and improvements in their businesses. Such accounts of the plans, problems, and achievements of individual men will give life to the figures and tables presented in this chapter. However, it is important first to demonstrate formally the extent and magnitude of the changes.

The data for these two chapters were taken from information collected during the final, intensive, follow-up interviews mentioned in Chapter 6. During the period March–May, 1967, interviews were conducted with 74 course participants[1] and 73 controls in the groupings described in Chapter 4. The interviews were conducted by Dr. David Winter, usually accompanied by Dr. Sara Winter and Shri V. Krishna Kumar, a research assistant who had accompanied Mr. Lasker and Shri Nadkarni on previous interviews. In most cases the interviews were held

1. Originally 78 people were trained. One died shortly after the course. Two were unavailable, but information about them was obtained from other businessmen in the community or from relatives. One was unavailable and no information could be obtained about him. Thus, usable information was gathered on 76 participants.

at the subject's place of business. Most were conducted in English, although in a very few cases it was necessary to work partly in Telugu or Tamil. Interviews lasted between 30 minutes and an hour and a half.

The procedure for each interview will be described in some detail. The interviewers appeared at the place of business, introduced themselves, and asked to talk with the subject. Sometimes the subject was busy or out, and so additional visits, often preceded by telephone calls, were necessary. The course participants immediately recognized the names and purposes of the interviewers, and so after a few minutes of greeting, offers of refreshments, and general conversation, the interview itself began. However, specific steps were taken to establish rapport with the control subjects. Those in Kakinada and Vellore had usually heard something about the courses or "the Harvard University project." Those from Rajahmundry had been interviewed by Shri Kumar one year before, and they recognized him. The first step with all control subjects was to hand them a printed business card giving the name and Harvard University relationship of the interviewer. The next step was to say that the interviewer was engaged in a study of economic development in the town, through talking with proprietors and managers of individual firms. Subjects were then given a letter of introduction, typed on Harvard University stationery and signed by Dr. McClelland. After they had read the letter, they usually asked: "Why do you want to talk with me?" or "What do you want to know?" The interviewer explained that he and several other businessmen from the town had been selected randomly. He very carefully explained that the project had no connection with the government, and that any information and especially figures on an individual or a firm would be treated as confidential and would never appear publicly or be shown to any government official. In all cases but a few, this introduction quickly established a cooperative and open atmosphere for the interview, which then proceeded.[2]

The questions naturally varied according to the situation. However, the following outline was the basis for each interview, and the specific questions listed below were asked in some form during each interview:

1. (History of the firm) Who founded this firm? When? What did it make or sell? What was the initial investment? How many employees did it have?

2. (Personal history) When did you join the firm? What was your title and what were your duties then? What changes in title and duties

2. The interviewers were in fact pleasantly surprised at the ease with which rapport could be built up, confirming the impressions of Berna (1960, p. 227).

have you had up to now? (If subject previously worked with another firm, ask these same questions about that job, and so on back to his first job.)

3. What changes have there been in this firm since it was founded, e.g., new units, new branches, new products, new machinery, new marketing techniques, expansions, investments?

(Ask the same question, probing more intensively, for the time period from 1960 to the present.)

When did this change happen? (Get month and year.)

Who had the idea? Who gave the approval? When was the change finally carried out?

(Probe on how much the subject had to do with this change.) What was the additional investment required?

4. What are the figures in 1966, 1964, and 1962[3] for the firm on the following items:

   Number of workers, including staff

   Total capital invested in the firm

   Total gross income or sales ("turnover") for that year

(If there are any changes in any of these figures from one date to the next, probe on why this change occurred. If the answer involves a major change as mentioned in question 3 above, get the details on such change.)

5. What are the present problems facing the firm? What are you doing about them?

6. What plans do you have for the firm? When will you carry out this plan?

7. Do you have any other sources of income; any other businesses?

8. What other activities, outside of your work, do you have—clubs, organizations, civic activities, charities?

Notes were taken during the interview and at the end of each day were written up into a report on each subject. The data to be presented below are taken from these reports.

Since the interviews are the principal source of data for the analyses and interpretations which follow, it is worthwhile to inquire how reliable the information reported in the interviews may be. The first issue is the accuracy of recollection of the subjects who were interviewed. Despite all the repeated testing and interviewing, unfortunately it did not prove possible to estimate, as fully as we had hoped, the accuracy of figures comparing the answers to the same questions asked on two different

3. For subjects in Vellore, the figures were obtained for the years 1967, 1965, and 1963.

occasions. It became apparent immediately that the financial data supplied on questionnaires by the course participants at the time that they started training at SIET Institute could not be compared with what they said in 1967 about the earlier period, because we could not tell which of their various enterprises many of them had chosen to provide financial data on for the questionnaires. Furthermore, the previous interviewers had not collected sufficiently precise financial data to permit checks on the reliability of the participants' memories. This left only the figures by interview obtained on two different occasions from the businessmen in Rajahmundry. Some of the figures were directly comparable. In March, 1966, Shri Kumar asked the participants to estimate what their business worth and gross income had been one year previously, i.e., in 1965. In April, 1967, Dr. Winter asked them for the same estimates as of two years previously. Since the queries both referred to the same time period (spring, 1965), the figures should be the same.

Eighteen men gave comparable estimates of 1965 capital worth on the same two subsequent occasions. The median absolute variation in estimate was 18 per cent. In 1966 their estimates of capital worth averaged Rs. 1.44 lakhs for 1965; in 1967, their estimates averaged Rs. 1.33 lakhs for the same time period. In other words, the more time that had elapsed since the period for which the estimates were being given, the lower the amount of capital they thought they had had in that period. Four gave exactly the same figure on the two occasions; nine gave a lower figure in 1967 than they had in 1966, and five gave a higher figure in 1967 than they had in 1966. But the average variation with sign taken into account is not great, being about 8 per cent.

Seventeen men gave comparable annual gross income figures on the two occasions. The median absolute variation in the estimates was 10 per cent, although two gave such greatly different figures that one suspects they had different business aggregates in mind. In 1966 they estimated their annual gross income to have averaged Rs. 1.34 lakhs for 1965; in 1967 their estimates for 1965 averaged Rs. 1.65 lakhs. As time went on they remembered their gross income as larger than they did in a previous year. In 1967, ten of them gave a larger estimate for their gross income in 1965 than they had in 1966, as contrasted with only three who gave a smaller estimate, and four who gave exactly the same figure on the two occasions.

In general one might conclude that estimates of capital vary within 20 per cent and decrease somewhat with elapsed time, whereas estimates of annual gross income vary within 10 per cent and increase somewhat with elapsed time. Unfortunately, no data permitted comparisons of current figures with estimates given later. So the errors are probably overestimated by our procedures here. Could these variations and time trends affect the conclusions to be drawn from the figures given in the 1967 interviews?

If subjects distort, and especially if they distort in such a way as to make their present performance more impressive, what will the effects be? Consider the data about capital investment, employees, gross income, and hours worked per day. Only the figures given in the 1967 interview will be used in subsequent tables. That is, these data for all subjects for all periods were gathered at the same time. Therefore, even though memory has distortion effects, it should not affect the validity of the comparison between course participants and controls. All men should remember gross income as relatively larger long ago than recently. However, it may be argued that the course participants would be more likely to distort current gross income in a favorable direction, since they were interviewed before, and since they have positive feelings about the course. Two things can be said in reply: (1) The interviewers tried to pin everyone down to specific facts and figures. In every case where appropriate, claims were checked and photographs taken of the actual improvement. (2) The position of the control subjects deserves careful consideration. In Kakinada and Vellore, they knew about the course, and might have been likely to distort their performances in a favorable direction so as to prove that they were "just as good" as the participants. The controls in Rajahmundry had been interviewed a year before, so that, as in Kakinada, their previous claims could be checked. Furthermore, the interviews were introduced as part of a project at Harvard University. The interviewers presented business cards and showed a letter of introduction from Harvard University. The study was explained as a study of the growth of firms in the community. It is certainly possible that if the course participants were biased, this explanation induced the control subjects to bias their answers in a favorable direction also. Obviously there is no sure guarantee of the reliability of the figures in the present study. In field research of this kind, one does what one can.

Measures of Increased Business Activity

The strategy of the project was to train a cross-section of men who were significant in the economic life of a town. As a result, the two groups of participants and the three control groups are very heterogeneous. They include men from foundries; men from firms that gather, process, pack, and export palmyra fiber; men from various small manufacturing firms; wholesale dealers; and retail merchants. There are also a few bankers. Most of the men are in charge of their firms, but some are younger partners who will not be making major business decisions for another few years. A few are salaried employees of national or regional firms. Thus it is apparent that the economic activities of all these men are not directly comparable. There is no one measure that can be used in every case, as increments in salary or number of promotions could be used to compare the employees of the large American company discussed in Chapter 2. A system for scoring business activity levels during a given time period from reports of a man's life and job performance was introduced in Chapter 2 to handle this same problem, in comparing managers from many different companies and with different kinds of jobs in Bombay, Mexico, Japan, and elsewhere. This scoring system was designed to reduce the activities of heterogeneous groups to a comparable measure, so that those who had received achievement motivation training could be compared with a control group. The scoring system specifies four different levels of business activity, each of which is defined by several specific, alternative criteria. These criteria are specific enough so that the coder can decide from a report whether the man has fulfilled them or not. They provide a rough measure of that man's economic or entrepreneurial effectiveness for two reasons: (1) They assess his own responsibility because they apply to that man's actions and not just events in the life of the firm, and (2) they are made up of actions that are likely to have an impact upon the economic performance of the firm.

While this system has advantages for comparing businessmen from diverse positions, it was developed primarily for managers in large corporations, and so had to be extended to fit the typical activities of proprietors and managers of small firms. Table 7.1 gives the extended activity level scoring system. This system was applied to the report on every subject, with course participants and controls mixed together to make sure that the standards of judgment were not shifting during the scoring. Activity level scores were assigned on the basis of specific statements or actions recorded in the reports; however, it is obvious that a good deal of knowledge of local conditions was necessary in order to understand and interpret these statements. Each subject was given an activity level score for the period of two years before the course and for the period of two years after the course. For the course participants, the actual date of the course was the dividing point. For control subjects

Table 7.1

Additional Criteria Used in Applying the Business Activity Level Scale in Kakinada, Rajahmundry, and Vellore (Also Consult Table 2.1)

Events Scored as −1

1. Responsible for major decrease in his firm's figures, failure or closing of the firm.

Events Scored as 0

1. Business failure, but man takes corrective action.
2. Reorganization of the firm, if for tax purposes or out of necessity; splitting up of joint family firm.
3. Routine decoration of shop or replacement of machinery.
4. Purchase of shares of stock or other investment for income only, i.e., a business in which the man is not actively involved.
5. Getting a new agency, unless it involves special trouble and initiative.

Events Scored as +2

1. Establishing a new business (not merely separation or re-organization of a prior business for tax or family purposes).
2. Expansion of the firm: new branches, new products, new machinery, new procedures. Does not include buying land or even machinery *per se*, unless it is definitely related to some planned activity of the man.

GENERAL NOTES:

1. If three people go into business together, all three get +2.
2. Do not score men who have a reputation of being a "successful businessman" as +1 or +2 just on the basis of their ability or reputation.
3. Activities are scored for the time period in which they are actually begun, and not just thought about. Often this is the time period in which some money is spent.

from Kakinada and Rajahmundry, June 1, 1964 was arbitrarily selected as the dividing point, since it fell between the second and third Kakinada courses. For control subjects from Vellore, April 1, 1965 was selected as the dividing point since it fell between the first and second Vellore courses. In the tables presented in this chapter, the period after the course will be labeled for convenience as 1964–66; but it should be understood that for all Vellore subjects, this period is actually 1965–67.

These comparative activity level scores are the first measure of the effects of the course. In addition, the activity level scores will be used in Chapter 9 as the basis for studying who changes after the course, i.e., what variables predict increased activity. This is because the activity level score is the most general and broadly comparable assessment that can be made on all subjects. It is less influenced by external economic conditions than are the economic measures that will be presented later. For all these purposes, the activity level scores have been combined as follows: The categories of +1 (e.g., plans), 0 (no change), and −1 (less activity) have been combined into the single category "inactive." This was done because after two years, the events scored as +1, such as plans or increased involvement in business, do not appear substantial and do not have any real effect on the firm's performance unless they have been followed by the kinds of specific actions that are scored +2. That is, a man may plan, but if after two years he has not taken any steps such as investing money or establishing a business, then one concludes that his plans had not been serious and he probably had not really changed. For present purposes, then, a score of "active" should be read as +2, that is, some specific activity which usually involves the expenditure or investment of money.[4]

Table 7.2 presents the results of these activity level scores. All the groups of course participants and controls are roughly at the same level before the course. That is, it appears that about one fifth of Indian businessmen are normally active in this sense during any two-year period. This is the baseline against which to assess the effects of the course. The participants from Kakinada (Group A) show a significant increase, so that during the two years after the course over half are active. The control subjects from Kakinada (Group B) and Rajahmundry (Group C) remain at about the same level of activity. Thus, significantly fewer of the men in these groups are active after the course than in Group A (the trained men). The participants from Vellore show a slightly smaller, though significant, increase after training, while the controls remain about the same, although these two groups are not significantly different after the course. The overall result seems clear: the course participants become considerably more active after the course, while the controls stay about the same.

To a psychologist, this strongly suggests that the course did change people, and these results fit in with earlier results from other achievement motivation courses reported in Chapter 2 and elsewhere (Cf. Kolb, 1965; Aronoff and Litwin, 1968). However, these results do not necessarily show that the more active behavior of those who took the course

4. Thus the activity level of the Kakinada participants before the course is lower in this table than reported in Chapter 6, because this table considers only the +2 category as active.

Table 7.2
Percentages of Entrepreneurs Classified as Active (+2) During Two-Year Periods

	Before Course 1962–1964	After Course 1964–1966	Significance of After-Before Levels
A. Kakinada, Trained in *n* Ach (N=51)*	18%	55%	$\chi^2 = 14.02$, p $<.001$
B. Kakinada, Controls (N=22)	18%	18%	
	Group A vs. Group B: $\chi^2 = 8.27$, p $<.01$		
C. Rajahmundry, Controls (N=35)	26%	31%	$\chi^2 = 0.07$, p = n.s.
	Group A vs. Group C: $\chi^2 = 4.62$, p $<.05$		
D. Vellore, Trained in *n* Ach (N=25)	17%	44%	$\chi^2 = 4.31$, p $<.05$
E. Vellore, Controls (N=16)	13%	19%	
	Group D vs. Group E: $\chi^2 = 2.76$, p $<.10$		
X. All Trained in *n* Ach (N=76)	18%	51%	$\chi^2 = 18.91$, p $<.001$
Y. All Controls (N=73)	22%	25%	
	Group X vs. Group Y: $\chi^2 = 11.15$, p $<.001$		

* Slight variation in the N due to death, unavailability of data, and so on.

has any economic effects. The activity level score is a psychological measure of a man's activity precisely because it is relatively uninfluenced by economic conditions such as price rises, raw materials shortages, and interest rates. Furthermore, it tends to equate big changes, such as starting a new factory, with relatively small changes, such as expanding a shop. Nevertheless, the purpose of this program was not only to change men but to produce effects on their economic output, and so to raise the economic standards of the community. To assess whether this purpose was fulfilled, a variety of specific "hard" economic measures is needed.

Measures of Economic Performance

How would increased achievement motivation show up in economic measures of the performance of a man or of a firm? Previous research evidence concludes that high achievement motivation leads specifically to success as an entrepreneur—that is, to energetic expansive business activity, rather than to greater short-run efficiency or greater wealth in a highly liquid form (see McClelland, 1961, Chapter 6). Thus any increase in achievement motivation should reflect itself specifically in measures of entrepreneurial functioning. While there is an immense literature on entrepreneurship, and some argument about what is the precise definition of an entrepreneur, there is general agreement that the entrepreneur, through *vigorous activity,* combines the factors of production—*labor* and *capital*—so as to produce an increased *output* of goods and services, thus increasing the total wealth or material welfare of the society (Marshall, 1920, pp. 293–98). The measures to be reported here are based on each of these components of entrepreneurship: changes in activity, labor, capital, and output.

HOURS WORKED

It is difficult to measure how vigorous and energetic a man's behavior is, and careful long-term observations of the behavior of one hundred fifty businessmen were out of the question. However, one crude measure of a man's activity is the number of hours a day that he spends at his work. Of course, working longer hours doesn't necessarily mean working better or more vigorously. In fact, a more effective entrepreneur might be able to accomplish more work in less time. So if a man's achievement motivation increased, he might not necessarily spend more time at work: conceivably he could do better in less time, and have more leisure for other things, such as his family and community activities. However, the average businessman in this study reported working a little over eight hours, and the businesses are small enough so that if the man worked more hours, it would very likely have a direct impact on the performance of his firm. Thus increases in hours worked will be considered one sign of more vigorous activity. All subjects were asked how many hours a day they worked during each of the three time periods. The interviewers probed so as to distinguish between the standard working hours for employees and staff and the man's own time at work.

Table 7.3 presents the results. Before the course, about 10 per cent of the course participants and the controls report that they worked longer hours in 1964 than in 1962. However, after the course, twice as many participants report working longer hours, while the proportion working longer among the controls decreases slightly. To the extent that spending more time on the job is a first requirement of more vigorous activity and enhanced entrepreneurship, the course participants become more vigorous in their activity.

Table 7.3
Percentages of Entrepreneurs Working Longer Hours at the End of Two-Year Periods

	Before Course 1962–64	After Course 1964–66	Significance of After-Before Levels
X. All Trained in n Ach (1964) (N=61)*	7%	20%	$\chi^2 = 8.61$, p $<.01$
Y. All Controls (N=44)	11%	7%	

Group X vs. Group Y: $\chi^2 = 6.25$, p $<.02$

* The Ns are those on whom this information could be obtained.

NEW FIRMS ESTABLISHED

A more direct measure of an entrepreneur's vigorous and innovative activity is whether he creates new firms and business ventures. The establishment of a new venture is extensive and difficult. It involves planning, usually some setbacks, and finally, some successes. Many Indian businessmen, if asked, say that they have plans or would like to establish a new firm, although these plans are usually rather vague. Often a man has a desire to start some new business, but takes no steps to do so and makes no definite attempt for several years. Hence these plans and desires remain in limbo. The first step in starting a new venture, then, is to make a definite attempt. Information is gathered, and calculations of available capital and possible market have to be made. On the basis of these calculations, the plans are then either initiated or given up. Naturally there are many obstacles to starting a new business, particularly in India: lack of capital, obtaining government approval for various licenses, uncertain markets, and so on. Thus a man who becomes serious about starting a new venture will first make a definite attempt. He will calculate, apply for a license, try to raise the capital, and so forth. Initially he may not be able to start the venture. However, he has at least converted a vague desire into a definite plan, and has taken some steps to carry out that plan. He may subsequently report that the plan was given up, or that it was unsuccessful, and he may make another definite attempt in the future. Given the difficulties of starting, it is likely that he will have to make several such unsuccessful attempts (see Chapter 6). Paradoxically, then, the number of definite attempts that he makes, without succeeding, is some measure of his entrepreneurial activity. An attempt that has become definite enough to be disposed of, even negatively, is the first step in converting vague hopes into definite action. Hence the first measure of new business ventures established is actually a measure of attempts which did not succeed.

Table 7.4 presents a comparison of the trained and control groups

Table 7.4
Percentages of Entrepreneurs* Making Unsuccessful Attempts to Start New Businesses,** 1964–66

A. Kakinada, Trained in n Ach (N=51)		31%
B. Kakinada, Controls (N=22)	Group A vs. Group B:	9% $x^2 = 4.11, p < .05$
C. Rajahmundry, Controls (N=35)	Group A vs. Group C:	6% $x^2 = 8.26, p < .01$
D. Vellore, Trained in n Ach (N=25)		12%
E. Vellore, Controls (N=16)	Group D vs. Group E:	6% $p = $ n.s.
X. All trained in n Ach (N=76)		25%
Y. All Controls (N=73)	Group X vs. Group Y:	7% $x^2 = 9.08, p < .01$

* There were cases in Kakinada where several men tried to start one business. Each such joint attempt is counted only once, i.e., as though it had been attempted by one man. Where one man made several attempts, only one is counted. This is conservative, but was felt necessary to avoid artificial inflation of the figures.

** A "new business" is defined as a firm which is separate, both physically and financially, from the man's present business. It must be involved with a different product. Separations for tax purposes, or arising from the partition of joint families, are not counted. Branches are counted only if they are located more than thirty miles away, and require separate management.

on this measure. When the interviews were conducted, the importance of unsuccessful attempts was not so clear, and the interviewers did not probe carefully for such attempts during the time period before the course. Thus, data for the period after the course only are presented. It is clear from the table that the course participants made more attempts which did not succeed to start new business ventures during this period than did the controls. To be sure, the controls have a lot of plans—"to increase sales," "to expand into mill stores," and so forth. They mention difficulties, but report no specific steps taken to investigate and overcome these difficulties. Thus they have not really given up the plans, but say vaguely that they hope to carry them out some day.

The second and more important measure of creating new business ventures is, of course, the number of new firms that are actually started. Table 7.5 presents comparative data for the groups of course participants

Table 7.5
Percentages of Entrepreneurs* Starting New Businesses** During Two-Year Periods

	Before Course 1962–64	After Course 1964–66	Significance of After-Before Levels
A. Kakinada, Trained in *n* Ach (N = 51)	6%	27%	$\chi^2 = 8.73$, p < .01
B. Kakinada, Controls (N = 22)	5%	5%	
	Group A. vs. Group B: $\chi^2 = 4.94$, p < .05		
C. Rajahmundry, Controls (N = 35)	9%	14%	$\chi^2 = 0.14$,† p = n.s.
	Group A vs. Group C: $\chi^2 = 2.09$, p < .20		
D. Vellore, Trained in *n* Ach (N = 25)	0%	12%	$\chi^2 = 1.34$,† p = n.s.
E. Vellore, Controls (N = 16)	6%	0%	
	Group D vs. Group E: $\chi^2 = 6.80$, p < .01		
X. All Trained in *n* Ach (N = 76)	4%	22%	$\chi^2 = 10.88$, p < .001
Y. All Controls (N = 73)	7%	8%	
	Group X vs. Group Y: $\chi^2 = 5.71$, p < .02		

* There were two cases in Kakinada where three course participants joined to start a new business. These two are each counted as a single business, i.e., as though it had been started by only one man. This is conservative, but was felt necessary to avoid artificial inflation of the number of businesses.

** New business defined as in Table 7.4, Note 2.

† Corrected for continuity.

and controls. The figures for the controls and the participants before the course suggest that normally about one businessman in twenty actually starts a new business venture during a two-year period. However, both groups of course participants show increases after the course, although the Vellore increase is not significant because of the small numbers involved. The combined increase is highly significant. Between 1964 and 1966, almost one man in four who had been trained in achievement motivation started a new business. In comparison, the controls remain at about the same level as in 1962–64.

So far, it seems clear that the course participants are behaving as better entrepreneurs than the controls after the course. They work longer and they make more definite attempts—both successful and unsuccessful—to establish new business ventures. However, it can readily be argued that the starting of new business ventures *per se* is not necessarily an improvement in economic terms. It may simply lead to a proliferation of small firms, each operating at an uneconomic level and each spreading the available technical and other resources too thin. (See Berna, 1960, p. 131). There is no reason why several small firms that do not grow are of greater economic benefit than a few larger firms (Berna, 1960, pp. 158–60). This argument can ultimately be answered only after several years. There are some indications that this is not the case with the course participants, however. One of the extraordinary effects of the course, to be discussed in the next chapter, is that in some cases men who got to know each other through the courses and the subsequent Entrepreneurs Associations combined to start new enterprises —an event which was almost nonexistent in the control groups. For the present, it is necessary to determine whether the increased entrepreneurial activity of the course participants, both in their old and in their new firms, represents an increase in the economic measures of entrepreneurial performance: new labor and new capital mobilized, and greater output. To what extent are these changes reflected in hard economic facts?

Answers to this question are the basis of the rest of this chapter. In assessing economic effects, only those businessmen in all groups who are in charge of their businesses will be considered. The reason is simple. If we know that a man is in charge of his firm, it is relatively safe and easy to attribute changes in the firm's employment, capital, and output to his actions, or at least to his final decision. But if a man is not in charge (is a son of the proprietor, a lesser partner, or a salaried employee), it is difficult to estimate what proportion of the firm's improvement figures reasonably can be attributed to his efforts. So it seems wisest to ignore such cases. Note that the various groups of participants are approximately comparable to their control groups in proportion of men who are in charge of the firm, as well as in proportion who are in industry and trade, as reported in Chapter 4. Hence the figures that are reported here should be considered the economic effects of the course only for men in charge of their firm. It is apparent that any future courses which hope to attain these effects would therefore have to be restricted to such men.

CAPITAL INVESTED

The provision or mobilization of capital is obviously central to the role of the entrepreneur. All subjects interviewed were asked about the total capital investment in their firms at three different points in time. However, their replies and figures presented several problems. First, it was not clear whether subjects were giving the actual investments that they had made, the increments of capital from whatever source (e.g., loans and advances), the increase in worth of the business, which is partly affected by rising prices, or the total increase of fixed and working capital (including stocks on hand). These distinctions are certainly clear conceptually, but they are very hard to get at in an interview. Furthermore, the careful investigation of books and records that would be necessary to untangle these different figures simply was not possible. Therefore, in considering increased mobilization of capital, the following rules were adopted for analysis of the interview data:

1. Only additional investments that are for some specified purpose, such as a new business, an expansion of a shop, or new machinery, are counted.[5] That is, increases in "total capital" are not considered unless the subject can specify the purpose for which the increase was used. Note that whenever a subject reported an increase in the total capital invested in the firm, the interviewer probed to discover such specific purposes. Increases in stocks on hand are not counted. They may only be a response to inflation, and do not directly create real wealth.

2. Not counted are investments in shares of stock or analogous investments where the primary purpose of the investor is to obtain income, and which are not a part of production or distribution in which the subject has some active involvement. Such investments may be highly successful as speculation and add to an individual's wealth. However, a man's speculation does not contribute directly to the community's real wealth unless he is the entrepreneur—i.e., combines his own efforts with the capital and labor. Moreover, investments in luxury goods are not counted. This is a conservative way of defining productive investment.

3. In general, funds put into moneylending are not counted, since it is unclear whether these contribute directly to the production and distribution of goods. (They often finance elaborate marriage functions and the purchase of luxury goods.) Furthermore, the amounts of such funds are usually vague and hard to verify. However, if lending funds are intended for the finance of some specified good, such as trucks, then they contribute to production and distribution and are counted. Thus,

5. If new machinery has been ordered, only the amount actually paid as a deposit is counted.

the measure of increased capital investment used here corresponds approximately to specific increases in productive fixed capital.

There is another problem in trying to assess how much investment is made by each subject. Often men are involved in joint business ventures with several partners. Sometimes they go into business for themselves, but obtain most or all of the capital from some other source, such as a relative or bank. Sometimes they provide the capital for someone else's venture. Therefore, the following rules were adopted in determining how much of an investment could be credited to a given person:

1. A man who is in complete charge of a firm (existing or new) receives credit for all the capital mobilized by that firm for some specific purpose, whether it is from the firm's profits, his own funds, or a bank or other lender.

2. If a man joins with several other partners in a new venture, or in an expansion of a previous one, he is credited with his share only. The distinction between this and number 1 above is that here the man is not the prime mover for the investment. Nevertheless, he must take some active involvement in the venture; otherwise it is considered investment for income on his part and is not counted at all.

3. If a man provides capital for someone else's venture, and takes some active part in the establishment or management of that venture, the amount that he invests is credited to him.

These rules attempt to include only investment that is entrepreneurial in the sense of being combined with the man's own vigorous activity. Some economists (e.g., Richardson, 1960) define entrepreneur in broader terms, so as to include the investor who simply purchases shares of stock in a firm. For present purposes, the term is applied more strictly. In summary, these rules attempt to define and classify specific increments of productive fixed capital which a man has mobilized in one way or another, and with which he is involved in an active way. These standards seem to be the most appropriate ones for judging the effects of the course.

Table 7.6 gives the comparative results. By the above criteria, about one third of all subjects in charge of their businesses make such specific investments during the period before the course. During the period after the course, the proportion of control subjects making such investments goes up slightly, although not significantly. However, the proportion of course participants increases significantly, so that after the course almost three quarters of them make such investments. The purposes for which they make these investments are as follows: nine men invested in new factories, ten in a new distribution business, nine in a substantial

Table 7.6

Percentages of Entrepreneurs in Charge of Firm Making Specific Fixed Capital Investment During Two-Year Periods

	Before Course 1962–64	After Course 1964–66	Significance of After–Before Levels
A. Kakinada, Trained in n Ach (N = 33)**	36%	78%	$\chi^2 = 12.75$, p $<$ .001
B. Kakinada, Controls (N = 15)	33%	40%	
	Group A vs. Group B: $\chi^2 = 6.80$, p $<$ .01		
C. Rajahmundry, Controls (N = 21)	33%	52%	$\chi^2 = 1.56$, p $=$ n.s.
	Group A vs. Group C: $\chi^2 = 3.96$, p $<$ .05		
D. Vellore, Trained in n Ach (N = 11)	18%	64%	$\chi^2 = 3.29,^*$ p $<$ .10
E. Vellore, Controls (N = 9)	13%	13%	
	Group D vs. Group E: $\chi^2 = 3.71,^*$ p $<$ .10		
X. All trained in n Ach (N = 47)	32%	74%	$\chi^2 = 17.09$, p $<$ .001
Y. All Controls (N = 45)	29%	40%	
	Group X vs. Group Y: $\chi^2 = 11.18$, p $<$ .001		

* Corrected for continuity.
** Ns represent the number of entrepreneurs in charge of their business at the end of 1966, from whom any investment data could be obtained.

expansion or renovation of their present shops or factories, and eight in purchase or construction of new machinery (not replacements).

Table 7.7 shows the total amounts of these investments, both in terms of group aggregates and in terms of investment per individual entrepreneur. The Kakinada participants invest significantly more after the course than do the Kakinada and Rajahmundry controls (p = .015, Mann-Whitney U test). How much more do they invest? That is, how much investment does the course mobilize? First it is necessary to estimate the ordinary level of investment as a baseline. Obviously the amount that a person invests in his business varies over time. If he invests in one period, then he probably has to consolidate in the next, and so does not make a further investment. Considering the figures from all the course participants before the course and all the controls before and after, the approximate investment per entrepreneur per time period ranges between Rs. 7,000 and Rs. 16,000. Thus, each course participant who is in charge of his business invests at least an extra Rs. 8,000

Table 7.7

Amount of Specific Fixed Capital Investment During Two-Year Periods
(in Thousands of Rupees)

	BEFORE COURSE, 1962–64		AFTER COURSE, 1964–66	
	Absolute Investment	Investment per Entrepreneur	Absolute Investment	Investment per Entrepreneur
A. Kakinada, Trained in *n* Ach (N = 36)	297	8.25	1007	28.00
B. Kakinada, Controls (N = 15)	244.5	16.30	233	15.50
C. Rajahmundry, (N = 21)	436.5	20.70	297.5	14.20
D. Vellore, Trained in *n* Ach (N = 11)	17	1.54	122.5	11.10
E. Vellore, Controls (N = 9)	50	5.50	18	2.00
X. All Trained in *n* Ach (N = 47)	314	6.68	1129.5	24.03
Y. All Controls (N = 45)	731	16.24	548.5	12.19

after the course, conservatively calculating Rs. 16,000 as the "normal" investment. Considering only the Kakinada participants and the Kakinada and Rajahmundry controls,[6] the ordinary range is between Rs. 8,000 and Rs. 20,000; the extra investment per participant is again Rs. 8,000 after the course, conservatively calculating Rs. 20,000 as the "normal" amount. Thus the effect of the course can be estimated at increasing investment by at least Rs. 8,000 over a two-year period per man who is in charge of his business. The aggregate increased investment due to the course so far is therefore Rs. 8,000 times 47 participants in charge of their business, or Rs. 376,000.[7]

From Table 7.7 it appears that the post-course amount of investment has almost doubled the ordinary rate. From Table 7.6 it further appears that the number of people making such investments has doubled. This suggests that the course achieves its effect not simply by drawing

6. The Kakinada and Rajahmundry groups have more personal capital to begin with, as noted in Chapter 4.

7. In Chapter 12, this table will be considered together with estimates of the cost of giving the course, in order to estimate the rupees of private capital mobilized per rupee of cost.

more money out of a few people who are already regular investors. Rather, the course increases the domain of people in the community who are willing to invest. It draws more people and more money into the production and distribution sector of the economy. This is an important point. Many writers (Lynton and Stepanek, 1963; Lewis, 1964, pp. 32–38) point out that India's problem is not so much a lack of wealth. In most districts, there is a considerable sum which for one reason or another is "frozen" in land, luxury possessions, and similar nonproductive assets. Therefore a good deal could be achieved without external supply of capital if only these frozen assets could be drawn into productive investment. It appears that the course has had precisely this effect. Chapter 8 will describe in detail some actual cases where this has happened. Chapter 12 will consider some of the implications of these findings for economic development policy.

These are some obvious questions about how productive, in the sense of goods and services, this new investment really is. First, it should be noted that investment was defined so as to exclude anything that might be considered primarily for consumption, such as houses or luxury goods; it included only specifiable investments, that is, money spent for which the entrepreneur could give a purpose. There is a more general question, however: Are these new investments economically appropriate for the economy of Kakinada and Vellore or for the economy of India as a whole? Are they better than any conceivable alternative use of the same funds, such as having the government take the funds through taxation and then invest them in public-sector enterprises? This is not the place to discuss the relative merits of public versus private investment. However, such an argument would have to demonstrate, first, that the public sector could in fact have mobilized these funds through effective increased taxation. Then it would have to demonstrate that having collected more money, the public sector could successfully invest the funds in productive enterprises. Finally, it would have to demonstrate that the resulting public sector enterprises make more efficient use of the funds than the private sector enterprises that are already under way here. All of these points about public enterprise in India are currently being debated (see Lewis, 1964, Chapter 8, esp. pp: 237–42).

Thus, the issue of whether these investments in Kakinada and Vellore are not as socially beneficial as some conceivable optimal investment program is academic, until those who propose some other optimal program can specify precisely how it will be carried out and then can make it come to pass. The position here is that a less than optimal improvement that can be carried out is better than a theoretical optimum which remains a plan. Even the general argument is not relevant to the principal findings of this chapter: that achievement motivation training does improve the enterpreneurial performance of individuals, and that this training could as easily be given to public-sector managers as to private-sector businessmen. The question of most efficient social and economic organization is not at issue; the evaluation of the performance of individual entrepreneurs is the purpose of this project.

However, another cricitism of the results might argue that the increased investments may be inappropriate from the perspective of the society and might divert India's scarce resources from more useful purposes (Cf. Sinha, 1967, and Chapter 3). Hence the overall effects would be harmful. There is no way to resolve this question without a careful specification of each additional resource that the participants mobilized and then a careful evaluation of how "scarce" it is and how important other uses for it would be. Again, the position here is that a scarce resource that is actually being used is probably of greater benefit than a theoretically better plan for using that resource. It is, however, by no means clear what resources are genuinely scarce in Kakinada and Vellore. As suggested above, capital may not be so scarce. In many sectors of the Indian economy, there is stagnation rather than scarcity. That is, resources are on hand which are not being used at all. Thus, for example, if the Indian cotton textile industry is producing output which is not fully consumed (see Reddaway, 1962, pp. 40–41), then an entrepreneur who expands his textile shop and increases his sales promotion so that people will buy more cloth rather than other things may be diverting pressure from consumer goods that are genuinely scarce, such as gold, gasoline, or luxury items. Of course it might also be true that he is simply taking customers away from other shops. What is needed is a thorough study of what goods are scarce, and what nonscarce goods can be and are substituted for them by increased retail promotion. Thus, increased investments in distribution and retail trade may well reduce the pressure on scarce resources, by "mopping up" consumer purchasing power with goods readily available, although at first such investments in retail trade might seem wasteful of scarce resources and therefore extravagant.

LABOR

While the argument about use of scarce resources cannot be evaluated fully without a good deal more knowledge about the Indian economy, and especially the economy of the districts discussed in this study, it is clear that there is one resource that is over-abundant in India today

—namely, labor. To the extent that the course increases employment, it is certainly not straining any scarce resource. It would further be helping to solve what many writers believe to be the most pervasive problem of the Indian economy (see Galbraith, 1962, pp. 24–25; Reddaway, 1962, pp. 24–25). Indeed, the most basic function of the entrepreneur is to combine capital with labor, so that improved enterpreneurial performance should be reflected in increased employment. To be sure, it is often thought that the entrepreneur's task is to increase the efficiency of production through capital-intensive technologies, and consequently to reduce the amount of labor used per unit of output. Whether this argument is relevant to the problems of developing countries, such as India, where unemployment is great has been debated by economists (cf. Sen, 1960; Myint, 1964, pp. 136–42; Lewis, 1964, pp. 58–62). For present purposes, however, the following propositions seem true: (1) Improved entrepreneurial performance here should be reflected in increased employment. That is, generally the increase in output will add workers much faster than improved efficiency will reduce workers. (2) For the kinds and scale of businesses under consideration here, namely small-scale enterprises employing fewer than fifty workers, the so-called economics of mechanization probably do not play a significant part over the ranges of increased investment and output here reported. (3) Even if mechanization could be introduced, its relatively great cost versus the relatively small cost of employing more labor in the industries here considered (given prevailing wages)[8] suggests that increased use of labor is more economical. In fact, the switch to advanced, highly mechanized equipment and processes may reflect a desire for prestige, rather than a consideration of economic production. (4) Moreover, any increase in employment will produce vitally important social benefits. With these considerations, the effects of the course upon employment will now be considered.

Most subjects interviewed had either the same or more employees in 1966 than they had in 1964. All the groups are compared in Table 7.8. About a third of the men in each group employed more workers in 1964 than they did in 1962. After the course, this proportion goes up significantly to well over one half among the Kakinada participants and to two thirds in Vellore. The proportions of the control groups stay about the same, although there is an insignificant increase in the

8. The average daily wage for unskilled and semiskilled workers in East Godavari district ranges between Rs. 1.75 and Rs. 3 ($.26 and $.41 respectively). *District Census Handbook, East Godavari District* (1961), Part 2, p. 26. The wage rates for Kakinada and Rajahmundry cities are probably somewhat higher.

Table 7.8

Percentages of Entrepreneurs in Charge of Firm Employing More People at the End of Two-Year Periods

	Before Course 1962–64	*After Course 1964–66*	*Signicance of After–Before Levels*
A. Kakinada, Trained in *n* Ach (N = 33)**	32%	58%	$\chi^2 = 4.13$, p $<$ .05
B. Kakinada, Controls (N = 14)	23%	21%	
	Group A vs. Group B: $\chi^2 = 5.16$, p $<$ .05		
C. Rajahmundry, Controls (N = 24)	35%	42%	$\chi^2 = 0.20$, p = n.s.
	Group A vs. Group C: $\chi^2 = 1.41$, p$<$ .30		
D. Vellore, Trained in *n* Ach (N = 11)	44%	64%	$\chi^2 = 0.00,^*$ p = n.s.
E. Vellore, Controls (N = 8)	33%	25%	
	Group D vs. Group E: $\chi^2 = 1.44,^*$ p $<$ .30		
X. All Trained in *n* Ach (N = 44)	35%	59%	$\chi^2 = 4.88$, p $<$ .05
Y. All Controls (N = 46)	31%	33%	
	Group X vs. Group Y: $\chi^2 = 6.36$, p $<$ .02		

* Corrected for continuity.

** Ns represent the number of entrepreneurs in charge during the 1964–66 period on whom data concerning employment could be obtained. The actual N is slightly lower in each group during the 1962–64 period. Percentages are calculated on the basis of the actual N for each period.

Rajahmundry group. The proportion of all course participants who employed more people in 1966 than they did in 1964 is significantly higher than the proportion of all controls who did so.

Table 7.9 shows the total amount of increased employment. The average number of new jobs per entrepreneur per two-year period is higher during the period 1964–66 than during the period 1962–64 for almost all groups. That is, there seems to be a general tendency for all businesses to provide more new jobs since 1962 and 1964. However, the Kakinada course participants provide almost twice as many new jobs per entrepreneur per two-year period after the course than do the controls from Kakinada or Rajahmundry. Before the course, the participants and the controls were about the same. Thus, the best estimate of the number of new jobs per entrepreneur per two-year period that can be directly attributed to the effect of the course is 6.62 (Kakinada participants' average 1964–66) minus the estimated base rate of 3.30 (Kakinada

Table 7.9
Amount of Increased Employment* During Two-Year Periods

	BEFORE COURSE, 1962–64		AFTER COURSE, 1964–66	
	Absolute Increase of Jobs	Increased Jobs Per Entrepreneur Per Two-Year Period**	Absolute Increase of Jobs	Increased Jobs Per Entrepreneur Per Two-Year Period**
A. Kakinada, Trained in *n* Ach (N = 31 Before, 33 After)	46	1.48	218	6.62
B. Kakinada, Controls (N = 13 Before, 14 After)	7	.06	47	3.36
C. Rajahmundry, Controls (N = 20 Before, 24 After)	31	1.54	79	3.30
D. Vellore, Trained in *n* Ach (N = 9 Before, 11 After)	12	1.34	40	3.64
E. Vellore, Controls (N = 6 Before, 8 After)	6	1.00	0	.00
X. All Trained in *n* Ach (N = 40 Before, 44 After)	58	1.46	258	5.86
Y. All Controls (N = 39 Before, 46 After)	44	1.14	126	2.74

* Only real jobs in existence as of end of 1966 are counted, not potential jobs of projects under way. Seasonal or part-time jobs are counted at their full-time equivalents.
** Calculated on the basis of the actual N for each period.

and Rajahmundry controls, 1962–64), or about 3.32. That is, in Kakinada the course led to more than three extra new jobs per man in charge per two-year period. So far the aggregate increased employment in Kakinada due to the course is 3.32 times 33, or about 110 new jobs. In Vellore, the figure for the control group after the course (0 new jobs) is probably not a true figure. A better estimate of the base rate of new employment could probably be obtained by taking the Vellore figures during 1962–64 for participants (1.34 new jobs). Thus in Vellore, about 2.3 jobs per entrepreneur per two-year period (3.64—1.34) can be attributed to the course effects. The total number of jobs created in Vellore is 2.3 times 11, or about 25 new jobs. In summary, the course seems to have generated about 135 new jobs[9] during a two-year period. There is no reason to assume that this is a final figure. That is, the course participants may well go on increasing employment at a higher rate than the controls.

INCREASED GROSS INCOME

So far, the effects of the course on some principal aspects of the entrepreneurial function have been studied. Course participants are more active, they attempt to start and actually do start more new ventures, and they mobilize increased amounts of capital and labor. Since the entrepreneur's function is to combine these factors of production in order to achieve increased output of goods and services, the participants should show increased output. Table 7.10 shows that a substantial proportion

Table 7.10
Percentages of Entrepreneurs in Charge of Firm* Having Increased Gross Income During Two-Year Periods

	Before Course 1962–64	After Course 1964–66
A. Kakinada, Trained in n Ach (N = 27)	75%	82%
B. Kakinada, Controls (N = 12)	50%	67%
C. Rajahmundry, Controls (N = 20)	67%	90%
D. Vellore, Trained in n Ach (N = 8)	75%	75%
E. Vellore, Controls (N = 6)	40%	50%
X. All Trained in n Ach (N = 35)	75%	80%
Y. All Controls (N = 38)	57%	76%

* Ns are the number of entrepreneurs in charge in 1964 on whom data could be obtained. There is some variation in the N between the two time periods due to availability of data and entry of new businesses.

of all groups show increased output (gross income) both during the period before the course and during the two years after. This proportion

9. In Chapter 12, this table will be considered together with estimates of the cost of giving the course, in order to estimate the rupee cost per new job created.

increased from 1962–64 to 1964–66 in almost all of the groups. Hence it is apparent that the simple measure of increased gross income could show no striking differences between the trained and the control groups. There are probably several reasons for this. The figures for gross income may be less accurate than those for new investments or new employees, since there was no direct way of checking them. However, the most obvious cause of this general increase in gross income is simply increased prices. India has been subject to considerable inflation, at least since the later 1950s (see Ghosh, 1964, p. 552). Thus it is not surprising that most businessmen would have greater income in monetary terms.

Given conditions of inflation, the course participants might nevertheless show relatively greater increases in gross income. However, this is not directly the case. If changes in gross income during the period 1964–66 are arranged in order of magnitude and then divided at the median, there is no tendency for the course participants to be above that median. Such a presentation, however, considers only the magnitude of the increase and does not take into account the initial figure or starting point of the firm. Thus a firm with initial gross income of Rs. 50,000 and an increase of Rs. 25,000 may be growing faster than a firm starting at Rs. 500,000 and increasing to Rs. 600,000. Therefore, the absolute increases in gross income were converted to percentage figures, with 1962 as the base for 1962–64, and 1964 as the base for 1964–66. When this is done, more of the course participants are above the median of percent gross income change after the course as compared with their positions before the course. As can be seen from the top of Table 7.11, the difference between the groups after the course is not quite statistically significant. However, the use of per cent increase in gross income presents a problem. Although there is virtually no correlation of base income with size of increase ($r = +.03$), the conversion of the increase to percentage figures introduces a substantial negative correlation with the base ($r = -.43$). Thus the conversion to percentage introduces a bias; the lower the initial base, the more likely it is that the per cent increase will be larger. McClelland (1961, pp. 87–89) discusses this point and suggests evaluating gains by means of a regression line. In the present case, 1964 base gross income and 1964–66 increase in gross income were plotted for all subjects. A regression line that described the relationship between the two variables and that split the combined subjects into two equal parts was then plotted. The course participants tend significantly to be above the line, while the controls tend to be below it, as reported in the bottom of Table 7.11. That is, the course participants tend to have relatively larger increases in gross income from 1964 to 1966 than do the controls, given the base from which each man

Table 7.11

Percentages of Entrepreneurs in Charge of Firm* Having Per Cent Gross Income Increases Above Median** During Two-Year Periods

	ABOVE MEDIAN % GROSS INCOME INCREASE	
	Before Course 1962–64	After Course 1964–66
All Trained in *n* Ach	52%	61%
All Controls	43%	38%
		$\chi^2 = 3.57$
		$p < .10$

	ABOVE THE REGRESSION LINE OF 1964–66 GROSS INCOME INCREASE ON 1964 BASE
All Trained in *n* Ach	63%
All Controls	36%
	$\chi^2 = 4.44$
	$p < .05$

* See note to Table 7.10.
** Median calculated for both groups combined, separately for the two time periods.

started. So there is some evidence that the improved entrepreneurial performance of participants is reflected in relatively greater increased output or gross income figures. However, two years is probably too short a time for the major increases in capital and employment to show through fully as increases in gross income. Most of the important changes, such as expansion, new branches, or new enterprises, had been in operation for less than a year at the time of the final interviews.

Summary of the Economic Effects of the Course

Analysis of several measures of individual behavior and economic effects demonstrated that the participants in achievement motivation courses showed significant improvement in many aspects of entrepreneurial performance, both as compared with themselves before the course and as compared with three matched groups of controls. Course participants show more active business behavior. Specifically, they work longer hours. They make more definite attempts to start new business ventures, and they actually start more such ventures. They make more specific investments in new, fixed, productive capital. They employ more workers. Finally, they tend to have relatively larger percentage increases in the gross income of their firms. Thus by measures of all the basic aspects of the entrepreneurial function, they have become improved entrepreneurs. The aggregate effects of the courses include, to date, the mobilization of approximately Rs. 376,000 of specific new capital investments and about 135 new jobs. Measured by these figures, the courses certainly seem to have had an economic effect. The next chapter will present some accounts of the ways in which individuals changed their business performance.

CHAPTER 8

EFFECTS OF THE COURSES: SOME INDIVIDUAL CASES

From the figures and analyses presented in Chapter 7, it seems clear that the course participants showed significant and important improvements after the course. Yet the aggregate figures do not convey a very full sense of what happened to individual businessmen. How did they change? What new plans did they make? How did they carry out these plans? What new risks were involved? What difficulties and obstacles did they face and how did they deal with them? In what ways did they have to change their plans in order to adapt to conditions? This chapter will present accounts of the activities of several course participants during the two years after the course, in order to illustrate the typical kinds of things that were achieved and to convey a sense of the environment in which the participants acted.

Improvements of Existing Businesses

Many participants made important changes in their existing businesses, such as renovating and enlarging a shop, opening a new branch, adding a new product, or purchasing additional machinery. Such changes are certainly less spectacular than starting a new business or opening a new factory; yet they are in most cases a clear departure from the routine history of the firm. For example, one man was the proprietor of a successful retail store that had been established by his father before World War II. His father had expanded the store after the war, and at the same time had taken up the manufacture of some simple and basic scientific equipment on a small scale, more or less as a sideline. Scientific equipment sales grew rapidly about ten years before the course when the firm was awarded supply contracts for various schools and colleges. Clearly this man was soundly established and doing well at the time of the course; however, both businesses had been running at a relatively constant level for several years. After the course, the man made several changes in the scientific equipment firm. First, he hired a salesman to travel and take orders. As a result, sales went up almost by 100 per cent. Partly because of this increase in sales, he then expanded manufacturing by constructing new, separate manufacturing sheds, and purchasing additional machinery. Shortly thereafter he was approached by a local charitable agency which employed handicapped workers. Their business had slackened, and they asked him for assistance in setting up some program for employing their workers. In consultation with this agency, he worked out a plan whereby the handicapped workers could manufacture some simple equipment that was closely related to the apparatus that he himself was already making. Thus he could handle sales through his existing outlets. Having taken these steps, he is now planning further expansion of his scientific equipment manufacture by moving it to a larger, independent site.

Now, this man has not done anything that is revolutionary or spectacular. Appointing a salesman, investing more in sheds and machinery, collaborating with another organization—these are rather simple and basic steps that are well within the scope of most small firms in India. The point is, however, that he did take these steps. He could have taken them at any point during the last ten years, and he may even have planned to do so. Yet it was only after the course that he acted. Similarly, many other well-established firms are in a position to make such elementary improvements, and their owners often talk about their plans to do so; yet as pointed out in chapter 7 (see table 7.4), these plans usually remain unfulfilled. So one basic effect of the course is that it moves participants to effort and action on projects that they had in mind for many years. Many of these projects do not require major inputs of capital or technology, but only need the commitment and action of the owner. That is, they are projects that are already within the scope of the man. Individually, their economic effects may not seem large; yet they are important changes, given the scope and resources of the men involved.

Establishing a New Firm in a Familiar Line of Business

Many participants established new firms which were related to their previous lines of business in some way. That is, they drew upon the knowledge and experience that they already possessed. Some had been sons or younger brothers in a family firm or managers working under the owners of a larger firm, while many were already in charge of their own firm. One man who owned a retail bicycle shop joined with others to start a company that loaned funds to other firms for the purchase of trucks and other motor vehicles. This company is able to finance purchase of more than ten vehicles a year, costing around Rs. 35,000 each. It therefore makes an important contribution to transport and distribution facilities in the region, which are largely dependent on road transport. Railways, while extensive by the standards of developing countries, do not begin to handle the needs of carrying the basic crops of the area to a central place, let alone transporting the supplies needed within the area, such as fertilizer. In fact, the state government has been concerned about expanding road transport, even to the point of considering setting up state-owned networks of vehicle fleets. Thus, any improvements in transport represent the creation of a vitally needed resource that has a wide economic impact throughout the area.

Another young man had had a successful career for several years as a manager in various large factories that processed agricultural products. After the course, he gave serious thought to starting his own manufacturing business. He visited the local Small Industries Service Institute (SISI)[1] to get information, read up on various possibilities, and made investigations into local resources and markets. Initially he decided that a manufacturing enterprise at that time would involve too high a risk because of difficulties with capital and raw materials. So he planned first to set up a series of wholesale and retail distribution firms. Then, he joined together with several sets of partners in five different towns in the district, to establish one distribution firm with branches in each town.

1. The Small Industries Service Institutes (SISIs) were established in the early 1960s by the Government of India as part of a comprehensive program to aid small industries throughout India. There is at least one SISI in each state. Typically, SISIs provide advice, technical and commercial information, and training to small businessmen from the area.

The firm as a whole employs about one hundred people. At the beginning, each branch handled construction materials and related products through several major agency-franchises that he had obtained. He planned to expand into the manufacture and mixing of fertilizer, and after one year received the necessary licenses. When the firm begins production, it will add another twenty employees. At about the same time, he joined with other partners to set up a bottling company which would have a local concession for bottling a national soft drink. He established the contact with the national firm through various friends. The plant was under construction in 1967. Although the course participant was responsible for organizing both the distribution firm and the bottling company, he spent a good deal of time finding experienced managers, and has put the day-to-day management in their hands. Consequently he himself now manages another large factory.

Clearly this man has always been vigorous and enterprising; and even without the course, he probably would have established some sort of firm sooner or later. The point is that only after the course did he take the actual first steps, such as collecting information and investigating possibilities, which resulted in getting the new firms started. Thus one important effect of the course may have been to speed up the natural or existing rate at which men act in an entrepreneurial way. Things that would have come to pass sooner or later, perhaps, are now happening sooner.

Establishing a New Industry

No doubt the expansion and improvement of retail trade and distribution is an important economic effect of the course, but it seems that the direct increase of actual production through the establishment of factories would be a more striking and immediate economic benefit. Increases in industrial production expand the resources available, instead of merely improving the efficiency with which these resources are allocated and distributed. Even more significant for the growth of industry and production is the establishment of industrial factories by men who were successful traders or merchants. Why is this type of enterprise important? Berna (1960, pp. 49–56) notes that industrial firms established by merchants are likely to have better capital resources than those founded by artisans or former factory workers. Later (pp. 158–60) he notes that industrial firms that do not grow from small to medium or large industries are usually held back by lack of capital resources. Hence any program would achieve important and beneficial results if it could encourage merchants to go into industry.

This happened in several instances among the course participants. One man had been a highly successful and respected dealer in household electrical products. For some time before the course, he had wanted to start a small-scale factory for light manufacturing. He kept putting off any definite steps. As has been noted above, this is typical of the vague plans that many businessmen in India have. Immediately after the course, however, he started gathering the necessary capital—from his own funds, from bank loans, and from friends and relatives. He set out very soon to manufacture some products, but could not manufacture the complete line until he had obtained the necessary licenses, which took over one year. He conducted a vigorous sales policy, sending out samples and publicity to dealers, and hiring a traveling sales representative. He believes in paying his staff and workers well—almost 50 per cent more than usual rates—with liberal increases over time. One of his successful salesmen had virtually doubled his salary in two years. Consequently the employees work hard, and he himself can be away from the factory during most of the day to look after his retail stores.

The quantitative economic effects of this man's activities are shown in Table 8.1, which gives comparative information before and after the

Table 8.1
Growth of One Man's Retail and Light Manufacturing Businesses

	1962	1964	1966
Household Equipment Retail Firm			
Capital*	100	100	150
Employees	3	7	7
Sales	300 units	350 units	450 units
Light Manufacturing Firm			
Capital	—	Rs. 15,000**	Rs. 60,000
Employees	—	4**	12
Sales	—	—	Rs. 110,000

* Expressed as a ratio with 1962 = base of 100. Increase due to opening new branch.
** Figures for shortly after the course (mid-1964).

course. The table shows the sales improvement in the retail business and the effects of starting the manufacturing firm: Rs. 60,000 of new investment, twelve new jobs, and over Rs. 100,000 of yearly sales, after two years.

One constant problem was getting metal containers at a reasonable price and in regular quantities. First he bought used containers, but the supply was irregular. Then he worked out an arrangement with a local metal fabricator to make and supply them. If they used new iron sheet, they would have the problem of quotas. Therefore they began to reclaim old oil and tar drums, which are cheaper and have no quota. The metal fabricator has taken on additional employees, and is able to produce containers for sale in other towns also. So the participant has stimulated activity in another man.

This man has obviously shown considerable ingenuity and continuing effort in overcoming the difficult problems which attend the beginning of any industrial venture. He has expanded his capital through bank loans and investment by friends, and is now planning larger scale production and a wider assortment of products. Already he has purchased a motor, and he is preparing to get some additional equipment manufactured locally in order to improve the quality and consistency of his products. He also is arranging for larger premises.

Another participant was the eldest son of an important family in his town. His ancestors had been important landowners and had played a major role in the history of the town. Before the course, he spent his time supervising the cultivation on family lands, overseeing the processing of agricultural products in mills, and looking after numerous charitable institutions that had been founded by his ancestors. Certainly these are common, reasonable, and worthy activities for someone from his background. However this man clearly had the resources and ability to become involved in industry, as do so many men like him in India. He had had vague thoughts about industry, but lacked any experience and indeed did not know many of the industrialists in his town. At the course, however, he met such people, probably for the first time, and continued to meet with them afterwards. This was not just a new friendship group; the men spent their time talking about setting up an industry and gathering information. One man in the group was the manager of a local branch of a bank, and he spent a lot of time going over the financial aspects of the plans. This in itself is striking, since it is rather unusual behavior for a bank manager. (One bank manager in the control group, when asked whether he ever gave such advice outside of working hours, replied that "A bank man can help industries only by loaning money, not by any advice.")

Together, this group investigated several projects. They did not jump at the first idea that came along, but in fact made some careful calculations. They invited technical advice from various outside experts. Finally the entrepreneur decided to manufacture sugar by the *khandasari* process,[2] and purchased and repaired a mill.

The mill had produced sugar previously, but the equipment was in such bad repair that it could not operate. Hence it represented idle or unused resources, which this man restored to a productive state. The mill now employs more than one hundred fifty men, most of them for about four months during the production season. For the most part, these employees usually work in agriculture, if they work at all, and are normally idle after the crops are harvested. By providing additional cash employment during the refining season, the participant has directly helped to alleviate the problem of "disguised unemployment" (see Nurkse, 1953, chapter 1), so prevalent in India, at no cost to the output of the agricultural sector. He was advised and assisted by another course participant who had extensive experience in foundries. He himself spent several months during the season at the mill, learning and overseeing its operations. This, however, is only a first step. He has already purchased the site for a steel rerolling mill, has had a bank loan approved, and with the advice of others in the group is planning to begin construction.

This man is perhaps the most striking example of change among the course participants. His entire background was in agriculture, charities, and the support of religious affairs. He had enjoyed considerable prestige in the town. Although he had ability and resources, it is unlikely that he ever would have started an industrial venture. This is not because he thought that industry was beneath him, or because he wasn't interested in a new venture—two explanations that are often cited for the reluctance of agricultural and commercial men to enter industry. Rather, it was simply that the industrial world was outside his domain of experience, knowledge, and friends. In the course, he was brought together with businessmen and industrialists. Because of the special climate of the course, in which openness, cooperation, and mutual assistance were strongly emphasized (see Chapter 5), both he and the already established businessmen began to spend time and make plans together. This is an important effect of the achievement motivation course that may not be at first apparent. People who share time and space with each other often do come to trust and collaborate with each other. The course provides an opportunity for spending time together; but perhaps more

2. The *khandasari* process for manufacturing sugar requires much less capital than the vacuum pan method used in large factories, yet gives almost comparable yields from the cane. The *khandasari* process was introduced to Andhra Pradesh State from North India in 1958. See C. Parasuram, "Khandasari Sugar Industry," *Progress and growth of small scale industries in East Godavari District*, Kakinada: Office of the Collector, 1963.

important, it provides a rationale and a framework for doing so—namely, the economic growth of the town.

Collaboration on a Joint New Enterprise

The previous example suggests the importance of collaboration among several different men as a way of bringing new talent and resources into business and industrial activity. Indeed, a modern economy is built on the joint-stock company, which is probably the most sophisticated development of this principle of collaboration. Yet it is often characteristic of developing economies that cooperation and collaboration very seldom occur naturally. Many writers suggest that business collaboration in India is difficult because people do not trust each other enough (Carstairs, 1957; Chaudhuri, 1966; Minturn and Hitchcock, 1963). Berna points out that many small firms do not grow because their owners are reluctant to gain access to increased capital through sharing ownership (1960, pp. 157–58); but that when ownership is shared, growth is often very rapid (p. 162). Collaboration broadens the base of resources beyond what any one man, or one joint family, can draw upon. It further increases the stock of knowledge, skills, and contacts. Thus it is important to present and discuss some examples of collaborative enterprise that occurred among the course participants.

One man who took the course was experienced in paper-making. He had obtained small grants from the Khadi and Village Industries Commission to establish a handmade paper factory as a cottage industry.[3] After several years, however, he could not bring the factory into production. For one thing, he never really had enough capital to put the enterprise on a sound financial basis. Another difficulty was that the machinery supplied was defective, and to get it fixed involved a long and rather fruitless correspondence with a factory several hundred miles away. At the course, he discussed his difficulties with other participants. One foundry owner, who had achieved a considerable reputation for his own activity and for encouraging others, took up the problem. He encouraged another participant, who was successful as a merchant and as a private

3. Cottage industries produce a variety of things such as cloth, paper, leather, finished apparel, crafts, and the like, through intensive use of hand labor without machines or electricity. Production takes place in relatively small units, dispersed throughout villages. The cottage industry movement is associated with the philosophy of Gandhi (1955), who felt that it had important moral benefits and that it avoided the evils of an industrial society. Gandhi felt that cottage industries would preserve the ideal of an India composed of thousands of relatively self-sufficient villages. In addition, the hand-spun cloth (khadi) movement was an important political tool against the British.

banker, to join in with some capital. Obviously to the banker, this use of his money involved a greater risk than in banking, where security was demanded and where return was generally both good and steady. Still, the banker was intrigued because of the course, and the amount required was within what he was willing to invest as a trial. The foundry owner agreed to produce the necessary machinery in his foundry as his share of the enterprise. The paper-maker supplied the technology, and agreed to oversee the factory. It took over a year to complete arrangements with the Khadi and Village Industries Commission and to erect the small factory. When production commences this enterprise will bring into use some resources originally created by the Khadi Commission but which had in fact been idle or wasted. It will employ at least five men.

This collaboration is especially interesting, not only because each partner's contribution to the whole is so distinct, but also because in the normal course of things it is most unlikely that these three partners ever would have met each other, let alone have collaborated on a joint industrial venture. Their backgrounds are quite different. One had roots in the *khadi* movement, which developed from Gandhi's ideal of a decentralized society focused on hand-made crafts and production in individual villages (see Gandhi, 1955). He had spent much of his life as a *patwari*, or village record-keeper. One was a self-made man in the classic sense: without much formal education, he had started his foundry over thirty years ago with his own skill and very little capital. With continuous effort and great intelligence, he had built up a successful business and a good reputation for being able to execute difficult and unusual casting orders. Finally, one was a highly educated, sophisticated, and urbane banker who was among the leading commercial figures in the community. Considering the usual patterns of social interaction in an Indian town (or almost any place else, for that matter), one would predict that these men would probably never even meet each other. One certainly would not expect that they would understand each other's plans, abilities, and points of view. The general problem, then, is as follows: Any town or region is divided into different social groups according to background, occupation, traditions, and even a variety of other differences such as family networks, religious communities, and similar ties. This segmentation occurs in any society, but it probably occurs more extensively in developing societies (cf. Geertz, 1963). More precisely, in developing societies this segmentation is often on the basis of attributes that are ascribed rather than achieved; that is, attributes that are not rational with respect to the economic system. As a result, the sum total of economic resources, potential skills, and technical knowledge in a town or a region is actually further fragmented into smaller groups, each of which may coexist with other groups, but may never have communication with them. Economic growth is hindered because there are, in effect, a large number of small pools of the required resources. Collaboration among the different groups is difficult because, lacking contact, they tend to be suspicious or ignorant of each other. Obviously the course did not bring about a complete change. Nevertheless, it did bring together men of very different backgrounds and experience in an open, frank, and supportive climate. Having participated together in an impressive experience far removed from their usual life, they are now bound together by ties not unlike those in any group that has gone through an important experience or initiation together. When they returned to their towns, these ties were kept alive through the Entrepreneurs Associations. The new friendship groups were given direction by the explicit content of the courses—namely improvement of entrepreneurial performance and the economic growth of the town. Consequently, men of diverse backgrounds actually planned new ventures and in some cases carried them out. Of course, these ties are frail and perhaps temporary. To capitalize on this effect would require additional support and probably further efforts. Nevertheless, the experience with the courses has at least demonstrated that something can be done to increase the effective size of the pool of talent and resources from which mutual plans, exchange, and activities arise.

There is another case of collaboration, mentioned in Chapter 6, that deserves further discussion. One course participant, a cinema house owner, had done quite well before the course and had every reason to be satisfied with himself. His business was successful; he was respected in the town for his cultural and civic activities. However, he reported that after the course he felt restless. First he executed some minor theater renovations that he had planned well before the course but had been continually putting off. Then he started thinking about new lines of business with another course participant, whom he had known before the course. They worked out details of several possible projects. For example, they considered manufacturing concrete pipes, and visited factories that were already producing them. They consulted with SISI personnel. However, raw materials and quota problems seemed too great, so they dropped the idea. Then they considered assembling umbrellas. Again the problems seemed too great. They actually worked out the details of four specific projects, always drawing upon the SISI for information and advice.

The plans that did not succeed are noteworthy, for several reasons:

First, they demonstrate that while the course does lead to greater activity and the establishment of more new ventures, it does not lead men to attempt to set up the first attractive project that comes along. There are numerous instances where men gave up a plan after calculating the economic conditions, the problems, and the resources available. For example, another course participant wanted to manufacture a basic ingredient of ceramics products, as mentioned in Chapter 6. First he talked to firms that purchased this material. They advised against it, on the grounds that such a business was not likely to succeed under present circumstances. He himself calculated that such a factory would not be profitable, largely because a government-owned factory in a nearby town would be meeting much of the demand of the region. The second point about the theater owner's activities is that he spent a good deal of time and effort working out calculations and getting appropriate information. That is, he turned from planning or aspiration to activities that were instrumental for realizing these plans. He modified his behavior when the calculations showed that the plans would probably not work out. Moreover, he used the resources and assistance that was provided by the government through the SISI. That is, he sought help from sources that were able to give expert advice, rather than only from his friends. Thus this man was behaving as an entrepreneur even before he ultimately established a business, during the interval between planning and execution. Several initial plans did not work out; nevertheless he persisted until he was able finally to set up a new venture.

Many other participants also showed this persistence through difficulties and initial setbacks. One man organized a group of participants that investigated several different schemes. First, they sought technical advice on setting up a steel rerolling mill, but the advisor was ultimately not willing to move to town to work on the project. Then they made sustained efforts to purchase a nearby leather factory that had been closed and was going to be sold by the government. This plan came to naught when the government decided to reopen the factory and run it. The point is that many participants are still making plans and investigating possibilities, even though they have been disappointed several times. Moreover, most of the men who succeeded in carrying out some activity, new venture, or expansion also reported at least one and often several instances of plans that were not successful and had to be abandoned. There are many difficulties in the way of establishing a new venture or improving one's entrepreneurial performance, in India as elsewhere. The natural reaction to such difficulties is to give up, after one or two attempts. At least that is the common pattern among the control subjects who were interviewed. However, the course participants seem to be more persistent; they are willing to keep going and consider yet another possibility. Thus it is no surprise that they are more successful in establishing new ventures.

To return to the theater owner, after giving up several plans, he and his new partner finally decided to print rolls of tickets for cinema houses. This was a business closely related to his present activity, and therefore probably a realistic plan. The market showed good potential, since even the smallest town in India usually has at least one cinema house, and cities of 100,000 generally have between eight and ten. Printing rolls of tickets required a special type of printing press that had to be imported. Normally this is an insuperable obstacle to an Indian small businessman, because import restrictions are severe. However, because the partner's firm processed and exported agricultural products, thus earning foreign exchange, it had a small import allowance. This quota was placed at the disposal of the ticket-printing venture, and so the necessary equipment could be imported,[4] although that involved a delay of one and a half years. Another partner was added in order to make available additional capital. Here, then, is an example of a relatively simple venture that was closely related to the present line of business of a successful businessman. It will supply a product that is necessary in an expanding Indian industry. Yet even to arrive at this venture required two years of trial and error, of collaboration, and of delays while the necessary equipment arrived.

What do all these cases show? They are among the most interesting examples of new ventures and improvements that the course participants accomplished over a two-year period, although there are numerous other instances not mentioned here. These cases suggest how long and complicated the process of setting up a new venture can be, from the initial plan to the final production. First there are plans. Then come calculation, gathering information, and seeking assistance. Then capital must be available and necessary licenses obtained. At these stages there are usually setbacks: not enough capital, government restrictions, delays,

4. To be sure, this venture required some foreign exchange, and therefore may not have been as optimal, for India as a whole, as some other use of that amount of foreign exchange. However, it must be remembered that the exporting firm would have had the quota *in any case;* therefore the real question is whether this use is better, in the sense of creating more new resources, than whatever else the exporting firm would have done with the funds. The roll-ticket printing machinery will produce at least Rs. 100,000 of gross income and create at least four jobs. It is difficult to know what alternative uses the exporting firm would have selected. Most likely they would have imported replacements for their existing machinery. Output might have been increased, but certainly not as much as with the ticket-printing enterprise.

and even flaws in the initial plan. Finally there are often long delays while the machinery which is ordered arrives. At every stage, difficulties arise and there are very good reasons for giving up completely. Thus it is not surprising that among the control subjects most plans to start some new business remain just vague plans. The usual rate of starting successful ventures is rather low. All of this is true in spite of the great strides taken by the Government of India to improve the situation of small industries, through credit, information, and incentives. Furthermore it seems reasonable that while additional efforts by the government and others to improve the situation will be made, they will by no means remove these obstacles. Yet the course participants were more persistent than the control subjects in overcoming the obstacles. They made significantly more attempts, they calculated, they changed their goals, they made use of the facilities already provided by the government; and they succeeded significantly more often! One can further predict that as government efforts to make the environment easier to expand and increase—through more liberal credit, better information, and the removal of delays and obstacles—these course participants will be even more successful than they are now, relative to the control subjects. They will be first in line to take advantage of new facilities.

In addition to changing the participants so that they were better able to deal with difficulties inherent in the situation of small industry, the course also seemed to promote some positive effects that played an important part in their improved performance. It created new friendship groups, so that men were drawn together, got to know and trust each other, and ultimately collaborated. In this sense, the course increased the rationality of existing resources and skills through breaking down segmental barriers to their use. It also introduced men to a new conception of themselves, so that a highly successful trader, private banker, or agriculturalist began to think of himself as a potential industrialist. Hence it drew new resources into the industrial sector. These two effects —collaboration among men of different backgrounds and experiences, and industrial ventures among men who had been in other activities— almost never occurred among the controls. All these effects, then, suggest the ways in which the course changed participants so that they were able to act on their economic and social environment in ways that produced the significant economic improvements discussed in the previous chapter.

CHAPTER 9

CHARACTERISTICS OF THE COURSE PARTICIPANTS WHO CHANGED

Which men changed as a result of the course? Can they be precisely identified? That is, are there certain personal or social characteristics that enable some men, more than others, to improve their entrepreneurial behavior after the *n* Ach training and thus enhance their economic importance? This chapter will summarize the statistical relationships between various aspects of the participants' backgrounds, social positions, and personalities and their performance after the course. Chapter 10 will explore in greater detail how the course affected some particular men, and why they did or did not subsequently change.

The question of who changed is first of all of theoretical interest. The changing of adult behavior is fast becoming an important concern in many fields of psychology, as pointed out in Chapter 2. Yet we have very little carefully tested theory about who changes, in what circumstances, and how. Consequently, it is important to explore the effects of the course in order to answer some questions about change. We know what happened at an overall level; now we shall investigate the particular men to whom it happened.

There is a second and compelling reason to find out who changed. If we can determine who is most likely to benefit from an achievement motivation development course, then we can select those persons for future courses. Obviously this is important for any future attempts to develop entrepreneurs, but it has a further significance which is even greater. Nowadays, many are concerned with so-called obstacles to change in the developing countries. Their conclusions are often based on their own observations, sometimes reinforced by appeals to "common sense" and superficial popular impressions about the particular culture or country. Typically, a developing country's religious beliefs or cultural practices are judged to be obstacles to development because the observer decides, or feels, that they generate a state of mind incompatible with what he believes to be the necessary preconditions for development. The conclusions of Ronald Segal, an English political journalist who travelled around India for three months, are typical of this type of analysis (1967, p. 158): "The problem . . . involves no less than changing the ageless character of Indian custom, of making vital to the Indian people the community and not the caste, all India's bodies and not each separate soul, the world of the gutter and the dam and not the world of the horoscope."

Others with more extensive experience of India often come to the same general conclusion, although whether they assign responsibility to Hindu religion as a belief system (Kapp, 1963; Mishra, 1962) or to the Hindu "basic personality" (Carstairs, 1957; Chaudhuri, 1966) varies.

Although their conclusions sound sophisticated, many writers have simply compared the Indian businessman or worker or society (admittedly less developed) with its counterpart in the West or in Japan. Rarely was an attempt made to discover who did change, and why, within India. For example, it may seem perfectly obvious that Hindu fatalism inhibits rational planning for the future and that this fatalism must therefore be changed if India is to develop. Yet Weber (1904) argued convincingly that fatalism, as it was interpreted in Calvinist theology, was an important concomitant of development in the West. So on a priori grounds we cannot be sure of the effects of any particular religious belief. One suspects that many books about obstacles to development in India simply reflect what their authors found to be most striking or most irritating about the country and therefore called an obstacle. In this sense, India is truly a projective screen for writers both Indian and Western. Therefore, such books have been rather effectively and justifiably criticized by other social scientists (Singer, 1966a, Singh,

1967). That there are cultural, social, and personal obstacles to development in India certainly cannot be denied; but which institutions and values actually do retard change, and by how much?

It may seem audacious to argue that the present study can finally decide any of these questions. Certainly our experience of India is less than that of many others. The data of this study were collected from 150 businessmen in three towns of South India. Furthermore, these data were collected as a part of the evaluation of courses, and not as an overall investigation of Indian culture and economic development. But this may be an important advantage. Some aspects of Indian society, while impressive to the observer, may not have much direct bearing on economic development. Thus it does not follow that the Indian economy is retarded because there are numerous *sadhus,* men who have renounced the material world in order to seek *moksha,* inner salvation. Similarly it may not be relevant to present purposes that thousands of lower-class workers in Calcutta experience life as hopeless misery— though it certainly is tragic. Neither of these two groups takes any major decisions about the course of industry and commerce in India. Rather it is the entrepreneurs, managers, and planners who will be responsible for Indian economic development in this generation. Thus our study is concerned with one of the most strategic sectors of Indian society. It is important to distinguish this sector from the society as a whole—to ask what the entrepreneurs think about the material world and inner salvation instead of what the *sadhus* think. Our conclusions are drawn from a careful analysis of a unique attempt to create change through increasing the achievement motivation of precisely these entrepreneurs and managers. We have shown in the previous two chapters that such changes occur. If we can now determine the distinguishing psychological, social, and cultural attributes of the men who change, then we will be able to give a more precise assessment of the effects of various aspects of Hindu religion and Indian society on change. We can ask of any particular aspect whether it promotes or retards behavior change and economic development *among entrepreneurs.* Of course our conclusions must remain tentative. Yet because they are based on a systematic study of entrepreneurs who have changed, they are important quite out of proportion to the small size of the sample and the limited scope of the inquiry.

The first step in this assessment is to work out a single measure of change that can be applied to each of the participants. As pointed out previously, these men are in different business situations; they have different opportunities; and they face different problems. The Business

Activity Level score, as described in Chapters 2 and 7, is a measure created to facilitate the comparison of all participants. It is the measure of performance before and after the course which is least likely to be affected by the economic or social conditions of any particular business, since it reduces many different kinds of activity to a simple coding of "active" or "inactive." For this reason, the comparisons in this chapter between those who changed and those who did not will be based on Business Activity Level scores.

We have defined Changers as those businessmen who were inactive $(-1, 0, +1)$ before the course and active $(+2)$ afterwards. Those who were inactive during both periods are classified as Inactives. When the participants from Kakinada and Vellore are combined, there are 27 Changers and 34 Inactives. Ten participants were active both before and after the course. Perhaps they were more active afterwards, but the simplest way to handle these cases is to exclude them from the analysis. Seven participants had still other patterns: two were less active after the course, and five could not be rated for one of the time periods. Again, the simplest policy seemed to be to omit them from the analysis. Thus the findings reported in this chapter are based on a comparison of the 27 Changers and the 34 Inactives.

Information about the characteristics possibly related to change came from several different sources. From the course itself there was a questionnaire containing biographical information, Semantic Differential ratings of Real Self and Ideal Self, Thematic Apperception Tests (TATs), and "Who Am I?" questionnaires. Other information about psychological, social, and cultural matters was collected during the visits made to Kakinada and Vellore described in Chapter 6. Mr. Harry Lasker gave questionnaires concerning values and practices, particularly as they were related to Hinduism and the Indian family structure. Mr. Joel Cohen asked more about family structure, household arrangements, and subcaste membership. Finally, Dr. David Winter obtained some data missing after the previous visits, collected economic figures, and secured information about the participants' precise role in the management of their firms.

Situational Factors in Change

It would seem reasonable that the men who changed after the course were those who had the most scope or opportunity to change—those who could control their activities and thus realize their plans. Actually, having the scope to change can mean several different things. First, it means simply being in charge of a business. Second, it can mean being in charge of one's family. A man might formally be in charge of a business, and yet live in a joint family where his father or elder brother makes virtually all the decisions. Finally, having the scope to change can mean simply having enough money or other resources to be able to carry out plans. We shall consider in turn each of these aspects of the scope to change.

Table 9.1 presents the comparative percentages of Changers and Inactives who are in positions of control in their business and their family. Control of one's business simply means making the major decisions affecting the firm. However, there are two different aspects to being in control of one's family. In a joint family, there is usually one person who makes the final decisions both in business and in other family matters. He is referred to as the *kartā*, a term derived from Sanskrit meaning doer or accomplisher. Normally the oldest male in a

Table 9.1
Percentages of Changers and Inactives in Control in Business or Family

	Changers* (N = 27)	Inactives** (N = 34)	Significance of Differences
In Charge of Business	78%	38%	$x^2 = 9.54$, p < .01 ϕ coefficient = .40
Kartā Role in Family	52%	26%	$x^2 = 4.24$, p < .05
Not in Joint Family	54%	25%	$x^2 = 5.21$, p < .05
Decision-Maker in Family (*Kartā* role or not in joint family)	77%	39%	$x^2 = 8.31$, p < .01
In Charge of Business *or* Decision-Maker in Family	92%	50%	$x^2 = 12.00$, p < .001
In Charge of Business *and* Decision-Maker in Family	62%	26%	$x^2 = 7.45$, p < .01

* Changers are those participants who were −1, 0, or +1 before the course and +2 afterwards.
** Inactives are those participants who were −1, 0, or +1 before and after the course.

household is considered to be the *kartā*: the father of the family, if he is alive, or else the eldest son. Other sons may enter the family firm and take increasing responsibility for business and family matters, but so long as the father is alive, he makes all final decisions. Later, so long as two or more surviving sons live in a joint family, the elder of the brothers normally continues to make all final decisions. Thus a man could be in control of his family in one of two ways: he could occupy the *kartā* role within the joint family, or he could move out of the joint family and live on his own. In either case, he would be the decision-maker in his family.

It seems clear from Table 9.1 that being in charge of the business is very highly associated with changing after the course. Over three quarters of the Changers were in charge of their businesses. Being a decision-maker in the family (*kartā* role, or else not living in a joint family) is almost as highly related to change. Virtually all of the Changers (92 per cent) were either in charge of their business or were decision-makers in their families, and well over half were in charge of both. Not surprisingly, being in charge of the business is highly related to being a decision-maker in the family, as shown in Table 9.2. Since

Table 9.2
Relationship Between Being in Charge of Business and Being a Decision-Maker in Family

	DECISION-MAKER IN FAMILY	
	Yes	*No*
In Charge of Business	24	8
Not in Charge	8	19

$$\chi^2 = 12.14$$
$$p < .001$$
$$\phi \text{ coefficient} = .45$$

most of the firms involved in this study are family firms, the person who is in charge of the family is in charge of the firm, and vice versa. Therefore the question arises as to which is more important. If a man is in charge of his business, does it make any difference whether he is also in charge of his family? This question is hard to answer with the small number of cases in this study, but the data in Table 9.3 suggest some tentative conclusions. In Table 9.3, the course participants are classified according to their position of control, and then the per cent of each classification that was active before and after the course is shown.

The first conclusion that can be drawn from the table is that those men who are in charge of their business were more active before the course than those who are not. However, there is no difference in activity levels before the course between men who are decision-makers in their families and men who are not. Thus it appears that there is a general relationship between control of business and business activity, but not between control of family and business activity. If control of family

Table 9.3
Percentages of Course Participants* in Various Situations Classified as Active (+2) During Two-Year Periods

	Before Course *1962–64*	*After Course* *1964–66*	*Significance of* *After-Before Levels*
In Charge of Business			$x^2 = 15.76$
(N = 46)	26%	67%	p < .001
Not in Charge of Business			$x^2 = 5.58$**
(N = 30)	3%	30%	p < .02
	$x^2 = 6.09$	$x^2 = 10.18$	
	p < .02	p < .01	
Decision-Maker in Family			$x^2 = 20.17$
(N = 40)	15%	65%	p < .001
Not Decision-Maker in Family			$x^2 = 2.52$
(N = 35)	19%	34%	p < .20
	$x^2 = 0.14$	$x^2 = 5.94$	
	p = n.s.	p < .02	
In Charge of Business and Decision-Maker in Family			
(N = 32)	22%	66%	
Not Decision-Maker in Family			
(N = 13)	38%	69%	
	$x^2 = 1.30$	$x^2 = 0.05$	
	p = n.s.	p = n.s.	

* The Ns in this table are larger because all subjects are included, not just those classified as Changers or Inactives.
** Corrected for continuity.

appears to be related to change, it is probably because family control is highly associated with business control. This is confirmed by dividing the men in control of their businesses into those who were family decision-makers and those who were not, as shown in the last part of Table 9.3. In both categories the increase in the percentage of men active after the course is about the same. Family control makes little difference in activity, as compared with business control.

Table 9.4 shows that the main effects of the course, as described in Chapter 7 (Table 7.2), are considerably attenuated among those participants who are not in charge of their businesses.

It is apparent, then, that men who are in charge of their business are

Table 9.4
Percentages of Participants and Controls Not in Charge of Business Classified as Active (+2) During Two-Year Periods

	Before Course 1962–64	After Course 1964–66	Significance of After-Before Levels
A. Kakinada, Trained in n Ach (N = 15)	0%	38%	$x^2 = 4.78*$ $p < .05$
B. Kakinada, Controls (N = 6)	17%	17%	$p = $ n.s.
C. Rajahmundry, Controls (N = 8)	0%	13%	$p = $ n.s.
D. Vellore, Trained in n Ach (N = 13)	8%	27%	$x^2 = 0.21*$ $p = $ n.s.
E. Vellore, Controls (N = 8)	13%	25%	$p = $ n.s.
X. All Trained in n Ach (N = 30)	4%	30%	$x^2 = 5.58*$ $p < .02$
Y. All Controls (N = 22)	9%	18%	$x^2 = 0.20*$ $p = $ n.s.

Group X vs Group Y: $x^2 = 0.42*$
$p = $ n.s.

* Corrected for continuity.

more likely to change after the course than men who are not. The reason is undoubtedly the nature of the small businesses in Kakinada and Vellore. The man in charge of a small firm in Kakinada and Vellore normally runs it completely. He initiates most activities and usually has complete say about any new proposals or any changes in policy. Many of the Inactive participants who were not in charge of their businesses spoke of ideas that they had had, or plans that they had proposed, only to discover that the man in charge of the firm simply would not permit them to carry them out. Moreover, six of the eight men not in charge who did change after the course became active by establishing their own firms. So we may conclude that the course is most likely to change those men who run their businesses, or who are in large and decentralized firms that permit them scope for independent action. Of course this is the situation after about two years: it may be that the course will have long-term effects even on those who are not presently in charge of their businesses.

Although being in charge of the firm is related to activity, and especially activity after the course, all the experimental and control groups were carefully matched on this variable (see Chapter 4). Thus this relationship does not affect the data and conclusions about the overall effects of the course presented in Chapter 7. However, it is important that we control for the effects of being in charge of a business before proceeding further. For example, such things as age, education, and even certain values might at first appear to be associated with change, but are in fact associated only with being in charge of a business. Therefore, in order to determine the independent relationships of any other variables to change, we shall consider in the rest of this chapter only those Changers (N = 21) and Inactives (N = 13) who are in charge of their businesses.

One further aspect of the scope or opportunity for change is financial resources. Intuitively, it might seem that men who start new businesses or expand old businesses would necessarily have greater financial resources than those who do not. That is, the men with money will be the ones who expand their business. It is very difficult to get reliable estimates of individual wealth in India. Yet our findings, as presented in Table 9.5, show that this is not the case for the men and firms of this

Table 9.5

Initial Financial Resources of Changers and Inactives Who Are in Charge of Their Businesses*

	Changers	*Inactives*	
Gross Income of Firm in 1964			
Above Median (= Rs. 238,000/year)	8	7	$x^2 = 2.40$ $p < .20$
Below Median	12	3	
Estimate of Capital Available *from Firm and Personal Sources*			
Above Median (= Rs. 100,000/year)	11	5	$x^2 = 0.57$ $p =$ n.s.
Below Median	9	7	

* Ns are reduced because accurate information was not available in some cases.

study. Those in charge of their firms who became active after the course were not necessarily from firms with the largest gross income, nor did they necessarily appear to have the greatest financial resources in the form of business capital and personal wealth.

How can these results be understood? The intuitive belief that it is mainly the rich men who expand their firms is probably over-influenced by cases of a few wealthy businessmen who do start firms. It is easy to forget about the larger number of equally wealthy men who are content to do nothing with their money except invest it in luxury goods. We may also forget about those men without great resources who nevertheless do something, though perhaps on a smaller scale. Several men in this study did manage to get capital from relatives, friends, banks, members of the same subcaste group—a few thousand rupees from each, often with great difficulty and delay.

While it may be true that there was no strong tendency for the wealthy men to be more likely than the less wealthy men to change after the course, nevertheless it may be argued that a man's wealth does determine the size of the new or expanded venture that he can mount, at least in the short term. Surely only the rich men are able to make changes that have appreciable economic importance. The changes made by men who did not possess considerable resources might technically qualify as activity, under the scoring system rules; but if they are of minor economic importance, we might as well still conclude that it takes wealthy men to produce wealth, even if it does not take wealthy men to produce change. Two further findings, while undoubtedly subject to error, are important here. If men in charge of their businesses are ranked on a careful estimate of their available personal and business wealth in 1964, and then ranked on the additional capital investment that they mobilized between 1964 and 1966, the correlation between the two rankings is only $+ .12$. Furthermore, rankings on the number of employees in 1964 and on increase in employees from 1964 to 1966 correlate only $+ .10$. Neither of these two rank-order correlations even approaches significance. So it seems that it was not necessarily even the wealthiest or largest businessmen who made the economically most important changes. Thus our conclusion is clear: While one might suppose that the men with the greatest resources would be most ready to make big changes, this did not happen among the cases in our study.

Of course, finance is not irrelevant: many men could not carry out their plans because of difficulties in raising capital. Much can be done to improve the availability of capital to small industry in India or any other developing country. However, we suggest that the effects of increased availability of capital will be very considerably enhanced if the motivation of the entrepreneurs is taken into account and changed. This kind of policy recommendation will be discussed further in Chapter 12.

Table 9.6

Changers and Inactives in Charge of Their Businesses by Type of Firm in 1964*

	Changers	*Inactives*	
Industry	8	1	$\chi^2 = 1.96$**
			$p < .20$
Commerce	12	10	

* Ns are reduced because some men were in positions that could not be classified as either industry or commerce.

** Corrected for continuity.

One additional finding about business environment is of interest. Table 9.6 shows that there is a trend, though not statistically significant, for Changers to be more often in industry rather than in commerce, although there are many Changers in commerce.

What of the more general social background of the participants? In India, caste is a sociological factor that might relate to change. Traditionally, each caste group is supposed to have its own occupation. Thus, Brahmins are priests and scholars, Kshatriyas are warriors and rulers, Vaisyas are merchants and traders, and Sudras are craftsmen (Minturn and Hitchcock, 1963). Do these traditions affect the performance of participants after the course? Table 9.7 shows that there is no strong

Table 9.7

Varna Groupings* of Subcastes of Changers and Inactives in Charge of Their Businesses

	Changers	*Inactives*
Brahmin	3	4
Kshatriya	9	1
Vaisya	5	4
Others**	4	4
	$\chi^2 = 5.04$, df $=3$	
	$p < .20$	
Kshatriya	9	1
All Others	12	12
	$\chi^2 = 3.24$,† df $= 1$	
	$p < .10$	

* Subcaste memberships reported by all subjects were grouped into the *varna* categories (see Minturn and Hitchcock, 1963) by Indian informants. In some cases, there was some initial disagreement about the *varna* to which a particular subcaste belonged, but this was resolved after discussion.

** Includes Sudra, Muslim, Christian, and unspecified.

† Corrected for continuity.

relationship between a participant's *varna* (caste grouping) and whether he changes after the course. Some Changers come from each of the caste groups. There is a slight tendency for Kshatriyas to be more active than all other groups after the course, but this trend is not statistically significant. Thus we may conclude that regardless of the importance of caste-occupational specialities for traditional Indian religion and society, they are not closely related to change after achievement motivation training in the modern commercial and industrial sector of India.

Studies of the diffusion of change through groups and social systems emphasize the importance of friendship patterns and sociometric relationships (Menzel and Katz, 1955; Katz and Lazarsfeld, 1955; Rogers, 1961). Within a group or community, change generally flows along the lines of friendship or influence. Mr. Joel Cohen recorded the responses to the following question of all course participants whom he interviewed: "Are you friends with any members of the Kakinada (Vellore) Entrepreneurs Association now?" With these data, the relationship between each participant and every other participant was plotted. When, for example, participant A names participant B and vice versa, then a mutual friendship bond (MFB) exists between the two. From diffusion theory we would predict that Changers would have more mutual friendship bonds with other active participants than would Inactives. That is, the changes after the course occur in patterns that are related to who spends time with whom. Since men in charge of their businesses tend to have more MFBs with both active and inactive participants, we must again consider only those Changers and Inactives who are in charge of their businesses.

Table 9.8 shows that in Kakinada, the Changers do indeed have

Table 9.8

Number of Mutual Friendship Bonds (MFBs) with Participants Who Were Active After the Course for Changers and Inactives in Charge of Their Businesses (Kakinada Only)

	Changers	*Inactives*
Three or More MFB with Active Participants	8	3
Fewer than Three MFB with Active Participants	3	7

$p < .10$ (Fisher exact test)

more MFBs with participants who were active after the course than the Inactives do. (Actives include both Changers and those active before and after the course.) This difference did not hold up in Vellore, partly because most participants had MFBs with all of the other participants from their particular batch. Hence we can say that there is some evidence that change after the course was related to sociometric relationships, at least in Kakinada. Of course, we cannot tell from these data whether the friendship bonds caused the spread of change, or whether the participants who were active after the course began to spend more time with each other. Furthermore, the finding could not be confirmed in Vellore, where all participants tended to list all members of the batch with which they had been trained. Thus we cannot form any firm conclusion from the data and can only suggest that friendship patterns and communication networks—in short, a "new reference group" (Chapter 2)—were probably important in producing changes after the course.

Personal, Psychological, and Cultural Values as Factors in Change

What individual characteristics are associated with change after the course? Table 9.9 shows that differences in age and education between

Table 9.9

Age and Education of Changers and Inactives Who Are in Charge of Their Businesses

	Changers N = 21	*Inactives* N = 13	*t* (C-I)	*p*
Age in 1964	39.0	38.9	.03	n.s.
Total Years of Education	12.1	13.8	−1.20	n.s.

Changers and Inactives are not statistically significant. The older and more experienced businessmen are not more likely to change than the younger and perhaps more vigorous men.

Much more interesting and compelling is the question of what personality characteristics, such as beliefs, values, and motives predict change after the course. As we pointed out at the beginning of this chapter, we can evaluate many common assertions about certain beliefs that allegedly inhibit change in India. If Changers show more (or less) of a particular value or practice than Inactives do, we would tentatively conclude that the particular value or practice was related to change. If there were no differences between the groups, we would doubt the relationship. Obviously this study cannot finally test or prove anything about the values that relate to change. The sample is small. There is no guarantee that the right questions were asked, or that questions were asked in the right way and with the right choice of words. There is no sure protection against the effects of response set (Crowne and Marlowe, 1964), or a host of other factors which tend to contaminate the results of questionnaire studies. However, precisely because there is so little evidence about the values and practices of small businessmen who do change to become better entrepreneurs, we firmly believe that our information and analysis are valuable.

Mr. Harry Lasker constructed a values questionnaire which contained a wide variety of items reflecting elements of Hindu belief and practice. These items were drawn from the extensive literature on Indian personality and society and were given their final form with the assistance of several Indian social scientists. First, there were 17 Likert-type items, asking the respondent to express agreement or disagreement. The responses were factor-analyzed and rotated,[1] resulting in five scales which seem to tap many important aspects of Indian values. The labels given to these factors suggest these aspects:

A. Cautious Fatalism
B. Respect for Powerful Others
C. Traditionalism
D. Conformity to Caste Rules
E. Submissive Conflict Avoidance

Table 9.10 presents the comparative factor scores, together with the scores on each individual item, for the Changers and Inactives who were in charge of their businesses. It is apparent that there are virtually no significant differences between the two groups on any factor or on any individual item. The differences on items 47 and 49, which barely approach statistical significance, might suggest that the Changers are slightly more optimistic or that they believe in the value of obsessive hard work. However, it is quite likely that these differences could have arisen by chance. Certainly the answers to the Likert-type items do not present any pattern of clearcut and obvious differences.

Verbal responses to direct questions do not always present a profound picture of personality, or even of values. Are there any differences in actual practices? Do the Changers spend less time on religious activities? Do they tend less often to consult a guru (spiritual leader) or an astrologer? Are they less bound than Inactives by caste rules about eating, drinking, or intermarriage? Do they act on a belief in the emancipation of women? Lasker also included many items asking about these and other practices. Table 9.11 presents the comparative results. Again,

1. Rotation according to Kaiser's Varimax criterion (Couch, 1966).

Table 9.10

Values and Beliefs of Changers and Inactives Who Are in Charge of Their Businesses

ITEM*	MEAN SCORES**			
	(N = 20) Changer	(N = 12) Inactive	(C-I) t	p
A. Cautious Fatalism	5.74	4.79	1.13	n.s.
41. It is simply better not to try something when the chances of success are not good.	2.15	2.08	.16	n.s.
43. Man's power and abilities are only limited.	1.80	1.42	.74	n.s.
47. There is nothing worse than a failure, no matter how small.	1.80	1.08	1.90	.07
B. Respect for Powerful Others	12.15	10.35	1.21	n.s.
39. Every event in a man's life has already been settled and determined by his fate.	2.21	2.00	.42	n.s.
44. When one is not sure that one can carry out a task successfully it is better to pass the responsibility on to someone else.	2.55	1.92	1.68	n.s.
45. An older person has the right to tell younger people what to do.	2.30	2.00	.66	n.s.
46. A basic tragedy is that man proposes, but God disposes.	2.60	2.08	1.12	n.s.
50. It is better to follow the leadership of wise elders than to do what one thinks is best.	2.45	2.33	.24	n.s.
C. Traditionalism	5.25	5.42	−.27	n.s.
40. Those of our social customs for which we do not have proper explanation should not be strictly obeyed simply because they are time honored.	2.80	2.75	.13	n.s.
42. A man should always do what he thinks is best, even if this means making enemies of the members of his caste or family.	2.45	2.67	−.52	n.s.

Table 9.10 (continued)

ITEM*	MEAN SCORES**			
	(N = 20) Changer	(N = 12) Inactive	(C-I) t	p
D. Conformity to Caste Rules	2.10	1.50	1.09	n.s.
35. Generally speaking, a man should not begin a business which is not a traditional occupation for his caste.	.85	.58	.91	n.s.
48. The caste system often keeps me from doing things I would like to do.	1.25	.92	.88	n.s.
E. Submissive Conflict Avoidance	6.55	5.92	.61	n.s.
37. One should always obey one's supervisors, even when they are wrong.	1.20	.92	.77	n.s.
38. It is better to keep silent when you know what you would say would result in disagreement and conflict.	2.35	2.33	.04	n.s.
51. It is not good to think about problems and difficulties; eventually they will take care of themselves.	1.65	1.50	.36	n.s.
52. Planning only makes a person unhappy since your plans hardly ever work out anyway.	1.32	1.17	.35	n.s.
49. The "impossible" can be accomplished if one works hard enough.	3.30	2.75	1.92	.06

* Item numbers are taken from Lasker (1966, Appendix 5).
** Items are scored as follows: strongly agree = +4
                      agree   = +3
                      neutral   = +2
                      disagree   = +1
                      strongly
                         disagree   = 0

the overwhelming conclusions are negative. There seem to be very few consistent patterns of difference between the practices of the Changers and those of the Inactives in the areas of Subordination, Dependence, Caste Rules, Religious Behavior, and Feminism. Statistically significant differences emerged on only three items, and while among so many items they could have arisen by chance, nevertheless they do deserve some comment. The Changers tend more often to employ relatives in their businesses (Item 30). This may indicate simply that they come more often from family-owned businesses. However, at least it contradicts the notion that the Changers would be less nepotistic and hence more rational in their choice of employees.

The two differences in religious behavior seem easier to interpret. The Changers tend, although not significantly at the usual level, to make pilgrimages less often to Tirupati[2] (Item 20). Also, they more readily agree that diseased cows should be killed (Item 23). Thus while there are no differences in everyday religious behavior, when the matter concerns an extraordinary effort, such as a pilgrimage, the Changers are less likely to make the effort. Similarly, while the Changers do not eat beef or any kind of meat more readily, they do more often favor killing diseased cows. Ordinarily they may revere and protect cows; only in special cases do their opinions differ. So the religious modernity of Changers holds only in a special and restricted sense. To our considerable surprise, we did not find any great overall differences in the areas of economic rationality or traditionalism. Indeed, the Inactives tended to answer most of the values and practices questions in the more "modern" or "rational" direction, although not to a statistically significant degree.

What can we conclude from these rather astonishing results? The Changers have made significant economic improvements and are going about their businesses in improved ways; yet they do not appear to be different in their verbally expressed values. Do these results simply show that we did not ask enough questions or did not cover all the significant aspects of Hindu belief and practice? Such an explanation cannot be ruled out. Yet upon reflection, our own observations of Changers and Inactives support the questionnaire findings. For every highly modernized, sophisticated Changer who spoke to us in fluent English, there seemed to be a devout Hindu wearing a *kurta* or *lungi*, who spoke broken English haltingly, but who nevertheless had made observable and important improvements in his business after the course. Moreover, just as there were some traditional, orthodox men who did not change, so also were there highly educated, Westernized men who made eloquent excuses for their inactivity. So first impressions and a priori ideas can be wrong; herein lies the value of systematic comparison of all Changers

---

2. Tirupati is a Pilgrimage center near Madras, about 300 miles from Kakinada and 60 miles from Vellore. The difference held true, however, among participants from both cities.

Table 9.11

Social, Religious, and Family Behavior of Changers and Inactives Who Are in Charge of Their Businesses

| | AGREEING OR ANSWERING "YES"** | | | | | |
| | CHANGERS | | INACTIVES | | | |
ITEM*	%	No.	%	No.	χ^2	p
A. Subordination/Superordination						
36. Would you offer advice to an older relative about how to run his business?	73	(15)	80	(10)		n.s.
7. Do you permit your children to smoke in your presence?	33	(18)	42	(12)		n.s.
8. Do you smoke in the presence of your elders (father)?	18	(17)	20	(10)		n.s.
15. Was your marriage largely arranged by your parents? (vs. asking your opinion or letting you choose yourself.)	65	(20)	45	(11)	1.94†	<.20
16. Was (Will be) your son's marriage largely arranged by you? (vs. asking his opinion or letting him choose himself).	5	(19)	9	(11)		n.s.
B. Dependence						
9. In making plans in following areas, what percentage of the time do you consult your elders in the family?						
Religious (more than 10%)	30	(20)	27	(11)		n.s.
Family (more than 30%)	50	(20)	33	(12)		n.s.
Business (more than 50%)	35	(20)	20	(12)		n.s.
10. What percentage of decisions does your wife make in the following areas?						
Religious (more than 50%)	44	(18)	60	(10)		n.s.
Family (more than 50%)	28	(18)	30	(10)		n.s.
Business (more than 10%)	22	(18)	30	(10)		n.s.
27. Do you have a guru?	30	(20)	30	(10)		n.s.
25. Do you consult a horoscope/astrologer?	60	(20)	80	(10)		n.s.
If so, for what percentage of decisions in the following areas:						
Family (more than 30%)	25	(12)	50	(8)		n.s.
Business (more than 10%)	33	(12)	63	(8)		n.s.
C. Caste Rules and Practices						
14. Would you be willing to eat food with someone of a lower caste?	100	(20)	100	(12)		n.s.

Table **9.11** (continued)

ITEM*	AGREEING OR ANSWERING "YES"**				χ^2	p
	CHANGERS		INACTIVES			
	%	No.	%	No.		
12. Would you be willing to eat food prepared by someone from a lower caste?	75	(20)	92	(12)		n.s.
17. Would you permit your daughter to marry outside her caste?	45	(20)	33	(12)		n.s.
29. Are you active in any caste or religious organizations?	10	(20)	25	(12)		n.s.
24. Have you broken any traditions of your caste or family?	35	(20)	55	(11)	1.10	n.s.
30. Do you have any relatives in your business?	43	(21)	8	(12)	4.33	<.05
33. Would you employ a Muslim?	94	(17)	83	(12)		n.s.

D. Religious Behavior

ITEM						
13. Are you willing to eat or drink:						
Meat	50	(20)	58	(12)		n.s.
Liquor	45	(20)	58	(12)		n.s.
19. Have you been to a temple to worship (within the last month)?	58	(19)	91	(11)	1.60	n.s.
20. How often do you go to Tirupati? (Every year or oftener).	16	(19)	42	(12)	2.57	<.20
22. After an important success or recovery from disease do you make an offering to God?	50	(20)	27	(11)		n.s.
23. Do you believe that diseased cows should be killed?	68	(19)	8	(12)	10.70	<.01
18. Are all elaborate ceremonies in an Indian wedding necessary? (vs. do you believe the wedding should be simplified?)	26	(19)	30	(10)		n.s.
26. Do you observe Rahukal, a period in the day when you should not conduct any business?	50	(20)	20	(12)	1.94	<.20

E. Feminism

ITEM						
5. Do you send your children to coeducational schools?	85	(20)	92	(12)		n.s.
6. Do you plan to give as much education to your daughters as you would give to your sons?	80	(20)	100	(12)		n.s.

[265]

Table 9.11 (continued)

	AGREEING OR ANSWERING "YES"**					
	CHANGERS		INACTIVES			
ITEM*	%	No.	%	No.	χ^2	p
11. Does your wife eat her meals with you?	74	(19)	64	(11)		n.s.
32. Would you employ a woman in your business?	60	(20)	45	(11)		n.s.

* Item numbers taken from Lasker (1966, Appendix 5).
** The numbers in parentheses are the total N for each question.
† Corrections for continuity are made when appropriate.

and Inactives. If we take these findings seriously, we must be prepared to admit that the connections between traditional values and modernization are neither so obviously true nor so simple as they might be thought to be. We must consider again what many anthropologists have long claimed: that change usually is consolidated not by the disruption and destruction of so-called traditional values, but rather by their reinterpretation or resynthesis together with new actions (Singer, 1966b). A man can begin to act differently and yet hold traditional beliefs. Whatever dissonance one would expect from this combination is handled by reinterpreting the old beliefs so that they do not conflict with the new actions. Usually it is not handled by directly abandoning the old beliefs. In fact, abandonment of old beliefs often leads not to modernity but to confusion and cultural inertia (Shils, 1961). Thus the notion that change can be, or must be, consistent with and harmonized with traditional values is not a naive, sentimental hope, but to some extent is a fact about those people who changed in our study.

How can commercial and industrial change fit in with traditional Hindu values? Here we can only suggest some ideas drawn from Weber and others (Weber, 1920–21; Bendix, 1962). Consider Weber's discussion of Calvinism. Calvinism asserts quite bluntly that a man's actions in this world do not have any power to determine his salvation in the next world: salvation is absolutely predetermined. Yet a man should not be anxious about his status. Therefore, Calvinism condones and recommends worldly economic success as a sign of confidence that one is indeed a member of the elect and destined for salvation. In fact, the elected person has an obligation to transform this world as a sign of his salvation, rather than as a precondition for it. So according to Weber, fatalism in Calvinism encourages vigorous economic activity.

Hinduism likewise emphasizes the absolute predetermination of a man's status in the next world (*karma*), although this status is related to the performance of his caste duties (*dharma*)in this world. Yet even a man's life and the performance of his *dharma* are the result of previous lives. So Hinduism likewise is fatalistic. It stresses that men have obligations in this life that are related to their status in the next. In Hinduism these obligations are absolutely necessary, while in Calvinism they are only psychologically necessary and do not have any inherent efficacy. What, then, are the differences between the two systems? A very important difference concerns who has the right to specify and interpret a man's obligations. In Calvinism, specification and interpretation are the responsibility of the individual; in Hinduism, they are the exclusive prerogative of the Brahmins. Historically, the Brahmins interpreted the *dharma* of all castes so as to reinforce their own dominant, authoritative position (Bendix, 1962, pp. 152–72). Consequently, Hinduism tended to produce a relatively rigid hierarchy of status-quo power, especially during the times of greatest Brahmin ascendency. Yet the Brahmin monopoly of interpretation has varied during Indian history. In modern times, commercial and industrial culture have promoted the spread of literacy and education, which in turn has implicitly encouraged individual interpretation of religious duties. This emphasis upon individual interpretation fosters achievement motivation and leads to active economic development (McClelland, 1961, p. 370). It would be fascinating to explore this theme throughout Indian history, to establish whether the early periods of great economic activity in India (e.g., the period of Ashoka and the first few centuries of the Christian era) were in fact those periods of relatively low interpretative authority of the Brahmins. Of course, such historical speculations are beyond the scope of this study.

Our results suggest that fatalistic religious beliefs by themselves do not necessarily inhibit commercial and economic growth. The manner and source of their interpretation may be far more important than the beliefs themselves. Given new interpretations, so-called traditional beliefs may encourage economic activity, while abruptly removing the beliefs may produce people who are confused and interested only in the superficial prestige symbols of modern industrial culture. To what extent these results are general can be debated. They do not necessarily hold for all varieties of traditional values. At any rate, our results certainly support the more limited conclusion that there is little payoff in selecting men for achievement motivation courses on the basis of their values and practices alone.

In spite of the negative results so far, we may still feel that the

Changers must be different, psychologically, from the Inactives, even if these differences are expressed in deeper and more subtle ways than can be detected by values questionnaires. Psychologists often feel that they can make sensitive clinical assessments of men, even though it is usually very difficult to work out any precise criteria against which to validate these assessments (OSS Assessment Staff, 1949). In the present case, the criterion is more specific: Did the man make significant entrepreneurial improvements in his business during a two-year period? Dr. Elliott Danzig, who was one of the principal trainers in the first two Kakinada courses, predicted shortly after the courses whether each participant would change. Table 9.12 shows the relationship between

Table 9.12

Business Growth Predictions by Course Trainer for Changers and Inactives in Charge of Their Businesses

Prediction of Business Growth*	Changers	Inactives
Likely	11	1
Unlikely	2	4

$$\chi^2 = 4.19^{**}$$
$$p < .05$$

* Predictions made by Dr. Elliott Danzig in 1964, after course, for Kakinada courses 1 and 2.
** Corrected for continuity.

these predictions and our subsequent classification as Changer or Inactive. The predictions were reasonably accurate, suggesting that it is possible to tell in some way who will change. Yet Danzig's predictions were made on a "global" basis; he had come to know each man rather well in formal and informal situations lasting over many days. It is not clear what cues he was using to make the predictions, and in any case, they were made after the course. So the practical question of choosing the most receptive men in advance remains. What differences were there before the course?

The participants were given a form of the Semantic Differential Test (Osgood, Suci, and Tannenbaum, 1957) at the beginning and end of the training, in which they rated the concepts "Myself" and "The person I would like to be" on twenty linear scales consisting of adjective pairs such as "Good . . . . . Bad," "Fast . . . . . Slow," and so forth. Each rating was converted to a 0–7 scale in which 7 represented the more favorable end of the scale. Table 9.13 shows differences in the way the Changers and Inactives in charge rated themselves on the three

Table 9.13

Mean Before and After Ratings of Self and Ideal Self on the Semantic Differential Test for Changers and Inactives in Charge of Their Businesses

Dimension	MYSELF		PERSON I WOULD LIKE TO BE		REAL-IDEAL SELF DISCREPANCY	
	Changers (N = 18)†	Inactives (N = 10)	Changers (N = 16)	Inactives (N = 10)	Changers (N = 16)	Inactives (N = 10)
Evaluation[a]						
Before	5.8	5.8	6.6	6.3	−.8	−.5
After	6.1	6.3	6.6	6.6	−.5	−.3
Potency[b]						
Before	4.5	4.7	5.3	5.3	−.8	−.6
After	4.6	5.2	5.3	5.7	−.7	−.5
Activity[c]						
Before	4.8*	5.4	6.2	5.8	−1.4*	−.4
After	5.3	6.1	6.3	6.2	−1.0*	−.2
Overall Self-Esteem[d]						
Before	5.0	5.3	6.0	5.8 .	−1.0*	−.5
After	5.2*	5.8	6.0	6.1	−.8	−.3

† There is some variation in N due to missing observations.
* Difference between Changers and Inactives on this concept significant at p < .05.
a. Mean rating for *good, useful, pleasant.*
b. Mean rating for *large, hard, deep, bright.*
c. Mean rating for *fast, active.*
d. Mean rating for all adjectives on the Evaluative, Potency, and Activity dimensions.

main dimensions used by Osgood, *et al.* (1957). In general, all of the Inactives rated themselves more favorably both before and after training. This shows up in a number of significant differences in the table. Before training, the Inactives rated themselves as slightly more Potent and significantly more Active (*t* = 2.48, p < .05). Furthermore, the training improved their opinion of themselves on each dimension more than for the Changers, so that afterwards, significantly more Inactives than Changers (eight out of ten, or 80 per cent as against three out of eighteen, or 16 per cent) had an overall Self-Esteem score of 5.5 or higher. The chi-square test of the difference, corrected for continuity, is 8.58, p < .01. Shri Nadkarni's impression, reported in Chapter 6, is borne out by these statistics: there seem to be more men among the Inactives who "talked a good game," who reported that they felt much stronger and more active and who thought they were greatly helped by the training. These men seem to be more open to suggestion from whatever source it comes, but they are not as likely to stay changed. The long-run Changers

—those who become really active—have, in contrast, a more modest view of themselves at the outset, and report less of a change in themselves after training.

The same trend shows up in the discrepancies between the ratings for the Real and Ideal Self. Before training, the Changers report a larger gap between what they are and what they would like to be, particularly in the Activity dimension. Eleven out of 16 show a gap of one scale point or more, contrasted with only 3 out of 11 of the Inactives $x^2 = 4.84$, p $< .05$). The gap persists after the training. On overall Self-Esteem before training, the difference is also significant: only 2 out of 10 of the Inactives show a gap of .75 scale points in discrepancy score, compared with 11 out of 16 of the Changers ($x^2 = 5.9$, p $< .05$). In other words, the Changers are more dissatisfied with their self-image at the outset and in some sense want to change more, particularly to become more "active," whereas those who remain Inactive start out and keep a more favorable and satisfied view of themselves.

Since the Changers report greater dissatisfaction with themselves at the outset, it might be thought that they are men with higher initial n Achievement, which leads them to profit more from the training. This can be easily checked, since each participant took a Thematic Apperception Test (TAT) at the very beginning of the course, before he had been introduced to the n Achievement scoring system. However, the Changers and Inactives did not differ in initial n Achievement. If anything, the Inactives had slightly higher scores (p $= .17$, Mann-Whitney U test). So it is clear that initial n Achievement does not predict change. That is, the course does not simply improve those men who are already high in achievement motivation.

Nevertheless, the initial TATs are a source of data to test other hypotheses about psychological differences between Changers and Inactives. Lasker (1966), working with preliminary criteria for measuring change, suggested that the Changers wrote initial TAT stories that were specific and that contained actions explicitly related to goals, rather than stories about diffuse goal states. In contrast, Inactives tended to write stories that stressed conflict avoidance through acquiescence to authority or through abandoning a goal in favor of group consensus. Inactives also stressed "defensive" themes, such as rectifying personal faults or avoiding loss. Building on this preliminary formulation and using more precise criteria of change, Mr. Stuart Pizer attempted to construct a more comprehensive scoring system that would predict who changed after the course. He started with Tests of Insight (French, 1958a) by the participants in the earlier Bombay courses, comparing those who had changed with those who had remained inactive. The resulting scoring system was organized around the concept of efficacy (White, 1959), and had the following major categories (see Appendix I for the complete scoring system):

1. Is the principal goal of the hero one which involves continuing action, or is it a state of being or essence?
2. Does the hero possess resources of his own? Or does the outcome depend on the resources of others? Does the hero lack resources?
3. Does the story use words such as "Life," "World," "the People," etc., which suggest a vague, global setting?
4. Does the hero initiate the action, or does he act because of the wishes or demands of others?
5. Does the hero avoid problems?

Activity goals, inner resources, the lack of vague global words, initiative, and problem-solving were prior characteristics that were associated with change after the course in the Bombay sample. However, the same coding system applied to the initial TATs of the Kakinada and Vellore Changers and Inactives did not yield the expected difference. In fact, the Changers averaged lower on the TAT measure of efficacy than the Inactives—just the reverse of what happened in Bombay (see Table 11.3). Perhaps the Test of Insight used in Bombay produces different types of stories than those written to pictures, as in Kakinada and Vellore. At any rate, the scoring system derived from the Bombay stories did not show the expected differences when applied to the initial TAT stories of the men from Kakinada and Vellore.

However, the participants were also asked to write a series of answers to the question "Who Am I?" at the beginning of the course, and again over a year later during Mr. Joel Cohen's visit. The Pizer scoring system was applied to these protocols, and yielded quite significant differences between the Changer and Inactive groups, as shown in Table 9.14. The overall efficacy scores of the Changers in Kakinada and Vellore, while low compared to Bombay, are significantly higher than those of the Inactives. This significant difference between the two groups was still present in the second administration of the "Who Am I? in January, 1966, over a year after the course. This suggests that the efficacy scoring system measures a genuine prior difference between the two groups, something which is not changed or affected by the course. What does the efficacy score mean? It does not relate to a person's manifest or verbal values, nor to his *n* Achievement. Rather, it is a style of describing his goals and actions in terms of efficacy and problem-solving. The potential changer is a man who thinks about and describes himself in

Table 9.14
Efficacy Scores* on "Who Am I?" Test of Changers and Inactives in Charge of Their Businesses

	Changers N = 20	Inactives N = 12	Significance of Difference
Score of 0 or higher at beginning of *n* Achievement course	75%	25%	$\chi^2 = 7.61$ $p < .01$
Score of 0 or higher in January, 1966	71%	33%	$\chi^2 = 3.88$ $p < .05$

* See Appendix I for a complete description of this scoring system.

ways that involve autonomous action, rather than contemplation of a goal state. He thinks about initiating actions by himself, rather than waiting for the situation or other people to push him into action. He is aware of his own internal resources. Finally, when a problem arises, he does not retreat into vague global fantasies, nor does he avoid the problem, but he thinks about how to solve it. The potential changer thinks of himself as a person who is able to have an effect on the world.

The efficacy pattern of thinking is subtle because it does not show up in answers to direct questions. Probably most people, when directly asked, would say that they think of themselves as able to initiate actions and solve problems. The Changers, however, spontaneously describe themselves in this way. Furthermore, the sense of efficacy is profound, because it seems to be related to important changes after the course. In the course, a participant's attention is focused on some specific goal, such as expanding or improving his business. Men accustomed to viewing themselves as functioning with efficacy respond by taking concrete action. These findings relate to data analyzed and reported by S. Winter, Griffith, and Kolb (1968), which suggest that the people who change as a result of self-directed projects in small groups tend to describe themselves and their goals in concrete, active words.

SUMMARY

Achievement motivation training is especially likely to change men who are in charge of their businesses, probably because they have the scope and independence to carry out new ideas and plans. Furthermore, if a man already is somewhat dissatisfied with himself, but sees himself as someone who can initiate specific action to solve specific problems, he is likely to respond to the training with specific and visible activity.

Beyond these findings, there appear to be no important differences between those who changed and those who remained inactive. The Changers did not have more money. They were not more Western, nor were they less committed to Hindu beliefs and practices. These findings cast some doubt on many common theories about the relationship of traditional values to change. They further suggest that it is not necessarily the wealthy men who will make the most important efforts to initiate and improve economic activity. To be sure, many of the findings reported in this chapter are negative. We cannot discount the possibility that they are due to the inadequacy or incompleteness of our data. They need to be checked in further studies, and must remain provisional. Meanwhile, it is important to describe in greater detail some of the particular businessmen who took the course—to give some life to the tables and statistics so far reported. Thus the next chapter will present some case studies.

CHAPTER 10

CASE STUDIES

by Sara K. Winter

How does an achievement motivation training course change individuals' behavior? Why do some businessmen respond more positively to the course than others? These questions have been considered in Chapter 9 with discussion of data from the sample as a whole. In this chapter we take a clinical approach. Through an examination of the impact of the course on four individual businessmen, we seek to discover not merely which factors predict change following achievement training, but how and why these factors are important. The four case studies presented here are intended to communicate the effects of the course to the reader more vividly than the tables and statistics of previous chapters, and to develop hypotheses about individual differences in response to achievement motivation training in the Indian context.

The four men described here include three Changers and one Inactive after training. The first three were selected for intensive study because they founded new businesses after the course; the third man was of particular interest because he was one of the few course participants who was active after the course while continuing to work under his father's direction in the family firm. The fourth individual, an older man still under the domination of his father in a traditional joint family, was selected as representative of men not in control of their firms on whom the course had no discernible impact.

Clinical interviews with the four men were conducted in English by Dr. Sara Winter. During the last few days of the final follow-up visit to the community, after a friendly acquaintance had been established through social visits and through the standard follow-up interviews, Mrs. Winter requested time "to learn more about you personally, not just about your business activities, as before." Misgivings about the men's willingness to discuss personal subjects with a Western female interviewer proved to be unfounded; all the businessmen seemed flattered and interested in the chance to talk further about themselves. Mrs. Winter interviewed each man in his home or place of business for from two to four hours. Since tape-recording was impractical, she took extensive handwritten notes which were transcribed immediately after each interview.

The case material presented here is drawn from these interview responses and from interview and psychological test data collected at the time of training and in earlier follow-up visits. The data included in the chapter are selected from a much larger body of material, and certain changes have been introduced to conceal the identities of the men studied. For each case, we first present the data on past and present life and then offer interpretive comments and hypotheses about the reasons for the individual's particular response to achievement training.

Case #1—N

N is a muscular, broad-shouldered, 39-year-old businessman with curly hair and a relaxed, open smile. At the time of the course he owned a prosperous optical supply retail shop, founded by himself a number of years before on the main street. He lived with his wife, two teen-aged daughters and a six-year-old son in a comfortable but not ostentatious home. His caste is Kshatriya.

We were interested in interviewing N in detail because of his notable business activity after the course. Although he had made several expansions and improvements in his business between 1950 and 1961, at the time of the achievement training there had been no changes in his firm in several years. After the course, however, N decided to become a manufacturer. Turning the routine management of his retail business over to a hired manager, he founded a small factory to manufacture a product useful in building construction. N worked persistently for over a year to overcome difficulties with licensing and procurement of raw materials, displaying a good deal of ingenuity and initiative in solving practical problems. He was unusual among the Indian businessmen in the sample in his willingness to delegate responsibility to his employees. By the time of final follow-up, the factory employed ten workers and had been in production for eight months. N proudly demonstrated for Dr. and Mrs. Winter a motor-driven drilling apparatus he had installed just in time for their follow-up visit.

N was relaxed and thoughtful in the interview with Mrs. Winter. Pausing reflectively to consider his answers to the questions, he seemed genuinely interested in thinking about his life, his personality, and how he had come to be the way he was. His emotions flowed freely as he recalled happy or unhappy events from childhood, or spoke with great pride of his children's educational accomplishments. In his soft-spoken but definite manner he conveyed a strong sense of well-being, of satisfaction with his life and especially with his recent business accomplishments.

Family and Childhood. N's father, who had only a few years of education, was an orphan who moved at the age of 13 to another village to take up cultivation of lands belonging to a distant relative. N's mother had no formal schooling at all. There were four children of whom N was the youngest; his brother was six years older and his sisters, three and nine years older than he. When N was three years old his father died suddenly, leaving his mother and brother to manage the family lands as best they could.

N liked being the youngest child: "It was a good thing, because everybody was sympathetic toward me." His early recollections are "vague shadows of my father, giving me candy or something when I was about three," and "complete memories of all my early school days." He recalls his mother's readying him for school and his own excitement at beginning classes. Another early memory concerns a time when all the children were asked to bring two rupees to class for a festival occasion, but N's mother had only one rupee to spare. He can still recall vividly his embarrassment at not being able to participate with the others. N's older sister is remembered as warm and loving; she married very young and moved away, but returned to visit N and the family from time to time.

N's brother and sisters studied only through the third grade, but N loved school and made truly extraordinary efforts to continue his education. After completing three grades in his own village he walked a mile daily to the higher school in the next village for the next two years. Then, until he was 13, he walked four miles daily to attend the next grades in a larger town. Since N was the only child in his village to do this, he was the object of much curiosity and favorable attention. Although his mother joined in the general approval of his efforts, she found it hard to understand why N did not choose to spend his time playing like all the other boys. N recalls that at the age of 11, cold and wet as he crossed the fields in monsoon time on his way to school, he would think, "Only two years more, then I can go to the big city." Even now, looking back on this experience, he finds it hard to understand the source of his unusually strong motivation to get an education.

Adolescence and Adulthood.   At age 13, however, a less happy period began when N moved to a large city to live in the household of an older male cousin and to attend high school. His cousin supervised his studies daily, forcing N to stay up late each night with his books. N lost interest, didn't concentrate on his work, and for the first time in his life failed his examinations. The following year he moved elsewhere, prepared on his own, and passed the tests. "Under my own self I worked very hard." After studying the Hindi language by himself for an interim year, he entered the university with financial help from the cousin's family. "But my friends were not interested in the work, and neither was I. I neglected my work." Again he failed his exams.

At the age of 17, N was concerned and unhappy, wondering what to do with his life. He thought of travel to distant places: "I wanted to fly away." Unable to obtain a passport because of World War II, he was pressed into a routine job in his cousin's firm. N worked two years as a clerk, unhappily "just working," dissatisfied, and considering alternatives. His cousin arranged a marriage in an attempt to make N settle down. The night before the wedding N "cried all night," uncomfortable about the burden of responsibility implied in marriage but unwilling to oppose directly his cousin's will.

After marriage N found his wife pleasant, but still felt unsettled and oppressed. He traveled alone to North India, took several jobs in optical manufacturing companies, and finally decided to take a course in lens grinding and engineering. His mother's continuing support is shown in the fact that "she took a great deal of trouble to send money." After graduation he took a job with a medium-sized firm which stationed him in the town where he now lives. His wife joined him, his first child was born, and N began to feel more satisfied with life. After going into business for himself in 1955, he experienced more and more pleasure in his job. The years 1955 to 1960 were a period of continual expansion of the retail firm. N also founded a "cultural club" to put on musical performances and read plays. Most of his friends today are drawn from this circle rather than from his business associates.

Family. N's marriage has worked well. Although his wife has very little education, he frequently speaks to her about his business affairs: "I just developed the habit of talking to her about all things." With N's encouragement, his wife has taught herself to read at home, using their daughters' schoolbooks. At present N's mother visits the family for a few months each year and gets along harmoniously with his wife. Other relatives live far away.

N is currently very proud of his daughters' school successes, particularly those of his elder girl who is a student in medical college and plans to practice medicine in a village after she finishes her education. He would be willing for his daughters to select husbands for themselves, but comments with some amusement that they seem more inclined to let him choose for them. N takes it for granted that his young son will decide for himself his course of higher study and his eventual occupation. Recalling his own difficulties with his cousin during adolescence, N now believes "in freedom for my children, so they feel the responsibility from themselves, and not from me."

Present Opinions and Interests. In his present work, N says that he likes best making innovations and solving problems in his new firm, and likes least the routine work in connection with his old retail business. Asked to recall a problem and how he surmounted it, N mentioned difficulties with licensing and financing encountered as he set up his new firm. "If it weren't for you people coming around, I would never have done it so fast." Since the achievement course, he says that he sets specific goals for himself to overcome his tendency toward procrastination. By making promises to others that he will finish a task by a given time, N says he is more likely to get things done.

N feels that his strongest points are "sincerity," "not telling lies," and the fact that "I try to be punctual." His weakest points are "my short temper," and "idleness . . . I tend to postpone things." Asked whether fate or will is more important in life, N answers promptly. "My will is all. For instance, I told you people I would get a new motor and now I have done it. If anyone thinks and believes in will, he can do things." If N were turned into an animal, he would like to be "a lion, because it will be the strongest in the forest, and have no fear. No other animal will kill it." He would least like to be "a crocodile or a python—because of its shape."

At the start of the achievement training course, N listed the following experiences as most satisfying in his life:

1. I got myself entered in the high school independently, when there was nobody studying in my village.
2. I was being loved by my teachers and friends to a great extent because I am sincere in work.
3. I wanted to see the country as a whole and find out customs and manners of the people, and could succeed in it.
4. I could succeed in securing a place in the optical course.
5. I stood first in the final examination.
6. I started the cultural club to improve dance, drama, and music in the state.
7. I tried to improve the business.
8. I wanted to learn Hindi and learnt it.
9. I wanted to start my own business and did so.

On the Semantic Differential Test he described himself as "good," "successful," and "satisfied" as the course began, but expressed a wish to become more "active." His goals established during the course included founding a new industry; expanding his old firm; "being loved by all to a great extent"; and "studying things relating to my new business, and try to stand on my own legs." Goals regarding power, status, and spiritual life seemed less prominent for N than goals dealing with achievement and affection.

The most unhappy period in N's life, he feels, was when he was studying for his examinations under his cousin's direction. The happiest time was "in the SIET Institute [at the achievement course] . . . because every day I was thinking, learning new things, and we all seemed young again." N feels that the best age to be is "between twenty and thirty. Before twenty it's just boyhood; you don't know things. From twenty to thirty there are no family burdens. If you have children they are small only, no encumbrances. After thirty, the burdens pile on." N goes on to say that at present his friends counsel him to pay more attention to his responsibility to accumulate money for school fees, his daughters' dowries, and the like. "People say to me, you should think of it now." N seems somewhat oppressed by these suggestions; he is anxious for his children to succeed, but dislikes feeling as though his own period of active life is over.

INTERPRETATION

N's case is particularly interesting in dispelling the stereotype that every boy in a small, traditional Indian village grows up with the passivity, fatalism, and otherworldliness so often described in the literature on Hindu culture and personality. N's life history testifies to his strong sense of individuality and to the fact that independence, autonomy, and personal achievements have been important to him since childhood. His self-concept might be summarized as "I am a man who sets goals and achieves them." It is interesting to hypothesize how this came to be.

The early death of N's father is doubtless an important factor. In reviewing N's case material, the idea that father-absence could have encouraged N's sense of autonomy seemed paradoxical, since in a Western achievement-oriented culture father-absence implies that the son is left without a model for masculine, instrumental achievement behavior. But the fact that N's father's absence did not appear to have produced this effect caused us to examine the picture more critically, especially when we learned that the two other businessmen in the larger sample who were most outstanding in their degree of autonomous activity in adulthood had also grown up in fatherless homes. We began to speculate that father-absence in the Indian context might produce exactly the opposite effect from that in the West.

We reasoned here that in a typical Indian joint family (as in the case of X, below), the father directs, supervises, and controls his son's activities so extensively that the child's autonomy is expressly inhibited. Further, the traditional Indian father exerts strict control over his wife's activities outside the home, with the effect that she in turn invests a large proportion of her energy in loving and caring for her sons. As ties of dependency between mother and son increase, it becomes unlikely that the son will take pleasure in autonomous achievement. It can be argued, then, that dependence and lack of initiative will be fostered in a son when his father is present in the home.

N's experience as youngest son in a fatherless family, in contrast, allowed him a good deal of autonomy and independence early in life. Without a father to provide for the family, it was naturally seen as important that the children receive enough education to be able to maintain themselves in the world on their own. N's elder brother, of course, had to terminate his schooling early to assist his mother with the lands, but as the youngest of four children N was relatively free of these family duties. Moreover, N's mother's responsibilities for maintaining the family prevented her, on the one hand, from fostering an unduly strong dependence in her son, and on the other hand, from controlling his every action so that autonomy would be inhibited. Mother and elder sister were warm toward N, but to a great degree he seems to have won their love by his actions as an increasingly autonomous individual. As his accomplishments were recognized by teachers and others in the village, doing well on his own became more and more satisfying. Autonomous achievement became a central characteristic of his personality, important partly in itself, partly as a means of winning approval from adults, and partly as a way of feeling secure in the absence of an all-embracing family group.

Pleasure in achievement is notable in N's current self-concept, but several other salient features of his achievement drive should be noted as well. First, N reports a good deal of difficulty in working under direct supervision. The period in his life marked by the greatest confusion and failure was the time when his older cousin undertook to direct his life. In enjoining N to study, providing him with a job, and arranging his marriage, the cousin was acting in a way most Indians would see as highly helpful. For N, however, accustomed to taking the initiative, this exterior control was upsetting and debilitating. We can hypothesize that his continued need for adults' interest and approval prevented him from direct defiance of authority, but that his sense of security and self-respect was undercut by his cousin's domination. Ever since that period of his life, N has arranged to be free from direct supervision and control.

A second notable attribute is the high value N places on his differentness: the uniqueness of his educational accomplishments, his opposition to traditional practices of his caste, his unusual plans for his daughters' education, his tradition-breaking in dealings with his present employees. All of N's current achievements are colored by his pleasure in not doing things the usual way, in thinking and acting for himself.

Although N's answers indicate that he sees himself as a very independent individual, further evidence suggests a theme of continued need for others as well. While N does not seek the help of male authority-figures, we note that he was very willing to turn to his mother for financial help in completing his education. Currently, he regularly discusses business problems with his wife. N looked forward to the visits of people connected with the achievement motivation project and seemed eager to describe his business activities to the visitors in great detail. We may hypothesize that the approval and interest of other people is still an important motivator for N, and that he achieves most productively when he is on his own, but when others take an active and approving interest in his accomplishments.

The Effects of Achievement Training for N. At the time of the course, N was basically a satisfied man, but we got the impression that he had lost some of the zest characteristic of his early adult life. For the previous few years he had formulated vague plans for business changes but had been plagued by procrastination and had taken no action. His thoughts had turned increasingly toward plans for his children's education and he had begun to worry a bit about the money that would be necessary for tuition and for his daughters' dowries. Since these concerns are typical for men of his age and station in life, he found it increasingly difficult to look on himself as a "different" and "special" man. Just as his friendships during college had been personally rewarding but had interfered with his sense of satisfaction in studies, now his association with other "solid citizens" in the community influenced him toward stability and even stagnation. In the eyes of everyone else N was doing well, yet it had been some time since he had taken unusual, innovative action of the sort which had given him his greatest pleasure early in life.

N describes his two-week stay at the SIET institute as a "second youth." The phrase is apt, for we can view the achievement training course as reawakening in N the motivation that had led him to enjoy autonomous achievement through childhood and early adulthood. The course gave N a message that he basically wanted to hear: it was still possible and highly desirable at his age to take risks and start anew. At the training course it was persuasively argued that middle age need not be, as his peers counseled, a period of gradual retirement from activity and concentration on security and the needs of his children. Since N was already familiar with the satisfactions which could come from risk-taking, innovation, and autonomous activity, this message was welcome. We hypothesize here that the achievement motivation ideology functioned as an important inspiration for N. Encouragement of risk is one course input that appears to have been important in influencing him to become entrepreneurially active after the course.

A second course input that appears important is the "interested but distant" nature of the authority structure associated with achievement training. We have hypothesized that for N, achievements are partially motivated by the desire to win the approval of admired people. We have also noted N's difficulty in working under too-direct control. In this light it appears important that the achievement-training course introduced authority figures (the course instructors, Dr. McClelland, the follow-up personnel) into N's life, but did so in a manner which did not curb his sense of personal autonomy. The SIET instructors were warm and encouraging but made it clear that plans were to be developed and carried out on the initiative of the course participants themselves. Prestigious follow-up visitors, arriving at regular intervals, were interested in N's progress but did not interfere in his day-to-day activities. N could combat his tendency to procrastinate by setting targets to be accomplished in time to display innovations to the visitors. Periodic follow-up by prestigious authorities, then, should be noted as another important attribute of the training course for N.

A final course input presumably important in N's case is the fact that achievement motivation ideology is not grounded in the Indian tradition. We have noted N's enjoyment of being different, of distinguishing himself from the beliefs and practices of his caste and town. Viewing himself as an "achiever," clearly different from most of Indian businessmen, was undoubtedly gratifying to him for this reason. It is not surprising that N was never deeply involved in the activities of the Entrepreneurs Association, or that he established his manufacturing concern alone rather than in collaboration with other course participants. The uniqueness and novelty of the *n* Achievement ideology were important for him; the involvement of some of his peers in achievement activities after the course was probably, if anything, a negative input in his case.

Case #2—B

B is a medium-sized, round-faced, soft-spoken man with a dark complexion and a broad smile. At the age of 37 he occupies a prominent social position in the town because he is the eldest son of an extremely rich and highly-respected landholding Vaisya family. At the time of the achievement training course, B lived with his aged, bedridden father, his mother, his wife, his three children, two younger brothers, and three unmarried teen-aged sisters in a large, elegant house near the outskirts of the town. He devoted full time to the management of several charitable institutions which had been run by the family for several generations.

We were interested in studying B in more detail because of the major change in his life which followed achievement training. After the *n* Achievement course, B decided to become a large-scale manufacturer. In collaboration with another course participant who provided the technical expertise, B purchased an industrial firm and invested a large sum to put the plant into better working condition. He devoted a good deal of time and energy to the project, first working to convince his mother and sisters to loan him money from the family stocks, and then making extended trips to the plant to oversee the work of getting it into operation. Although B had previously been unacquainted with the small businessmen of the community, after the course his home became a frequent meeting place for course participants interested in discussing their business plans. At the time of final follow-up, the plant was in production, and B was completing plans with his collaborator for establishing a second industry, a large graphite processing plant. B's business activity was especially noteworthy because no member of his family had previously invested capital in an entrepreneurial venture.

B was easy-going, good-natured, and cooperative in the interview with Mrs. Winter, but he experienced a good deal of difficulty with some of the questions. Though his English was not fluent, this did not seem to be the major problem. Rather, one got the feeling that the point of the interview eluded him; thinking and talking about his personal history and inner life seemed alien in the extreme. For example, when asked about his earliest memories or about strong and weak points in his personality, B looked baffled, paused, laughed, and seemed unable to come up with any answers. He tried hard to provide the information requested, but he appeared to be an unimaginative and unintellectual man who is unaccustomed to introspection.

Childhood. B grew up in the substantial house where his family still lives. He was the oldest of three sons, with three older sisters and three sisters younger than the boys. In addition to the nine siblings, the family included grandparents, several other relatives, and a large number of servants and clerks who were employed to administer the family charities. As is the case today, a member of this large family had surprisingly little contact with the ordinary life of the community. Tradespeople visited the household when their services were needed, and neither adults nor children considered it appropriate to spend time mingling with the ordinary townspeople. At the present time the family philosophy of life (as communicated primarily by other family members) seems to be that the traditions of the family are best carried on by an aloof bearing in the community and by the gracious administration of a large number of charities.

B describes himself as a "calm" child. His only memory of his early years is that "we were not allowed to go out of the house, so there was no chance to mix with other people. . . . If you go out they fear you will mix with other types of people, and the family face will go down." B reports having little contact with his father during childhood: "He was not taking care of us; mother was all." B's mother is not recalled as highly indulgent, however. Mother "has something of a temper, she is not so calm as my father." B's mother was a stern taskmaster in regard to his education: "My mother gave punishments for every failure, even for weekly tests in school . . . beating, scolding, everything." But she also praised him "for good marks, and for prizes I won in school." As a child, B was urged to dress himself, bathe himself, and otherwise do without parental help (his sisters, in contrast, report with pride that the servants did such things for them throughout childhood). "I learned that I myself could get it done," B recalls.

Education.   B attended a private school in the town. He was never an outstanding student, but "I liked school, I had so many friends there, all kinds of associations." Despite diligent work B failed his high-school entrance exams, but under his mother's close supervision he was able to pass eventually. B had no definite plans for higher education, but was able to obtain a place in a university business course. "I can't say I studied hard, I just passed it." After his studies, it never occurred to B to seek employment. "My place was just to look after our family affairs, for we ourselves give jobs to so many people."

Work history.   Within the sphere of family activities it appears that B took on a good deal of personal responsibility relatively early in life. While still a student he assumed the management of certain family lands, and after his education he was given the direction of some large shelters where poor people could sleep and be fed. Describing his work, he says, "Whether or not I am getting good results, I try to pay attention, know the most, know how best we can perform, learning from others and from practical experience. If a problem comes up I try to meet it, find a better way." It seems that as B's father grew older and his health began to decline, responsibility was gradually shifted onto B's shoulders.

Marriage.   B was married at 18 to the daughter of another prosperous local family. He liked his bride, and found her "not quarrelsome with me." Faced with the typical sort of conflict between his wife and mother within the joint family, B refused to take sides: "How can I be on this side or that side?" In 1965, B moved with his wife and children to a separate residence. The move appears to have been amicable, and he and his children still frequently spend time in the old family home. In contrast to his father's policy of restricting the female family members' movements outside the home, B is agreeable to his wife's shopping and visiting in the community.

Current Interests and Personality.   Religion is important to B: he prays twice daily, visits the temple often, and conforms strictly to dietary laws. For him the religious life means devotion to charitable works and maintaining his family's benevolent activities. In filling out his goal questionnaire at the time of the course, for example, B listed more separate goals under the "religion" heading than any other, and all these goals dealt with helping others in concrete, material ways.

At the time of the *n* Achievement course, B listed the following experiences as most satisfying in his life: "educational success," "managing the family charities," and "supervising agricultural cultivation on my own." The happiest time in his life was "no one time, but when the season is good in agriculture, and when the charities are running well and all the people are getting benefits." B can specify no one accomplishment as his best, but says "all the charities and activities that I have done by my own effort make me proud." Despite this pride in his own accomplishment, however, B responded to the interviewing question about the relative importance of fate versus will with the strong affirmation that "we have belief in fate, everything will be according to our fate." He went on to document a list of personal accomplishments, but to affirm again that "in all these things, fate will be guiding us."

In the interview, B could not think of any special strong points or weak points in his personality. "How can I tell you? You must ask others." When asked about efforts to improve himself, he replied readily: "After my education, we didn't have proper relations with so many people, so I tried to mingle with people, and to have good connections with them."

With the exception of the religious goals mentioned above, all B's entries in the goal questionnaire dealt with specific plans for starting a new industry. In his TAT stories the most prominent theme was determined effort toward achievement. For example, B told the following story in response to a picture of a man at a drawing board, looking at a photograph of several people.

> The man in the picture has determined to construct a house. Whether he gets a good plan or not he is trying to draw. With his own efforts and his friends' help he has drawn a good plan and constructed the house. He is feeling joy for his success and remembering his helpful friends in the photo.

All B's stories, interestingly enough, were similar to this one in describing help by friends as an important element in achievement success.

INTERPRETATION

It would be difficult to understand B's personality outside the context of his family customs and traditions. While every man defines himself to some extent in terms of his station in life, an unusually large proportion of B's feelings, interests, and activities appear to be centered in a contented acceptance of his role as the son of an important and charitable family within the community. B views himself as an instrument of fate, put on earth to fulfill his duties of carrying on the family traditions. He strikes one as a psychologically uncomplicated man whose principal satisfaction is his sense that he is discharging well the duties appropriate to his position in the community.

It is important to note, however, that for B an acceptance of fate does not negate the importance of doing his job well. For a Westerner, the achievement ethic of "accomplishing as much as possible as well as possible" is most frequently grounded in a belief in the importance and efficacy of one's own free will. B, as we have seen, would put the matter somewhat differently: he considers that it is his fated duty not only to work hard in the affairs of the world, but also to do as well as possible. The ultimate results may be in the hands of fate, but he feels a personal obligation to strive for excellence and he experiences personal satisfaction when his job is well done.

As in N's case, it is possible to see in B's family background the sources of his values of personal excellence and achievement. Like N, B was not overshadowed by paternal domination; his father appears to have been scarcely present as an important figure during the early years. B's mother, the primary agent of his socialization, seems to have placed consistent emphasis on responsibility and achievement. It is somewhat puzzling how B, growing up with six sisters in a female-dominated household, avoided developing a more feminine personality orientation. The mother-daughter ties in this family appear unusually close, and perhaps B's mother fostered greater dependence in her daughters than in her sons. Sex-role differentiation was strong, and the parental feeling was presumably that boys should be trained to manage responsibly the duties of the family in the world. In any case, although the evidence is slight, we see no signs of a feminine identification in B; for example, he describes himself as "calm," like his father and in sharp contradiction to his mother.

Before the course, then, B already had several important characteristics of the high achiever. He established definite standards of excellence for himself, paid attention to feedback in his work, and took pleasure in a job well done. His activities, however, were confined to those traditional in the family. Since his philosophy of life emphasized the fulfillment of obligations, B had little motivation to undertake activities beyond the sphere of "what our family ought to do." Further, as a rather unimaginative person, it seems unlikely that he would have the ability to develop plans that represented a radical break with family tradition.

It should be noted, however, that in one important respect B did not simply mirror his family's interests and values. From boyhood he seems to have been somewhat unhappy with the isolation from others in the town imposed on him by the family position. In school he had enjoyed friendships with many boys, and after completion of his schooling he had taken an unusual step in going out to his "inferiors" in the city to build acquaintances across caste and class lines. B's desire to have greater contact with nonfamily members may be one reason he was attracted by the idea of achievement training.

Effects of the Course for B. We have speculated that even before the achievement training course, B possessed many of the personal qualities necessary to make him a satisfied and successful businessman. Why, then, had he not already become an entrepreneur? We can speculate that one important reason was sociological; members of B's family had never considered business activity as appropriate to their obligations and duties, to their "fate" or *dharma*. A second possible reason is B's lack of technical knowledge about business; for this reason alone it was difficult for him to translate vague desires into concrete plans.

The achievement training course removed both of these barriers and thus cleared the way for B's business activity. First, business activity was presented as important and desirable. This input was probably not crucial for B; we have seen that even before the course, he had had vague thoughts that he would like to begin some business activity. More vital was the opportunity the course gave B to meet with other men who could contribute what he lacked: practical intelligence, imagination, and knowledge about the mechanics of initiating business activity. We have suggested that achievement training appealed to B initially because of the opportunity it gave him to have warm, friendly contact with peers from whom he was customarily cut off by his family position. The peer group input of the course was attractive to B in two ways: intrinsically, and as a means for finding a collaborator who could instruct him in the details of business operation. After the course, B was delighted with his new friendships. As his home became the meeting place for other entrepreneurs, his interest in business was sustained and he could receive continued advice and suggestions from men more experienced than he in business activity. Secure in his social position, and accustomed to turning to his family staff members for practical advice, B found working with the other entrepreneurs easy and congenial. The peer contacts and the support of this new business-oriented reference group were the important course input in his case.

Case #3—D

D is a handsome, slim, boyish-looking man of twenty-seven of the Vaisya caste. He lives with his father, mother, wife, three children, and a young nephew in a modest house. At the time of the course he worked under his father's direction in the family firm, a retail radio shop on Main Street. D was selected for study because he was one of the few men not in control of their firms who was nonetheless rated active after the course. His business activity, undertaken as a sideline while he continued to help his father in the store, was the founding of a local ice-cream concession in collaboration with a man his own age who had not attended the course. At the time of follow-up, the ice-cream agency had been operating profitably for four months. D and his friend were about to hire their first employee, and were making plans for expanding their activities to a nearby town.

D's intelligence and psychological-mindedness made him a pleasant subject for the clinical interview. He appeared to enjoy talking about his interests and experiences; after asking a few initial questions about the purpose of the interview, he responded to Mrs. Winter's inquiries directly and nondefensively. D experienced some difficulty in recalling details from his very early years, which was surprising in the light of the introspectiveness and imagination he displayed elsewhere in the interview. When the questions were finished, he took the opportunity to ask for information about friendship, courtship, and marriage in America.

Family and Childhood. D's family during childhood consisted of his father, mother, uncle, aunt, and maternal grandmother. D and his two sisters, three and four years older, were the only children. D was happy to have only two siblings, since "with a smaller family we can enjoy more education and comforts." He plans to limit his own family to three children.

D describes his father as prone to speak his mind. "He gets provoked with harsh words for others . . . whatever he has to say, he doesn't keep it in his mind but talks it openly." D's mother, on the other hand, is easygoing, calm and "God-minded . . . prayer is important." D considers that he resembles his mother in temperament. Though he is less religious than his mother, he generally conceals this fact since he does not like to upset her.

D's mother was absent from the home during most of his early childhood due to a severe illness. "My sisters and I were angry . . . we never had regular contact with her." His father played relatively little part in his early upbringing: "He was not very lovable to the children. He loved us, but would never take us up or lull us." D was cared for primarily by his grandmother, although he does not describe this relationship as particularly close or intense.

D as a child was "jolly-going, not so naughty." "I was careful, I didn't dare to go with naughty boys. I was just going on with my education, coming home, having food, and so on." He recalls being forced to attend school at the age of six. "Previously I had enjoyed all the homely comforts, so I did not like to go." His grandmother forced a servant to carry him bodily to class. "I would run home from school, causing much trouble."

D remembers no notable punishment during childhood. He was praised "by neighbors, aunt and uncle, for my intelligence." His tutor's mother also thought highly of his intellectual gifts. D was not encouraged to be independent during childhood. "Up to six years others are dressing me. . . . Tuition and direction were used to keep my routine and to guide my studies."

Education and Employment. D often shirked his homework during elementary school, but passed his tests easily anyway. His family, distressed at his poor study habits, supervised his work carefully and hired tutors to stand over him as he prepared for exams. A turning point came at the age of 14 when, D says, "I realized myself that I should start studying." Mother and father were leaving town for a festival in a married sister's village, just as D was preparing for an important test. D's tutor's mother was instructed by the parents to stand over him to make sure he did the work. After their departure, however, he insisted on working on his own. "Why should I be caretaken by others? I'll do it myself," he thought. "Spoon-feeding is unnecessary at this level."

D recalls two difficult decisions during the next few years. First was the necessity of choosing between a difficult high-school math course, as preparation for the highly desirable engineering or medical university program, and an easier general mathematics curriculum. "I wanted the difficult course but people said it would be too hard. All my friends, my bosom friends all through school, chose the easier one." D went along with his classmates, but ever since has felt "worry that I unnecessarily took the wrong path." His marks were so high that he feels now that he could have succeeded in what he really wanted in the first place.

D subsequently entered the university program in commerce, feeling that his father had gone to so much trouble to educate him that he should follow a business course which might be helpful to the family firm. After graduation, he faced the second difficult decision: whether to do graduate study in accounting, which he found highly interesting and which would lead to a good job in some large firm, or to terminate his education and join his father's business. "I was too much worried, thinking through the night what to do." While his father left the decision up to D, D felt great pressure to enter the family firm. Non-family members could not be trusted to carry on the business; since D was the only son, his moving away would mean that the business would come to an end. After struggling for weeks with the problem, D finally made his decision. "Why not help my father? So to safeguard the business and the livelihood, I sacrificed my studies."

D still appears to experience some regret over this decision, but he is moderately satisfied with his work in his father's firm. He likes best his duty of looking after correspondence, since this is interesting and allows him to develop and improve his knowledge of English. He likes least "working from morning to night if my father is not there. I feel botheration about the weight of responsibility." D still feels "young and inexperienced" in the firm, and turns to his father for advice on dealing diplomatically with customers.

Marriage and Children.   D proudly introduced his lovely wife before the interview. While speaking with Mrs. Winter he dwelt at length on his satisfaction with the marriage, which was arranged after D had inspected more than a dozen girls, looking for the proper combination of beauty and education. "I was very particular." He described his pleasure at their opportunity to travel to Northern India for a honeymoon, and his approval of the new furniture obtained for their room in the family home. His wife is "calm-going and adjusted with the entire household." Disputes between D's mother and wife are few; he tries not to take sides, but "to please both." D does not discuss business with his wife unless she asks, but then is glad to explain.

D is proud of his young son and daughter and the new baby. Plans for their future are naturally still vague, but D feels his daughter should be well educated and perhaps should become a doctor. "She should have good behavior and a decent life; I'm not so particular about tradition. Now the old traditions about women are coming down," D notes approvingly.

Present Opinions and Interests.   During university and afterwards, D enjoyed spending his leisure hours walking, talking, and drinking coffee with a small group of close friends. This pattern continued until about a year ago, when several of the friends moved away from the community and D found himself spending more time at home. His partner in the new ice-cream agency is a young man whom he met through his friendship group. "He was a friend's brother, so day by day I became intimate with him, and thought he would be a good partner."

Religion is not too important in D's present life, but "all the women believe it, so I go along—I have no courage." This is in contrast to his father's blunt rejection of religious customs and concerns. D believes in fate as more important than will. "Although will may have effect, fate has ruled for me, and there has been no trouble for me so far." As his personal strong point, D mentions, "I have no vices, no smoking or drinking. . . . I am having a smooth business without hardship . . . and I am satisfactory with wife and family." When asked about weak points D recalled his anger during childhood over the fact that he had little contact with his mother during her long illness. He attempted personal change only once, about two years ago. "I wanted to make new friends, and to be famous in the society, but couldn't do it because of the routine of the business. So I joined a club." If D were to be an animal he would like to be "a prince's dog . . . because good care is taken of him, just like a baby." He would least want to be a snake, "because a man can't be careful against it . . . even if he is on guard, he can be bitten."

D's response to the achievement training course was noteworthy. At the start of the training he expressed a marked skepticism. "I am a self-depending man," he asserted in his initial "Who Am I?" statement, explaining further that he was the sort of person who would consider new ideas very carefully before allowing himself to be convinced. His final "Who Am I?" statement, in contrast, began: "Now I am a man with achievement motivation." D went on to express his commitment to things learned in the course, and to state that he had become inspired to be an achiever "by contact with people who were nothing at the start of their business, but great industrialists now." As the course ended, D's enthusiasm about achievement motivation was high, but he seemed vague about how the course material could be applied to his own life plans. In his goal inventory, for example, D noted vaguely that he wanted to expand his business or start an industry. He listed three more definite goals relating to status and respect, six goals relating to friendship, and four goals relating to use of his leisure time.

INTERPRETATION

Dependency appears to be an important theme in D's life history. Evidence for his desire to be protected and taken care of is prominent in the case material, from his early memory of wanting to stay at home rather than go to school, to his present wish to be "a prince's dog," cared for like a baby. We note his present reluctance to disagree with wife and mother and stand up to his own opinions about religion; his dislike of being given full responsibility in the family firm, even for a short period of time; and his satisfaction, rather atypical for educated young Indians, with living in his parents' home. D seems to be hesitant to stand on his own two feet and confront the world on his own.

Yet equally prominent in D's case history is a theme of discomfort with and denial of these dependency needs. The greatest crisis in his life thus far was the difficult decision as to whether or not to join the family firm. His final choice—to stay under his father's wing—is an expression of the desire for continued protection. Yet D is evidently uncomfortable with this aspect of the decision, as evidenced by his statement, in one of the biographical questionnaires, "I joined my father's firm in order to retain my independence." Similar discomfort with the notion that he likes to lean on others is suggested in the "Who Am I?" statement quoted above, where D argues lengthily for his "self-dependence." It is evidently a matter of some importance to him that he see himself as not easily swayed by others.

In this light, the acts in D's life which are apparently most independent when examined closely may be viewed as counterdependent actions, motivated by D's desire to convince himself that he is able to rely on himself rather than others. It is interesting, for example, that D's independence regarding study habits was asserted at the very moment when the protection of his parents ("spoon-feeding") was withdrawn as his parents abandoned him to attend his sister's wedding. Perhaps D, unwilling to admit how much he did wish his parents' direction at this difficult time, chose a course of extreme independence in an effort to convince himself that he really could get along alone. We might speculate that his early resistance to the ideas in the achievement training course arose as he felt himself strongly tempted to agree with everything that was being said.

We may summarize that there is little indication that D experiences satisfaction in independent, autonomous achievement of the sort characteristic of N or even of A. Rather he seems most satisfied when responsibility is carried by stronger figures but when he can avoid direct awareness of this state of affairs. How did D come to be so different from N and from A in this respect? The most important factor appears to be a childhood ill-suited to the development of a basic sense of trust in his own abilities. D never experienced the sort of warm relationship with his mother that could serve as the foundation for a strong sense of security later in life. Since his mother was seriously ill during his early childhood, we presume that he was denied the kind of maternal relationship which in Erikson's terms (1950) is essential for the development of the child's basic trust in his own powers. Currently, D seems to view the world with a good deal of distrust and suspicion—as, for example, in his statement quoted above about why he would not like to be a snake. His lack of trust in his abilities is further suggested by his reluctance in adolescence to risk failure in the math course for which he was actually qualified.

Whether or not these speculations about D's lack of basic trust are well founded, it seems clear that at the present time he is not primarily achievement-oriented. Instead he is motivated toward a somewhat guarded dependence on his father, mother, and wife; toward affiliative satisfactions with his wife and friends; and toward attaining status and prestige, particularly in the eyes of important older people. Other attributes which should be noted are D's pride in his intelligence, his interest in learning, and his continued desire to view himself as a person who does things for himself.

D's Response to Achievement Training. After some initial skepticism, presumably motivated by the desire not to appear too dependent on authority, D's response to the achievement training course was highly enthusiastic. We can speculate that the attractive features of the training course for him were (a) the prestigious authorities who "spoon-fed" him with time, attention, reading materials, approval, and the like; (b) the intellectual respectability of the achievement motivation ideology; and (c) the presence of prestigious older businessmen as members of his group. It was doubtless also important to D that he attended the course but his father did not, since thus he could view the training as an avenue of partial independence from his father's business path. For all these reasons, D found the message of the course highly convincing.

In our analysis of D's personality we have suggested some of the reasons why this enthusiasm was not followed by D's leaving the family firm after the training course. In the context of the Indian value of respect for one's father, this would have been a difficult step for any young man to take; for D it appeared to be quite impossible. In fact, our analysis of his character structure makes it rather surprising that he took any business action at all. That D's achievement motivation was radically changed by the training course seems an unlikely explanation for his business activity after the course, since his TAT in the follow-up period contained relatively little achievement imagery. In the light of a past history seemingly so discouraging to entrepreneurial actions, to what can we attribute D's business activity after the course?

First, it may be that the strength and definiteness of D's commitment to achievement motivation immediately after the course created sufficient cognitive dissonance that he was motivated to act in accordance with his self-proclaimed principles. In his "Who Am I?" statement after the course, D committed himself voluntarily and publicly to the statement that he had high achievement motivation and planned to undertake business activity. Unlike some of the businessmen who failed to act on similar statements, D places a high value on logical thinking and internal consistency. Dissonance theorists would argue that the very definiteness of his commitment made it likely that he would undertake action in support of his views.

Second, membership in the Entrepreneurs Association was gratifying to D both for the status and prestige it implied and for the chance to associate with important older businessmen who might be of assistance to him. As a young person he perhaps felt it necessary to reinforce his sense of belonging to the group by actually becoming an entrepreneur, rather than sitting on the sidelines at meetings.

Third, it is probably important that D embarked in business at the suggestion of a friend. In this way he could be both dependent (on the friend's ideas and initiative) and independent (from the family business) at the same time. Moreover, the process of making contacts in the distribution of ice cream involved D in the sort of friendly, sociable visits within the community that he had always found pleasurable. Thus, the particular type of business activity that D selected appears to be rewarding to him for its affiliation satisfactions, entirely apart from any achievement connotations.

In summary, then, D can be viewed as a young man rather low in independence and achievement motivation, who started a new business after the training course mainly from a desire for status, respect, and affiliation. The important course inputs in his case appear to have been the attention and concern of the prestigious course leaders and his membership in the Entrepreneurs Association after training.

Case #4—X

X is a tall, wiry 46-year-old Brahmin. Jumpy and erratic in his movements, he talks quickly in a loud, forceful tone. At the time of the course, X lived with his wife, four children and 11 other relatives in the home of his vigorous 80-year-old father. Adjoining the house is the family business, a factory employing 25 people, founded by X's father many years ago. Since X's father retains full responsibility for business decisions, X's duties in the firm are relatively few. He spends several hours each day at the local Vedanta society lodge in meditation, study, and philosophical conversation with friends. After the achievement motivation training course, X attended a few meetings of the Entrepreneurs Association but took no steps toward new business activity.

Although X was aware that the purpose of our follow-up visit was to learn of new businesses founded by course participants, he seemed unembarrassed at having no business progress to report. On the contrary, X was eager to talk to the Western visitors. As an expert on "the way to do things in India," he delivered long, didactic lectures on Indian values, customs, and philosophies, contrasting these sharply with what he portrayed as the dangerously misguided ways of the West. He was particularly anxious to convince us that the immorality, delinquency, and gangsterism common today in America were due to Americans' laissez-faire attitudes toward marriage and the raising of children. The virulence of X's opposition to Western emancipation of women contrasted dramatically with his cordiality to Mrs. Winter and his cooperation about being interviewed. He appeared to enjoy the interview situation partially as a chance to expound his own values and partially as an opportunity to convince a Western woman that she was a prisoner of her misguided culture.

During the interview X was guarded when he sensed that a question was aimed at eliciting personal information. He would laugh nervously, counter with questions of his own, or evade the point by launching another forceful explanation of "Indian practices." He seemed eager to convince the interviewer that his strong and weak points were not his alone, but rather were characteristic of the system of which he is a part. Throughout the interview X plied Mrs. Winter with coffee and sweetmeats so insistently that it was impossible to refuse. The interview was interrupted twice when X called his daughter and niece into the room and delivered a monologue on their characters, in illustration of some of his general points, while the girls stood painfully by. For Mrs. Winter, the interview with X was an unusual, somewhat uncomfortable, but fascinating experience.

Family and Childhood. X's father, a business-college graduate, is described as vigorous and forceful, "leading an exceptionally disciplined life." X's mother, who died in his late adolescence, was "queen of the household" but was never allowed to step outside the home. X's only brother, younger than himself, died in 1966.

X describes himself as closest to his mother during childhood, and more like his mother than his father, who was "always angry." Until the age of four, he explained, "the mother is all to the son . . . the mother doesn't give the father a chance to scold the boy, beat or punish." His earliest memory is of crying and then of being breast-fed, "at the age of three or so."

Later memories deal with the relationship to his father. At about the age of seven, X and a cousin decided to stay home from school and were "beaten black and blue" when his father discovered them together at home. X returned to this incident later in the interview when asked about childhood fears: "On seeing my father I was damned frightened, and on a good number of occasions I had fear of my father." His up-bringing was "strict." "Before the age of 15, wherever I go, I should be in the notice of the parents." Asked whether he was ever encouraged to do things on his own, X was quick to explain that "generally the mother will assist boys. Even to teen-agers she will be assisting, particularly for girls. For myself also, up to age ten my mother was assisting with the bath." He appears to have had no duties or work responsibilities as a child.

Education. X did not like school very much because "thirty years ago we were terribly fearing our teachers. Teachers were whipping and scolding . . . I used to go to school fearing strong discipline." He was interested in university study but was not admitted, "a sad point." After completing his schooling, X reports, "I had no need for plans. My father was in business, so I was confident of the place there."

Marriage and Family. X was married at 19 to a distant relative. Describing the marital relationship, he expounded at length on Indian women's obedience to men: "There is generally no scope for tension between the husband and wife. The woman doesn't have her own views, so is always guided in every aspect. The man tames her, guides her, maintains peace. Her duty is to worship the man as a god."

X described in a general way the inevitable tensions between a man's mother and his wife in the joint family, and explained that throughout his marriage he took his mother's side in such disagreements since "affection to mother plays a major part," especially during the first five or six years of marriage.

In raising children, X explained, "parents play a major part as long as they can." He is developing plans for his sons' educations and careers. His oldest daughter, now married, wished to continue her education but was prohibited from doing so by X and her husband-to-be, who told her that eight years of school was enough. The only "weak point" admitted to by X is his tendency to "become irritated, make a fuss . . . I will yell at my son for not studying, then later think it is bad, and realize." Generally, however, X is proud of the way he lives up to the parental responsibility to arrange his children's lives in every detail.

Present Interests.   In contrast to his volubility on family matters, X had little to say about his business career. "The business is my father's; it is one man's personal empire." X asks no one for advice because "in India there is jealousy . . . no man likes to see another get ahead, so we will not expose ourselves and expect cooperation." He has no preference for one aspect of work over another. "My father attends to work at the plant but is becoming older, so I feel it is my duty to go outside and attend to selling, canvassing, and purchasing materials."

In X's view his main strong point is that "I like to help others. If a friend has a problem I can give constructive suggestions or criticisms, to help with the worry." Asked for other strong points, he replied, "I can help myself. I can help others . . . no, that is the same as the one I said before. I can volunteer my services to anyone who asks. And also I like to have a disciplined life, both physically and mentally." Apart from the "weak point" mentioned above, his anger at his sons, X could think of no flaws in his character. He attempts to improve himself "through meditation, constantly."

The happiest time in X's life was his wedding night; the unhappiest, "the day of my mother's demise." What age is it best to be? "Childhood is the best age! There are no botherations, troubles or worries, we are free all the 24 hours, from birth to the fifth year. We treat the baby as equal to God." What makes him angry? "Whatever happens opposed to my feeling!" When questioned about examples, X added that he expects his children to study until ten o'clock nightly. If he returns home and finds them sleeping he beats them, "in their own interest only."

If X had to become an animal he would choose to be an elephant, "for its majesty, because it is the strongest, and also a vegetarian." He would dislike being a mosquito "because it sucks the blood and brings impurity, and causes unhealth in the healthy body." X digressed at this point in the interview to explain the importance of a number of Brahmin ritual practices in assuring a calm, tranquil, and disciplined life.

The integration of family, religious, and personal concerns in X's life is well illustrated, finally, by a quotation from the "Who Am I?" statement he wrote at the start of the achievement course:

> Being born in a middle class family, I need not struggle for my basic needs. But, when it comes to personal prosperity and achievements, I have to struggle. I begin to think. The thoughts go higher and higher. I see no limit. I begin to compare with others. I find myself very small, but I fear to admit this fact. I have come to know that there is a Most High, say God, or any other. One day or other I can become as High as Himself. I have got enough good education, and am given good chances to prosper. But, still I crave to be more useful to me as well as others. I feel it is my duty to drive out despondency, bring out harmony, merry [sic] and joy. I am an industrialist of small scale, with a burning desire to develop.

INTERPRETATION

If the organizing theme of D's case history is dependence, that of X's is power. To an unusual degree even within Indian culture, his personality is centered around a wish for and interest in domination of other people. This concern is reflected in many aspects of the case material: in X's satisfying experiences of domination of others; in his insistence that women should be controlled by men; in his stress on the power available to him through religion; in his portrait of infancy as pleasurable because "we treat the baby as God"; and even in his choice of the elephant as favorite animal "for its majesty, and because it is the strongest." How can we understand the intensity of this power drive in X's life?

It should be noted that X is concerned with power of two quite different varieties. First we see a concern with actual instrumental dominance of other people (especially women, children, and people who have stood in his way). X rationalizes his desire for this sort of power by characterizing it as typical for his family, his caste group, and for India as a whole. Second, X appears to seek a sort of fantasy-power in which actual domination of others is less salient than the feeling of being satisfied, tranquil, and capable of bringing about all that he desires, by thinking alone. In this category we would place his religious aspiration to bring himself into harmony with the universe through the power of his meditations. X is unambivalent about the desirability of this type of power.

To understand the sources of these power concerns we must consider X's experience in his traditionally organized joint family. For the first few years X was "treated as God" by a warm, ever-present mother.

In this extreme early maternal indulgence, we can infer that X was waited on hand and foot, given whatever he desired, and indulged whenever he cried. His wish was sufficient to bring immediate gratification.

At the age of four or five, however, X entered his father's sphere of influence and experienced a traumatic end to this previously absolute power. X's relationship to his strict, traditional male parent was necessarily characterized by total respect and subordination, accompanied by a good deal of unexpressed anger and fear. X complied with his father's demands, experiencing vividly his own weakness and lack of potency under the paternal domination.

Traces of these two important relationships, to his mother and his father, can be seen in X's present personality. The early experience of power to command instant indulgence from his mother through thinking alone seems to have persisted in the form of X's present belief in the power of mind to influence the world and provide harmony and peace of spirit. X still sees wishing and thinking as the preferred and most effective methods for achieving satisfaction and power. "When it comes to personal prosperity and achievements, I have to struggle. *I begin to think* . . . thoughts go higher and higher, I see no limit," he says. We can speculate that the strength of early indulgence has short-circuited for X the process of achieving effects through instrumental activity in the world.

X's response to his father's domination can be seen as the source of his current concerns with control over other people. It appears that X dealt with and partially mastered his fear and anger toward his father by developing a fairly strong identification with the harsh, aggressive paternal role. Thus today X describes himself as quick-tempered and severe with his own children. As was noted above, X is somewhat ambivalent about these aspects of his present personality; he does not emphasize directly the resemblances between his father's behavior and his own. Evidently the fact that he still must respect and obey his father is uncomfortable for him. Yet we see him handling these feelings by acting his father's part toward his own children, with the effect that the pattern will doubtless be perpetuated in the next generation. We view X today, then, as identifying somewhat ambivalently with his father's dominant temperament and role as a means of compensating for his actual position of continued powerlessness vis-à-vis his father in the joint family.

But interestingly enough, X's relationship with his father appears to be less central to his personality formation than his relationship with his mother. X is somewhat disapproving toward those elements in his present behavior that we have attributed to his identification with his father. No such hesitancy appears, however, as he describes with pride his acts of helping, giving to, assisting, or directing the lives of younger, weaker, or more helpless individuals. The case material suggests that X is pleased to think of himself as a superior and respected figure who controls the lives of younger and more helpless people through his ability to give. This view of himself as powerful through the ability to give can be seen as evidence of X's identification with the maternal role on a more profound level than the identification with father referred to earlier.

We have already suggested that X found the experience of infantile indulgence profoundly satisfying. It would appear, then, that to him the maternal role implies the power to grant to others the best experience imaginable: total and immediate gratification. Women, in short, automatically possess the greatest possible power.

It now becomes clearer why X strongly insists that women (who apparently, in Indian culture, possess very little social influence over adult men) be firmly and continually put in their place by men. It is absolutely essential for X that women be subordinated, lest he give way to his strong unconscious desire to slip back into the state of being dominated by women, which represents the most complete pleasure he can imagine. Thus we hypothesize that X counters his longing to subordinate himself to women in two ways: by taking on the maternal "giving" role himself, and by firmly enforcing his dominance over women of the family in the day-to-day routine.

To summarize again, we see X's personality as centered around efforts to obtain a sense of power in the face of long-term experiences of powerlessness vis-à-vis both parents. He responds to his father's daily domination by identifying (on a fairly superficial level) with a harsh male role. On a deeper level, however, X perceives women as possessing the most profoundly attractive sort of power, the power to gratify dependent desires. X finds the female "power to give" both intensely attractive and intensely threatening. He deals with these feelings in two ways: by himself taking the feminine role of giving, and by investing a good deal of energy in exerting superficial control over the daily activities of women in his family.

We dwell at length on this psychological complex not merely for its importance in X's individual life history; our assumption is that X's pattern may be rather typical in Indian life. Observers of Indian culture have remarked on the high degree of maternal indulgence characteristic of child-rearing in the joint family (Carstairs, 1957; Minturn and Lambert, 1964), and on the infrequency of Indian men's autonomous behavior in opposition to their fathers. The notion that Indian men attribute unusual power to the female role is supported both by Indians' notable restrictions on females' daily activities and by their exaggerated devotion to such maternal symbols as goddesses, "Mother India," and the all-giving cow. The power implied in the giving role is familiar to and gratifying to many Indian men; Westerners working in India are frequently puzzled and somewhat irritated at the manner in which a young Indian will place himself in a position of dependence on the Westerner. He assumes that the other man will be gratified (as the Indian would be in the same situation) by the power satisfactions associated with the ability to be of assistance. Thus themes important in X's individual history appear to be writ large in Hindu culture.

Carrying the parallel one step further, we may hypothesize that X exemplifies (although with some exaggeration) the modal personality of the Indian male brought up in a traditional joint family. The typical Indian male, in this view, would be a female-identified individual (cf. Minturn and Lambert, 1964) for whom power concerns are central. His power needs are expressed primarily through helping and giving to weaker individuals. A sense of personal efficacy is achieved mainly through this helping dominance of others, but secondarily through a development and reliance on the power of the mind to bring gratification in fantasy, with real-world success seen as much less important. The extreme love of money and material possessions, which has struck some Western observers as paradoxical in the Indian context, is founded not in the Protestant ethic that worldly success is important in itself, but rather in the Indian's desire to accumulate resources with which he can control others through giving.

In summary, we suggest that the Indian male seeks two kinds of power: power over others through giving and power over the world or reality through the instrument of fantasy. The Indian social network, focused around mutual obligations for a charitable dominance that is received with respectful and grateful subordination, can be seen as the social expression of the first sort of power. Indian philosophy, with its teaching that the world of the mind is ultimately more meaningful than the world of action, is understandable as an expression of the second form of power.

This formulation contrasts sharply, of course, with what is generally accepted as male modal personality in a Western, achievement-oriented culture. The Western pattern would be a male-identified man whose sense of efficacy is achieved through instrumental activity in the world.

Action is more important and real to him than fantasy, and achievement needs are more prominent than needs for power. Persons in positions of power seek not to perpetuate their subordinates' dependence upon them, but rather to encourage autonomous behavior. Thus the network of social relationship generated by individuals with this personality constellation is more conducive to the development of n Achievement and a value on personal responsibility than is the hypothesized Indian model.

Effects of Achievement Training for X.   Returning now to X's case, we can speculate on the reasons why the n Achievement training course appears to have had little effect. As has been suggested, for X to have become an achiever would have required a radical reorganization of deeply rooted aspects of his personality. Entrepreneurial activity after the course would also have been difficult for X, because his father retains full control over the resources of the family firm. For these reasons alone, it is understandable that the training course failed to bring about change.

Beyond these factors, we can imagine that any course expressly identified as "behavior change" would be unattractive to X in the light of his unwillingness to bow to others' authority. His power needs would be threatened by the idea of outside figures proposing changes in his behavior or personality. Any authoritarian structure would arouse the sort of resentful compliance (with little internalization) characteristic of his present relationship with his father, while more democratically oriented authority would be insufficiently powerful to elicit X's respect.

Since X is self-consciously anti-Western in his political, religious, and economic ideology, the n Achievement theories were hardly calculated to motivate him toward behavior change. It seems unlikely that the Entrepreneurs Association would become an important reference group for X after the course, both because of his prior attachment to the Vedanta group and because relationships with superiors and subordinates appear to be more important in his life than dealings with peers. Finally, X stated openly at the course that the trust and openness toward others advocated by the SIET instructors "would never work in India." The implication is that he was unwilling to reveal enough of himself to instructors or peers to allow them a position of potential influence over his life.

SUMMARY COMMENTS

In reviewing these four case studies, it would be gratifying if we could identify some particular aspect of achievement motivation training to which we could attribute all favorable responses to the courses. The picture, of course, is not that clear. A clinical psychologist, attempting to pay full attention to the unique elements in each case, finds it particularly difficult to point to common features that are important in all cases; differences among individuals seem so much more striking than similarities among them. A further difficulty lies in the fact that case studies that include information on the early lives of the subjects are bound to emphasize elements of continuity and consistency in personality, at the expense of recognizing the possibility of change in adult life. Continuity between childhood and adulthood is so undeniable, that one is tempted to stress it at the expense of the subtle and complicated ways in which lives may be altered by later experiences and events.

In the light of these considerations, the first conclusion to be drawn from these case studies is almost a truism: no single input of the achievement training courses can be cited as basic for the three Changers described here. Individuals seem to have responded positively to the training courses for different reasons. All of the following inputs (and potentially others as well) were important in one or another of the cases studied: the democratic authority structure of the courses, the prestige of both the instructors and the other participants, the bonds of friendship formed at the courses, the information provided about practical details of entrepreneurial activity, the intellectual appeal of the achievement-motivation ideology, and the creation of a new reference group afterwards in the home community. It is unfortunate but not surprising that no single aspect is the magic wand that can be waved over every course participant to bring about entrepreneurial activity.

A second conclusion is that the training courses did not achieve their effects by deep-seated transformation of the motivation of the participants. Rather, it appears that the courses affected individuals by accentuating, building upon, or focusing potential for entrepreneurial activity which was already there. It is not astonishing that personalities in which dependency, affiliation, or power concerns have been primary for decades cannot be radically transformed by a two-week training course. Where the courses are successful, their effects appear to be achieved by building on a basis laid down in the childhood, adolescence, and adulthood of the individual participant. One heartening fact, from the point of view of those interested in further achievement training in non-Western cultures, is that the cases described here suggest that individuals with personality structures conducive to n Achievement do exist even outside the ideology, family structure, and values that

Westerners have conventionally associated with the Protestant ethic model for achievement. (See the conclusions of Chapter 9.)

If prior life history and personality structure are vital in determining response to achievement training, a pressing question remains. Can any general conclusions be drawn about what types of individuals will be most responsive to courses of this kind? What do the four cases reported here tell us about crucial antecedents to a positive response to achievement training?

Modern or Western values, as opposed to traditional values, while important to a degree, appear to be less crucial in this regard than we might previously have suspected. It is true that N, the most modern man described, is also the highest achiever, and that X, the most traditional, did not appear to change as a result of the course. Yet D, who was committed to education and modern values, was far less active after the course than B, who came from a highly traditional family and espoused a devoutly religious belief that fate is more important than man's will. Dietary practices, observance of caste and religious customs, or belief in astrology do not necessarily betoken a personality structure inimical to the message of achievement training.

One cluster of traditional Indian beliefs, however, may possibly suggest a character structure or family background uncongenial with entrepreneurial initiative. We refer here to intense opposition to the emancipation of women or to granting women significant social power. As was suggested in the comments on X's case, such attitudes may be a sensitive indicator that the individual is both threatened by and attracted to a feminine image of power. This connotes, in turn, the presence of a latent female identification and a desire for the social role of "powerful giver." For such a person, the exercise of control over subordinates is likely to be more rewarding than the achievement of successes in the economic world. We infer further that for a man preoccupied with enforcing his domination over women, the sense of personal autonomy is likely to be so weak that achievement behavior is unlikely. The importance of attitudes toward women in relation to achievement behavior receives tentative support from the trend reported in Table 9.10, showing that Inactives were even less willing than Changers to grant women social power by allowing them to work in their businesses (Item 32).

The crucial childhood antecedent of later achievement behavior, insofar as it can be identified in the cases considered here, is probably the development throughout an individual's life of the sense that pleasure can come from autonomy and from personal responsibility for actions.

For this, a modicum of personal autonomy and independence in childhood appears essential. We can imagine that this autonomy is best brought about by a moderate amount of maternal infantile gratification, the minimum necessary for a sense of basic trust in the child (Erikson, 1950), and by a degree of independence of the young boy from paternal supervision and control. In addition, there should be some encouragement of the son's independence and some reward for his autonomous behavior.

In the Indian context, these requirements are best met by a mother less indulgent than the average and a father who is physically absent or relatively uninvolved in the upbringing of his son. This formulation is supported by Bradburn's finding that Turkish boys whose fathers had been absent in the war during their childhood grew up with higher achievement motivation than did those with paternal models present at home (McClelland, 1961). In a culture that places such a high value on respect for and obedience to the father, it appears that the father must be absent in some way, if the son is to experience an appreciable degree of independence and autonomy in the early years.

The foregoing paragraphs might erroneously be taken to suggest that achievement training only succeeds for individuals whose achievement motivation is already high due to a fortuitous family structure or pattern of child-rearing. On the contrary, this pessimistic conclusion is unjustified for at least three reasons. First, original n Ach score does not predict which men will become active after the course (see Chapter 9). But even if this score were not a valid index of the autonomy and independence we have argued is essential for business activity, we should point secondly to the case material presented here for D. This suggests that achievement training can elicit entrepreneurial behavior even in a young man whose background clearly does not fit the model outlined above. While a background including autonomy may be the best basis for business activity following the course, D's case suggests that achievement training can foster business activity even in individuals for whom the childhood antecedents of achievement behavior are largely lacking.

Third, it should be emphasized that even individuals with backgrounds closely resembling the ideal model outlined above may not spontaneously turn to entrepreneurial activity in the Indian context without the stimulus of an achievement motivation training course. In a nation dominated by the Protestant ethic, most young men high in initiative, autonomy, and a preference for moderate risks presumably find it relatively easy to place themselves in occupational situations where these qualities can be brought into play to good effect. Since the dominant cultural values are in support of achievement behavior, successful entrepreneurial activity is rewarded, and one can predict that a successful business career will continue and even accelerate throughout a man's life. In a nation such as India, however, in which entrepreneurial activity receives much less historical and current cultural support, there may be a good deal of latent entrepreneurial talent that is never put to use. One important function of achievement motivation training courses is to locate such individuals as N, whose business initiative had "run down" in middle age, or B, who because of his family position had scarcely considered entrepreneurial activity. An effective achievement training course can convert latent personal resources of the sort possessed by these two men into productive economic activity, simply through practical assistance, prestigious inspiration, and the increasing of a businessman's perceived probability of business success.

CHAPTER 11

THE PSYCHOLOGICAL
IMPACT OF ACHIEVEMENT
MOTIVATION TRAINING

The case studies of individual businessmen have raised some interesting general questions: How did the courses affect people psychologically? What happens to businessmen who undergo achievement motivation training? What educational inputs are particularly effective? In what ways are they effective? Different aspects of the training appealed particularly to different individuals, but can any generalizations be drawn as to what factor or combination of factors is most effective in producing changes in activity level? Beyond that question lies another of greater psychological importance. Granted a change in activity level, what produced it? That is, what personality characteristics were modified by the courses sufficiently to account for changes in activity level? Was motivation to achieve really changed? Or are the results more simply accounted for in terms of some "prestige suggestion" effect?

The general purpose of this chapter is to bring together and examine any evidence that bears on why and how motivation training works. Unfortunately the evidence is scattered and not as systematic as one could wish for. It seldom permits clear-cut testing of a particular hypothesis.

Yet in its totality it does render some explanations of how the courses worked more likely, and others less likely. The evidence consists of two kinds of information: variations in course results or yields, which can be attributed to variations in educational inputs; and changes in personality characteristics of the trained men, which might be considered responsible for changes in business activity levels. That is, we can try to isolate the course inputs that had the most effect on activity levels, and then study the personality changes which were the result of training and which presumably were instrumental in producing the changes in activity levels.

Variations in Course Yields

In early studies of the effectiveness of achievement motivation training, some information was gathered on comparative yields in activity levels of courses varying greatly in educational inputs (see Table 2.2). To this can now be added the results of the four courses given for businessmen from Kakinada, the two courses for men from Vellore, and data from six more courses not yet mentioned—two brief capsule courses given by SIET Institute for businessmen in Hyderabad, and four courses given for businessmen in Barcelona, Spain. But before we turn to a comparison of the effects of these courses, it is necessary to give some attention to defining the yield measure so that it is comparable across courses. The only conceivable measure that can be used is the very crude activity rating described first in Chapter 2 and refined for application to Kakinada and Vellore in Chapter 7. It is more open to bias than salary raises, money invested, or new jobs created; but unfortunately such measures were not always applicable to the activities of participants in courses other than those given in Kakinada and Vellore. Aside from the fact that it is the only measure that provides comparability across the samples, the activity level score can be defended in its own right on a variety of grounds. The fact that the judges can take everything into account can lead to more valid as well as less valid judgments. Thus a salary increase might seem to be objective, but a judge reading detailed notes of the circumstances of the raise can discover that the raise was due entirely to the fact that the man's father owned the business and arranged for his son's promotion. In such a case the son would get no increased score on the activity level index, even though the more "objective" measure of salary increase would indicate that he had been doing better. Thus it should be remembered that the rating schedule, particularly for the +2 score, requires that the judge be able to identify some specific new activity that the man has undertaken himself, which has significant financial consequences. It is not based on a general impression or report that the man is "more active." Finally, while it certainly could be argued that despite all attempts at honesty, the judges were biased in favor of giving higher ratings to those who had been trained in *n* Ach than to untrained men, it is hard to see how this bias could have produced the large variations in course yields to be reported below. The activity ratings for individuals were made before the course yields could be computed, and afterwards they were obviously not revised. What is more, early comparisons of yields of various courses were made in terms of the crude, uncorrected activity level scores, as in Table 2.2, so that the authors were for some time under several misapprehensions as to which were the effective courses. Further analysis of the data showed that two corrections in the raw yield scores had to be made, one major and one minor.

The single most important factor determining whether *n* Ach training was effective turned out to be not in the training or in the individual, but in the participant's situation. In other words, what mattered most was whether a man was "in charge" or not, as the results in Chapter 9 have already suggested. Table 11.1 brings together activity scores for those in charge and not in charge in all courses. For the man in a position of responsibility—that is, with an opportunity to initiate changes in life—the effects of *n* Ach training are large and highly significant. For those with no opportunity (i.e., those judged not to be in charge of anything), the effects of *n* Ach training are small and not statistically significant across all Indian courses. In other words, if our courses had been attended entirely or largely by men who were not in a position to do anything in their businesses, it would have been unlikely that *n* Ach training could have been shown to have any effect whatsoever. The point seems obvious: a man cannot convert increased motivation into increased activity unless he has a real opportunity to do so. However, the point was not so obvious to the authors that they had built it into the research design in advance. They discovered it only after all the data were in and the more detailed analyses for Kakinada and Vellore were made, as reported in Chapter 7. Figures in Table 11.1 include those already reported in Chapter 7 for those two towns plus the ratings for those in charge and not in charge from the Bombay and Hyderabad courses. The authors were not unaware that opportunities could exert a modifying influence, but as psychologists they were perhaps more

Table 11.1

Average Business Activity Levels in Two-Year Periods after Courses for Men in Charge and Not in Charge (from All Samples)

	IN CHARGE		NOT IN CHARGE			
	N	Mean	N	Mean	Difference	p
Trained in *n* Ach	70*	1.39	45†	.71	.68	<.01
Not Trained in *n* Ach	60**	.57	34††	.38	.21	n.s.
Differential		.82		.33		
p		<.001		<.20		

* Thirty-one from Kakinada, 11 from Vellore, 10 from Hyderabad, 18 from Bombay.
** Sixteen from Kakinada, 8 from Vellore, 23 from Rajahmundry, and 13 from Bombay.
† Sixteen from Kakinada, 14 from Vellore, 4 from Hyderabad, 11 from Bombay.
†† Six from Kakinada, 8 from Vellore, 12 from Rajahmundry, 8 from Bombay.

optimistic than sociologists or economists would be as to the extent to which a man with increased motivation could make opportunities for himself. At least so far as India is concerned, the figures in Table 11.1 make it clear that businessmen who are not in a position of authority cannot, on the average, convert a conceivable increase in motivation into an increased business activity level. The motivational training was not sufficiently strong to cause them to break loose from their position in the social structure and find opportunities for themselves. Clearly those sociologists are right who, like Eisenstadt (1963), have argued that the achievement motivation research neglects social-structural variables.

If being in charge is such an important determinant of activity levels after training, the composition of the group trained will also make a big difference in the average yields for the course. If one course, for instance, is made up almost entirely of men in charge, and another consists of men not in charge, comparing their average yields would reveal very little as to the educational power of the two courses. For example, in the first two courses from Kakinada, 77 per cent of the men were classified as in charge and the average yield score was 1.56. For the second two courses from Kakinada, only 55 per cent of the men were in charge and the average yield score was only .77. At least some of this large difference in yield might be due to having fewer men in charge in the second two courses, and it would be incorrect to attribute all the difference in yields to variations in the educational inputs in the two courses. Therefore, in order to make yield scores comparable from all the courses, activity levels are included only for those men in each course who were classified as in charge. Variations in yields for such men might more reasonably be attributed to variations in educational inputs than to variations in the opportunities available after the course.

One other small adjustment had to be made, when it was noted that men who were active before the course were also more likely to be active afterwards. For example, for 22 men who were scored $+2$ and in charge before training, the average activity level score after training was 1.59. For 48 men in charge who received a lower activity rating before the course (either 0 or $+1$), the average activity rating after the course was 1.30. The difference is not highly significant ($t = 1.36$, $p < .20$), but it still seems reasonable to correct for it, particularly since by chance a couple of courses included a higher than usual percentage of men who had been active before the course and who were thus more likely to be active afterwards. It seemed important to make all the samples roughly comparable on their activity ratings before the training by counting fewer men who received $+2$ ratings before the course, as explained in full in the notes to Table 11.2.

Table 11.2

Estimated Yields in Subsequent Activity Levels of Businessmen Participating in Various n Ach Courses (Men in Charge Only)

	COURSE INPUT RATINGS*				INPUT SUM	MEAN ACTIVITY RATINGS			
	Achieve-ment	Self-study	Goal Setting	Inter-personal		N	Before	After	% rated +2 After
Kakinada 1, 2	5.5	5	6	6	22.5	21	.35	1.61	81
Kakinada 3, 4	6	5	6	6	23	10**	.70	.90	40
Vellore 1, 2	6	5	6	6	23	11	.64	1.73	82
Hyderabad	4	2	4	0	10	10†	.60	1.06	40
Bombay	5.5	5	3	2	15.5	18	.65	1.39	67
Untrained Indian Businessmen					0	60††	.58	.57	28
Barcelona 1	3	3.5	2	0	8.5	13	.08†††	.85	38
Barcelona 2–4	5.5	5	6	4	20.5	19	.53	1.37	58
Rank Order Correlation with Yield Omitting Kakinada 3, 4	.96	.88	.82	.94	.96				

* Ratings are sums of 0–2 ratings on three inputs under each category. See Table 2.2.
** The actual number of cases was 12, but since an unusual number were active ($+2$) before the course, the scores for these five men were averaged and entered three times to make the Before activity level more comparable to other samples.
† The actual number of cases was 14, but since an unusual number were active ($+2$) before the course, the scores for these six men were averaged and entered twice to make the Before activity level more comparable to other samples.
†† Sixteen from Kakinada, eight from Vellore, 23 from Rajahmundry and 13 from Bombay.
††† Probably due in part to lack of information.

Table 11.2 shows corrected activity ratings for men who were exposed to seven different sets of n Ach courses and for a group of Indian businessmen who had received no motivational training at all. It has been necessary to pool the results of comparable courses to get large enough numbers of men in charge to provide reasonably stable average yield scores. For example, it was noted that the yield scores for courses 1 and 2 from Kakinada were very comparable, as were those for courses 3 and 4 from Kakinada and courses 1 and 2 from Vellore. Thus the scores are combined for these three pairs of courses in Table 11.2.

Also shown in the table are ratings of the strength of various educational inputs. They are summarized from the more complete ratings given in Appendix II to make gross comparisons among the courses easier. It will be recalled that 12 inputs in all are rated, three for each of the four major types of inputs: the achievement syndrome (A), self-study (S), goal-setting (G), and interpersonal supports (I). Thus the maximum score under any one of these major categories is six, which equals a rating of two, the maximum, for each of the three inputs under that heading. Obviously a category total could be obtained by a variety of combinations of subscores, but the number of course variations available is not sufficiently large to permit drawing any conclusions from these subcategory variations.

Two sets of courses, the yields of which are included in the table, have not so far been described. The SIET Institute staff offered two capsule weekend courses for local businessmen in Hyderabad in January and March, 1965. The amount of time devoted to the training is the lowest reported in the table: 12 to 15 hours spread over three days. Sessions ran roughly from 4:00 P.M. to 8:00–9:00 P.M. on Friday, Saturday, and Sunday afternoons. The courses obviously provided very little opportunity for self-study or for building interpersonal support. They were more in the nature of academic exercises which taught the n Ach scoring system, something about the research behind it, the action characteristics of men high in n Ach, and the importance of making concrete detailed plans for business activity over the next months. Nineteen men attended the first capsule course and fifteen the second. Their average age was 39 and average years of education 14.7. Seventy-eight per cent were in charge. On the whole, they worked for larger businesses, were somewhat better educated, and were more active than the samples of businessmen from Kakinada and Vellore. A number worked for large Indian businesses such as Voltas, Sarabhai Chemicals, and several major insurance companies. In this respect they are more comparable to the samples trained in the Bombay courses. Dr. David Winter was able to interview 13 of the 19 in the first course and a random sample of five from the fifteen who took the second course. By the time the sample was adjusted for precourse activity level and number in charge, the effective number of cases was reduced to ten.

At the bottom of Table 11.2 are shown the results for four courses conducted in Barcelona, Spain in March 1964 and in successive weeks in February, 1966. The instructors were Mr. José Fons-Boronat, who had attended the original AID-sponsored training course described in Chapter 3, and Father Luis Ramallo, a Jesuit priest who had been studying achievement motivation at Harvard under Dr. McClelland for eight years. Both faculty members came from the Barcelona area and Mr. Fons-Boronat was on the faculty at ESADE (Escuela Superior de Administracion y Direction de Empresas), a Catholic business school where the courses were held. The average age of the participants was 37.8 years, omitting a few university students present as observers. All courses were given at the school on five consecutive days in the late afternoon and early evening for a total of 25 to 30 hours of training. The educational setup and length of training were most like the training carried out in Bombay, although the courses were completed in fewer days.

Twenty-three men attended the first course, five of whom were students and faculty from the school and seven of whom were lawyers, most of them working for the government in the taxation department. This meant that only 11 of the 23 participants, or 48 per cent, were actually in business, which is the smallest percentage by far of any of the courses reported. In the figures reported in Table 11.2, the students and faculty have been discarded and only those lawyers and businessmen included who were judged to be in charge of some operation. The first course was clearly differentiated from the second, third, and fourth in its approach and content. In most respects it was like the Mexican *n* Ach course, the complete input ratings for which are given in Table 2.2. It was largely an academic exercise in which heavy emphasis was placed on *n* Ach research results, learning the *n* Ach scoring system, and considering whether any of the material might reasonably be applied by the individual to his own life. There was little or no delving into motives or group discussions of personal motives, which the faculty felt Spaniards would find difficult. There was also no concrete goal-setting for their own lives in the next months, since that particular input was not at that time in use.

The second through fourth courses were comparable to each other and more like the courses as they had developed in Kakinada and

Vellore. The second and third courses were small, attended by seven and nine individuals respectively, while the fourth was attended by 18 individuals. The total number of men in these courses was 34, of whom eight were students or faculty members who were discarded from the sample. Of the 26 remaining, 25 were in business and one was a lawyer. Thus the percentage of businessmen (74 per cent) was much higher than in the first course. Furthermore, in the fourth course several were in sales, advertising, and promotion, while none had been in these fields in the first course. Thus both in composition of the samples trained and in educational inputs, the second through fourth Barcelona courses would have to be regarded as much more likely to have an impact on the participants. There was quite a bit more self-study, much greater interpersonal warmth and support, and more specific training in goal-setting for their own life activities in the next months. Furthermore, particularly in the fourth course, which was by far the most successful, a solid in-group was formed which continued to meet regularly after the training. The group went so far as to start a company of its own, which according to its charter will be operated "according to the principles of achievement motivation as discovered by Professor McClelland of Harvard University." Some eleven men from this group have bought stock in the corporation; they have searched for a consumer product which they can make inexpensively and sell through the efforts of one of their members, who is the director-owner of an advertising agency. At latest report they were market-testing an ashtray with a sand-bag on the bottom, to see whether it had consumer appeal. If it does, they have plans to raise one million pesetas and manufacture and sell 250,000 a year. The final evaluation on the activities of the men who attended all the four courses in Barcelona was carried out by Mr. Fons-Boronat and Dr. McClelland in May, 1967, which is only 15 months after courses two through four were given, the shortest time period reflected in the table. Thus the score for courses two through four may in the end be somewhat higher. The same coding system was applied to the activity reports as was applied in India. Information was available on all but two of the businessmen trained.

With this background information on Table 11.2, it is now possible to turn to an examination of the comparative yields of various courses, in an attempt to draw inferences as to what makes them more or less effective. The first fact that stands out in Table 11.2 is that the third and fourth courses from Kakinada were much less effective on the average than either the first two courses from Kakinada (mean difference = .71, t = 1.96, p ~ .05) or the two courses from Vellore (mean difference = .83, t = 2.24, p < .05). The result is surprising because as the table also shows, the educational inputs were very nearly identical for these three pairs of courses. If anything, teaching the achievement syndrome improved steadily from the first pair of these courses to the last pair, as the staff grew more experienced. It might be thought that the dropping off in performance of those who attended the third and fourth courses from Kakinada was due to the fact that two of the key staff members in the early Kakinada work, Dr. Aziz Pabaney and Dr. Elliott Danzig, had had to leave when The Ford Foundation did not supply additional funds. However, neither they nor any other outside consultant was present for the two courses from Vellore, either. Unless one wants to fall back on an argument such as that the resulting relative deprivation was greater in Kakinada than Vellore, it is difficult to account for the poorer yield of Kakinada courses 3 and 4 in this way. It is necessary to look elsewhere for an explanation.

The staff did have the impression that the participants of the third and fourth groups from Kakinada were on the whole less influential than those in the first two courses. It may be remembered that they were considerably younger on the average (see Table 4.1). They contained a higher proportion of people who were not in charge (45 per cent vs. 23 per cent, respectively). It is true that the yield scores do not include the performance of those not in charge, but it seemed possible that the number of influential men in a group might be considered a prestige input which would effect how seriously all the participants took the training. When training groups of this sort gather for the first time, each participant tends to look around the room to see who else is there. As he discovers who the other participants are, he tends to be more or less impressed, depending on how many important people are present. It was this consideration that led the staff to work so hard in the early stages of each project to recruit as participants some of the key people in the town. They felt that if they did not succeed in getting any of the important people in the town, even those who went to the courses would take them less seriously. The staff operated on the assumption that since many influentials had been trained in earlier batches from Kakinada, later participants would still tend to define the training as very important. Yet the lower yield of the later courses from Kakinada suggested that this might not be true.

So each participant in all the six courses from the two towns was rated for his local importance. Two somewhat unrelated factors entered into the rating—his wealth and family position, and his actual performance as a leading man in the town. It was possible for a man to have an important position as a leader in a wealthy family, but not to be widely respected because he wasted his time and did not pay attention to business. Or, on the other hand, it was possible for a man to be very influential because of his excellence in performing his duties, although his family background might be quite modest. Ratings were given on a scale of A (very important) through C (relatively young, inexperienced, not particularly successful). Forty-seven per cent of the 30 men attending the first two courses from Kakinada received an A rating, and 41 per cent of the 27 men attending the first two courses from Vellore received an A rating. In contrast, only 3 out of the 22 men attending the second two courses in Kakinada, or 14 per cent, received an A rating. The difference is highly significant statistically ($x^2 = 6.34$, p < .02). The general impression of the staff that the later course from Kakinada contained fewer influential men seems backed up by this more careful rating. However, while some of the ratings (for Kakinada courses 1 and 2) were made before the difference in course yields was observed, others were not and could therefore be subject to rater bias.

Fortunately there was a more objective, though indirect, way of testing the hypothesis that the participants in K-3 and K-4 were somewhat less highly qualified than those in K-1 and K-2. Fluency in English could be checked easily by counting the number of words the subject produced spontaneously in a relatively short period of time in writing his initial TAT stories. The median number of words in these stories across all courses was 420. Fifty-two per cent of the men from the first two courses from Kakinada and 62 per cent of the men from the courses from Vellore scored above the median, as contrasted with only 29 per cent of the men in the third and fourth courses for Kakinada ($x^2 = 3.36$, p < .10). Clearly the participants in the later courses from Kakinada were less fluent in English, which of course might mean that they understood what was going on less well. Dr. Pareek, a staff member in all six courses, has in fact reported that he believes the participants in K-1 and K-2 and V-1 and V-2 had a somewhat better abstract and conceptual understanding of the course material than the participants in K-3 and K-4. But it is hard to believe that this was due wholly to a lack of ability in English, since their English was good enough for the sessions to be carried out in the usual way: they learned the scoring system just as well, they filled out the various forms as well, and so on. It seems likely that at least some of the lower level of understanding Dr. Pareek refers to is due to the lesser experience and importance of the men in the town. Those who were older, more experienced, more successful, and more influential were able to interpret the meaning of the courses in terms of their own lives more easily. Thus, the two interpretations of the meaning of the lower English fluency in K-3 and K-4 are not essentially different. Lower English fluency suggests lack of experience and influence or lack of ease in self-expression; it also suggests a lesser ability to comprehend, which could result from a lack of experience and influence. So it seems reasonably safe to conclude that the lower yield of K-3 and K-4 is due to the smaller proportion of influential men present, which in turn lowered the level of comprehension of the ideas presented and the expectation that the training would effectively change the individuals involved (see Proposition G-1, Chapter 2).[1]

That such an interpretation is not completely ad hoc is suggested by similar results reported in the well-known Coleman report, *Equality of Educational Opportunity in the United States* (1966). There too the data show that the influence of one's classmates is very strong in determining educational test yield scores. The proportion of children in a school from middle-class homes is strongly related to better test scores for all children in various grades. It is as if the children learn more when the whole atmosphere is better, regardless of their own backgrounds, either because peer group conversations are at a higher level or because greater expectation of improvement occurs where more children have higher status (Proposition G-1, Chapter 2).

The second conclusion to be drawn from Table 11.2 concerns the capsule courses given for businessmen from Hyderabad. Clearly the yield from these courses is significantly less than it is for K-1/K-2 and V-1/V-2 (mean difference = .61, t = 2.01, p < .05). In other words, a very brief course with fewer inputs, particularly in the self-study and interpersonal supports areas, is on the average less effective than a full-scale ten-day course containing influentials, as in the first two courses from Kakinada and Vellore. In a sense it is some satisfaction to the staff, though perhaps not at all surprising, that an intensive course taking up to 100 hours is more effective than a course lasting only 12 to 15 hours, with very little personal involvement of the staff with the participants. On the other hand, it cannot be argued that the capsule courses were totally ineffective, since the yield rating is almost significantly higher than the mean activity rating for untrained Indian businessmen in the same time period (t = 1.71, p < .10). The sample size is small; a num-

---

1. However, there is no direct relationship between TAT fluency and standing in the respective towns. The mean number of words for those receiving an A rating was 442 as compared with 415 for those with other ratings, but the difference does not approach significance.

ber of adjustments had to be made in it to make it comparable to the other samples; there is always the possibility that the evaluators favored those who had been trained. Yet our own bias all along was certainly against finding improvements after so short a course. We do not feel, in view of this result, that we can dismiss altogether the possibility that even a brief achievement motivation training course has some effect on subsequent business activity.

Comparisons among the Barcelona courses also support the same general conclusion that the greater the educational input, the higher the yield in activity ratings after the course. Clearly the later courses given in Barcelona were stronger in almost every respect than the first course—in appropriateness of the participants as well as in all four main types of educational inputs—and the yield from the later courses was almost significantly greater ($t = 1.49$, $p < .10$ in the predicted direction). The yield of the later Barcelona courses is very similar to the yield of the Bombay courses and they were fairly comparable on the input side—longer and stronger than the Hyderabad capsule courses but not as strong as the full-length courses for Kakinada and Vellore. In fact the simplest and most general conclusion suggested by the yield data in Table 11.2 is that the stronger and longer the educational inputs, the greater the yield in subsequent activity levels. If K-3 and K-4 are omitted on the grounds that the number of influentials present was significantly lower than in the other courses (which should be reflected in the G-1 input rating, but is not), the rank order of the sum of the input ratings is almost perfectly correlated with the yield scores for the various courses. The Spearman Rank Order Correlation is .96, $N = 7$, counting the untrained Indian businessmen as the lowest both on the input and output sides. Furthermore, the results from the early Mexican course seemed quite consistent. They have not been included in this table because it was not possible to decide who was in charge and to get a proper average yield score comparable to the other such scores given in Table 11.2. Nevertheless, on the input side the Mexican course scored the lowest and it seems reasonably safe to infer from the uncorrected yield score reported in Table 2.2 that even a corrected yield score would have been among the lowest.

Can anything more than this rough correlation between amounts of input and output be deduced from Table 11.2? Are any of the major categories of inputs either demonstrably essential or unessential? Consider first the achievement motivation instruction itself. The rank order of the strength of this educational input correlates more highly with the yield measures than does any other major category of inputs, but the differences are slight. There is a high degree of covariation among the various inputs, and it would therefore be unwise to put much weight on this observation. A more important question is whether achievement motivation training is necessary at all. This question has already been answered in part by data presented in Table 2.2. There it is shown that a company course not containing material on achievement motivation has a significantly lower yield in subsequent activity than a shorter course containing instruction in achievement motivation. Thus the low level generalization is confirmed that some courses can be given that will result in lower yields than courses containing achievement motivation instruction. But the opposite low level generalization is also probably true, to judge by the results of the self-study course given in Mexico, data for which are also reported in Table 2.2. There are likely to be some courses that will provide activity level yields as high as *n* Ach courses, even though they do not include *n* Ach instructions. Beyond these two extreme statements, little can be concluded from the statistical evidence. However, it ought to be realized that from the point of view of those offering the courses, achievement motivation provides the rationale for organizing the courses, the research data to back up the various exercises introduced, and the focus of all the educational inputs. Thus, if the achievement orientation is to be omitted, some other rationale must be developed for holding the courses.

Is achievement motivation instruction sufficient to produce significant activity changes? Probably not, to judge by the low yields of the early Mexican course and the first course in Barcelona, both of which concentrated almost exclusively on the academic presentation of the achievement motivation research, with very little goal-setting or personal involvement. On the other hand, the Hyderabad capsule courses may have produced a significant effect, even though the level of personal involvement was only slightly higher. The safest conclusion would appear to be that some minimal level of other inputs must be added to achievement motivation instruction for it to be significantly effective in changing behavior.

What about self-study? Is it necessary or sufficient to produce changes in activity levels? Here the evidence is not at all clear. The Mexican course, the first Barcelona course, and the Hyderabad courses were low in the self-study input and generally had lower yields than the courses with high self-study inputs, but the differences may have been due to other variables. Whether self-study is sufficient or not probably depends on its focus. It will be recalled from Table 2.2 that a self-study course organized in Mexico resulted in improved performance, though the change was not statistically significant. Even in this course, however, the purpose of the self-study was clearly related to making a better adjustment to work—that is, it was achievement-oriented or work-oriented. Other self-study courses such as those reported by Kolb, S. Winter, and Berlew (1968) do result in behavior change, particularly if they are combined with the third major input here, goal setting. But the goals achieved in these studies are not necessarily achievement goals; they often involve improvements in interpersonal or social behavior. It seems reasonable to infer that for self-study to affect business activity levels it would have to focus on work and achievement.

Probably the most important question that many psychologists would want to put to the data is whether they can all be accounted for by prestige suggestion. The studies reviewed in Chapter 2 point to suggestion as an extremely powerful force for inducing behavior change. Can the results of achievement motivation training be attributed exclusively to suggestion? Is it enough to get a group of people together and create in them a strong expectation that their activity level is going to change in the future? Almost certainly not, to judge by the variations in course yields reported in Table 11.2. All the prestige of Harvard and scientific research were behind the early Mexican course, the first Barcelona course, the K-3 and K-4 courses, or for that matter the public meetings attended by most of the untrained men from Kakinada, and yet none of these exposures was sufficient to produce a significant increase in activity level afterwards. Furthermore, the company course for the large U.S. firm reported in Table 2.2 probably had higher prestige than the "experimental" n Ach course, but the latter had a significantly higher activity yield than the former. Finally, the overall ratings on the goal-setting input correlated lowest of any of the four major classes of inputs with overall yield score in Table 11.2. Yet it would be a mistake to conclude that prestige factors play no role, as the comparison of K-3/K-4 with K-1/K-2 and V-1/V-2 has already made clear. To guard against indifference to the training, it is important to have some prestigious people as participants during the training. And it should also be noted that in none of the courses was the prestige factor at a really low level. Finally, the goal-setting input, as distinct from the prestige input, seems to be of considerable importance, to judge by the greater yield of the later Barcelona courses as compared with the earlier one. It could be argued that this concrete focusing on future activities was the major difference between the later Barcelona courses and the early one, and the difference in yields between the two is nearly significant. It will be recalled, for instance, that there was much future planning during the fourth Barcelona course, which resulted in repeated meetings after the course and in the creation of a whole new business enterprise, which was jointly owned by course alumni. It seems reasonable to conclude that this focusing on goal setting and future planning played an important role in the higher yield of the later Barcelona courses. It may also help explain why the Hyderabad capsule courses were more effective than the other two "academic-type" courses—the one in Mexico and the early one in Barcelona. Practically the only important difference in the capsule courses was that by this time the future-planning, goal-setting part of the course was much better developed and was used effectively in Hyderabad. It had not been so used in the earlier, academic courses.

Finally, does the retreat setting, with its greater opportunity for building interpersonal support, add materially to the effectiveness of the courses? While the differences are not statistically significant, it is suggestive that the courses with a retreat setting (K-1/K-2 and V-1/V-2) had higher yield scores than the Bombay or later Barcelona courses. These were in many ways similar in educational inputs, except for the fact that the participants did not live together while they were studying. On the other hand, the retreat setting is certainly not necessary to get a significant increase in activity level, since both the Bombay and later Barcelona courses produced increases without residential living arrangements.

In short, inspection of various course yields strongly suggests that no one of the various educational inputs is either absolutely necessary or sufficient by itself. Some kind of achievement orientation is probably the closest to being necessary, in the sense that it gives a focus to the instruction that is likely to yield changes in business achievement. Beyond this, one can only infer that a case can be made for the value of all the inputs, that in some sense they cumulate in their influence so that the overall course yield is greater, the larger the sum total of the educational inputs, becomes. Furthermore, there is some absolute minimum quantity of input below which it is not possible to go and still get a significant improvement in business activity level.

The next question is, if we opt for a simple cumulative model of course effectiveness, how can all these various factors enter in to produce the changes in activity level? It looks as though more than a change in achievement motivation must be involved. What are the long-term effects of the courses on the personality characteristics of the individuals who took them, particularly the active ones?

Personality Changes After Training

Obviously the courses in some way changed the men who were in charge of their businesses, since they were more active in business after they returned home. But how were they changed? What had happened inside of them, so to speak, to make them more active? We have been trying to infer what must have happened from variations in yields of various courses. Now let us turn to more direct measures of personality changes.

Achievement Motivation. The courses were intended to increase n Achievement. The staff expected that the average motivation to achieve would increase, and so did the participants. Since one of the main methods of developing n Achievement was to teach the participants to write stories containing achievement imagery, the average n Achievement score after the course was many times higher than it was before the course (see Figure 11.1). But how is such a rise to be interpreted? A naive behaviorist might argue that it represents an increase in motivation because the frequency with which a person can think along achievement lines *is* the motive, since it is the operational definition of the motive. But a skeptic might reply that thinking along achievement lines as instructed in the narrowly defined test situation might be one thing, whereas thinking along similar lines in everyday life might be quite another. The naive behaviorist need not be silenced altogether by this argument. He could reply that the increased level of business activity is itself direct evidence that some generalization of achievement thinking must have taken place from test situation to life. From this point of view, the change in achievement thinking is the link between the educational inputs and increased business activity levels. The only problem is that it is harder to understand why the other course inputs, not directly connected with n Ach thinking, also had an effect on course yields.

Some further light on the role that achievement thinking plays is provided by the n Achievement scores obtained in a third testing session, conducted by Dr. Winter, in his final interviews. He reminded each of the participants of the scoring system in which they had been instructed two to three years earlier, and asked them to write stories containing the maximum amount of achievement imagery and subcategories. In other words, this was a retention test, which measured their ability to recall what they had been taught and to include it in their stories in a way that would get them a high *n* Achievement score. The same pictures were used as had been used on the previous two tests. As Figure 11.1

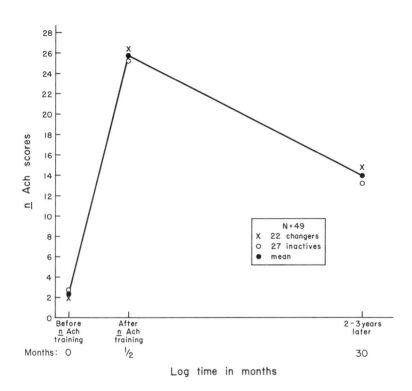

Figure 11.1

Average n Achievement Scores Before and After n Achievement Training and 2–3 Years Later

shows, their average *n* Achievement score was considerably lower than it had been right after training. The per cent of the gain from training which is retained (almost 60 per cent) is about what one would expect from other studies of memory for content over long periods of time (see for example, Stroud, 1946, p. 509). And certainly the average score is still far above what it was before training. All of these differences are highly significant statistically and could scarcely have arisen by chance. But what about the Changers? If the above theorizing is correct, shouldn't they recall more of the scoring system than the Inactives? It would seem reasonable to infer that those who were able to reproduce the achievement associative network most readily two to three years later were those who had been recalling and practicing achievement modes of thinking in the meantime; and if they were thinking more often along achievement lines, they might also be supposed to be the ones who were taking more achievement-related actions. However, the findings reported in Figure 11.1 clearly contradict such an hypothesis. It is true that the Changers scored higher in n Achievement just after training and on the retest two to three years later, but the differences are slight and insignificant. For all practical purposes the n Ach acquisition and retention curves for the Changers and Inactives are identical. If we consider only those in charge, the difference in the mean n Ach scores for the Changers and Inactives on the retest is slightly greater (14.72 vs. 12.00), but it is still nowhere near significance. Nor is there a greater tendency for the Changers to recall better the key instrumental aspects of the achievement action sequence, as might be predicted from the better economic performance of countries which focus on these aspects in their children's stories (see McClelland, 1961, Chapter 3). The n Ach measure itself does not support the hypothesis that the better acquisition or retention of the n Ach associative network is responsible for some people being active and others being inactive, given equal opportunity.

But one cannot dismiss n Achievement as unimportant either. First, one need not take the naive behaviorist view that the measure is the motive. It is at least conceivable that the measure is no longer a valid indicator of the strength of n Achievement precisely because it has become the object of instruction. Thus, whether it is actually recalled or not would seem to depend on other variables such as verbal facility, number of years of schooling, and so on. It is our impression from knowing the individuals who obtained these various scores that some of the active men whose scores dropped were "men of action" rather than words. They were less verbal, less fluent, more interested in doing things. In contrast, those who recalled the scoring system well were often people who were interested in ideas and had talked a good deal about the philosophy behind the course. Thus, ability to recall the scoring system may be influenced by other factors than the strength of the motive itself, conceived as a hypothetical construct, of which the TAT n Ach score is only one measure.

Second, it is important to remember that even at the third testing, nearly everyone recalled enough about achievement thinking to score high in n Achievement compared to naive, untrained men. For instance, of those in charge, only one of the 18 Changers scored below

+3, and only two of the ten Inactives did so. Thus practically all of them retained enough of the instruction about achievement thinking for it to facilitate action. According to this line of reasoning, some other factor would have to be invoked to explain why some who thought along these lines were blocked from becoming active. That is, one could still argue from these data that some minimum level of achievement thinking is necessary for activity, but not sufficient. Such a conclusion only serves to stimulate interest already aroused as to what factors besides n Ach were changed by the courses. The simplistic notion can no longer be entertained that all the courses did was to increase n Achievement, which in turn increased entrepreneurial activity, even though this notion was the one which originated the research project. The data require an expanded interpretation.

One other finding involving n Achievement deserves mention. In Chapter 9 it was pointed out that somewhat paradoxically, men who had been inactive before the course scored on the average higher in n Ach at the outset than those who had been active, though the difference is not significant. The contrast appears also in Figure 11.1 at the first point in the graph. At first consideration, this would seem to contradict the general expectation that men with high n Ach are the ones who are more active entrepreneurs. Yet as the discussion of the Atkinson and Feather theoretical model in Chapter 1 made clear, this depends very much on the opportunities available. According to that model, men with high n Ach will in fact be less active than men with low n Ach if opportunities for success are very low (see Figure 1.1, Chapter 1). One can argue that the prevailing opinion among the business community in India at the time this testing was done certainly was that the probability of success in business was quite low because of shortages of materials, government red tape, and the like. It is possible to check this somewhat paradoxical prediction once more with the present data by noting that those in charge have a much higher probability of success than those not in charge. Then the question once again becomes: How does a man with high n Ach react in a situation in which he has very low probability of success, as contrasted to one in which he has a high probability of success? The reversal predicted by the Atkinson/Feather model occurs. If we first consider only those men in charge, 12 out of 14 or 86 per cent of those high in n Ach at the third testing had been active to the extent of receiving at least a +1 score. In contrast, 9 out of 14 or 64 per cent of those low in n Ach among those in charge had been active at this level. In other words, when perceived probability of success is greater, as it should be when one is in charge, n Ach seems to be associated with greater activity. However, if we consider those men who are not in charge, 3 out of 12 or only 25 per cent of those high in n Ach had been active, whereas five out of ten or 50 per cent of those low in n Ach had been active at least to the planning stage. In other words, when opportunities seemed slight, men with high n Ach are more likely not to try than are those with low n Ach. The interaction χ^2 is only about 2.2, $p < .10$ in the predicted direction, but it is worth noting that this not-at-all obvious theoretical prediction does seem to be confirmed, at least at some marginal level of significance. The finding serves to underline the fact that n Ach will not always lead to greater persistence and hard work in the face of overwhelming obstacles.

Fluency and Self-Confidence. As mentioned in Chapter 6, Shri Nadkarni reported that he had noted several changes in the men when he interviewed them a couple of years after the training. They seemed more fluent, more willing to talk openly and freely about their thoughts and plans. If his impression were correct, it might be supposed that they would construct longer TAT stories in the third testing than they had in the first testing before the course. It was a simple matter to count the number of words used by each man before the course and in the final testing some two or three years later. However, on the average there was a slight decrease in the number of words used in the last testing. Among those in charge, for the subjects who became active the mean number of words dropped from 456 to 437 and for the inactive subjects from 482 to 477. None of these differences is significant, but if anything they show that the inactive subjects were somewhat more fluent at both time periods and also showed less of a drop from the before to the after testing. Of course the task may be too circumscribed to provide a good measure of Nadkarni's impressions of greater imaginativeness, but so far as it goes, it does not support the idea that the men had begun to imagine and think more freely and easily.

Shri Nadkarni also felt that the men had grown more self-confident in at least two senses. They seemed more willing to take risks, to "jump in" and make an investment, for instance, and of course the data in Chapter 7 bear out this impression directly. However, in discussing their activities the men were not talking so much in terms of achievement imagery as they were talking in terms of "proving oneself to oneself," of proving that they could do something even though others thought they couldn't. Both these impressions, and particularly the latter, suggested that the men's sense of power might have been increased by the training. So the Thematic Apperception Tests written before training and two to three years later were all scored for *n* Power, according to a system devised by Winter (1967) which codes particularly whether a person in a story is having impact on someone else. The impact may be shown either by the strong, vigorous action of the protagonist, by the concern he has for his reputation in the eyes of the world, or by an emotional response being aroused in the person influenced. People who fill their stories with such ideas are obviously concerned with the strength and power of a person and with his impact on others. For the 48 subjects from Kakinada and Vellore on whom tests were available, the mean *n* Power score rises from 3.25 before training to 5.23 two to three years later. The difference of 1.98 is significant ($t = 2.39$, $p < .05$). Part of this increase appears to be due to instruction in the *n* Ach scoring system, since before the course the correlation between *n* Ach and *n* Power was $- .15$ whereas afterwards, at the final testing, it rose to $+ .55$, $p. < .01$. In other words, in attempting to write assertive stories which would be scored for *n* Achievement, the men inadvertently introduced related themes that were scored for *n* Power. But what is especially interesting is that the increase in *n* Power scores is heavily concentrated in the group of men who were in charge but inactive. Their average *n* Power score went from 3.20 before training to 6.80 two to three years later, a difference which is highly significant ($t = 3.49$, $p < .001$). In contrast, the men who were in charge but became active went from an average score of 3.39 to 4.74, a difference which is not at all significant. The meaning of this contrast is illuminated by comparing it with the gains in *n* Ach scores in the same two groups. The Inactives in charge gained 9.96 points (from 2.68 to 12.64) whereas the Changers in charge gained more, going from 1.91 to 14.73, a difference of 12.82. In short, the Changers gained relatively more in *n* Ach than they did in *n* Power and the reverse was true of the Inactives.

This difference can be shown to be significant with a very crude statistic. The gain scores for *n* Ach and *n* Power were each divided evenly into thirds. Each man's gain score in each distribution was classified as belonging in the upper, middle, or lower third of the distribution of gain scores. Then it could be observed whether a man's gain score in the *n* Power distribution was relatively higher than his gain score in the *n* Ach distribution. Six of the 10 men who were in charge and inactive had higher *n* Power gain scores than *n* Ach gain scores, as contrasted with only 4 out of 17 of the men in charge who became active. This difference is unlikely to have arisen by chance ($p < .02$). In short, the courses stressed self-assertiveness, which tended to express itself both in power and achievement terms in their thinking, but the significant point is that those participants who tended to direct their thinking more toward n Power than n Ach were precisely those who, though in charge, were inactive after the course.

It seems reasonable to infer that one of the reasons why the Inactives were so is that they were confusing n Power with n Achievement. The courses were aimed at increasing self-assertiveness. Many of the educational inputs described in Chapter 5 were designed to make the men feel more powerful, more in charge of their fate, and less dependent on external resources. The self-assertiveness was supposed to be focused on doing things better, on improving one's business performance in the achievement sense, but it is not surprising to find that it produced an increase in a more generalized concern for power. Proving oneself to oneself might be considered more evidence of a power concern than an achievement concern narrowly defined. The fact that the power concern rose more among the Inactives in charge suggests a reason why they may have been inactive. It will be remembered from Chapter 9 that they viewed themselves as stronger and more active at the outset. So either by predisposition or by misunderstanding at the time of the training they were stimulated more to thoughts about general assertiveness than to a narrower concern with improved performance. As the case material in Chapter 10 makes clear, status in traditional Indian society is more closely tied to power and importance than it is to achievement. Thus, it could be expected that educational inputs designed to improve self-confidence in performance would stimulate some people's concern for power along traditional Indian lines.

Efficacy. From the description of the courses in Chapter 2 it will be recalled that they were aimed not only at changing motivation, but also at changing self-conception. The men at the outset seemed rather fatalistic about their chances of achieving very much in the business sphere because either they lacked resources, they were stopped by government regulations, or they did not feel strong enough to take risks on their own. Hence many of the training inputs were designed to make them feel more like origins than pawns. Is there evidence that their self-images did change, that they felt themselves to be more self-reliant, autonomous, and capable after the training? If so, it might help explain the increased activity level of some and the inactivity of others, even though both groups had learned the achievement motivation system equally well.

Some evidence on this point can be gathered from the "Who Am I?" exercise readministered by Mr. Joel Cohen on his visit to the towns approximately a year to eighteen months after training. As noted in Chapter 9, the answers to this exercise can be coded to yield Pizer's efficacy score: reflecting the extent to which the individual describes himself as interested in activity rather than essence goals, as relying on internal rather than external resources, as taking initiative, as solving problems rather than avoiding them, and so on. One simple question is whether the efficacy scores obtained in this way were higher on the whole some time after the training than they had been at the original testing. One might expect that they would be, if the courses had really increased perception of self as autonomous and self-reliant. Unfortunately, the trend is if anything in the opposite direction. Of the 48 men on whom scores were available from both testings, only 15 or 31 per cent gained in overall self-perceived efficacy scores, whereas 25 or 56 per cent had lower scores. If we assume that by chance there should have been an equal number of gains and losses, the deviation from this expectation approaches significance in the wrong direction ($x^2 = 2.5$, p < .15). Self-perceived efficacy may even decrease in the year or so after training. It will be recalled from Chapter 9 that those who subsequently became active perceived themselves as more efficacious in answering the "Who Am I?" question before the course as contrasted with those who were subsequently inactive. On the retest, the Changers had declined in average efficacy score (from 1.14 to .34); the Inactives had also decreased a bit (from $-$ 1.15 to $-$ 1.31). More of the former still describe themselves as more efficacious than the latter, though the size of the difference is reduced (see Table 9.14). There is nothing in any of these findings to support the notion that the training had so altered self-perception of efficacy as to make it easier for the Changers to take risks and be active. They had seen themselves as more efficacious all along.

However, if the men's TAT stories written in the final evaluation session for Dr. Winter are coded for efficacy according to the same system, quite a different result is obtained. Table 11.3 summarizes the relevant comparisons. Some years after the training all men produced stories in which the characters are described as more efficacious than the characters in the stories written before training. The general increase of 1.60 is nearly significant ($t = 1.88$, p <.10), and it could not be an indirect effect of increases in *n* Ach or *n* Power scores, since the efficacy score does not correlate significantly with *n* Ach ($r = .09$) or *n* Power ($r = .12$). What is more, the increase in the TAT efficacy score is heavily concentrated among the Changers and those in charge. Significantly more of the Changers, whether or not they were in charge,

Table 11.3

Personal Efficacy Scores in TAT Stories

	BEFORE TRAINING (B)			2–3 YEARS AFTER TRAINING (A)			
	N	Mean	Above Median (−3 and up)	N	Mean	Gain A–B	Men Increasing in Efficacy, A–B
Total Efficacy Score, All Subjects	47	−4.45		47	−2.85	+1.60**	
Changers	23	−5.13	30%	23	−2.57	+2.56†	74%
Inactives	24	−3.79	58%	24	−3.13	+ .66	38%
Changers vs.			$\chi^2 = 3.76$,				$\chi^2 = 11.53$,
Inactives:			$p \sim .05$				$p < .001$

* Men who increased their activity from less than +2 before training to +2 after-wards.

** $p < .10$.

† $p < .05$.

showed a gain in TAT efficacy scores (see Table 11.3) and also significantly more of those in charge gained, whether they were active or not (68 per cent of those in charge gained vs. 37 per cent of those not in charge, $\chi^2 = 7.9$, $p < .01$). As would be expected, therefore, the highest mean gain in efficacy is among those who were both Changers and in charge (mean gain = 3.33), whereas among Inactives not in charge there was a loss (average difference = − .14). The number of cases who were Changers but not in charge, is too small (N = 5) to provide a satisfactory test of the statistical significance of this interaction. But the implication seems very clear. After the course, though not before, TAT efficacy scores go along with being efficacious in the real world, that is, with being in charge and becoming active.

However, there are still some puzzles in these data. It seems particularly strange that the men who later became active were thinking somewhat less autonomously or efficaciously (in the TAT) before training (see Table 11.3). Only 30 per cent of them had high scores in TAT efficacy, as compared with 58 per cent of those who were later inactive ($p \sim .05$). Why should those who were having trouble in thinking autonomously before training be most likely to benefit from the instruction? The mystery deepens when it is recalled that these same men, when answering the "Who Am I?" exercise (WAI), describe themselves as more autonomous than those who are later inactive. As one would expect from these differences, the efficacy scores obtained from the "Who Am I?" exercise and from the TAT stories do not correlate significantly. The Changers seem to be contradicting themselves. On one measuring instrument they describe themselves as more efficacious, self-reliant, and autonomous, but on another measuring instrument they show that they tend to think along less efficacious, more fate-controlled lines. Training reverses these differences. Of the 18 Changers on whom both measures were available at both time periods, 11 or 61 per cent showed a loss in self-perceived (WAI) efficacy and a gain in TAT efficacy, as contrasted with only 5 out of 19 of the Inactives who showed this pattern. The difference is significant ($p < .05$). What sense can be made of these apparent contradictions?

One possible interpretation starts from the hypothesis that the answers to the "Who Am I?" exercise give a picture of a person's ego ideal, or ideal self-image. As he thinks quickly back over his life, he tends to introduce those characteristics or actions which fit best his self-image —describing himself in ways that show him to be more or less of an autonomous individual, depending on how important or salient this characteristic is to his self-image. The way he writes a TAT story, on the other hand, reveals the extent to which he actually thinks along the lines of being active, self-reliant, and autonomous. The contrast provided by the two measures is in a sense that between ends and means, between being considered efficacious by oneself and others and actually thinking and acting in efficacious ways. The Changers were concentrating before the course on the ideal of being considered efficacious (WAI), but they were less able than were the Inactives to display the means of achieving that goal by thinking and acting efficaciously (TAT). What the course did for them was to shift the emphasis from the goal to the means. This interpretation is supported by the findings on the Semantic Differential Test (see Table 9.13). The Changers started out with somewhat higher ideals for themselves, particularly on the Evaluative and Activity dimensions, but they considered themselves to fall even farther short of their ideals than the Inactives did. The message that the training successfully conveyed to them must have been something like this: "If you want to be such a good, active, and efficacious person, here is the way you can think and act like one." The message apparently didn't get through to the Inactives, because they had somewhat lower ideals to start with and were satisfied with their ability to meet them. While this interpretation may seem somewhat strained, it has the merit of being consistent with the case-study data presented in the previous chapter. What seemed to characterize the men who changed most was an initial interest in being self-reliant and autonomous that was somewhat atypical for their society. What they lacked was the understanding or the confidence to act and think in ways that would achieve that goal. And that is precisely what the courses gave them—some concrete ways of behaving that would bring them closer to what they wanted. So they were able to shift some of their attention from the goal to the means of achieving it, and in the process to come closer to achieving it than they had before.

REVIEW AND SUMMARY

What, then, has been learned about the psychological impact of motivation training? How does it work to increase the level of business activity? In a sense, the results do not lend themselves to any spectacular new insights into human personality or into the methods by which it may be changed. Perhaps more than anything else, they serve to correct any simple-minded notion that teaching n Achievement is sufficient to increase levels of entrepreneurial activity. The comparative yields of various training courses do not support this conclusion. Other training inputs are demonstrably important, and teaching n Ach alone is not sufficient. Nor do the personality change data support such a simple-minded hypothesis. The men who become active after the course on the whole do not retain better command of the n Ach associative network than those who are inactive. Above all, opportunity plays a major role in determining whether increased n Achievement leads to greater activity. For the men who were not in charge of their businesses, the n Ach increase had no significant effect, at least within the time period of the evaluations reported here. Furthermore, there is even a suggestion in the data, as the theoretical model predicts, that increasing n Ach when no opportunities exist will actually lead to less activity.

Clearly something more is involved in the training and its impact. What activates some men who are exposed to the training seems to involve that aspect of personality that we have called efficacy. A number of the educational inputs were designed to increase the participant's sense of personal efficacy—his feeling that he could rely on himself, take initiative, become activity-oriented rather than "goal-state" oriented, solve problems rather than avoid them. The self-study inputs promoted this feeling. To know oneself better, and to feel that one has some command of the methods by which one can go on understanding himself better, is certainly to increase one's sense of power over himself and his destiny. The goal-setting inputs also contribute to a sense of power and control, as do the interpersonal supports provided in some of the courses. Men come to feel that others think they are important and that what they do is important. All of this should increase a man's sense of personal efficacy. It does, but in selective ways. People do not describe themselves in the "Who Am I?" exercise after training as more efficacious. If anything, as they look back over their lives, they see that they have been somewhat less efficacious than the course made them feel they should be. On the other hand, they think along more efficacious lines in the TAT and show more overall self-esteem on the Semantic Differential Test. What seems to differentiate the Changers and the Inactives is that the former start out more dissatisfied with the level of their activity and learn to think more efficaciously. In other words, the effect of the training depends on the initial goals of the participant. Men in charge who wanted to be more active responded to training designed to make them feel like origins by learning to think more efficaciously and by increasing their business activity. Men like the Inactives in charge did not have so strong a desire to be more active; they converted the origin training into higher need for Power. Seen in these terms, the courses do not so much affect goals as they do the means of attaining them. Put in the language of personality theory, they do not increase or alter the ego ideal so much as they strengthen the ego, the adaptive mechanism by which the person achieves his goals. Thus, learning *n* Achievement becomes not so much the goal, as a means of making more explicit just how a person can become a more efficacious thinker and doer. To be sure, in real life such a clear-cut distinction between means and ends is not possible. Focusing on a means such as behaving like a person with high *n* Achievement may become almost a goal in itself, although so far as our findings are concerned, this did not turn out to be the case. Achievement motivation training worked best by strengthening the sense of efficacy among those men who already wanted it, by giving them concrete information as to the means by which they could overcome their felt discrepancy between real and ideal selves. And it worked at all only among those men who had some opportunities to display these new characteristics.

THE ROLE OF PSYCHOLOGICAL EDUCATION IN DEVELOPMENT

It is time to attempt a summary of what has been learned from our experiences in trying to accelerate economic growth by means of psychological education. Let us take a look at the simpler, more encouraging implications of the findings first, and then proceed to the more problematic ones. The most clear-cut conclusion to be drawn from the research is that adult behavior can be changed. Whether the change is conceived as involving personality, motivation, action, or the structure of response does not matter in one sense. In economic terms, what matters is that the change in people resulted in concrete increases in investment and employment. What is more, the business expansion was not in response to changes in the opportunity structure or to specific economic incentives or disincentives introduced by the government or the market in Kakinada or Vellore. If the trainers may be considered "developers" or "change agents," they had to go about their task completely empty-handed, so far as material aids were concerned. They could make available no special loans, no tax advantages, and no particular inside knowledge on where to get scarce materials. All they had to offer is what are usually considered to be "soft" educational inputs, yet these inputs had a greater effect on "hard" economic outcomes than many aid programs that have made available large material resources and incentives.

To understand in more general terms what happened, it is necessary to refer back to our model of economic development outlined in Chapter 1. There it is pointed out that most economists actually operate in terms of a theory of motivation which applies best and perhaps only to individuals with strong achievement motivation. That is, the theory assumes that people desire to improve, that they calculate "costs of reaching a given goal in relation to anticipation of rewards of reaching the goal," that they take into account "the probabilities or odds of reaching a given goal" and "the anticipated time-span between first effort for the given goal and payoff to be received when the goal is reached" (Whyte and Williams, 1968, p. 46). As we attempted to show in Chapter 1, these attributes—concern for improvement, maximization of gains, minimization of time and effort, weighing difficulties realistically— characterize people with strong achievement motivation. These attributes are taught in the courses, and they are the reasons why a businessman tends to take better advantage of existing economic opportunities once he has been trained. But they are not characteristic of all types of human motivation, contrary to what some economists believe. For instance, empirical studies of power motivation have shown that men who have a high need for Power seek different goals (e.g., rank and status), think in terms of different strategies of reaching the goals (e.g., by forming alliances), and spend money on possessions that reflect prestige (Winter, 1967). To give one example of what a difference this can make, consider an assumption basic to achievement motivation theory, namely that the greatest amount of approach behavior will occur when the probability of success is about .50, as illustrated in Figure 1.1. The curve also suggests that people high in achievement motivation will work less hard for a sure thing, which seems counter-intuitive in many situations, as Whyte and Williams (1968) point out. Does it really seem likely that a presidential candidate will work less hard if he is almost certain of winning than if he has only a fifty-fifty chance? Or that a peasant involved in a lawsuit over land will be more likely to take up the challenge in court if he has only a fifty-fifty chance of winning? The reason the examples appear to contradict the assumptions of the achievement motivation model in Figure 1.1 is that they do not involve achievement motivation. In both instances the concern is for Power, not

Achievement, and the risk-taking function for power motivation is almost certainly different from the one for achievement motivation, although it has not as yet been carefully worked out. Many development theories suffer from overly simplistic models of human motivation, models that often unconsciously assume the characteristics of achievement motivation. What this research purports to have shown is the peculiar relevance of these achievement characteristics to improved economic performance—a relevance which paradoxically was ignored by economic theorists because they incorrectly thought that all motivation had these achievement characteristics. What is significant, then, for the theory of economic development is our demonstration that not all people possess the characteristics of achievement motivation in a sufficient degree to respond to economic incentives, and that the structure of their response to opportunities can be altered by simple training methods.

Costs of Economic Increments
Produced by Psychological Education

The demonstration that achievement motivation training can produce economic changes would be trivial, or, as we pointed out in Chapter 1, tactically unimportant, if it turned out to be difficult, time-consuming, and costly as compared to changing opportunities. Certainly it did not turn out to be extremely difficult or time consuming. The duration of the training was only five to ten days. The instructors in the courses needed only about a month of prior training and preparation, and only one or two at the outset had advanced degrees in psychology. Few of the course participants had been to a university; most had had some secondary-school education, but a few had even less schooling. This suggests that psychological education of this type can be useful to those with limited education. In fact, the courses have a "cut-rate" image that disturbs representatives from American business schools, who have been working hard to convince underdeveloped countries that they need management-training institutes where entry is often restricted to college graduates and courses last anywhere from six months to two years. To avoid misunderstanding, it should be stressed that our courses make no attempt to impart skills which may take months to learn, nor are they aimed primarily at improving management effectiveness in large, well-established businesses. Rather their goal is to motivate entrepreneurs to start businesses and to learn whatever skills they need to promote their business goals effectively.

But what about costs? Table 12.1 has been prepared to estimate what

Table 12.1

Estimated Costs of Additional Jobs Created and Private Investment Mobilized in South Central India by Achievement Motivation Training

Annual Operating Expenses for Motivation Training Program (SIET Institute)

Six half-time staff members at a median salary of Rs. 1,500 per month	Rs. 54,000
Overhead at 30 per cent of salaries	16,200
Supporting costs (clerk-typist, supplies) at Rs. 400 per month	4,800
Travel costs for staff at Rs. 900 per course for twelve courses a year	10,800
Total costs:	Rs. 85,800

Number of Businessmen Trained

Twelve ten-day courses per year at fifteen trainees per course	180
Men in charge trained	150
Cost per trainee	Rs. 477
Cost per man in charge trained	Rs. 572

Additional Jobs

Created per man in charge trained	3.12*
Total additional jobs created	468
Cost per additional job created	Rs. 183

Additional Private Investment

Mobilized per man in charge trained	Rs. 11,840**
Total additional investment mobilized	Rs. 17.76 lakhs†
Cost to government of mobilizing additional private investment	4.85 per cent
Ratio of public to private investment	1:20
Average capital outlay (public and private) per job‡	Rs. 4,126

* This figure is taken from Table 7.9, as the difference in number of new employees per man in charge (1964–66) between the trained and control groups.

** This figure is taken from Table 7.7, as the difference in new investment mobilized per man in charge (1964–66) between the trained and control groups.

† One lakh = 100,000.

‡ This figure is the average total (not incremental) investment after the course for trained men in charge (Table 7.9) plus the cost per trainee given above, divided by the average number of new jobs created for trained men in charge (Table 7.7). The calculation is done in this way to facilitate direct comparison with the state government program described in Table 12.2.

the continuing costs to SIET Institute would have been to produce the incremental changes in economic performance reported in Chapter 7. The figures assume that the initial or start-up costs had been paid, as in fact they had been at the time the project was discontinued. That is, there were several staff members at SIET Institute who were fully trained and capable of continuing the courses and making the follow-up visits. In any case, the start-up costs were small because the major research applications had been disapproved: they certainly did not exceed $20,000, including travel money for all visitors from the United States and expenses to the Institute. What Table 12.1 does purport to show is what it would have cost the Institute to continue the program on an annual basis. Then, if we assume that the yield of subsequent courses would have been comparable to that of the early courses, we can calculate the costs of the yields obtained. This assumption seems to be justified, since Chapter 11 reported no decrease in yield for the two courses given in Vellore when no outside assistance was available to the Institute staff. The budget for the achievement motivation training program is shown simply as an additional activity for the Institute with staff members participating only part-time in motivation training. (Experience has shown that staff members need release from such emotionally demanding courses and also need to have some status as instructors in more conventional management fields.) Overhead has been set somewhat arbitrarily at 30 per cent of salaries. The remaining costs are based realistically on actual expenses incurred in giving the six courses at the Institute. We are indebted to Dr. Udai Pareek, formerly Director of Extension Training at SIET Institute, for help in making these estimates. It is further assumed that the trainees will pay their own transportation, board, and room as they did in the later courses at SIET Institute.

It is estimated that a staff of six trainers operating half-time each could comfortably run 12 ten-day courses in a year. If each course averages 15 participants, then the Institute could train 180 businessmen a year. Since the evidence in Chapter 11 conclusively shows that the effect of training is restricted primarily to businessmen who are in charge, it is further assumed that future participants would be selected largely, though not wholly, in terms of whether they were in a position to make some changes in their businesses. Arbitrarily it is assumed that about 80 per cent, or 150, of those trained would be in charge. The cost of training a man in charge then turns out to be Rs. 572. If it is estimated from previous experience that each such man will be responsible for creating 3.12 more new jobs than he would without training, then the training cost per additional job is Rs. 183, or about $25 at the 1968 rate of exchange.

Since each trained man in charge invests an additional Rs. 11,840, it can easily be calculated that the cost of stimulating this additional investment is 4.85 per cent. Or if the more conservative figure of Rs. 8,000 additional investment is used, as suggested in Chapter 7, then the cost is 7.2 per cent. To put it another way, for every rupee invested by the government in training costs, Rs. 14–20 are mobilized in private investment above what would be invested normally. Are these cost-benefit ratios favorable? Let us look at some comparative figures provided by Lynton and Stepanek (1963).

> . . . Government finance has not stimulated the productive investment of private funds in rural areas to anything like the amount expected and available. The most favorable ratio we have found has been Rs. 0.75 private funds for every Re. 1/- from government.
>
> This ratio is impossible to sustain. Were it possible to employ additional workers in productive industry for a total new capital outlay of Rs. 5,000 each, which is the average estimated investment for small mechanized industry, this ratio would call for nearly Rs. 3,000 per worker from the government, or Rs. 5,100 crores [= Rs. 51,000,000,000] for the seventeen million new workers during the third plan period, if they were all to be placed in such industry. Instead of Rs. 0.75 private to every Re. 1/- from government, the ratio has to become Rs. 4/- private to Re. 1/- from government, or higher still. Studies carried out by the economic investigation division of the CSIO in units outside the Okhla (Delhi) Industrial Estate show that this is quite possible. The prevailing ratio there is about Rs. 5/- private for every Re. 1/- of government funds. More recently a SIET Institute group reported the possibility of a 10 to 1 ratio in a rural area of Andhra Pradesh.

Thus the ratio of additional private investment stimulated to each government rupee invested obtained in this project is extremely favorable in relation to all the comparative standards given by Lynton and Stepanek. In fact, the ratio of 20 to 1 is double the most favorable ratio envisaged but not actually obtained. Moreover, their figures are substantiated by a report of estimated yields for an Andhra Pradesh state government intensive campaign to aid small industry through providing loans for hire-purchase (installment buying) of new equipment. The report was issued at about the same time that we were making the final evaluation of our project in the spring of 1967. Some of the published figures are laid out in Table 12.2 in a way that permits rough cost estimates of the type presented in Table 12.1. The average loan per unit was around Rs. 43,000, which of course does not represent the total cost to the government, because the expenses of operating the program and maintaining the government staff involved are not included. Even excluding these overhead costs, the government had to put out Rs. 3,500 for each new worker employed, or somewhat above what Lynton and

Table 12.2

Costs of Estimated Jobs Created and Estimated Private Investment Mobilized by an Intensive Hire-Purchase Campaign to Aid Small Industry in Andhra Pradesh, 1967

Number of units assisted reporting information	153
Total amount of assistance	Rs. 65.99 lakhs*
Overhead costs	?
Average loan per unit	Rs. 43,000
Jobs Created	
Total employment Before	1,543
After	3,401
Gain in employment	1,858
Average number of new jobs per unit	12.1
Cost to government per new job created	over Rs. 3,500
Private Investment Mobilized	
Total investment Before	Rs. 64.06 lakhs
After	Rs. 217.08 lakhs
Gain in investment	Rs. 153.02 lakhs
Privately mobilized investment total	Rs. 87.03 lakhs
Average private investment per unit	Rs. 57,000
Cost to government of mobilizing private investment	76 per cent
Ratio of public to private investment	1: 1.3
Average capital outlay (public and private) per job	Rs. 8,236

* One lakh = 100,000.
Adapted from data in *The Indian Express*, April 18, 1967.

Stepanek estimate, although this government aid went to industries that were more capital-intensive than average. While the government loans also succeeded in mobilizing private capital, the ratio was about as unfavorable as Lynton and Stepanek estimate—namely, for every government rupee expended, about Rs. 1.3 were mobilized from the private sector. Note that these figures are not incremental yields (as are the yields in Table 12.1), in the sense that one does not know how much of this private outlay would have been made anyway, without government expenditure. It should be recalled that the total private investment in Kakinada and Vellore was double the incremental investment attributable to achievement motivation training.

Even though the industries are more capital-intensive, the total capital outlay (public and private) per job in the hire-purchase campaign comes to the very high figure of over Rs. 8,200. This is considerably more than Lynton and Stepanek's estimate of Rs. 5,000 and about double the capital necessary for each new job created by the businessmen of Kakinada and Vellore when they were raising all the money themselves, without direct government aid. That is, the average total amount the trained men reported they had invested was about Rs. 24,000 (plus Rs. 572 training cost per entrepreneur as an additional public investment) and the average total number of jobs created was 5.86, yielding an estimated capital outlay per job of about Rs. 4,100. This figure is close to Lynton and Stepanek's estimate, but it is Rs. 4,000 less, per worker, than was required under the government loan plan.

Clearly, laying out government money can create employment and stimulate private investment, just as the economists argue it should, but the costs are prohibitive. They are too large to finance the employment and investment goals of the Third and Fourth Five Year Plans in India, and several times larger than the costs of producing the same economic effects by means of motivation training. It may be objected that some of the money raised by the trained businessmen in fact came from the government, so that the ratios are not so favorable as reported. Unfortunately, our records do not always show where the money raised came from, but it is very unlikely that more than a small fraction of it came from government sources. The sources mentioned were nearly always other members of the family or commercial banks. Even if all the money were ultimately from government sources, it is worth noting that when individuals themselves raise such money, they need considerably less capital to create a new job than they would if they were responding to government urging. Furthermore, as Lynton and Stepanek point out, "there are many signs in smaller towns and villages that the officials' very eagerness to spend government funds has driven underground any inclination local people may have felt to invest large amounts of their own funds. In short, except perhaps in the large towns, industrial development is more and more a government program when it needs to be a people's program." It is this exclusive concern with government support of small-scale industry that led an official to comment after the Andhra Pradesh campaign in 1967: "The growth of small-scale industry has suffered a severe setback in recent years due to cuts in the government budgets of allotments made for this purpose, in view of the diversion of resources for large scale and defense-oriented industry." As the present study has shown, such large-scale government investments are neither essential nor economical. Much smaller government expenditures for entrepreneurial training can stimulate employment and private investment at a far more favorable cost-effectiveness ratio. Thus one could argue that discontinuing the motivation training program at SIET

Institute set back the growth of small industry in the area much more severely, in terms of relative costs, than the cuts in government loan funds available.

It may be objected that motivation training produces an effect that is too small, although it is efficient. But the effect need not be small if training is instituted on a large scale through other management institutes already in existence throughout India or through Small Industries Service Institutes. Even if large-scale application increased the costs or decreased effectiveness, the ratios estimated in Table 12.1 are so favorable compared with those obtained by other methods that it would seem well worth trying.

It may be useful to introduce another point of comparison for the cost effectiveness of motivating training. There is much concern in India and other developing countries for increasing the income of subsistence farmers. After all, the argument goes, most of the population live in villages, and elaborate economic development plans often seem aimed primarily at increasing the incomes of the relatively few people who live in the cities. Thus many programs have been undertaken by government and private agencies in the past 15 to 20 years aimed at rural transformation or development. As an excellent example of such a program, let us look at the economic impact of Barpali Village Service, which was operated in the state of Orissa for ten years beginning in 1952, by the American Friends Service Committee. It supplied several dedicated staff members both from India and the United States who attempted to persuade the villagers to protect their water supply, to use latrines to control the spread of disease, to raise vegetables and poultry as cash crops, and to organize leatherworking and weaving cooperatives to increase their incomes. What distinguishes this project from many others is the care with which the villagers were consulted at every point about their needs and desires, the imaginativeness with which various plans were conceived and executed, and the serious attempt made by the AFSC at the end of the ten-year period to evaluate the impact of the pilot project. Dr. Thomas Fraser, an anthropologist who visited the village some time after the completion of the project, wrote up as carefully as he could what the effects of the various programs had been. (Fraser, 1966). He reports that while the Village Service did succeed in providing the villagers with a protected water supply by helping them build over 154 pump wells, its effect on family incomes several years after the completion of the project was less obvious. After several seasons, more and more of the villagers grew vegetables, but marketing them proved to be a problem because increasing quantities depressed local prices. Pure-bred Leghorn cocks were substituted for local cocks to improve the native chickens, which were scrawny and small. Even though at one time over 50 men had joined in the improvement scheme, and though it was obvious that the eggs from the hybrid birds were almost double the size of those obtained from the local strain, toward the end of the project "there was no trace of the improved poultry to be seen in the villages of Barpali *thana*" (Fraser, 1966, p. 203). The improved chickens required greater care; for instance, they needed to be fenced in because they could not run as fast as the local birds, and fell prey to the local dogs. In fact, the effort to improve the poultry strain nearly wiped out the chicken population.

Efforts to increase income by developing local cooperatives were scarcely more successful. A great deal of time was spent selecting the best weavers and organizing them into a weavers' cooperative to market locally produced cloth of high quality in urban centers in India, and even as far away as the United States. Despite considerable initial success, when Barpali Village Service withdrew, the local weaving group was unable to continue the carefully worked out project successfully, possibly because of the dominant management of the project technicians, who had set up an extensive system of "external relationships which were difficult for a rural organization to maintain" (Fraser, 1966, p. 209). The leathermakers' cooperative, which involved an outcast group that dealt with dead animals, shifted in midstream to a project for crushing the bones of the animals to make fertilizer. Local caste leadership took over this project and it continued after Barpali Village Service had withdrawn. While a careful cost-yield analysis is not really possible in this case, it is worth noting that the American Friends Service Committee invested upwards of $750,000 in the project over a ten-year period. While much of this went to improving health conditions rather than increasing local income, it would not be unreasonable to assume that at least half of it was invested to raise family incomes. Yet the project as a whole probably improved the incomes of fewer families than the actions of the one man described in Chapter 8 who, after taking the achievement motivation course, decided to buy up and rehabilitate an unused *khandasari* sugar mill, which employed seasonally 150 rural workers. When it is recalled that the cost of training this man was somewhere around $82 in contrast with the $300,000 invested in Barpali Village Service, the advantage of investing in direct training of individuals to take leadership seems overwhelming, as compared with giving technical advice and services. The conclusion is that if a planner is interested in improving the incomes of rural families, he should consider whether sometimes the best and most efficient way to do it is not directly, but indirectly through local business leaders.

The Importance of Cost-Yield Calculations

Estimates of the economic yield of Barpali Village Service are admittedly very crude, but at least an overall evaluation of the project was carried out. Surprisingly, even this amount of evaluation is rare for the numerous aid projects that have been supported over the past 20 years by private foundations and governments. It is almost impossible to find in the literature carefully calculated cost-yield ratios of either large or small projects. Everyone talks about the importance of evaluation, but apparently no one does anything about it. Yet the Ford and Rockefeller Foundations, the U.S. Agency for International Development, the United Nations, and many governments all over the world have spent billions of dollars trying to aid economic development apparently without serious evaluation of the cost-effectiveness of different types of investments.

The reason appears to be that the approach to development has been rational rather than empirical. It has seemed obvious that if rural people were to have better incomes, they would need roads so that they could get their produce to market. Why is it necessary to find out whether, after the road is built, they do in fact get more produce to market and get a better price for it? Or if a country is to develop modern business corporations, surely it needs advanced management training institutes to prepare local businessmen to run these corporations. Why is it necessary to see whether those who have been to the institutes actually perform better than those who have not? If a country is to invest its tax resources efficiently, surely it is obvious that foreign experts should be brought in, whatever the cost, to plan out the future economic development of the country, sector by sector, manpower requirement by manpower requirement. Why is it necessary to check up five years after the plans have been made to see whether the extent to which they have been realized in relation to their cost proves that the planning was an efficient procedure? If people who are near starvation are to eat better, surely it is rational to spend money on research to find a new and more protein-rich variety of wheat that can be locally grown. Is it necessary to spend even more money ten years later to find out if the new type of wheat is actually consumed?

Yet the literature is full of such "reasonable" investments that have not paid off, of roads built that do not get used to bring fish to market, of vegetables grown that cannot be marketed at a higher price, of better wheat flour that Indian women refuse to use because it is the wrong color. Probably there is a clear bias in such reports, because it makes for better journalism to expose the dramatic misfiring of some rationally conceived plan. In all likelihood the benefits of most such investments have been considerable. But the point is that the benefits relative to the costs have not been calculated and until they are, it will never be possible to decide prudently which type of investment is most likely to be effective in a given situation. Rational analysis is not by itself enough. It must be supplemented by systematic cost-yield calculations of the type presented here, based on actual experience.

Fortunately for us, the yield measures were built into the research design, partly because they were considered a continuation of the training and partly because we were trying to evaluate which combination of educational inputs would be most effective. Furthermore, we were not in the position of many economic planners, whose contributions to development seem so obvious that they do not need evidence to support them. Psychological education seemed like such an improbable economic input that evidence had to be collected to show its value.

Is Traditionalism a Serious Obstacle to Development?

When rational plans of the type mentioned above miscarry, the typical explanation is that people are "backward"—that is, that they have attitudes, norms, or institutions which keep them from doing what rational analysis says is to their advantage. For instance, Fraser (1966) explains the failure of the weavers' cooperative started by Barpali Village Service as being due in part to the fact that the project technicians were interested in selecting the best weavers, and therefore drew them from two different caste groups that could not work together. The norm of efficiency conflicted with caste traditionalism. He notes that raising poultry was a low-caste occupation and even those who engaged in it did not want to improve their performance, lest it prevent them from rising socially. It has always proved easy in post hoc analyses to find good reasons why people won't or can't do what they ought to do to improve their lives economically. There can be no doubt that such traditional difficulties are real. The problems facing the small businessmen in Kakinada and Vellore have already been enumerated at length in Chapters 3 and 6. They could not get licenses from the government for scarce raw materials. The extended family often forced an enterprising man to spend whatever he saved on supporting others rather than on investment in business expansion. Government assistance was spread too thin to have any effective impact. They had minimal technical or accounting skills, many of them probably being unable even to calculate whether they were making a profit or not. They belonged to different caste groups which ordinarily did not mix or cooperate. Many of them made their important decisions irrationally, by Western standards, after consulting an astrologer or perhaps a guru.

Yet they overcame these very real obstacles. What is more, traditional beliefs and practices did not turn out to interfere with whether they became active after the course (Chatper 9). The traditional individuals were just as likely to become active as the modern ones. How is it that people who were cautiously fatalistic, who avoided conflict, who did not believe in planning, and who strictly followed traditional caste rules were just as likely to expand their businesses after achievement motivation training as those who claimed to be modern on all of these issues? The result doesn't make much sense in terms of the Western, rational model of what it takes to be a modern, enterprising man. The conclusion seems compelling that much of what has been written about the changes in attitudes that are necessary for business improvement is misleading. It is motivated perhaps by a desire to explain why certain rationally conceived schemes for improvement have not worked. It does not seem to be necessary for a man to change his fatalistic attitude or his religious beliefs or practices to become an energetic entrepreneur. In other words, many of the obstacles to development are in the eye of the beholder, not in the psychology of the entrepreneurs involved. What does seem to be essential is that the man develop a strong faith in himself as an origin or agent of change, as someone who can solve problems efficaciously on his own. If he believes in himself, if he is motivated to change things, then he is undoubtedly an expert on how to carry out change within his social framework and within his traditional beliefs. The most effective strategy, in other words, appears to be to change the man's self-image by direct instruction on this key point, and then to leave the rest to him. This is in great contrast to the traditional strategy of trying to show him how some ways of doing things are better than others in the hope that indirectly and slowly he will decide on some rational basis to do the better things. Such an approach can only contribute to his feeling that he is a pawn: someone who doesn't know what is best and has to be shown by some outside expert. Thus, advice and assistance, however well intentioned or democratically offered, can weaken his self-confidence and strengthen his conviction that the real world is full of almost insurmountable obstacles. He may come to believe that he in particular will find it hard to overcome these obstacles because of his traditional, "irrational" beliefs and practices. Stress on the difficulties of development thus becomes one of the chief obstacles to development. It seems far more effective to convince a man directly that he can accomplish what he wants, that he can become a change agent, and then trust him to find ways within his traditional culture of accomplishing his aims. Under these circumstances, the much touted traditionalist obstacles to development turn out to be less serious than most observers have claimed.

The Promise of Psychological Education

To a psychologist, the most exciting implication of the results of this research is that adults apparently can be changed fairly easily by direct educational methods. Such a conclusion, if taken seriously, means a radical transformation of much current psychological theory. As we pointed out in Chapter 2, since Calvin and Freud, most personality psychologists have believed in a kind of predestination. What happens in the first few years of life to a few instincts has been thought to determine adult personality characteristics forever after. As the twig is bent, so grows the tree. Therefore adult personality could only be changed, if at all, by an elaborate, time-consuming reconstruction of early childhood dynamics. Yet adults clearly did change as a result of achievement motivation training. They spent their waking hours differently. They worked harder and longer. They changed what they spent their time thinking about. They raised capital, spent their money in different ways, hired new employees, bought land, let contracts to build additions to their shops or new factories, drank less at their clubs because they had less time to spend there, and so forth. Doubtless many psychologists will conclude that these changes are superficial, that they did not involve any deep personality transformation. Perhaps that is so, but we suspect that such a judgment is based at least in part on the fact that the transformations were brought about so quickly and easily. For among personality psychologists, it is tacitly assumed that if a characteristic changes quickly, it has to be superficial and if it shows great resistance to change, it must be deep. Such an assumption seems circular, and is probably misleading. The ease or difficulty of changing a personality or action characteristic may have as much to do with the technique employed to change it as with the depth of the characteristic itself. Certainly to us, and to the men themselves, the changes in their behavior often seemed quite profound.

The question, therefore, has naturally arisen as to whether this type of psychological education would be as effective in other situations. Certainly there are many other groups of disadvantaged individuals who appear to be unmotivated. Would the technique work as well for them? Quite naturally attention first turned to the unmotivated high school boys, for whom all the ordinary techniques of parental or school counseling and guidance seemed to be failing. Despite the fact that most such boys are not in a position to plan to go into business, for which n Achievement is supposed to be particularly suited, it was decided that the achievement motivation training course might build in them a sense that they were origins rather than pawns, much as it did in the case of the Kakinada businessmen. So a group of potential high-school dropouts or failures, 16 to 17 years of age, were taken to a country retreat for a five-day course patterned along the lines described in Chapter 2. Half of the boys dropped out of the motivation course, following the same pattern they had been showing in school; but among those who stayed, the changes in behavior a year and a half later were quite marked. Seven out of nine, as contrasted with three out of nine of their matched controls, showed a marked improvement in grades. Furthermore, all of them reported thinking very seriously about their vocational plans, as contrasted with practically none of the control boys, who reported that their chief concerns at the moment were sports, cars, and girls (McClelland, 1969). The results are not conclusive because the numbers are small and because of the number who dropped out.

Yet at least in some cases, the technique produced dramatic changes that other methods had failed to achieve. Extensive studies are now under way to try out the techniques on a large scale and to adapt them to the normal conditions of high-school education. One of the important side effects of the training in India is that Dr. Prayag Mehta of the National Institute of Education has introduced achievement motivation training for underachieving high-school students on an extensive scale.

Achievement motivation training has also been carried out with urban lower-class Negro Americans. A number of studies have documented the fact that lower-class Negroes are low in n Achievement (cf. Rosen, 1959) and that the Negro community as a whole has not been very entrepreneurial. So it was of particular interest to see whether achievement motivation could be developed in such a situation. Quite accidentally, Shri Nadkarni, the chief trainer in the project in India, made contact while he was in Boston with a club of Negro fathers from a ghetto area, who expressed interest in the training he had been giving in India. He arranged to run several courses for them along the usual lines, in a retreat setting outside Boston in the early spring of 1966. Sixteen out of 19 of the participants were black; most were in their early thirties, married, with children; many had extensive criminal records; and few had graduated from high school. Several were civil-rights leaders in the ghetto community. In a follow-up evaluation conducted approximately two years later, eight of the sixteen Negro men trained received a score of $+2$, according to the coding scheme used in Chapters 2 and 7, and the average business activity score for the group was 1.31, a yield from the training which is very similar to that obtained from the second through fourth courses given in Barcelona (See Table 11.2). For instance, one man bought two income properties and went into business for himself as a building contractor. Another entered night school to take a business degree at a nearby university and obtained a much better job. A third bought a car and no longer works exclusively as a construction foreman for another man, but now operates his own apartment-renovating business. A fourth expanded his photographic business, began a program series for the local educational television station, and helped form a new organization called the Massachusetts Achievement Trainers, Inc. (MAT). Several graduates of the courses felt that the type of training they had received would be valuable for other men in their situation. With Shri Nadkarni's help, several of them were given enough further training to become trainers themselves. The resulting company, MAT, has already successfully undertaken a number of motivation training jobs to prepare Negroes and other disadvantaged groups for employment and economic advancement. The organization began with seven part-time members and a capital investment of $350.00. During its first year of operation, 1966, the Roxbury area of Boston provided four small, short-term contracts. In two short years, MAT has grown into a non-profit corporation with nine board members, four provisional members, a full-time secretary, executive director and business manager, and numerous technical consultants. Training contracts are long-range and national in scope, and the financial worth of the organization has multiplied itself many times over.

One may be skeptical in attributing all of these changes to the achievement motivation training the men received since, of course, there were many other psychological and material inputs into the Negro ghetto area during this same period. But the similarity of the results to yields obtained in other courses suggests at least that the training was partly responsible for their improved performance. Certainly without the training the new organization, MAT, could never have been formed and would not now be providing similar types of motivation training for other disadvantaged adults.

This initial promising result also encouraged application of the technique on a wider scale under carefully controlled conditions in a Negro business community in Washington, D.C. Here the goal is to see whether achievement motivation training can energize a group of businessmen who, in their way, are as discouraged as the small businessmen in Kakinada and Vellore were. The obstacles to business expansion in the Negro community in America are much greater even than in small cities in India. But with changes in legislation and opportunities available for disadvantaged groups in the United States, it seemed worth trying to activate Negro business leadership to take more rapid advantage of changes in the opportunity structure. The training has been carried out, and some early follow-up results are available. It was interesting to observe that Negro American businessmen had even less confidence in themselves than the Indian businessmen. At the least sign of failure in any of the exercises, they would typically give up, withdraw, and define themselves as "no good," thus echoing what many whites have so often said about them. Therefore it has been necessary to build in special training devices, to find psychological factors which would heighten self-confidence and pride. One such factor which undoubtedly played a key role in the MAT training courses in the Boston area was the philosophy of Black Power, which strongly permeated the group. In fact, the Black Power movement can be seen psychologically as a rather emphatic assertion that one is an agent, rather than a pawn to be oppressed, or "helped," or otherwise pushed around by white people. As such, it is part of the psychological transformation needed to bring about improved economic performance, as we have argued in the case of the Indian businessmen. The Black Power philosophy may not appeal as much to middle-class Negroes, such as those trained in Washington. If so, then they must find some alternative means of becoming proud of themselves and their community, if they are to think of themselves as capable of improving their own position, rather than just creeping slowly forward as retreating whites let them.

Six months after the training, ten of the businessmen had formed a community investment corporation, "Capital City Investors, Inc.," of which total capitalization contributed by members was to be $30,000. It planned to invest in real estate—e.g., the purchase and rehabilitation of apartment buildings—or businesses such as plastics manufacturing, a shopping center, an automobile franchise, or a lumberyard. The company plans to retain 60 per cent ownership of anything in which it invests, selling shares for the remaining 40 per cent in those cases where additional capital is required. All of these possibilities were being actively researched in a manner exactly parallel to what happened in Kakinada. One man had invested in a beauty products franchise and had already made back his initial investment. Another, a printer, had joined in partnership with a nonparticipant to produce a line of greeting cards. A third man, who was part-owner of a beauty parlor, expanded into the selling of wigs. Eight new businesses had been started six months later as contrasted with none by a comparable untrained group of men. Early returns suggested that motivation training would increase business effectiveness as much in a black central city area in America as it did in small cities in India. Of the 49 men trained, 71 per cent had become unusually active after the courses as contrasted with only 27 per cent of the 63 men in a carefully matched untrained group of men. The trained businessmen had already invested $4200 on the average as contrasted with the $1400 invested on the average by the untrained men.

Similar achievement motivation courses have been conducted for a group of business leaders in McAlester, Oklahoma, under contract from the Economic Development Administration of the U.S. Department of Commerce. McAlester was chosen because it was the center of a region that had, in common with other economically underdeveloped areas of the country, a high rate of unemployment. A new economic base for employment had to be found, to replace marginal farmlands of declining importance.

Six months after the n Achievement training, 61 per cent of the 41 businessmen participants had become markedly more active, as contrasted with 24 per cent of the 59 untrained matched controls (Behavioral Science Center, 1968). The participants had decided to contribute to a capital fund which was to provide risk capital to small businesses. Most of the total capital had already been subscribed, and the first loan had been made. A wholesale dealer reduced his inventory obsolescence, and used the working capital thereby freed up to add a new product line. A bank employee set up a recreational business. Other, more elaborate ventures were in stages of advanced planning. But here the emphasis was more heavily on improving existing businesses, rather than investing in new ones as the black businessmen did. For the trained group of businessmen after six months, sales had increased $9500 on the average, as contrasted with $1800 on the average for their matched, untrained controls.

Psychological education is not restricted to achievement motivation training. Most of the techniques described in Chapter 2 are quite general. Only one of the four major types of educational inputs explicitly involves the achievement motivation syndrome. Therefore it has also seemed desirable to try and test the effectiveness of the general approach in another psychological area. Considerable recent empirical research has shown that a key motivational factor leading to alcoholism, both cross-culturally and individually, is a frustrated need for Power (see McClelland, *et al.*, 1970). As in the case of the achievement syndrome, years of research leading up to this conclusion had resulted in a number of measuring instruments and test situations which could be used to teach the alcoholic to see in more precise terms what his problem was and what he needed to do to overcome it. Thus, on an experimental basis, the Massachusetts Achievement Trainers group described above gave a number of long-weekend courses designed to help alcoholics. The chief difference between these courses and those involving achievement motivation was that the participants here learned how alcohol increased their fantasies of power and how they might find other methods of satisfying their power needs, which would not only be more socially acceptable but would also be less self-defeating. Again the follow-up has not been completed, and the courses themselves were probably little more successful than our early, fumbling attempts to teach achievement motivation in Mexico, but there have been a few startling personality and work transformations in participants. The results are inconclusive at this stage, but they tend to support the belief that the techniques of psychological education can be applied effectively in a number of different psychological areas, as well as among different types of unmotivated groups that need to develop self-esteem if they are to overcome their disadvantages.

Why is psychological education effective? How can such a short exposure in some cases produce such large and lasting changes in behavior? It is probably too soon to answer the question with any degree of theoretical sophistication. The answer may involve the differences between working with adults and working with children. Many people prefer to work with children: for example, they may believe that the only way to transform the Negro American community is to reach its children, before they are handicapped for life by their disadvantages. However, we have observed two distinct advantages of working with adults; these advantages may explain the effectiveness of psychological education. First, adults can understand what you are saying to them, but children often cannot. That is, our technique employs psychological explanations and requires participants to understand completely what is going on and why the trainers are doing what they are doing. It assumes, quite simply, that reason and understanding help a person change. The behavior of children, in contrast, has to be shaped indirectly and less effectively.

Second, children are so young—which is another way of saying both the child and the change agent have to wait a long time to see whether any of the educational interventions have had any effect. In contrast, adults are in a position to show the effects of their personality transformations immediately. An alcoholic can reduce his drinking tomorrow. A businessman can decide to seek a loan immediately. Adults are in a position to be agents, to test out new behaviors, to demonstrate to themselves that they are no longer pawns. To be sure, children have some freedom of action, but when they are very young it is quite limited and what they can do is not really the same as what the educator hopes he is preparing them to do effectively in later life. A child of eight or ten might, with considerable effort, be shaped gradually into someone showing the characteristics of higher achievement motivation, but many things can happen to him before he could display it in a relevant business situation. Why not work with adults who are in that situation, and to whom the motivation is relevant? To us it is no longer a self-evident truth that it is easier to produce long-range personality transformations in young children than it is in adults. For the adults can better understand what is going on and they are also in a better position to put the changes into effect immediately.

Did the Results Have Anything to Do with the Theory?

It is time to view the research findings somewhat more skeptically. So far we have concentrated on drawing out some of their most obvious and encouraging implications. However, that is only part of the story. Any objective observer would be troubled by doubts, difficulties, and objections that also need a careful airing.

To begin with, how can we be sure that our interpretation of the results is correct? We have analyzed what we did, or what we thought we did in the training courses and have calculated the ways in which men exposed to the courses behaved differently from those who were not. But how can we be sure that what we thought we did caused what they did? Is the whole psychological theory we have invoked necessary to explain the results? We have already argued in Chapter 11 that it is too easy to try to understand the results in terms of a simple increase in *n* Achievement levels among the trained businessmen. Rather it appeared as if the instruction in achievement motivation was one of the important means by which the men became convinced that they themselves were entirely capable of expanding their business activities. But doesn't such an interpretation raise even more insistently the question of whether the same result could not have been obtained without all of the elaborate psychological educational inputs described in Chapter 2? Couldn't the men have been activated simply by planning conferences, public exhortations made by prestigious outsiders, and periodic interviews on progress made by government extension workers? The issue is of vital practical importance because governments and other aid agencies seem far more likely to adopt such familiar activities than they are to learn the seemingly arcane techniques of psychological education.

Unfortunately, the conventional techniques of activation and planning do not seem to be sufficient. To prove the point it is only necessary to refer back to the tables in Chapter 7, showing the before and after activity levels of the Kakinada control subjects. Nearly all had been exposed to conventional activation inputs. That is, they had attended public meetings and heard the plans for Kakinada described in detail; they had participated in discussion groups organized around the theme of achievement motivation; they had individually been interviewed by a representative of the project about their personal interest in attending the courses. All of them had expressed a desire to undergo the motivation training. In short, they were exposed to many of the ordinary techniques used to arouse a community to further effort to improve their condition. Yet the results, as reported in Tables 7.7 and 7.9, clearly show that these men behaved no differently after such activation efforts than they had before, and certainly no differently from control businessmen in Rajahmundry who had not been exposed to any campaign to get them to improve their business activity. We had, in fact, expected that "talking up" achievement would spread to other businessmen in Kakinada particularly, even though they were prevented from actually attending the courses at SIET Institute. However, only those who were intensively exposed to the achievement motivation course actually showed significant improvements in business activity.

Furthermore, it is worth recalling for a moment what happened in the achievement motivation courses organized for potential high-school dropouts. About half these boys dropped out of the training after a day or two at the retreat center. How is this to be interpreted? They were exposed to prestigious educational leaders; they had learned something about the achievement syndrome; they had started on a self-improvement program. Yet somehow these inputs didn't take. They dropped out and showed no improvement in subsequent performance as compared to control subjects. In theoretical terms, what had gone wrong? Even the simple summative model of input effectiveness arrived at in Chapter 11 does not seem sufficient to explain the result. That is, one might argue that neither the Kakinada control businessmen nor the course dropouts had been exposed to a sufficient number of educational inputs for any change in their behavior to occur. Every input may add a little bit and a critical mass may be necessary to produce an effect. But such an interpretation is of little use in understanding the training dropouts, because they would not stay long enough to get exposed to more inputs. Apparently, putting on a course involves more than exposing some individuals to various combinations of psychological inputs, as suggested, for example, by Table 11.2. Successful course management is involved, and management suggests that training courses should be considered as social systems.

It then became apparent to us that we had been unconsciously thinking of what we had been doing in terms of the framework of a psychological experiment, because we were, after all, psychologists. Traditionally, the social-system aspects of the psychological experiment have been ignored because the model for it is the physical science experiment, in which the observer is outside the system that he is studying. Thus it has been considered desirable to pretend that the experimenter (or E) is in no way part of the experiment he is conducting: his thoughts, wishes and relationship to his "subjects" are not supposed to enter in to "distort" the results of the experiment. It was easy to accept this assumption so long as psychologists worked with animal subjects, but as they became involved in more and more social experiments of the type reported here, it became clearer that the experimenter was involved in some kind of a contract with his subjects—a contract that had certain of the attributes of a system. That is, the experimenter can alter the nature of the contract in a variety of subtle ways by the normative attitudes, expectations or biases that he brings to the situation (see, for example, Rosenthal and Jacobson, 1968), or by the "mix" of participants he induces to participate. This is illustrated in the discussion in Chapter 11 of how the third and fourth Kakinada courses differed from the first and second. The subjects can also alter it by the expectations they bring to it, or more dramatically by dropping out of the contract or not entering into it in the first place. This focuses attention on the nature of the contract and how it is managed, rather than exclusively on what is done once the contract is established.

The importance of this change in viewpoint is perhaps best illustrated by referring to Table 12.3, which is designed to show in the simplest

Table 12.3
The Functional Imperatives of a Social System, after Parsons
(cf. Black, 1961, p. 331)*

	Instrumental Activities	Consummatory States	Relevant Psychological Systems
Task Performance (External Orientation)	Adaptation (Technology) *Achievement syndrome* (A)	Goal Attainment *Goals of business expansion* (G)	Achievement Syndrome
System Maintenance (Internal Orientation)	Pattern Maintenance (Norms, tension management) *Self-study* (S)	Integration (System survival) *Interpersonal supports* (I)	Power Syndrome

* Major categories of course inputs are in italics.

possible fashion the functional imperatives of a social system as analyzed by Parsons. He argues that it is possible to distinguish two main functions of any social system—one oriented outwards toward the environment, which he labels task performance; and the other oriented inwards, which he labels system maintenance. The goals and means of attaining each differ. Thus a psychological experiment such as the achievement motivation training courses has two distinct aspects. The task performance aspect is to expose businessmen to certain psychological inputs with the goal of changing their business behavior. However, for this task to be performed, a system maintenance goal must also be achieved, that is, the course as a social system must survive. The means of promoting the goal of system survival (or integration) are the norms relating to the course contract and certain techniques for tension management used during the course. Clearly these means were inadequate to insure survival of the course, as far as concerns half of the high-school underachievers who started attending the sessions designed for them. Unfortunately, we have learned very little from this research that we can communicate explicitly about how to promote system maintenance. Our trainers must have been fairly effective at the practical level, or the courses would not have been carried out as well as they were. But we can say very little of a formal nature about the techniques of pattern maintenance employed or the exact nature of the optimal contract established between trainees and participants. In fact, we only identified this as a major problem for research and interpretation after the completion of the project.

However, Table 12.3 also serves to demonstrate that quite unconsciously we had introduced educational inputs that corresponded to the four functional imperatives of a social system. They are written in italics in each of the four boxes. The *achievement syndrome* (A) is the technical means by which the *Goals of business expansion* set by the participants (G) are to be achieved. These two classes of educational inputs relate to the task to be performed as a result of the creation of this miniature social system. On the other hand, the *self-study* (S) educational inputs seem designed in retrospect to help the person manage the tensions and value changes within himself and in his relations to others, which are likely to result from pursuing the task performance goal. Similarly the *interpersonal supports* (I) educational inputs seem designed to fulfill the requirement for integration either within the personality as a system or within the society to which the individual returns. Specifically, the Kakinada Entrepreneurs Association fulfilled an integrative function for the course alumni who were attempting to behave in new ways when they went back into their traditional social system. Thus the system maintenance problems were not wholly neglected in the courses, although we now believe we could have done a better job if at the time we had explicitly defined what we were doing in terms of this analysis.

That is, we believe that it is better to think of the research design not in terms of combinations of inputs, but in terms of certain functional requirements which must be met for optimal effectiveness of the training. Any one of these requirements can be met in a variety of ways. This seems to be an advance beyond the summative model of Chapter 11. It suggests that at least some minimal level of course inputs relevant to each of the four functional imperatives is necessary to achieve effectiveness; further, that even intensive attention given to two or three of the four prerequisites is not likely to be as effective as some attention to all of them. At a minimum we are convinced by our experience that exclusive attention to task performance without any attention to system maintenance is likely to result in complete failure of the enterprise. The participants will either not attend the course, drop out after it has started, or fail to maintain behavior changes once they have re-entered the old social system.

In short, our theoretical account of what we were doing and what happened is too limited. It was biased by our psychological background in the direction of neglecting the system requirements of putting on the course and maintaining their effects afterwards.

Why Was the Program Discontinued at SIET Institute?

The observer might well wonder why the program was dropped by SIET Institute if it was as successful as described in this book. In fact, our report so far resembles the hospital bulletin that said: "The operation was successful; the patient died." It is customary in such cases to explain failure of a program as being due to personality conflicts or particular local issues of no general significance to social science. There were such problems in the present instance, but on closer study they seem to transcend local significance and to point to a general problem that is often neglected in aid programs of all sorts. By its very nature, aid or intervention involves a power relationship between the agent and his target. The agent has goals of his own; in order to achieve them he may have to work through an institution that has goals of its own. Since the two sets of goals often conflict, and since the means of attaining them are different, a power problem often arises. The agent may require the institution to change so as to achieve his goals; the institution resists because it is pursuing certain system goals.

Again, Table 12.3 is helpful. In the light of this analytic scheme, the Harvard Entrepreneurial Motivation Project had almost exclusively a task orientation. Its goal was to produce change in business activity levels of individual businessmen; its means was psychological education of the achievement motivation variety. But obviously in order to achieve these goals the project had to be lodged within an Indian institution, in this case SIET Institute, which had been created to train government extension workers. The Harvard Project staff failed to consider seriously that SIET Institute had system maintenance problems of its own. It had to survive as a social system largely by continuing to get government appropriations and grants from The Ford Foundation. Certainly in order to continue to get public funds, it had to maintain certain norms generally applied by the Government of India to such organizations— norms, for instance, dealing with salary levels, vacations, and travel allowances. The Harvard or task orientation might be paraphrased like this: "The important thing is to get the job done; we have a terrifically difficult task in trying to persuade all these businessmen to come here for training and to put on an essentially new and untried type of course;

if we are to do it successfully, we must have the freedom to pay good staff people, and the flexibility to do things the way it is essential to have them done in order to succeed." The SIET Institute or system orientation might be expressed thus: "Whether this special training project succeeds or not is of little or no importance to the Institute; what is important is whether the Institute survives; that is, continues to get its appropriation from the government, which in turn depends on whether it performs the functions it is supposed to perform and follows the norms governing institutions of this sort." To symbolize this contrast by reference to Table 12.3, the task orientation has been labeled as implying in psychological terms the achievement syndrome. Emphasis is clearly on successful task performance, on concrete knowledge of results, and on using any technological means necessary to achieve the results. The system orientation, on the other hand, seems to involve psychological problems of authority, control, or power. In order for the social system to be maintained, some exercise of authority and control is clearly necessary. The two orientations were bound to conflict in the present instance. For example, it seemed to the regular staff members that those involved in the motivation training were getting some kind of special treatment, because of their association with an outside source of funds. Achievement motivation training was in no way central to the Institute's survival. In fact it was perceived by some as undercutting the Institute's main function, which was to train government extension workers; and as creating certain new problems for the government, such as an active group of businessmen who would keep pestering officials for scarce resources. Even the notion of research as an achievement enterprise does not fit well with system goals, for, as one official put it, if achievement motivation training worked, why not include it in the regular courses; and if we weren't sure about it, why waste time and money experimenting? Such questions naturally arise when the primary goal is to maintain a system free from doubts and threats to its stability. In the end the training was dropped, for a number of such reasons.

But the lesson is clear: in any intervention effort there is not only an achievement problem—succeeding in what you are trying to do—but also a power problem—finding an institutional base for carrying out the task. It is our belief that the experience at SIET Institute is by no means atypical of aid efforts and that far more of them fail because they fail to solve the power problem than because they fail in performing the task itself. The usual course of events is the same as it was at SIET Institute. The power problem was handled initially by the Principal Director of the Institute. He used his authority to welcome the aid project without either his or the project staff's worrying too much about possible conflict between the project and the Institute. If the director had stayed on, he doubtless would have found a way to reconcile the task and system goals, but the fact that he did not was in part a result of his tendency to be more innovative than was normative for a government official in his position. After all, he was a businessman, an outsider, and not a member of the Indian Administrative Service.

But the key point is that the power problem was solved initially in this case, as it often is in traditional societies, by exercising the personal authority of the head of the institution. And when he left, the project was discontinued essentially on the personal authority of his successor. In both cases, suitable group actions were taken, but they were based in large part on the personal authority of the director. Certainly one of the simplest ways to handle power problems in a social system is through personal leadership or charisma. Order is maintained in the system on the authority of the head man. While this is a general solution adopted to some degree in all societies, many observers feel that it is peculiarly adapted to India's tradition.[1] There the institution has been the shadow of a man. A classic Indian institution is the ashram, which forms around a powerful leader. When he dies, the ashram dissolves or eventually reforms around another leader. As we have seen, the man occupying the *kartā* role typically exercises the same kind of personal authority in the family. As the Indian children's stories analyzed for *The Achieving Society* (see also Chapter 2) and the case studies reported in Chapter 10 make abundantly clear, power problems in the Indian culture tend to be highly personalized. They occur between individuals rather than institutions, and the means of resolving them are interpersonal rather than impersonal and institutional.

A bureaucracy or a rule of laws and regulations is supposed to be the chief alternative to exercising control through personal leadership or charismatic authority. Certainly India has a well-developed bureaucratic system. Yet when the shift from personal to impersonal authority has not been fully made, the bureaucratic system can simply be used as a means of exercising the leader's authority. The rules may be used by the leader in whatever way he thinks is best to maintain his authority and the survival of the system. To some extent this is true of all institutions; we are talking about a matter of degree. For example, it seems fair to conclude from subsequent events that the Harvard project had more of a personalized power relationship to the director of the Institute than

---

1. For further discussion of the role of power-dependency problems in India and in development, see Pareek, 1966, 1967.

it did an institutional relationship to SIET Institute as a social system. Thus when the incumbent in the Principal Director role changed, the relationship did not continue as before; in fact, the new director may have felt that since the relationship had not been worked out with him personally, by definition it could no longer hold.

One can infer from this analysis that in societies characterized by personalized authority, it may be easier to get acceptance of an intervention program, but harder to build an institutionalized base for continuing the program. What makes for easy initial entrance into the system—personal authority—often creates problems in the long run. The person sponsoring the entry may move to another position or his initial acceptance of the project may have made entry so easy that a consideration of system problems created by the project may be completely neglected.

It is our conviction that the power problems involved in attempting to aid economic development have not been sufficiently recognized, analyzed, or studied and that they constitute one of the major reasons why many development efforts fail. After all, of what value is it to demonstrate the utility of achievement motivation education for promoting economic growth if there is no way to enter the authority systems or institutions in underdeveloped countries in order to get it widely used?

What Was the Community Impact of the Project?

In the early stages of planning for this project, as reported in Chapter 3, we had rather ambitious hopes of starting an achieving society, of showing in miniature how economic growth begins. Measured against such a goal, surely the project must be judged less than successful. Would a casual visitor to Kakinada today, for instance, be able to observe that it is more of an achieving society than Rajahmundry? Probably not. Aren't the results more statistical than "real"? Will the initial enthusiasm of the trained businessman last beyond the five years that have elapsed since they were trained? Or will our efforts, like so many others, simply disappear under the cross-pressures of the many macroeconomic and social factors that in the long run determine a community's progress?

We attempted to collect community economic figures for Kakinada, Rejahmundry, and Vellore, covering such things as overall employment, tax collections, electricity consumed, and the like. In view of the findings reported in Chapters 7 and 8, it seems hardly likely that such community indexes of economic growth would be affected by the actions of the trained entrepreneurs. For one thing, the major project plans of the Kakinada Entrepreneurs Association, such as the steel rerolling mill or the leather factory, were never realized. Also, some of the largest new enterprises mentioned in Chapter 8, such as the *khandasari* sugar mill and the truck finance company, were realized outside the city limits of Kakinada. Finally, the figures themselves as collected by the towns are not very reliable. The only ones that seemed genuinely comparable across time periods and towns are those for industrial and commercial electric power consumption as summarized in Table 12.4. These figures confirm

Table 12.4
Industrial and Commercial Electric Power Consumption in KWH Units for Comparable Time Periods in Kakinada and Rajahmundry

	Before training *June–November, 1963*	*After training* *June–November, 1965*	*Gain*
Kakinada	2,132,108	2,990,680	858,572
Rajahmundry	2,182,220	3,045,453	863,451

the impression that whatever happened in Kakinada, it was not large enough to affect such a community index as industrial and commerical electric power consumed. We chose a six-month period before training in both Kakinada and Rajahmundry to compare with a similar six-month period about a year and a half after training. The cities started at about the same level and increased in the two-year period by about the same amount. Moreover, there is some evidence that overall electricity consumption is allocated to various cities on a quota system, which prevents one city from getting more than its share. Certainly restrictions on electricity consumed were imposed both in Rajahmundry and Kakinada between November 1963 and June 1965.

But these figures reopen an important question already mentioned in Chapter 3. Is it not possible that by stimulating some businessmen to be more aggressive, we only succeeded in redistributing what business there was in a town like Kakinada? If one merchant air-conditions his sari shop so that he gets more business, we may credit him with increased business activity, but doesn't he simply take away business from other merchants, so that there is no net gain for the community as a whole? The community economic indexes were supposed to answer this question, but they did not. That forces us to fall back on case data which are helpful but not entirely conclusive. In many important instances it would be hard to argue that the businesses were simply taking away work from other people. The *khandasari* sugar factory that was activated had simply been unused and rusting for several years; with transport conditions the way they are in that section of rural India, it is difficult to imagine that the farmers could possibly have gotten their cane to other mills. Even if they did, it would have taken more effort and left less time for other presumably more productive economic activities. The truck finance business simply helped to fill a need for more rapid and efficient distribution of goods, as Chapter 8 pointed out. Even the air-conditioned sari shop may have a demonstration effect, for all we know. That is, other cloth merchants seeing that this man gets more business because of his air conditioner, might also install air conditioners, increasing the business for the supplier of air conditioners and perhaps even encouraging ladies to buy more saris because it is pleasanter to shop. We simply do not have enough evidence on the collective impact of the business improvements described in Chapters 7 and 8. What is needed is a thorough input-output analysis of the transactions carried on within a city like Kakinada, a study which was clearly beyond our means and competence.

Is Psychological Education Morally Justified?

The moral problems of intervening to change people's values and motives directly have been raised in Chapter 1 and elsewhere. Individuals have repeatedly told us that we couldn't change people's values and even if we could, we should not. One of the strongest beliefs in the American tradition is that people ought not to impose their values on others, that if they do so they are somehow violating the fundamental right of self-determination. As an amusing example of the conflicting value attitudes surrounding research of this sort, consider the case of the parents who were startled to discover that their son, after being exposed to achievement motivation training, suddenly gave up watching television in the evening and worked for hours on his math problems instead. They had been disturbed that he was not studying, and that nothing they could say seemed to interest him in his math. However, when they noted such a marked change in his behavior, apparently due to some mysterious psychological intervention, they became alarmed and wondered if we had "brainwashed" him.

Curiously enough, these doubts and moral objectives derive from a profound respect for the very psychological characteristic that our courses try to promote—namely, the conviction that an individual can and should be responsible for his own actions. When a boy suddenly starts studying beyond all previous expectations, the fear is that someone has gotten him to do it "against his will." Or when we speak of intervening to change one's values, the fear is that the target of the influence attempt is being treated like a pawn, something to be manipulated.

Yet careful review of our whole philosophy of psychological education would show that the problem is semantic rather than real. The term "intervention" sounds as if the techniques are aimed at manipulating people, but in fact a careful reading of how the techniques work shows that at every point they embody individual responsibility, initiative, and choice. The goal of the educational techniques is achieved only when the person accepts the fact that he alone can change his own behavior.

But there is still another bothersome aspect to the problem. A key moral theme in Western culture is that of individual responsibility. If we kill someone accidentally, we are not morally responsible. But if we kill him intentionally, we are certainly responsible for murder. If we actually try by psychological education to influence a person's motives and values, particularly if we can do it effectively, can we not be held more responsible if something goes wrong than if we didn't know what we were doing?

A teacher once told us that she knew she was undoubtedly influencing the values and motives of her pupils unconsciously all the time, but she certainly wanted no part of an effort to do it deliberately, lest she be held responsible for what her pupils did afterwards. But surely this is cowardice. A teacher simply cannot escape the responsibility for influencing students in one way or another. Surely it is better to know and to understand what one is doing, even though one cannot escape so easily from any later blame.

That brings up the practical question of whether the achievement motivation courses for men from Kakinada and Vellore had any detectable bad effects. A careful review of all 79 cases suggests that only for two men could we reasonably argue that the effects of the training were harmful. One was an older man who had been investing in impractical schemes all his life. He had some capital, and simply because he liked machinery, he tended to invest in machines that often did not get used to make products of economic value. After the training, it appeared that this tendency had been accentuated; that is, that he now had invested somewhat more money than previously in unproductive enterprises. Actually this judgment was hard to make and doubtless he himself would not agree with it, but to be fair, one might well conclude that in his case the motivation training had only raised his level of impractical investment and lost him more money.

In another instance, a young man had been psychologically depressed and disturbed because of a scandal involving a member of his family. He went to the course partly because he and some of his friends thought it might do him good. It did not. When he was seen in the final interview, he was very angry at the Americans and those who had given the course because his life had been one succession of failures ever since the training. He had been encouraged by the course to try out some schemes, all of which had failed, and quite naturally he blamed the project for what had happened. There is little doubt in the minds of those who know him that his problems are of a deep psychological nature and in no sense can be attributed to the course. Nevertheless, the course may well have made them worse.

Thus in honesty we should report that the training had negative consequences for two out of 79, or 2.5 per cent of the cases. As Bergin points out (1967), psychotherapy appears to make a much higher percentage of its patients worse. Against the failures, one must weigh, of course, the tremendous gains in success and satisfaction that upwards of two thirds of the trained men reported. It cannot be said that psychological education is wholly without risk, but in our experience the gains outweigh the risks many times over.

Implementing Development Plans

Like most research projects, this one will not serve to satisfy a reasonably persistent skeptic. It raises certain new questions, such as the power relations implicit in aid efforts, and leaves certain others unanswered, such as the impact on the community of increased entrepreneurial activity. Yet despite these doubts, many would like to know what has been learned from the project about practical implementation of economic development. Judgments must often be made on the basis of imperfect evidence. Does what happened in the business communities in Kakinada and Vellore suggest new practical procedures that might be followed in promoting economic growth?

A recurrent theme throughout the book has been that at least in theory, changes in opportunity structures ought to be combined with an attempt to change man's response to them. Material aids and psychological education should go hand in hand. If we have stressed the shortcomings of material aid by itself, it is because we have felt the need to make a serious case for psychological education. It is certainly not because we think that providing capital or tax benefits or high interest rates or technical assistance is of no value in promoting economic growth. Rather our conclusion is that the way in which these benefits are provided may undermine the motivation necessary to take full advantage of them, and that direct attempts to change the structure of response to them will pay off many times over in greater yields obtained from such benefits. While developers may assent to these propositions as probably true in theory, they might still legitimately wonder how the two approaches can be combined at the practical level.

To see how this might be done, let us consider for a moment the prevailing method of promoting development. It derives essentially from two main sources—the theory and empirical analysis of production (Cf. Brown, 1967) and management theory and practice. Both deal essentially with problems in optimal resource allocation in existing structures. At the macroeconomic level, economists have estimated with increasing accuracy the combination of such inputs as capital, labor, research and development, education, and the like, which will produce optimal growth rates of collective economic indicators. Similarly, at the level of the firm, management theory and experience attempt to specify how resources should be allocated as between marketing, production, personnel, and so on, to produce optimal growth in profits for the firm. In other words, neither is concerned directly with the problem of mobilization of resources. Rather they deal with optimal *allocation* of resources. A further assumption is implicitly made so far as development is concerned: that *optimal allocation of resources is the best way to mobilize resources.* The result is economic planning as an aid to development.

Typically, foreign economic experts are called into an underdeveloped country to work out a five-year plan. They begin by setting a target for a reasonable annual rate of desired growth in gross domestic product. Then, in order to achieve this goal, targets are set by various economic sectors such as mining, agriculture, construction, and industry. If these sectoral targets are to be achieved, plans must be made in further detail for a series of projects which are bankable or feasible and which, if carried out as planned, will produce the gross increases in levels of employment, capital, and income that are the targets for the plan. Much technical skill, time, effort, and money are necessary to work out such plans. Yet in the process very little attention is paid to the motivational problem implicit in getting the plans implemented.

Instead, planners typically tell governments what they "must" do if the plans are to be realized. The government must raise more money in taxes, yet not spend it all on increases in government salaries. Typical statements from such a planning document run as follows: "The development goals require that much more progress be made on expanding the yield of peasant subsistence agriculture." "The development goals of the government for the economy will also require the successful negotiation and efficient use of a very large additional volume of external loans, credits and direct investments, public or private." Realistic, well-conceived projects "must be executed" to attain development goals. Regional resources allocation decisions must be based on their relative rates of economic return to the nation. And so forth. The advice is certainly excellent, yet how is it to be implemented? Who will do all these things and why? The closest the planners come to answering such questions is to mention certain institutions that should be set up to "implement" the decisions, such as development banks, or public administration institutes that will train people to make such decisions. They also set manpower targets for training different types of high-level personnel. The assumption is that given such and such "human resources," people will do what the plans say they should.

Despite huge investments in this type of economic planning by public and private agencies all over the world, there has apparently been relatively little attempt to measure its cost effectiveness. On the other hand, informal evidence repeatedly has suggested that plans often fall far short of being realized because the motivational mechanisms necessary to implement them are not understood. The implementation figures for industrial projects in an African country presented in Table 12.5 are

Table 12.5
New Industrial Projects Planned and Realized During a Five-Year Plan in an African Country

	Total	Started	In Operation	Not Realized
Planned	95	15	20	60
Unplanned	37	14	23	—

probably typical of what happens. Only 37 per cent of the 95 planned projects started or in operation by the end of the five-year plan. The other 60 projects, which economists had spent a considerable amount of time demonstrating the need for and the feasibility of, had not been realized at all. On the other hand, 37 unplanned projects had been started, or slightly more than half the total number of projects realized altogether during the second five-year plan. At the very least, these figures suggest that the planning process is not very efficient. In fact, such shortfalls in the planning process have been so familiar in some countries, such as India, that there is general disillusionment with the whole planning process.

To point the way to a solution to this problem, it may be useful to draw on experience with an analogous problem in business management. It has been the practice of some large corporations to engage in long-range, careful economic planning. For instance, a soft-drink company may set as a target the optimum annual increase in sales, profits, or share of the market that it realistically expects it can achieve over the next few years. Then experts can work out in detail how many bottles of the product must be sold at what price and cost to achieve this goal. Then, typically, sales quotas are assigned to various regions, where the managers break up their overall quotas into route quotas assigned to particular salesmen. Motivationally speaking, the situation is exactly analogous to what happens in national planning for a country. Ideally, each person in the chain of command from the top to the bottom knows what he must do if the overall goals for the nation (or for the company) are to be achieved. In business terminology this process is sometimes called "top-down goal setting." Some corporations have found that it is no more effective in getting performance out of individuals than national planning has proved to be, using a similar goal-setting procedure. They therefore turned the process around and started with the route salesman, asking him to set the goals for increased performance that he realistically felt that he could achieve. These estimates were then collected by the regional managers and handed on up the hierarchy until they reached the top. Somewhat to the surprise of the planners at the top, the aggregate of the individual goals set from the bottom up often exceeded what they thought could be achieved working from the top down. And, of course, what pleased the companies even more was that the goals set from the bottom up were much more likely to be achieved than those set from the top down.

Can national, regional, or community planning also be organized to function from the bottom up? The experience we gained in Kakinada and Vellore suggests that it is possible. What was striking about the trained businessmen, in fact, was the amount of planning they personally engaged in. As data presented in Chapters 6 and 7 show, they often made several concrete plans before arriving at one that was successfully carried out. What is equally striking is that parallel to their planning activities was a whole planning mechanism supported by the Government of India that was scarcely linked at all to what they were doing. The Industries Department of the government of Andhra Pradesh and the Small Industries Service Institute in Hyderabad were busy providing loans to purchase equipment, technical advice, economic information, training for skilled workers, development of prototype designs, export promotional schemes, and so forth. For example, in Rajasthan, the National Small Industry Corporation

> had published a booklet containing about 30 schemes having po-tential for development requiring both indigenous and imported machines which could be adopted for implementation by small units in Rajasthan. These schemes were prepared on the basis of experience that the corporation had gained during the ten years of its working, and care was also taken to insure that almost all the schemes, in view of the acute scarcity of foreign exchange for import of raw materials, could be worked on locally available raw materials. (Nanjappa, 1966)

On the one hand, the Government of India was providing credit, plans, and technical advice, and on the other, individuals in Kakinada and Vellore were making their own plans based on their own past experience and local opportunities. Clearly what is needed is some mechanism for bringing these two efforts together. For our experience and the experi-ence of companies that have shifted to bottom-up goal setting show that plans made by the people who have to carry them out are much more likely to be realistic and to be carried out. The reason that plans made by outside experts are often not carried out seems to be that they are made by people who will not personally be called upon to execute them. This is not to say that the man at the bottom, the man who is going to have to implement the project, does not need information that experts can pro-vide. It does mean that the initiative should clearly be given to him from the outset, and planners should be in the position of simply providing him with information that enables him to make more realistic, useful, and efficient plans, which taken together will achieve national or com-munity goals.

In short, what seems to be needed to get better implementation of development plans is some kind of an implementation service, a group of trainers such as those on the staff of SIET Institute who could run business leadership seminars. It would be entirely feasible to make gov-ernment planning information fully available toward the end of the seminar when the men are engaged in setting their own concrete goals for the next few years.

Should such an implementing service be located in the public or private sector? The answer to this question will vary from country to country, but it is worth mentioning two possibilities, one of which is likely and unpromising, and the other less likely but more promising. Management training is well understood and widely supported in developing countries, so that it would be natural to add a course in achievement motivation to the repertoires of management training institutes. Such an approach would consider achievement motivation a skill that could be taught like any other, such as accounting, for example. But this approach would almost certainly be a mistake for two reasons. First, it is wholly individually oriented; it neglects almost entirely the structural or system aspects of the motivation seminars described above. Even though we did not understand these requirements very well at the time, it should be remembered that the participants in the SIET Institute courses thought of themselves as a small band who were going to work together for the good of their community, their own businesses, and the welfare of India. At a practical level, it is hard to see how some of these important motivational factors could be duplicated at a management training institute where a course in achievement motivation would take its place alongside a course in accounting.

Second, staff in a management training institute (or a motivation training service, let us say, attached to the Ministry of Planning) would normally not enter into a contract with the participants stating that the better the participants performed after training, the greater the reward for the staff or its institution would be. Yet this was clearly the nature of the contract we entered into with the participants in our achievement motivation training courses. They knew from the outset that we could not regard the training as successful until years later, when we had feedback in terms of their actual performance. In contrast, training is ordinarily regarded as a professional service and no one understands that payment for this service will be in proportion to its success. Once a man has been trained, his teacher has fulfilled his obligation as a professional and retains no further formal interest in whether the trainee performs better. Yet it seems clear from our data that the continued follow-up on the goals set was an important part of the success of the training. How can it be built into the training provided by a management institute or service, where normally interest in a participant stops when a course is over?

A possibility that has much in its favor is that achievement motivation training be attached to an institution providing credit—such as a bank, a development corporation, or a rural cooperative credit union. There are several advantages of such an association: (1) Such institutions are usually designed explicitly to speed economic growth. If they are private, their profit depends on expansion of commercial loans made. If they are public, the government and the plan usually see them as the primary means by which rapid economic growth is to be promoted. Their problem often is that they do not know how to perform their assigned function better. So in theory, they would be interested in achievement motivation training, if they could perceive it as a means of doing a better job. (2) A credit institution is necessarily interested in the long-term performance of someone to whom it has loaned money. It automatically gets continuous feedback over a period of time on how well he is doing, in terms of whether he is able to meet his payment schedule on the loan. Thus, trainers on the institution staff will get continuous feedback on whether their training is paying off in terms of reduced defaulting on payments, larger loans successfully managed, and so on. (3) By definition, the better the training, the greater the payoff for the credit institution. This is in direct contrast to a management training institute where there is no direct relationship between payoff to the institution and success of the training. (4) At a practical level, loan officers would have an opportunity to observe the course participants and their plans for ten days. So they would be in a better position than they usually are to judge the quality of the man and his plan and decide who should get how much credit. (5) Potential borrowers, for their part, should be interested in attending the seminars, not only for the personal benefit they might derive, but also for the improved access to credit and to information about projects the government plan favors. (6) Above all, business leadership seminars run by credit institutions would put motivation together with opportunities. The man who is making the plan is the one who is going to carry it out, which is ideal from the motivational point of view. Furthermore, he will carry it out after the structure of his response has been improved by training; with the benefit of the necessary credit; and with the information that experts think is relevant to his goals. It may take some time to convince a credit institution that it ought to engage in motivation training to increase its efficiency, and to find out whether such auspices would interfere with the effectiveness of the training, but the possibility deserves serious consideration.

The proposal is capable of being generalized to all situations in which material aid is offered. That is, motivation training could be provided in connection with loans not only for large businesses, but also for small businesses, for rural cooperative associations, or for farmers. One might argue that one of the main reasons for the success of the Comilla Rural Development project in East Pakistan is its emphasis on what we would call motivation training, that goes along with providing credit to local farmers' cooperatives. It is worth citing the experience of this successful project in some detail to give a concrete example of the advantages of interweaving material aid with psychological education.

> The opportunity to obtain inexpensive credit is the chief incentive that attracts villages to the program. [Operated by the Pakistan Academy for Rural Development in Comilla.] But in order to join, a group of cultivators must satisfy a number of demands from the Central Association. A local Cooperative has to be formed that draws wide, though by no means necessarily complete, support throughout the village. The Cooperative members must show that they can meet regularly and arrive at basic group decisions. They must raise collective funds, with savings contributed from all members no matter how poor, to be used as security against loans taken from the Central Association. And they must select several members to occupy specified leadership roles that serve to connect the village to the Central Association.
>
> Perhaps the most striking departure from ordinary efforts at rural development has been this emphasis on developing new local leadership. Rather than concentrating on sending extension officers and other government aid officials "into" villages, the Comilla program has encouraged village Cooperatives to choose their own leaders for specially created roles such as Cooperative "Organizer," "Accountant," and "Model Farmer." These men, whose past, present, and future lives are rooted in the village, are required to come at frequent and regular intervals (usually once a week) to the Central Association headquarters to discuss village problems, observe new methods and materials of farming, attend classes on subjects and skills directly related to their role, and transact business with the Central Cooperative Association credit office. (Schuman, 1967, pp. 4–5)

Obviously this program combines bottom-up goal setting with a material aid program (inexpensive loans), plus a required structural reorganization and frequent activation or motivation sessions for the leaders of the new structures. It has put together what we consider to be the main features of a successful development effort, although on the psychological education side, of course, its efforts were based on commonsense understanding, rather than detailed knowledge of achievement motivation. A successful aid program involves *motivation training, information, organization,* and an *improved opportunity structure.* Hopefully in the future more development efforts of all types will follow this pattern and will not try to produce changes merely by alterations in the environment, such as low-cost housing, racial integration of schools, job opportunities for unskilled and previously unemployable workers, and so on. Our findings suggest that spending 10 per cent of the total budget for such programs for motivation and organization should increase their yield several times over.

Social Determinism and Social Change

One of the curious paradoxes of recent history is that growth in the belief in social determinism has undermined the capacity of man to bring about social change. Freud cogently pointed out that man has suffered one blow after another to his pride and self-confidence from scientific discoveries of the past few centuries. First in the Copernican-Galilean revolution, he learned that the earth could not reasonably be considered the center of the universe. Instead, man lived on a small speck which revolved around the sun in an infinite universe. Next, Darwin demonstrated that man need not be considered the supreme creation, but rather was a byproduct of a process of natural selection over which he certainly had no control. Darwin, in fact, popularized the fashion in intellectual circles of conceiving of man as adapting to his environment. In its most general form, this conception of man's role in society and history has been called Social Darwinism. Marx and other economic theorists strengthened the view of man as a reactor by writing about his desires and aspirations as if they were wholly determined by economic conditions. The bourgeoisie "had to" search endlessly for profit if it was to survive. It "had to" exploit labor to make profits. Labor "had to" react violently against exploitation. The whole historical process was predetermined; man had no control over the social process of which he was the victim. Freud added to man's sense of helplessness, as he himself pointed out, by demonstrating that he is not master in his own household. Even when a man thinks he is exercising free will and self-control, his every choice is predetermined by unconscious forces of which he is completely unaware, according to Freud. Where in all this picture of social determinism was there a place for man as a creator rather than a creature, as an actor rather than a reactor, as an agent of change rather than a product of historical, social, and personal history?

The practical consequences of the stress on social determinism are very great. Consider the ghetto Negro American. If he is poor, out of work, with little ambition and poor work habits, he is told that he cannot help it, that his responses and his condition are the direct result of oppression, racial prejudice, a poor family structure, or perhaps the way welfare is provided him. Or consider the Indian businessman. He is told by his government and by foreign experts that his situation is practically hopeless—there is not enough foreign exchange to buy scarce resources; he is tradition-ridden in ways that will prevent him from acting efficiently; the extended family stifles enterprise; there are major rigidities in market structure and the supply of labor, and so on. None of these problems is his fault. Nor is there anything much that he can do about them. He can only adjust as best he can. Or consider the Indian subsistence farmer. A recent publication put out by a Government of India society concerned with his plight starts out with the following sentence: "The average Indian farmer is poor and backward." Once again the pamphlet is quick to point out that his troubles are not his fault. He is a creature of tradition and economic and environmental circumstances beyond his control.

All of these deterministic analyses can be justified, but one of their unintended consequences is that they may convince the people described that in fact they can do nothing to change their condition, that the environment must change first. In other words, describing people's reactions as determined can be a self-fulfilling prophecy, as Rosenthal's work has so clearly shown (Rosenthal, 1966; Rosenthal and Jacobson, 1968). If teachers believe that their children are incapable of learning, in fact the children are incapable of learning. It may be morally or scientifically correct for a teacher to believe that a Negro child cannot learn because of his unfortunate early upbringing and racial discrimination, but nevertheless her very belief that he is a pawn of circumstances beyond his control makes it more likely that he will act like a pawn. In his analysis of race relations in America, Silberman (1964) calls this process "welfare colonialism," and argues that though it may be well intentioned, it actually increases dependency. If the Indian farmer or businessman believes what people say about how backward he is and why, he will behave in a backward, passive way. Yet he has the capacity to change what seems to be his predetermined response, as the Kakinada and Vellore businessmen showed. If there is one general conclusion that we hope will be drawn from the studies reported in this book, it is that man is not as predetermined in what he can do as social scientists and historians sometimes think. He has greater freedom to act, to change the structure of his response, and find opportunities in his environment than the traditional forms of social analysis would lead him to believe.

If man's confidence in himself derived from his former conviction that he was created, looked after, and guided by an all-powerful God, where will it come from now that in popular terminology, "God is dead"? Where will he get the confidence to believe that he can act and change the course of events when he is told almost daily by the social scientists that he is not free to act, that his every reaction is predetermined by his personal and social history? Two experiences point the way to an answer to these questions. First, it is a curious paradox that the most deterministic of contemporary psychologists—namely the neo-behaviorists, followers of B. F. Skinner—are the most confident that they can create a new Utopia. The more they think they know about man, the more they think he is capable of anything. It is true that they talk in terms of creating an environment that will shape man's behavior optimally according to deterministic laws. Yet someone must act, must make the decision to create the environment and design the environment that will predetermine the best response from the individuals who live in it. Where does the creator, the prime mover, get his confidence to act? From science, of course. Knowledge is the new source of power. Somehow, by thoroughly understanding how we are determined, we gain the confidence to act so as to transcend determinism.

Moreover, this is precisely what happened in Kakinada. A large source of the new confidence the businessmen gained came from their conviction, based on carefully marshalled scientific evidence, that they understood themselves and how they had to think and act if they were to attain their new goals. Scientific knowledge is the new God, the new source of man's conviction that he has the competence to act. Yet in another sense, of course, it is a very old God, a conviction that there are certain immutable laws which exist outside of man in the universe and which, if known and obeyed, give man the power to shape his destiny.

SCORING MANUAL FOR SENSE OF EFFICACY

by Stuart A. Pizer

I. *Goal: Being vs. Doing*

Does the hero want an end state in which he is continuously engaging in some *activity*, doing something, or is his goal to attain a state of being, or *essence*, that does not entail particular activity? When the hero reaches his goal will he be performing, generating action, doing something more or less continuously, or will he be in a condition, position, state of being? Is the end a process or a product?

1.
    A. Look for statement of hero's goal, usually introduced by words indicating: want, wish, interest in, like, desire, cherish, in order to.
    B. Goal can be inferred from phrases like "he is *never content to . . .*"
    C. Not every instance of the word *like* indicates *want*; "he likes money" is not scored, without further elaboration. Look for the *because*-phrase after *like*; for example:
        He likes money (not scored for goal).
        He likes money because it is a sign of affluence (scored essence).
        He likes money because it enables him to travel (scored activity).
    D. When there is an awkward or extended statement of the hero's goal, contract to "he wants," (e.g., "he is interested in securing the job at the literary magazine because in that way he will be in the position to write poetry" is contracted to "he wants to write poetry").
    E. Not every "wants" indicates a goal statement: e.g., "even when he wants to make a point, he doesn't offend"—this is a statement of attribute, not goal.
    F. Take gerundive form of verb following "experience of" or "satisfaction

of" as the *verb* of sentence (e.g., "he wants the *experience of painting*" = "he wants *to paint*").

G. When the goal is not specified enough to score at all, don't score, even if a "want" word is present.

2. Decide next what type of goal is wanted, whether it is *essence* or *activity*. If there is ambiguity over whether the goal is activity or essence (but not ambiguity over whether there is a goal indicated at all), score *essence*.

A. Essence Goal (EG): a label, an identity, a state of mind, a position in life, a change of state.
Examples: he wants
> to be an artist
> to be a successful businessman
> to be the founder of a business
> to be an important man
> to have a lot of money
> to be a respected citizen
> to escape from misery and suffering
> to clean up the slums
> to reach the top
> to be a leader

B. Activity (AG): action; performing; attaining a position in which the hero can *do* what he wants to *do*. A *passacaglia* structure to the story (usually signalled by words like always, whenever, usually) can change an essence goal to an activity goal: for example:
"He is absorbed in solving the job's problems"—scored essence goal.
"He is always absorbed in solving problems that arise in his job"—scored activity goal.
Examples: He wants
> to paint
> to run things for or by himself
> to use his calculating mind to solve problems
> to take risks
> to help others
> to continue to found businesses

C. Note subtle accents or qualifications of goal statement that make it essence rather than activity (or vice versa).
Examples:
> "He wants to run a business of his own" (activity goal).
> "He wants to satisfy himself of his ability to run a business of his own" (essence goal).

D. The statement of *wants* may be clarified or modified by its context or by elaboration elsewhere in the story. For example, "he wants to be a painter" would be scored *essence goal*. But, presence earlier in the story of "he enjoys doing some creative work alone" modifies *want* statement to score as *activity goal*.

Examples:
Activity Goal:

> (Who Am I?) Since from childhood I have an aspiration for acquiring knowledge, I still continue to read law even at this age of 35 years. I am eager to help financially to poor students who have got a real aspiration for education.

> (TAT) He thinks he could do better if he applied his abilities fully to his own advantage. He wants full expression of his personality into action.

> (TAT) He perhaps wants to express his ideals or his emotions on canvas —this is where he feels he can confide the most.

> (Who Am I?) I am interested in the collection of articles and fond of driving fast cars.

Essence Goal:

> (TAT) He wants to achieve success and head a large organization and give a comfortable life to his family—all the opportunities which he himself did not get.

> (TAT) Now he thinks that he can go on his own and establish his own business. He wants to have satisfaction of his ability to do so.

> (Who Am I?) In the future I want to become an industrialist.

> (Who Am I?) I feel that I lack real ambition. I want to change my mental outlook; I want to do something to prove to my satisfaction that I can do something.

II. *Locus of Resources*

A. Internal (IR): Score if hero is described as *able, competent, prepared, experienced,* or if specific powers, capabilities, or counteractions of weaknesses relevant to the present situation are enumerated (e.g., "His perceptiveness and understanding of others make him a good organizer of committees"; "A man of many limitations . . . but by God . . . he can work wonders within these limitations"). Score internal if hero can control or deal successfully with external resources (e.g., "he is certain that he can persuade the other committeemen who must vote on the issue").

B. External (ER): Score if outcome depends upon the resources of others, even if strengths of hero are also enumerated.

C. Lack (LR): Score if the story explicitly states that the hero lacks specific capabilities relevant to the situation at hand (e.g., "He just doesn't have the courage to face his boss").

D. Note: Do not score Lack of Resources if hero fails to accomplish desired result unless specified that the reason is an inadequacy of the hero's or an external factor. For example:

> "He fails" (don't score)
> "He fails because he is poorly prepared" (score LR)
> "He fails because help doesn't come in time" (score ER)

Examples:

1. Internal Resources:

    (Who Am I?) I work always with determination and courage . . . so I am always confident of achieving anything I want.

    (TAT) Dinesh has a keen mind and is above average in intelligence . . . With adequate qualifications and experience no wonder he can be successful in his job.

2. External Resources:

    (Who Am I?) Now I wish to start a business. Now I am in lack of capital. If enough capital is found, I will start an industry. If the department helps with financial aid I can start my business.

    (TAT) He wants other people to join him in his work and if he has a big team he will be able to achieve his aim.

3. Lack of Resources:

    (TAT) When his wife opposes, Ram thinks that he is doing something wrong. Even if he has any point he does not have courage to make his point.

    (Who Am I?) I am not able to make ends meet for want of capital.

    (Who Am I?) Now I am trying for a small scale industry. I am in need of better managerial efficiency and organizing capacity.

III. Global Stage (GS):

Hero exists in vaguely defined, unfocused stage. Scored for use of capitalized form (or implied capitalized form) of words: World, The Universe, The People, Society, Life (but not more specific expressions like "his life").

Examples:

    (TAT) He wants to obtain more satisfatcion from life's offerings.
    (TAT) The world he feels is not just the four walls of an office.
    (TAT) Life is to him "lily-like."
    (Who Am I?) I am one in the vast humanity of the world.
    (TAT) He wishes to modify humanity with his art.

IV. Initiative vs. Compliance

Who defines the task or problem? Does the hero start the ball rolling? Or do others start the ball rolling? Is the hero proactive or reactive? Does the hero see himself as the originator or source of action, or is he essentially a pawn acted upon and moved by individuals or forces external to himself?

A. Initiative (I): Score only for presence of cue words: decides, initiates resolves, focuses, determines, creates, etc.

B. Compliance (C):

1. Someone else defines problem for hero, entrusts work to him, assigns task.
2. Hero is supported, encouraged, criticized, controlled, compelled, pressured or under the disposal of . . .
3. Hero attempts to prove himself to others, win acceptance or popularity (unless achieving popularity is specified as instrumental toward attaining a goal such as elected office). A promotion as a reward from others, not as a goal, is scored.
4. Hero is directly responsive to the demands of others. There is not merely a demand, but a response to demands that suggests that the demands of others have a claim upon you.

If the hero transforms the demands of others, or actively mediates to accommodate his own needs or desires, don't score.

Examples:

"My wife is displeased; I must satisfy her" (C)

"I have a misunderstanding with my wife; I must help her understand" (don't score Compliance).

5. Help is not scored here because it does not define the task or problem.

Examples:

Initiative:

(TAT) After considering various factors he made up his mind to change his job.

(Who Am I?) At age twenty-five I started a new business. I constructed a baling press (pressing palmyra fiber into bales) and opened a fuel depot.

Compliance:

(Who Am I?) I am under complete control of my father, meaning I have no independence in business.

(Who Am I?) To my disappointment I became a lawyer at my father's pressure.

(TAT) He is a person who gets carried away by the decisions of others and can be easily dominated.

(TAT) If Dinesh keeps on doing hard work like he is doing of the last fifteen years the management will certainly put him as the head of the organization.

V. *Problem-solving vs. Problem-avoidance*

A. Problem-solving (PS):

Score for presence of conditional clauses, introduced by such cues as: if, so that, when, since, because. Conditional clauses indicate an attempt to clarify or specify logical sequential connections within a sentence.

B. Problem-avoidance (PA):

1. Score if hero becomes *depressed* or *apathetic* in the face of a problem or obstacle.

2. Score if hero *gives up, gives in*, or *quits*.
3. Score if hero does not give in but remains unhappy about the problem; *suffers* without attempting to remedy the problem.
4. One manner of avoiding difficulties is a withdrawal from reality. Score if hero attempts to escape "far from the madding crowd" by entering a world of fantasy, reverie, meditation, or seclusion.
   "Hameed was a successful young man with a good job . . . He took up painting, quit his job, and became reticent and withdrawn."
5. Score for sudden, unexplained, or unjustified, *deus ex machina* positive ending, or for improbable hyperbolic success story (e.g., "He was good at math in school . . . He became *famous* as a trouble-shooter . . . now whenever there is a problem or bottleneck people consult him").
6. Score if hero is described as a "gentle Jesus type" possessing "conflict-avoiding" personal qualities; gentle, sincere, good-natured, does not make enemies, likeable, tender, etc.
7. Score if hero is left at the end confused, uncertain, indecisive, or unresolved.

Examples:
Problem-solving:
   (TAT) If he plans well and keeps his balance Ramesh is likely to succeed.
   (TAT) He made a success of his business as all his capabilities he used on his previous job stood him in good stead.
   (TAT) If Ram continues to follow this trait he will be in the lawbooks of the management and his family life will become miserable.
   (Who Am I?) Since I am closely watching the accounting procedure of merchants, I was tempted to trade by joining the motivation training course of the SIET Institute.

Problem-avoidance:
   (TAT) It appears Ram will fail to convince her. He will not work overtime and will land himself in financial trouble. Ram should assert his authority.
   (TAT) He will remain a confused person, moving on the edge.
   (TAT) Ram will continue as before dominated by his wife.
   (TAT) Well, what's the use of thinking about it. You never know with women anyway.
   (TAT) His sincerity will definitely make him famous.
   (Who Am I?) I desire to be obedient to the elders . . . and become famous in Vellore.
   (Who Am I?) I am always good to all people and never like to hear bad words.

Summary of scoring categories:
   1. (EG)   Essence Goal (− 1)
   2. (AG)   Activity Goal (+ 1)
   3. (IR)   Internal Locus of Resources (+ 1)
   4. (ER)   External Locus of Resources (− 1)

5. (LR)   Lack of Resources (-1)
6. (GS)   Global Stage (-1)
7. (I)   Initiative $(+1)$
8. (C)   Compliance (-1)
9. (PS)   Problem-Solving $(+1)$
10. (PA) Problem-Avoidance (-1)

APPENDIX II

Input Ratings for Achievement Motivation Development Courses for Businessmen Trained in India, Spain, the United States, and Mexico

	Date	ACH. SYNDROME			SELF-STUDY			GOAL SETTING			INTERPERSONAL SUPPORTS			Input Total	Number Trained[1]
		Fantasy	Action	Cases	Career	Motives	Values	Prestige	Plan	Ach. Check up	Warmth	Re-treat	Ref. group		
Kakinada 1, 2	2-4/64	1.5[2]	2	2	2	2	1	2	2	2	2	2	2	22.5	30
Kakinada 3, 4	7-10/64	2	2	2	2	2	1	2	2	2	2	2	2	23	22
Vellore	2-4/65	2	2	2	2	2	1	2	2	2	2	2	2	23	26
Hyderabad 1, 2	1-3/65	2	2	0	2	0	0	2	2	0	0	0	0	10	34
Bombay	2/63	1.5	2	2	2	2	1	2	0	1	2	0	0	15.5	29
Barcelona 1	3/64	2	1	0	2	1	.5	2	0	0	0	0	0	8.5	18
Barcelona 2-4	2/66	2	2	1.5	2	2	1	2	2	2	2	0	2	20.5	26
U.S. Firm	10/62	2	2	1	2	2	0	2	2	0	2	2	0	17	11
Mexico	8/61	1.5	2	0	1	0	1	2	0	0	0	0	0	7.5	13
Total															209

1. Excluding students and observers.
2. Rated so that 0 = not present; 1 = partly present; 2 = fully present.

BIBLIOGRAPHY

Allport, G. W. The ego in contemporary psychology. *Psychological Review,* 1943, **50**, 451–78.

Andrews, J. D. W. The achievement motive and life style among Harvard freshmen. Unpublished Ph.D. thesis, Harvard University, 1966.

———. The achievement motive in two types of organizations. *Journal of Personality and Social Psychology,* 1967, **6**, 163–68.

Aronoff, J., and Litwin, G. Achievement motivation training and executive advancement. *Journal of Applied Behavioral Science,* 1968 (in press).

Atkinson, J. W. Motivational determinants of risk-taking behavior. *Psychological Review,* 1957, **64**, 359–72.

——— (Ed.), *Motives in fantasy, action and society.* Princeton, N.J.: D. Van Nostrand Co., 1958.

———. *An introduction to motivation.* Princeton, N.J.: D. Van Nostrand Co., 1964.

———, and Feather, N. T. (Eds.), *A theory of achievement motivation.* New York: John Wiley & Sons, Inc., 1966.

———, and Reitman, W. R. Performance as a function of motive strength and expectancy of goal attainment. *Journal of Abnormal and Social Psychology,* 1956, **53**, 361–66.

Bandura, A., and Walters, R. H. *Social learning and personality development.* New York: Holt, Rinehart & Winston, 1963.

Bauer, R. A. The obstinate audience: The influence process from the point of view of social communication. *American Psychologist*, 1964, **19**, 319–29.

Becker, G. S. *Human capital*. New York: Columbia University Press, 1964.

Behavioral Science Center. Business leadership training: a three-month evaluation. Boston: Sterling Institute, 1968.

Bendix, R. *Max Weber—An intellectual portrait*. Garden City, N.Y.: Doubleday, 1962 (Anchor Book).

Benedict, Ruth. *The chrysanthemum and the sword*. Boston: Houghton Mifflin Company, 1946.

Berelson, B., and Steiner, G. A. *Human behavior: An inventory of scientific findings*. New York: Harcourt, Brace & World, 1964.

Bergin, A. Some implications of psychotherapy research for therapeutic practice. *Journal of Abnormal Psychology*, 1966, **71**, 235–46.

Berna, J. *Industrial entrepreneurship in Madras state*. New York: Asia Publishing House, 1960.

Black, M. (Ed.), *The social theories of Talcott Parsons*. Englewood Cliffs, N.J.: Prentice-Hall, Inc., 1961.

Bradford, L., Gibb, J., and Benne, K. (Eds.), *T-group theory and training method*. New York: John Wiley & Sons, Inc., 1964.

Brown, M. (Ed.), *The theory and empirical analysis of production*. New York: Columbia University Press, 1967.

Brown, R. W. *Words and things*. New York: The Free Press, 1958.

Browning, R. P., and Jacob, H. Power motivation and the political personality. *Public Opinion Quarterly*, 1964, **28**, 75–90.

Burnstein, E., Moulton, R., and Liberty, P. Prestige *vs.* excellence as determinants of role attractiveness. *American Sociological Review*, 1963, **28**, 212–19.

Burris, R. W. The effect of counseling on achievement motivation. Unpublished doctoral dissertation, University of Indiana, 1958.

Carstairs, G. M. *The twice born*. London: Hogarth Press, 1957.

Caudill, W. *The psychiatric hospital as a small society*. Cambridge, Mass.: Harvard University Press, 1958.

Chaudhuri, N. C. *The continent of Circe*. Bombay: Jaico Publishing House, 1966.

Cohen, A. R. *Attitude change and social influence*. New York: Basic Books, 1964.

Coleman, J. S., et al. *Equality of educational opportunity*. Washington: U.S. Government Printing Office, 1966.

Couch, A. S. The data-text system. A computer language for social science research. Preliminary manual. Harvard University, Department of Social Relations, 1966.

Crowne, D. P., and Marlowe, D. *The approval motive*. New York: John Wiley & Sons, Inc., 1964.

Danzig, E. R. The creative thinking process. *The Chemist*, 1953, **30**, 11, 525–28.

———, and Nadkarni, M. *A manual for instructors*. Hyderabad, India: SIET Institute, 1964.

deCharms, R. *Personal causation*. New York: Academic Press, 1968.

Douvan, E. Social status and success striving. *Journal of Abnormal and Social Psychology*, 1956, **52**, 219–23.

Eisenstadt, S. N. The need for achievement. *Economic Development and Cultural Change*, 1963, **4**, 420–32.

Ends, E. J., and Page, C. W. A study of three types of group psychotherapy with hospitalized male inebriates. *Quarterly Journal on Alcohol*, 1957, **18**, 263–77.

Erikson, E. H. *Childhood and society*. New York: W. W. Norton & Company, Inc., 1950.

Eysenck, H. J. The effects of psychotherapy: an evaluation. *Journal of Consulting Psychology*, 1952, **16**, 319–24.

———. The effects of psychotherapy. In H. J. Eysenck (Ed.), *Handbook of abnormal psychology*. New York: Basic Books, 1960.

Feather, N. T. The relationship of persistence at a task and expectation of success and achievement-related motives. *Journal of Abnormal and Social Psychology*, 1961, **63**, 552–61.

Festinger, L. *A theory of cognitive dissonance*. New York: Harper & Row, Publishers, 1957.

Flinn, M. W. *The origins of the industrial revolution*. London: Longmans, Green & Co., Inc., 1966.

Foster, G. M. Peasant society and the image of the limited good. *American Anthropologist*, 1965, 67, **2**, 293–315.

Frank, J. *Persuasion and healing*. Baltimore: The Johns Hopkins Press, 1961.

Fraser, T. M., Jr. Sociocultural parameters in directed change. In A. H. Niehoff (Ed.), *A casebook of social change*. Chicago: Aldine, 1966, pp. 193–216.

French, Elizabeth G. Motivation as a variable in work partner selection. *Journal of Abnormal and Social Psychology*, 1956, **53**, 96–99.

———. Development of a measure of complex motivation. In J. W. Atkinson (Ed.), *Motives in fantasy, action and society*. Princeton, N.J.: D. Van Nostrand Co., 1958, pp. 242–48 (a).

———. Effects of the interaction of motivation and feedback on task performance. In J. W. Atkinson (Ed.), *Motives in fantasy, action and society*. Princeton, N.J.: D. Van Nostrand Co., 1958, pp. 400–08 (b).

Freud, S. *Civilization and its discontents*. 1930. Garden City, N.Y.: Doubleday, 1958 (Anchor Book).

Galbraith, J. K. *Economic development in perspective*. Cambridge, Mass.: Harvard University Press, 1962.

Gandhi, M. K. *Khadi (Hand-spun cloth). Why and how*. Ahmedabad, India: Navajivan Publishing House, 1955.

Geertz, C. Primordial sentiments and civil politics in the new states. In C. Geertz (Ed.), *Old societies and new states*. New York: The Free Press, 1963.

Ghosh, A. *Indian economy: its nature and problems*. Calcutta: World Press, 1964.

Hagen, E. *On the theory of social change.* Homewood, Ill.: Dorsey Press, 1962.

Harbison, F., and Myers, C. A. *Education, manpower, and economic growth.* New York: McGraw-Hill Book Company, 1964.

Heckhausen, H. Eine rahmentheorie der motivation in zehn thesen. *Zeitschrift für experimentelle und angewandte psychologie,* 1963, **X**/4, 604–26.

———. *The anatomy of achievement motivation.* New York and London: Academic Press, 1967.

Horton, W. R. G. The boundaries of explanation in social anthropology. *Man,* 1963, **43**, 10–11.

Hovland, C. I. Human learning and retention. In S. S. Stevens (Ed.), *Handbook of experimental psychology.* New York: John Wiley & Sons, Inc., 1951.

———, Janis, I. L., and Kelley, H. H. *Communication and persuasion: psychological studies of opinion change.* New Haven: Yale University Press, 1953.

Inkeles, A. The modernization of man. Ch. 10 in M. Weiner (Ed.), *Modernization: The dynamics of growth.* New York: Basic Books, 1966, pp. 138–50.

Kagan, J. On the need for relativism. *American Psychologist,* 1967, **22**, 131–42.

———, and Moss, H. A. *Birth to maturity.* New York: John Wiley & Sons, Inc., 1962.

Kapp, K. W. *Hindu culture, economic development, and economic planning in India.* Bombay and New York: Asia Publishing House, 1963.

Kardiner, A., *et al. The psychological frontiers of society.* New York: Columbia University Press, 1945.

Katz, E., and Lazarsfeld, P. F. *Personal influence.* New York: The Free Press, 1955.

Kausler, D. H. Aspiration level as a determinant of performance. *Journal of Personality,* 1959, **27**, 346–51.

Kelly, G. A. *The psychology of personal constructs.* New York: W. W. Norton & Company, Inc., 1955.

Kluckhohn, Florence R., and Strodtbeck, F. L. *Variations in value orientations.* New York: Harper & Row, Publishers, 1961.

Kock, S. W. Management and motivation. Summary of a doctoral thesis presented at the Swedish School of Economics, Helsingfors, Finland, 1965.

Kolb, D. Achievement motivation training for underachieving high-school boys. *Journal of Personality and Social Psychology,* 1965, **2**, 783–92.

———, Winter, Sara K., and Berlew, D. E. Self-directed change: Two studies. *Journal of Applied Behavioral Sciences,* 1968 (in press).

Kolp, P. Navaho economic change. Unpublished Ph.D. thesis, Massachusetts Institute of Technology, 1965.

Korzybski, A. *Science and sanity.* Lancaster, Pa.: Science Press, 1941.

Kuznets, S. *Six lectures on economic growth.* New York: The Free Press, 1959.

Lasker, H. M. Factors affecting responses to achievement motivation training in India. Unpublished A.B. thesis, Department of Social Relations, Harvard College, 1966.

LeVine, R. *Dreams and deeds: Achievement motivation in Nigeria.* Chicago: University of Chicago Press, 1966.

Lewis, J. P. *Quiet crisis in India.* Garden City, N.Y.: Doubleday, 1964 (Anchor Book).

Lewis, O. *Children of Sanchez.* New York: Random House, 1961.

Litwin, G. H., and Ciarlo, J. A. Achievement motivation and risk taking in a business setting. *Technical Report,* The Behavioral Research Service, General Electric Company, New York City, 1959.

Lynton, R. P., and Pareek, U. *Training for development.* Homewood, Ill.: R. D. Irwin and Dorsey Press, 1967.

———, and Stepanek, J. *Industrialization beyond the metropolis: a new look at India.* Hyderabad, India: SIET Institute, 1963.

McClelland, D. C. *Personality.* New York: Holt, Rinehart & Winston, 1951.

———. Methods of measuring human motivation. In J. W. Atkinson (Ed.), *Motives in fantasy, action and society.* Princeton, N.J.: D. Van Nostrand Co., 1958, Ch. 1.

———. *The achieving society.* Princeton, N.J.: D. Van Nostrand Co., 1961.

———. Motivational patterns in Southeast Asia with special reference to the Chinese case. *Journal of Social Issues,* 1963, **19,** 1, 6–19.

———. *The roots of consciousness.* Princeton, N.J.: D. Van Nostrand Co., 1964.

———. N Achievement and entrepreneurship: A longitudinal study. *Journal of Personality and Social Psychology,* 1965, **1,** 389–92 (a).

———. Toward a theory of motive acquisition. *American Psychologist,* **20,** 5, 1965, 321–33 (b).

———. Does education accelerate economic growth? *Economic Development and Cultural Change,* 1966, **14,** 257–78 (a).

———. Longitudinal trends in the relation of thought to action. *Journal of Consulting Psychology,* 1966, **30,** 479–83 (b).

———. The role of achievement orientation in the transfer of technology. In W. H. Gruber, and D. G. Marquis (Eds.), *The human factor in the transfer of technology.* Cambridge, Mass.: M.I.T. Press, 1968.

———. Achievement motivation training for potential high school dropouts. Harvard University, Department of Social Relations, unpublished paper, 1969.

———, Atkinson, J. W., Clark, R. A., and Lowell, E. L. *The achievement motive.* New York: Appleton-Century-Crofts, 1953.

———, Kalin, R., Wanner, H. E., and Davis, W. *Alcohol, power, and inhibition.* Princeton, N.J.: D. Van Nostrand Co., 1970 (in press).

McGeoch, J. A., and Irion, A. L. *The psychology of human learning.* (2nd ed.) New York: Longmans, Green & Co., Inc., 1952.

Marshall, A. *Principles of economics.* (8th ed.) London: Macmillan & Co., Ltd., 1920.

Mehta, P. Level of *n* Achievement in high school boys. *Indian Educational Review,* 1967, **II**, 2, 36–70.

Menzel, H., and Katz, E. Social relations and innovation in the medical profession: The epidemiology of a new drug. *Public Opinion Quarterly,* 1955, **29**, 337–52.

Mierke, K. *Wille und Leistung.* Göttingen: Verlag für Psychologie, 1955.

Mills, T. M. *Group transformation.* Englewood Cliffs, N.J.: Prentice-Hall, 1964.

Milnor, J. Games against nature. In R. M. Thrall, C. H. Coombs, and R. L. Davis (Eds.), *Decision processes.* New York: John Wiley & Sons, Inc., 1954.

Minturn, L., and Hitchcock, J. T. The Rajputs of Khalapur, India. In B. B. Whiting (Ed.), *Six cultures.* New York: John Wiley & Sons, Inc., 1963.

Minturn, L., and Lambert, W. *Mothers of six cultures—Or: Antecedents of child rearing.* New York: John Wiley & Sons, Inc., 1964.

Mishra, V. *Hinduism and economic growth.* Bombay: Oxford University Press, 1962.

Murray, H. A. An American Icarus. In A. Burton and R. E. Harris (Eds.), *Clinical studies of personality,* Vol. 2, New York: Harper & Row, Publishers, 1955.

Myint, H. *The economics of the developing countries.* New York and Washington: Praeger, 1965.

Nair, K. *Blossoms in the dust.* London: Duckworth, 1961.

Nanjappa, K. L. *How to manufacture entrepreneurs in backward areas.* New Delhi, India: National Small Industries Corporation, 1966.

Nurkse, R. *Problems of capital formation in underdeveloped countries.* Oxford: Blackwell, 1953.

Ogilvie, D. Psychodynamics of fantasized flight: A study of people and folktales. Unpublished Ph.D. thesis, Harvard University, 1967.

Orne, M. On the social psychology of the psychological experiment: with particular reference to demand characteristics and their implications. *American Psychologist,* 1962, **17**, 776–83.

Osborn, A. F. *Applied imagination: principles of creative thinking.* New York: Charles Scribner's Sons, 1953.

Osgood, C. D., Suci, G. J., and Tannenbaum, P. H. *The measurement of meaning.* Urbana: University of Illinois Press, 1957.

OSS Assessment Staff. *Assessment of men.* New York: Holt, Rinehart & Winston, 1948.

Papanek, G. S. The development of entrepreneurship. *American Economic Review,* 1962, **52**, 46–58.

Pareek, U. Impediments to development: a psychocultural analysis. In N. Prasad, and B. N. Juyal (Eds.), *Impediments to development in developing countries.* Varanasi: Gandhian Institute of Studies, 1966.

———. A motivational paradigm of development. *Indian Educational Review,* 1967, **2**, 105–11.

Pool, I. deS. Communication and development. In M. Weiner (Ed.), *Modernization: The dynamics of growth.* New York: Basic Books, 1966, Ch. 7.

Reddaway, W. B. *The development of the Indian economy.* London: Allen & Unwin, 1962.

Richardson, G. B. *Information and investment.* London: Oxford University Press, 1960.

Roethlisberger, F. J., and Dickson, W. J. *Management and the worker.* Cambridge, Mass.: Harvard University Press, 1947.

Rogers, C. R. *On becoming a person.* Boston: Houghton Mifflin Company, 1961.

————, and Dymond, R. D. (Eds.), *Psychotherapy and personality change.* Chicago: University of Chicago Press, 1954.

Rogers, E. M. *Diffusion of innovations.* New York: The Free Press, 1961.

————, and Neill, R. E. *Achievement motivation among Colombian peasants.* East Lansing, Michigan: Michigan State University, Department of Communication, 1966.

Rosen, B. C. Race, ethnicity and the achievement syndrome. *American Sociological Review,* 1959, **24,** 47–60.

————, and D'Andrade, R. G. The psychological origins of achievement motivation. *Sociometry,* 1959, **22,** 185–218.

Rosenthal, R. On the social psychology of the psychological experiment: The experimenter's hypothesis as unintended determinant of experimental results. *American Scientist,* 1963, **51,** 268–83.

————. *Experimenter effects in behavioral research.* New York: Appleton-Century-Crofts, 1966.

————, and Jacobson, Lenore, *Pygmalion in the classroom: teacher expectation and pupils' intellectual development.* New York: Holt, Rinehart & Winston, 1968.

Rostow, W. W. *The process of economic growth.* New York: W. W. Norton & Company, Inc., 1952.

Saint Ignatius. *Spiritual exercises.* Translated by L. J. Puhl. Westminster, Md.: The Newman Press, 1960.

Sarason, I. Empirical findings and theoretical problems in the use of anxiety scales. *Psychological Bulletin,* 1960, **57,** 403–15.

Schmookler, J. *Invention and economic growth.* Cambridge, Mass.: Harvard University Press, 1966.

Schuman, H. *Economic development and individual change: A social psychological study of the Comilla experiment in Pakistan.* Cambridge, Mass.: Harvard University Center for International Affairs, 1967.

Sears, R. R., Maccoby, E. E., and Levin, H. *Patterns of child rearing.* New York: Harper & Row, Publishers, 1957.

Segal, R. *The anguish of India.* New York: New American Library, 1966 (Signet Books).

Sen, A. K. *Choice of technique.* Oxford: Basil Blackwell, 1960.

Sheppard, H. L., and Belitsky, A. H. *The job hunt.* Baltimore, Md.: Johns Hopkins Press, 1966.

Shils, E. *The intellectual between tradition and modernity: the Indian situation*. The Hague: Mouton, 1961.

Silberman, C. E. *Crisis in black and white*. New York: Random House, 1964.

Singer, M. Religion and social change in India: The Max Weber thesis, phase three. *Economic development and cultural change*, 1966, **14**, 497–505 (a).

————. The modernization of religious beliefs. In M. Weiner (Ed.), *Modernization*. New York: Basic Books, 1966, Ch. 4 (b).

Singh, A. K. Hindu culture and economic development in India. *Conspectus* (Quarterly journal of the India International Centre, New Delhi), 1967, **1**, 9–32.

Sinha, J. B. P. *Effects of n Ach/n Cooperation on group output and interpersonal relations under limited/unlimited resource conditions*. Patna, India: A. N. S. Institute of Social Studies, 1967.

Skinner, B. F. *Science and human behavior*. New York: The Macmillan Company, 1953.

Skolnick, Arlene. Motivational imagery and behavior over twenty years. *Journal of Consulting Psychology*, 1966, **30**, 463–78.

Slater, P. *Microcosm: Structural, psychological and religious evolution in groups*. New York: John Wiley & Sons, Inc., 1966.

Smelser, N. J. The modernization of social relations. In M. Weiner (Ed.), *Modernization: The dynamics of growth*. New York: Basic Books, 1966.

Stroud, J. B. *Psychology in education*. London: Longmans, Green & Co., Inc., 1946.

Wainer, H. A., and Rubin, I. M. Motivation of R & D entrepreneurs: Determinants of company success. Unpublished paper, Massachusetts Institute of Technology, Alfred P. Sloan School of Management, 1967.

Weber, M. *The protestant ethic and the spirit of capitalism*. 1904. New York: Charles Scribner's Sons, 1958.

————. *The religion of India*. 1920–21. New York: The Free Press, 1958.

Weiner, M. (Ed.), *Modernization: The dynamics of growth*. New York: Basic Books, 1966.

Wharton, C. J., Jr., Modernizing subsistence agriculture. In M. Weiner (Ed.), *Modernization: The dynamics of growth*. New York: Basic Books, 1966.

White, R. W. Motivation reconsidered: the concept of competence. *Psychological Review*, 1959, **66**, 297–333.

Whiting, J. W. M. Socialization process and personality. In F. L. K. Hsu (Ed.), *Psychological Anthropology*. Homewood, Ill.: Dorsey Press, 1961.

————, Chasdi, E. H., Antonovsky, H. F., and Ayres, B. C. The learning of values. In E. Z. Vogt and E. M. Albert (Eds.), *People of Rimrock: A study of values in five cultures*. Cambridge, Mass.: Harvard University Press, 1966, Ch. 4.

Whyte, W. F., and Williams, L. K. Toward an integrated theory of development: economic and non-economic variables in rural development. Ithaca,

N.Y.: Cornell University, School of Industrial and Labor Relations, ILR Paperback No. 5, February 1968.

Wilhelm, D. Priorities for effective development. In J. D. Montgomery and A. Smithies (Eds.), *Public policy,* Vol. 15, pp. 304–22. Cambridge, Mass.: Harvard University Press, 1966.

Winter, D. G. Power motivation in thought and action. Unpublished Ph.D. Thesis, Harvard University, 1967.

Winter, Sara K., Griffith, J., and Kolb, D. A. The capacity for self-direction. *Journal of Consulting Psychology,* 1968, **32,** 35–41.

INDEX

[397]